The Economics of Speed

Willem Vaessen

The Economics of Speed

Assessing the Financial Impact of the Just-in-Time Concept in the Chemical-Pharmaceutical Industry

PETER LANG
Bern · Berlin · Frankfurt a.M. · New York · Paris · Wien

Die Deutsche Bibliothek – CIP-Einheitsaufnahme

Vaessen, Willem:
The economics of speed : assessing the financial impact of the just-in-time concept in the chemical-pharmaceutical industry / Willem Vaessen. - Bern ; Berlin ; Frankfurt a.M. ; New York ; Paris ; Wien : Lang, 1991
ISBN 3-261-04489-6

Printed in Switzerland

Abstract

The topic of this thesis lies in the ambiguity of its title. In traditional manufacturing, the notion of speed and its scope are open to fruitful re-interpretation. Aesop's fable about the tortoise and the hare illustrates the point. The speed of the hare is not sufficient to let it beat its competitor the tortoise, which proceeds at a steady pace to win the race. This paradox is commonplace by now. But, does the tortoise at the same time make more effective and efficient use of the resources that are available to it?

A central and unresolved issue in modern manufacturing remains the economics of speed. This thesis addresses this issue by critically examining and evaluating the application of the just-in-time concept in the chemical-pharmaceutical industry. To this end, this thesis develops a framework for assessing the impact of the just-in-time concept and then applies this framework to an actual case in the industry.

The framework puts two complementary methods into contrast. It demonstrates the use of visual interactive simulation modelling as implemented in ProfiSEE and then compares the advantages and limitations of this operations research technique with a rough-cut financial analysis. A structurally simpler model, dubbed QED for Quick *et* Dirty or Quite Easily Done, performs the financial analysis forming the core of this thesis. This financial model, however, does take into account a much broader range of decisions and contexts, and lends itself to sensitivity analysis.

The outstanding feature of this model is that it translates common measures of speed into financial terms. In this fashion, the analysis differentiates a classical capacity-oriented operation from its flow-oriented counterpart, a just-in-time operation. The results of the analysis show that the tortoise not only wins the race, but also wastes less resources in doing so. QED.

Table of Contents

Acknowledgements

I am grateful to many people. Naturally, it is a sincere pleasure to acknowledge my indebtedness to those who have provided me with the necessary data and information, those with whom I could discuss the ideas developed in this thesis, and those who supported the projects on which this thesis is based and allocated the necessary resources.

During the period this thesis was written, I worked as a full-time analyst in the Operations Research department of CIBA–GEIGY AG, Basel. This organization bore the costs of the resources that were required for carrying out the work presented here. I take the liberty of singling out several individuals in this organization: I would like to thank the head of Information Services, Dr. Hans-Jürgen Poschet, and the head of OR, Dr. Lothar Seinige, for the most generous support that I received during the past years, and in particular also the time I could spend on this work. Dr. Seinige ensured a relaxed and effective working environment, which contributed in no small part to the successful completion of this work. Dr. Rudolf Furtwängler, head of the Stein works, I would like to thank for his initial approval and his subsequent support of the projects that form the basis of the industrial case study embedded in this thesis, as well as his frank and critical assessment of the economics of the just-in-time concept. I also express my special thanks to the leaders and team members of these projects for their diligent and thoughtful contribution. This work would not have been possible without the genuine interest and enthusiasm of Mr. Aldo Grüninger, head of logistics of the pharmaceutical division. Mr. Grüninger, who has also played a key role in the company-wide supply chain management improvement project, will find that my work contains some of the ideas that he has been propagating for some time.

The publication of this book is partially subsidized by the pharmaceutical division of CIBA–GEIGY. I would like to thank Dr. Rico Brauchbar, head of technical operations, and Mr. Aldo Grüninger for this financial contribution.

Almost singlehandedly, Mr. Hans-Martin Mosner re-implemented the prototype of ProfiSEE, a visual interactive simulation tool originally designed and implemented by the author, and described in chapter IV. Mr. Mosner is a top-notch software engineer and highly proficient in Smalltalk-80, the development environment of ProfiSEE. I gladly acknowledge his critical contribution. In addition, I benefited from discussions with my colleagues in the Operations Research department and the numerous users of ProfiSEE. In particular, I want to mention Dr. Klaus Braun, who took over the responsibility for ProfiSEE after I left the Operations Research department. Early encouragement and interest, I received from Mr. Francois Veillon, head of the former Expert Systems group at CIBA–GEIGY, who shared the floor of R-1360 with me during the quiet hours.

Besides Smalltalk-80, which is a product of Parc Place systems, ProfiSEE makes heavy use of The Analyst, which is a product of Xerox Special Information Systems, also written in Smalltalk-80. The costs of the development of ProfiSEE and the software mentioned above were funded by CIBA–GEIGY.

This publication is a doctoral dissertation accepted by the centre for business studies (*Wirtschaftswissenschaftliches Zentrum*) at the university of Basel, Switzerland. The thesis defense took place on June 21, 1991. Professor Dr. Wilhelm Hill was my research supervisor. Professor Dr. Friedrich Rosenkranz was the co-referee. I would like to thank both my academic advisors for their comments and constructive criticism. I am especially grateful to Professor Hill for his guidance, good sense of humor, and, in particular, also for suggesting the basic approach of the rough-cut financial model QED, which builds the core of the analysis presented in this thesis, and discussing its development and application. Using Microsoft's Excel, I designed and implemented this financial model.

I have made a diligent effort to refer to the work of other researchers in a clear and accurate manner. The text, including any grammatical mistakes, the numerous diagrams and graphs are my responsibility, except where indicated otherwise.

Section 8.5 of this book stems from two interviews with Mr. H.R. Aerni and Mr. Thomas Rotzler of F. Hoffmann-La Roche AG, Basel. I express my gratitude to them for the permission to include this worthwhile section on the just-in-time project of this pharmaceutical company at its Kaiseraugst works in Switzerland.

Mr. Fergus Byrne and Mr. Tim Mantle of Coopers & Lybrand Deloitte, UK, shared their views on the subject of just-in-time and MRP II with me. Mr. Mantle also commented on the section 5.8 and the plausibility of the results of QED.

Dr. Ulrich Fincke of McKinsey & Company, Düsseldorf, is the person who most influenced my initial decision to write a dissertation on the subject of just-in-time. Since then, four years have passed. Upon completion of the final draft, Helen Knutti, my wife, displayed her subtle understanding of the just-in-time concept. She made me a present of Nadolny's *Die Entdeckung der Langsamkeit* (literally, the discovery of slowness), which retells the story of John Franklin and his attempt to find the Northwest Passage. As Franklin eventually discovered, the flagships of the British admiralty were ill-suited for his fateful venture. Years later, Amundsen adopted other means to succeed. But that is a different story.

Foreword

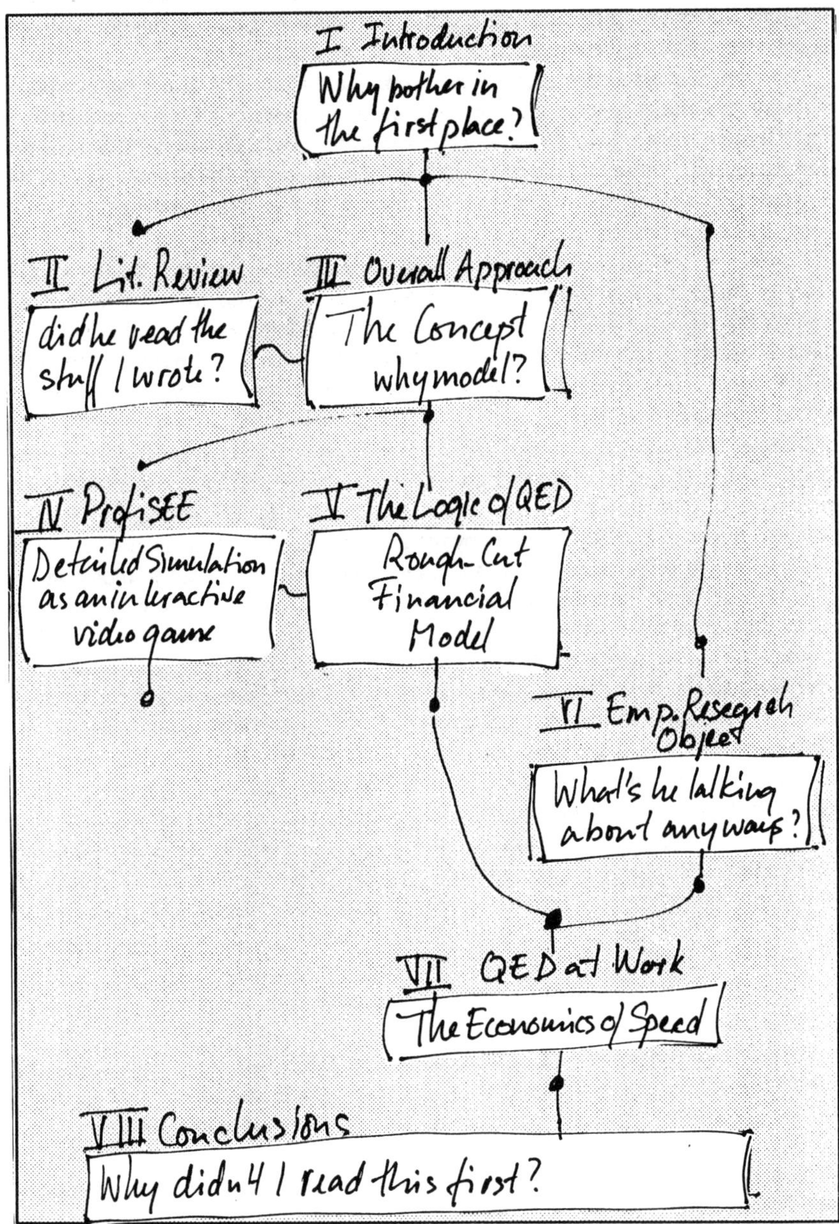

Figure 0.1: The sketch of contents. Forewords forewarn.

This is a long thesis. It is not a master piece in creative or technical writing. At times, the English is turgid, the subject matter dry and spiked with supplementary details. To make up for these qualities, there are plenty of explanatory and illustrative diagrams providing visual relief. For starters, I do recommend both the sketch and the table of contents.

The work is divided into 8 chapters of unequal length. The first chapter tries to motivate the reader to proceed with the remaining chapters. If the reader doesn't find the arguments in favour of the relevance of the topic convincing, he or she may go directly to chapter 6, which describes and analyzes an actual case in the pharmaceutical-chemical industry. This chapter in particular amplifies the basic points in the first chapter.

Chapter 2 reviews some selected publications on or related to the topic. The body of literature is already too large that I can pretend to have read it all. Particularly important are the sections on accounting and investment appraisals, on the one hand, and formal models investigating the nonfinancial aspect of the just-in-time concept, on the other hand. The remaining chapters, I view as an attempt to bridge between these two.

Chapter 3 presents the overall approach for assessing the impact of the just-in-time concept. The chapter starts, however, by asking what it is that this thesis sets out to prove. One component of the overall approach for answering the principle research question is QED. This acronym stands either for Quick *et* Dirty or for Quite Easily Done to emphasize that it avoids elaborate mathematical formulations or complex operations research methods. The second component is a workbench for visual interactive simulation modeling. ProfiSEE, as it is called, is a kind of interactive video game that the user constructs to gain a more detailed understanding of manufacturing process in the chemical-pharmaceutical industry. Chapter 3 argues that these two components complement each other.

Chapter 4 describes the role and characteristics of ProfiSEE in further detail. To enhance the understanding of this role, the chapter also covers the nature of facility design in the batch process industry and the important issue of line balancing. But as shown by the sketch of contents, it is largely a dead end in terms of the links to the remaining chapters. It is inessential for understanding what follows. The reader who is not interested in simulation modeling may safely decide to gloss over this chapter, especially sections 4.5 through 4.9. ProfiSEE happens to have been the author's pet project.

Chapter 5 is in the center of the sketch of contents. This is no accident. It explains the logic and role of QED.

Chapter 6 provides the empirical substance for QED. Besides a case study of a classical capacity-oriented operation in the pharmaceutical industry, it includes a proposed solution for a flow-oriented alternative reflecting the key elements of the just-in-time concept.

Chapter 7 merges the input provided by the two preceding chapters. It presents and analyzes the results of a fairly extensive range of experiments comparing the basic alternatives. This thesis would not deserve its title without these results and analysis.

The final chapter is a compulsory one—not for the reader, but for the author of a Ph.D. thesis. It summarizes the previous results and conclusions, draws attention to some current trends in the industry to substantiate these conclusions, pinpoints a prime managerial dilemma that arises, notes the strategic impact, and, finally, puts the just-in-time concept in a slightly broader perspective.

Basel
January 1991

List of Figures

Experimental Charts

List of Tables

1 Introduction

1.1 Purpose of the Research

A central and unresolved issue in modern manufacturing remains the economics of speed. This thesis addresses this issue by critically examining and evaluating the application of the just-in-time concept in the chemical-pharmaceutical industry. To this end this thesis develops a framework for assessing the impact of the just-in-time concept and then applies this framework to an actual case in the industry.

The most important part of this framework is a model that translates low-level decisions variables and common measures of speed into financial terms. Using this model, it is possible to differentiate a traditional capacity-oriented manufacturing operation in the industry from a flow-oriented alternative in a manner that establishes the economics of speed.

1.2 Relevance of the Research

1.2.1 In General

Hayes et al. [1985] discuss the questioning of the neoclassical model of economic growth, which correlates some measure of economic growth to a range of macro-economic variables. They refer to other research which shows that the explanatory power of the model declined at the same time as industrial productivity to justify the renewed interest in productivity at the micro level and in particular in their own research, which I summarize below. This concern with productivity in the factory has lead to what Skinner [1986], writing about the ill-conceived focus on direct-labor efficiency, dubbed the "productivity paradox." Low labour costs make for a dull competitive edge. "[Q]uality, reliable delivery, short lead times, customer service, rapid product introduction, flexible capacity, and efficient capital deployment—these, not cost reduction, are the primary operational source of advantage in today's competitive environment [ibid., p. 56]." Of course, they may also result in cost reductions, but that is not the point. Besides being ineffective, conventional productivity and cost-cutting approaches may also not be aligned with the manufacturing strategy.

The attention currently being paid to just-in-time manufacturing is the result, on the one hand, of "[t]he rediscovery of logistics [Sharman 1984]" as an important element of manufacturing strategy; and, of course, the phenomenal success of the Japanese automobile industry, on the other hand. Sharman and others, e.g. [Wildemann 1986b; Jäger 1988], argue for an integrated view of logistics that covers the planning and control of information and material flows up and down the entire logistics chain, ranging from suppliers of raw materials to customers for finished goods. Logistics can no longer be equated with physical distribution or materials management in the narrow sense. Just-in-time embodies this modern view of logistics.

Sharman [1984, p. 74] estimates overall logistics cost in manufacturing industries to range from 15% to 30% of sales—as shown by the figures in chapter 7, this range is far too high for the pharmaceutical industry. Due to the increasing complexity of logistics and the fact that the added value is typically declining relative to the costs of materials and distribution [ibid., p. 72], this percentage is likely to be on the increase. Furthermore, as Sharman writes, "... these costs are sensitive to factors that either lie beyond management's control or have proven especially hard to cut." He, as well as others, point out that the different functional areas in an organization share the responsibility for setting inventory levels: "... [L]ogistics constitutes a strand running through all the traditional functional responsibilities." The "functional" search for excellence tends to lead local optima, the global consequences of which are examined in [Meyersiek et al. 1984]. Their analysis of the annual reports of the 300 largest German companies over a period of six years (1978 to 1981) reveals that current assets as a percentage of total assets increased from 51.4% to 55%[1], while at the same time *Eigenkapitalrendite* (literally, the return on a company's equity capital, i.e. the ratio of net profit after tax and equity—non-borrowed—capital) fell from 9.6% to 4.4%. The analysis of Meyersick et al. attributes 85% of this decline to additional capital costs.[2] Unfortunately, the authors neglect to specify to what extent increased interest rates played a role.

Hayes et al. [1985] also report on the link between stock levels and productivity. On the basis of an in-depth study of twelve factories, they regress each factory's monthly total factor productivity (TFP) against a variety of managerial policy variables, including quality and work-in-process (WIP) [p. 5] and conclude, "[T]he relationships observed ... were about the same no matter how we defined this variable [WIP] and had a greater impact on TFP than would have resulted simply from changing the amount of capital invested in WIP [pp. 9-10]."

[1] Remarkable is also the distribution of the percentage: For 30% of these companies the share is more than 70%.

[2] "Die Verschlechterung der Eigenkapitalrendite ... ist nach dieser Varianzanalyse zu fast 85% auf die Verminderung des Finanzierungsbeitrages zurückzuführen - verursacht durch das Ansteigen des absoluten Betrages für Fremdfinanzierung und die Zinssteigerungen in dieser Periode [Meyersiek et al. 1984, pp. 19-20]." It is perhaps no accident that both articles quoted in this paragraph were written by members of McKinsey & Company.

1.2.2 In Particular

'Just-in-time-production' ist ein brennendes Thema für die chemische Industrie. Nicht nur wirtschaftliche Interessen, sondern auch ökologische und sicherheitstechnische Forderungen zwingen uns, unsere Warenlager möglichst niedrig und unsere Transportwege möglichst kurz zu halten.[3]

Hans-Jürgen Poschet

This introductory quotation expresses the concern of management with the different socioeconomic dimensions of the issues the just-in-time concept affects. The population at large in the region of Basel obviously shares this concern.[4] Thus, it may seem that the relevance of the topic is established and that there is no further need to belabour the point. This is not so.

This thesis needs to focus on the economics of the just-in-time concept in the particular case of the chemical-pharmaceutical industry because it is far from obvious that it's application is a lucrative proposition. A quick look at the composition of the balance sheet as published in the annual report of CIBA–GEIGY would reveal this. Now, it may be argued that these figures are misleading. CIBA–GEIGY valuates inventories at variable product cost (VPC), as opposed to total product cost (TPC). TPC includes the period costs of labour and fixed production assets. Instead, the figures taken from the analysis of the industrial case examined in this thesis—see chapter 6 and specifically §6.3.4—will suffice to make the point:

- fixed production assets at current depreciated value: 32 M.SFr.
- total amount of tied-up capital in stocks at TPC: 18 M.SFr.

The subsequent investigation shows that, depending on the size of the operation, the application of a radical version of the just-in-time concept will require a minimum of 25% more production assets than its classical counterpart. To counterbalance this increase, it is necessary to achieve an inventory reduction of more than 40%. This is a drastic reduction in view of the fact that during the past 15 years total inventory coverage of pharmaceutical products in the parent company has gone down from ca. 12 to 7 months.

If we believe the gurus, just-in-time is a philosophy that strives for the elimination of all waste. Is the additional production capacity that the just-in-time concept requires not waste? It is not surprising that the just-in-time concept puts a lot of

---

[3]"Just-in-time production is a burning topic for the chemical industry. Not just economic considerations, but also environmental and safety requirements force us to keep our inventories as low as possible and our transportation routes as short as possible." These words, dated April 15, 1987, form the introductory paragraph of a letter to Prof. Wilhelm Hill, written on my behalf. Dr. Poschet is a senior director at CIBA–GEIGY. The choice of the word burning is a subtle reference to the near disaster that occurred in Basel half a year earlier when a warehouse full of chemicals burnt down.

[4]See the article in the Basler Zeitung of June 26, 1990 [no. 146, p. 23] on the announcement of CIBA–GEIGY not to proceed with the construction of a central warehouse for 50'000 pallets.

emphasis on creating free capacity by eliminating activities wasteful of capacity and making good use of old equipment. But the question still stands.

The actual size and composition of the balance sheet, and the return on assets employed is a consequence of the specific manufacturing strategy that is in place. This strategy in turn translates into specific decisions on low-level factors. These factors include the horizontal and vertical segmentation of a manufacturing operation, campaign and lot sizing policies, equipment technology, planning and control systems and procedures, and the organizational structure.

There is a large body of research that investigates the impact of these factors. It is known, for example, that reducing production and order quantities is of paramount importance for successfully implementing just-in-time manufacturing. Krajewski et al. [1987] have demonstrated that setup times shape the manufacturing environment. "Simultaneously reducing setup times and lot sizes is found to be the single most effective way to cut inventory levels and improve customer service." Their research suggests that the choice of a production and inventory control system is less important than the factors shaping the manufacturing environment. This kind of insight is valuable.

However, the available research predominantly ignores the financial aspects. In particular, it doesn't examine the link between low-level decision variables and high-level financial performance indicators. This thesis therefore attempts to bridge part of the gap.

2 The Just-in-Time Concept in the Academic Literature[5]

2.1 Introduction

Publications on just-in-time start appearing only at the beginning of the 1980's. In a recent review of the literature relating to the just-in-time concept, Sohal et al. [1989] claim the late 1970's as the starting point, and indeed the first article, [Sugimore et al.], written by members of the production control department at Toyota Motor Co., appears already in 1977. But, as indicated by the references cited in [Sohal et al., ibid], the next article doesn't appear until four years later.

In 1982 Schonberger [1982a, p. 1] writes, " ... only about three authors have published articles in English on Japanese parts supply and production methods ...." On the basis of tours of several manufacturing facilities Hayes [1981], one of the authors referred to, describes the different elements of the "factory of the present," noting that "[f]or the most part Japanese factories are *not* the modern structures filled with highly sophisticated equipment that I (and others in the group) expected them to be." Although Hayes quotes a senior manager who refers to inventory as the "root of all evil," he doesn't mention kanban or any other just-in-time production system and the central role these play. Schonberger [1982b, p. 10] further notes that several best-selling books on Japanese management techniques also failed to mention just-in-time. I estimate that since the discoveries of these "pioneers" over 500 articles have been published on the subject.[6] We may fruitfully surmise, why the Western world took so long to recognize the role of just-in-time.

The topics of the publications on the subject of just-in-time proper that are discussed in this chapter conveniently fall into four categories:

- general reviews and descriptions of the concepts and philosophy
- motivation behind the concept and its impact
- formal mathematical or simulation models of specific aspects of the concept
- just-in-time acquisition of materials, and supplier relations

The last one of these four may seem unusual; the share of publications that concentrates solely on this issue is surprisingly large. Also included in the review are some selected publications on manufacturing strategy in general and cost accounting. These concern the second of the categories listed and are therefore particularly relevant for this thesis.

---

[5]This chapter is largely based on an unpublished discussion paper entitled "Just-in-time strategies in the chemical and pharmaceutical industry: current research opportunities." It was last revised in March, 1989. Where necessary a few more recent references have been included. Readers who are familiar with the contents of this paper will therefore find little that is new in this chapter. There is a substantial amount of discussion of further publications in the subsequent chapters.

[6]Some of these might strike the European reader as amusing: "The JIT concept is not a radical departure from traditional manufacturing methods, nor is it a mystical extension of the Japanese culture. In fact, its roots are as American as the proverbial apple pie, or more exactly, Henry Ford's pioneering manufacturing methods, typified by the assembly line [Dornan 1987, p. 60]." Dornan is right, of course: Toyota management and, especially Taiichi Ohno, see §2.2, were thoroughly familiar with the work of Ford.

2.2 A Short History of Just-in-Time

This chapter would not be complete without a reference to the work of Taiichi Ohno, the originator of the just-in-time concept. His book—*The Toyota Production System: Beyond Large-Scale Production*—may well become the counterpart of Henry Ford's *Today and Tomorrow.* It was first published in Japanese in 1978 and not translated into English until ten years later. The first thing that ought to strike the reader of this book when he or she examines its inside cover is that the history of just-in-time isn't quite as short as most Western business people would guess: the development and implementation of the concept goes back to the 1940's, the conception of the original ideas even further. This history also includes some significant failures. The publisher notes in his foreword that for the longest time nothing was recorded about the improvement process not only, as Ohno claims, to prevent the process from crystallizing and blocking further improvements, but also out of fear that Toyota's competition in the U.S and elsewhere would recognize the secret of Toyota's success. As indicated in the previous section, this fear, if it existed, would have been unfounded.

The two pillars that support the Toyota production system are just-in-time and autonomation—"automation with a human touch," [Ohno 1988, p. 4]. Ohno views the Toyota production system as one that is based on a philosophy instilling a company-wide attitude that establishes a continual improvement process. This process focuses on understanding and eliminating the causes of waste along the time line that starts with customer demand and ends with cash received.

As investigated in [Williams et al. 1989, pp. 97-99], the common assumption that the Japanese industry has realized continual stock reductions is simply wrong: "There was an heroic era of stock reduction from 1955 to 1969 when the Japanese manufacturers took out three weeks of stocks and reduced their sales cover from 9.2 to 6.2 weeks. But, in the past 20 years, the Japanese have not managed any steady improvement in their turnover stock ratios." In the face of stringent market requirements, they still had to improve to maintain these ratios. Using further census data as a basis, Williams et al. [ibid] show that Japanese manufacturers were at the same time making more effective use of existing production capacity. Their approximative, but plausible arithmetic shows the investment saving in terms of net annual output to be very impressive. "In our view, the precondition of financial saving in Japan was an all round competence in production and marketing; while the motive to achieve savings was supplied by the trajectory of manufacturing expansion and growth. [ibid, p. 100]"

The Toyota production system, as described by Ohno and Sugimore et al. [1977], includes elements that come under the heading of total quality management[7] (TQM). It will become clear that this thesis excludes such elements from consideration; not because they are irrelevant, but for a purely practical reason, namely, to narrow the boundary of the topic.

[7] In 1976, the number of employee improvement proposals had increased to 380'000 or 15 per employee, of these 83% were accepted.

2.3 Terminology

The subject of just-in-time hardly requires an introduction[8]. Today, one will find articles about the subject in the business section of a local newspaper. It does not surprise, however, that the concept crops up in different incarnations and so it appears useful to clarify the subject matter. Those already familiar with the subject can safely skip all of this section except for the last few paragraphs, which delineates the term as used in the remainder of the present work. A recent publication of Wildemann [1988a], written with managers and potential practitioners in mind, provides a fine overview of the just-in-time concept. Unfortunately, it is only available in German.

The dictionary of APICS[9] Inc [Anonymous 1984, p. 15], presumably an authoritative source, defines the concept in terms of one of its most tangible goals:

> JUST-IN-TIME – A logistics approach designed to result in minimum inventory by having material arrive at each operation just in time to be used. The implication is that each operation is closely synchronized with the subsequent ones to make that possible. In the narrow sense, just-in-time refers to the movement of material so as to have only the necessary material at the necessary place at the necessary time. In the broad sense, it refers to all the activities of manufacturing which make the just-in-time movement of material possible.

As such, this definition would be more suitable for the concept Zero Inventories (ZI), see the definition of APICS below, which in practice is often used interchangeably with just-in-time. The use of terms ZI and stockless production, which gained currency due to Hall, a prominent member of APICS, and the title of his popular publication [1983], has lead to the common erroneous view that just-in-time is in essence a stock reduction programme. In addition, the utopian overtones of the two terms tend to be even stronger than those of just-in-time. Be this as it may, the distinction drawn above between the narrow and the broad sense is most pertinent.

Only in the narrow and superficial sense do most other modern materials management and logistics concepts—MRP II[10] being the prime example—overlap

---

[8]Several readers of the earlier version of the paper on which this chapter is based suggested the inclusion of a section defining unfamiliar terminology. In an attempt to turn this chapter into a readable one for those not familiar with the current literature on manufacturing practice, I present and discuss some of the major terms in this section. Other terms are briefly explained in the body of the text or in the footnotes as they crop up.

[9]American Production and Inventory Control Society. This society led the MRP II crusade.

[10] "Manufacturing Resource Planning (MRP II) – A method for the effective planning of all resources of a manufacturing company. *Ideally,* [my italics] it addresses operational planning in units, financial planning in dollars, and has a simulation capability to answer 'what if' questions. It is made up of a variety of functions, each linked together: Business Planning, Production Planning, Master Production Scheduling, Material Requirements Planning and the execution support systems for capacity and material. ... Manufacturing Resource Planning is a direct outgrowth and extension of closed-loop MRP" [Anonymous 1984, p. 18].

with just-in-time. Any successful application of the MRP II philosophy must culminate in the implementation of a sophisticated E.D.P. system and its integration in the organizational environment. The E.D.P. system is in effect the dominant component. Substantial resources need to be committed to it.

Kanban, the original Japanese just-in-time method of production, does not require an E.D.P. system; it typically uses cards as information carriers. Inventory is kept insight in standard containers located on predetermined places on the factory floor; not "out of sight, out of mind" in a fully automated warehouse. The numbers of kanbans, the Japanese word for card, in circulation controls the amount of work-in-process. Among the critical features of the kanban system are the use of the pull principle, its simplicity and drastically reduced changeover times to allow small lot and campaign sizes. Implementing kanban generally requires a careful segmentation of the functional grouping of work centers into U-shaped cells to streamline the material and information flows in a factory. These are the kinds of activity meant in the broad sense of the term just-in-time quoted above.

It is worthwhile to dwell upon the implications of the careless use of the term kanban which equates it with just-in-time concepts in general. It is necessary to draw a clear distinction between kanban and just-in-time manufacturing. Particularly in the published German literature, the terms are used interchangeably. Referring to just-in-time, Fleischmann [1988, p. 351] writes, "[d]ieses aus Japan stammende Steuerungssystem, auch Kanban-System genannt .... ." Krüger [1986, p. 15, pp. 125-129] quotes, among others, *nota bene*, Schonberger to support his view of kanban as the central component. The upshot appears to be a clear case of *pars pro toto*—the part being interchangeable. Schonberger [1982b, p. 57] writes,

> The prevailing view of JIT is as an inventory-control system. It is not uncommon to find just-in-time used synonymously with *kanban*, which is the name for a specific Japanese inventory-replenishment system developed by Toyota. *Stockless production* is another term that is sometimes used. Kanban is indeed one device for moving toward JIT production, ... But I view just-in-time production management as much more: ....

Several other authors point out this misconception [Hahn et al. 1983, p. 3; Loebe 1986, p. 45].

"Material Requirements Planning – A set of techniques which uses bills of material, inventory data and the master production schedule to calculate requirements for materials. It makes recommendations to release replenishment orders for material. Further since it is time-phased, it makes recommendations to re-schedule open orders when due dates and need dates are not in phase. Originally seen as merely a better way to order inventory, today it is thought of as primarily a scheduling technique, i.e., a method for establishing and maintaining valid due dates on orders." [ibid, p. 18]. Closed-loop MRP, as the term implies, provides for the feedback between the various execution functions that play a role.

The literature on MRP II and its predecessors is vast and does not fall within the scope of this paper. Experience has shown that most companies have great implementation difficulties. The economics of MRP II continues to be the subject of debate. Its pertinent characteristics with reference to just-in-time are that (1) it does not entail a restructuring of the production facilities and the associated material flows, instead it tends to cement existing structures, (2) it is in its very essence a push system with a central locus of control, (3) the operational discipline it requires can only be enforced centrally.

This question of terminology is not purely academic. Currently open research questions concern just-in-time concepts both at the intra- and the inter-factory level. This is especially relevant in the chemical and pharmaceutical industry where the symptoms and problems appear and often lie at the inter-factory level. Within a dyestuff factory, for example, the application of the group technology concept may have led to production lines which require little or no work-in-process. The research presented in this thesis couldn't get off the ground if kanban and just-in-time were to be equated. Just-in-time concepts offer a broad perspective covering the logistical function as a whole. Kanban is one mechanism facilitating a transparent flow of information and goods in the factory. It is most suitable at the intra-factory level.[11] This is not to repudiate that kanban is as effective as it is simple—there is ample evidence to support that.

A second problem which follows from equating kanban and just-in-time is that it shuts the door on the wide-open research question whether just-in-time and MRP II systems are compatible [Schonberger 1982a, p. 10]. The integration of production units that have been converted to operate according to just-in-time principles with other parts of the manufacturing environment and with existing, and usually diverse production planning and control systems is a critical success factor. The difficulties, which are easily underestimated, are due to the inherent nature of complex E.D.P. systems, more precisely, their resistance to adaptation and their concomitant propensity to inhibit institutional change. For a brief discussion of the role of central E.D.P. systems, see §2.9.

The APICS definition provided for ZI [ibid, p. 33] covers the broad sense:

> ZERO INVENTORIES – A philosophy of manufacturing based on planned elimination of all waste and consistent improvement of productivity. It encompasses the successful execution of all manufacturing activities required to produce a final product, from design engineering to delivery and including all stages of conversion from raw material onward. The primary elements of zero inventories are to have only the required inventory when needed; to improve quality to zero defects; to reduce lead times by reducing set-up times, queue lengths, and lot sizes; and to incrementally [sic] revise the operations themselves to accomplish these things at minimum cost. In the broad sense it applies to all forms of manufacturing, job shop and process as well as repetitive.

This definition captures the scope and the multi-faceted nature of just-in-time. The IBM corporation prefers to use the noteworthy term Continuous Flow Manufacturing (CFM). Perhaps Heraklit will prove to be right again: Everything flows. IBM's term emphasizes that the goal of just-in-time is not primarily to reduce stocks but rather to keep stocks flowing. The German term *Umlaufvermögen*[12] is the source of some irony in this context since stocks are stocked all most all of the time and hence stock the flow of goods.

---

[11]The kanban system can of course also be used to transmit information between factories, or between a manufacturer and its suppliers, see [Mondon 1981].

[12]Literally, assets in circulation: *laufen* means to run. Correctly translated, current assets.

In view of the above, the current literature and a large number of published case studies, see Wildemann [1986a], the following definition should adequately serve the purposes of the research presented in this thesis:

> Just-in-time is a multi-faceted[13] productivity improvement programme applicable to a broad range of manufacturing environments, covering the inter- as well as the intra-factory level. It entails a change of traditional manufacturing practices and principles and, in general, a major overhaul of the parts of the organization encompassing the manufacturing process as a whole in view of attaining a system that is more responsive to the markets consuming its products. Just-in-time strives to resolve the predominant dichotomy between functional units in large organizations, in particular the conflicts of interest between logistics, production and purchasing departments. The just-in-time programme as it has been applied in industry consists of several interdependent components. Among the major ones are:
>
> - reduction of changeover—setup and cleanup—times, lot and campaign sizes;
> - product segmentation and reorganization of factory layouts to create product-oriented material flows (keywords: cellular manufacturing, group technology);
> - reduction of variability and imbalance in production processes
> - application of the pull-principle at all levels (i.e. demand-driven production)
> - integration with materials management systems;
> - quality and process control[14] at the source;
> - raw material acquisition based on partnerships with few suppliers
> - design for manufacturability

One important, albeit obvious, implication is that just-in-time is a manufacturing concept that concerns the *modus operandi* of several different departments in large organizations; besides logistics and production, it concerns the central units responsible for material acquisition and physical distribution.

[13]The term holistic also springs to mind. If the English word had been wholistic I might have used it. The German equivalent *ganzheitlich* avoids the association with holy.

[14]*Sicherung* – as opposed to *Kontrolle*.

2.4 Manufacturing Strategy

> A manufacturing strategy describes the competitive leverage required of—and made possibly by—the production function. It analyzes the entire manufacturing function relative to its ability to provide such leverage, on which task it then focuses each element of manufacturing structure. It also allows the *structure* to be managed, not just the short-term, operational details of cost, quality and delivery. And it spells out an internally consistent set of structural decisions designed to forge manufacturing into a strategic weapon. ... [Skinner 1986, p. 58]

Fine and Hax [1985] provide a framework and methodology for viewing just-in-time from the perspective of manufacturing strategy. The corporate strategic planning process for production must consider four dimensions: cost, quality, delivery and flexibility [Wheelwright 1981, quoted in the paper of Fine and Hax], which entail significant tradeoffs. Just-in-time affects all four dimensions, albeit flexibility mainly to the extent of product mix and volume changes. Fine and Hax base the "complex web of decisions" posed by formulating a comprehensive manufacturing strategy on nine decision categories: facilities, capacity, vertical integration, processes and technologies, scope and new products, human resources, quality, infrastructure, and vendor relations [Fine et al. 1985, pp. 31-36]. Again, a switch to just-in-time manufacturing requires decisions that fall into each one of these categories. This has obviously consequences for the limitations of the research presented in this thesis, since I do not intend to address all of these.

The simple concept of efficient frontier, as used, for example, by Rosenfield et al. [1985], is a step towards understanding the nature of the tradeoffs between the four strategic dimensions. It shows the implications of these tradeoffs on possible logistics structures in an industry, and hence on strategy. Rosenfield et al. systematically examine the cost-service trade-off, and focus on one aspect of service, namely delivery speed.

In this case, the efficient frontier consists of those possible logistics configurations that are not dominated in both cost and delivery by others. "The slowest but least costly system is to custom produce, keeping all raw material at supplier locations. The fastest and most expensive is to store local finished goods inventories. ... [C]entral production from raw-material stocks combined with air delivery to the customer would not be efficient for bulky, low-value-added products [p. 49]." Operations research models typically improve the cost or the service level to move a firm to the frontier.[15] They rarely change the shape—see below—of the frontier. A recent inventory and distribution policy study carried out at CIBA–GEIGY, see [Fincke et al., 1988], is no exception. The concept is illustrated in Figure 2.1a.

Rosenfield et al. identify three groups of factors which determine the shape of the efficient frontier: "[T]he nature of demand and product variety, transportation economics, and the structure of the value-added chain [1985, p. 50]." This

---

[15]The kind of mandate that departments carrying out operations research projects have prohibits this.

underscores the necessity of including cost-based factors and measures for gaining a deeper understanding in particular of just-in-time, see also [Fincke et al. 1988]. It is quite surprising in this regard that a relatively large body of research on production and inventory management completely ignores cost-based factors, or at least assumes that these can be accounted for trivially—not to speak of overall productivity measures.

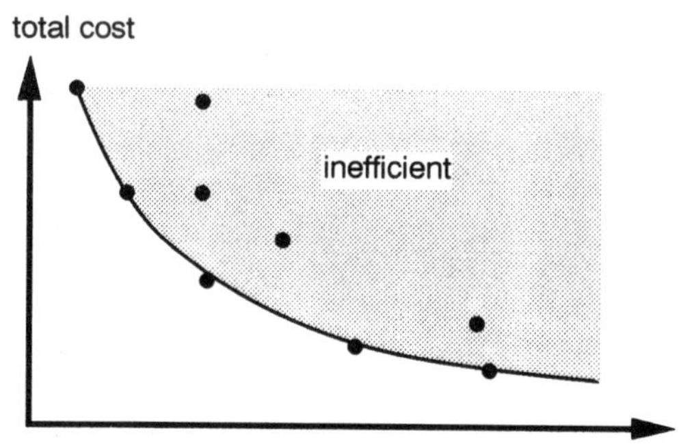

Figure 2.1a: A cost-delivery frontier. Logistics strategies that do not place a firm on the efficient frontier are inefficient. Source: [Rosenfield et al., 1985].

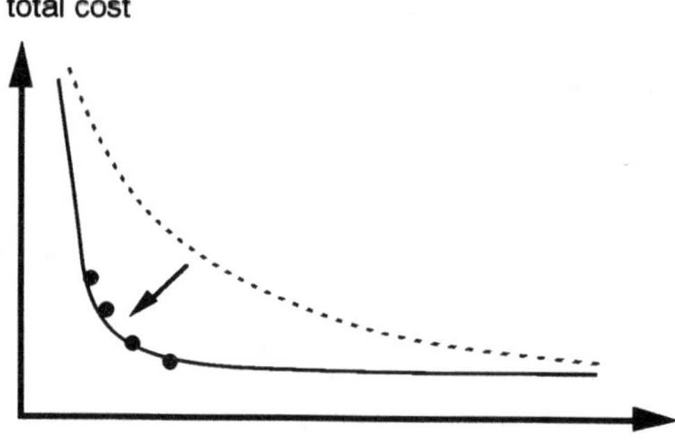

Figure 2.1b: A shift in the efficient frontier. This occurs when a firm can provide better service at equal or lower cost through, for example, the use of communications technology. Competitors move closer together as the elbow becomes sharper. Such a shift requires a new process, or technology or system, see [ibid, pp. 49-50].

The structure of the value-added chain is important in it own right in the context of introducing just-in-time concepts. The so-called value-added curve, which displays the relation of the overall throughput time for each level in the logistics chain and the associated product cost, is a simple and valuable piece of information for setting the focus and direction of the initial efforts, see [Wildemann 1988a, pp. 177-179]. It indicates, for example, at which level a reduction in throughput time may result in the largest cost advantage, i.e. it identifies the "low-hanging fruits." See §6.2.5 for a specific example and discussion.

The introduction of just-in-time or new technology typically results in a shift of the efficient frontier towards the origin, as illustrated in Figure 2.1b, much in the same way quality and cost can be improved at the same time—"quality is free" as Crosby proclaims.

What's the value of a given service level to the customer? Rosenfield et al. [1985, pp. 54-55] introduce a curve which represents the maximum amount a buyer is willing to pay for a certain level of service, see Figure 2.1c. This curve, together with the position of the competition, determines where a firm should position itself. The shape of the curve, the subject of considerable empirical research, is important in the context of just-in-time. How long is a customer willing to wait for a delivery? Does this depend on the size of the order? For a discussion, see [Fincke et al., 1988]. Just-in-time delivery also means that large, relatively infrequent orders, should be delivered just when they are really wanted. Should large orders be encouraged by offering rebates?

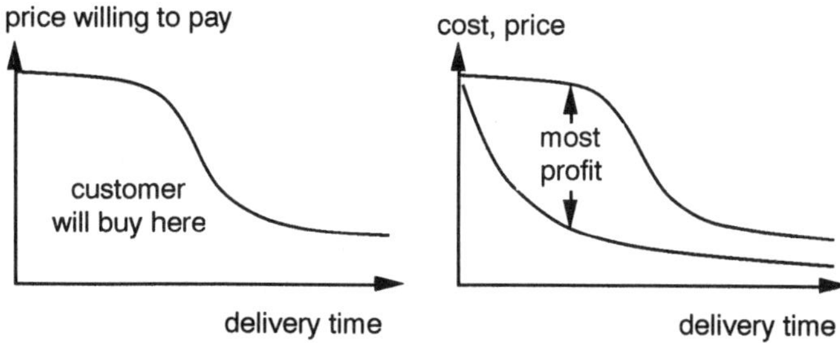

Figure 2.1c: The buyer's willingness-to-pay curve (left) determines together with the efficient frontier where the maximum profit could be obtained (right).

Measuring the utility of a particular performance criteria for customers is clearly an interesting, and at the same difficult and laborious task. However, it is not germane to the topic of the proposed research and could not be carried out within time frame set for it.

2.5 Just-in-Time in General

Turning from the broader strategic framework, to the literature on just-in-time proper, one finds that relatively few articles add new insight to the subject. Hall's Zero Inventories [1983] still stands as a good introduction to the subject. Many articles are very general: they describe the major characteristics of just-in-time and the requirements for implementation. Some merely regurgitate what could have been read elsewhere. Few are critical. Together, they contain the collected experience of the practitioners of just-in-time. The abundant and substantial claims for productivity improvements require scrutiny as close as the emperor's new clothing. This holds true for more sophisticated clothes like MRP II as well. The point is that causal models supporting these claims are scarce.

In general, it appears that there is no major controversial issue. I could criticize Aggarwal [1985] for his comments in an article subtitled "Making sense of production operations systems" in the Harvard Business Review: "Kanban's core objective is to obtain low-cost, high-quality, on-time production. To achieve this, the system attempts to eliminate stock between the successive processes and to minimize any idle equipment, facilities, or workers [ibid., p. 9]." Aggarwal emphasizes aspects that lead back to the productivity paradox mentioned earlier. Perhaps, Schonberger et al. [1984d] overstate their case in an article titled "Reinventing inventory control" when they write, "[t]he foundations of classical inventory control [theory] weaken as Western industry comes to understand the very different approach, developed in Japan, ... [ibid., p. 76]." Under the narrow interpretation of the concept, it could be argued that just-in-time is not bringing about a paradigm change; it's a question of rethinking parameters that were previously taken as exogenous, that is to say, constant. But, are these key issues?

2.6 Cost Accounting and Capital Investment Appraisals

"One Cost System isn't enough"
[Kaplan 1988]

Cost accounting may at a first glance appear to be unrelated to the subject at hand. However, the measurement of individual product costs and the evaluation of investments in flexible equipment rely heavily on the cost system and procedures in use and clearly are pertinent issues, that are drawing attention in the recent literature on cost accounting. The erosion of traditional accounting models is evident in manufacturing environments where the market has turned flexibility, quality and innovation into critical success factors. A brief review of some selected articles is therefore in order.

Kaplan [1988], first of all, points out that cost systems need to address three different functions: value assets, in particluar stocks, for financial and tax statements; provide timely feedback to production and logistics managers to control operations; and measure individual product costs. Purpose and scope of these functions are so diverse that several, possibly decentralized, cost systems are currently a necessity. The economics of information processing systems permit this development. Kaplan [ibid.] argues that more experience needs to be gained, before a single system fulfilling all the demands placed by the different functions can be designed. In addition, many manufacturing environments require specific solutions. At present, external requirements hamper effective internal use of accounting systems.

For operational control, the frequency of the reported information, the fluctuation and allocation of costs, and the use of nonfinancial measurements, must be taken into account—see also Kaplan [1984]. A typical question is whether a work center to which costs are allocated has control over these within the time horizon of the decisions to be based on the reported information. Nonfinancial measurements such as defect rates, throughput times, inventory levels—not just average and highly aggregated values—are especially important statistics for operating and systematically improving just-in-time environments. As discussed already in §1.2.1, these are becoming increasingly useful productivity indicators. At the same time, the effectiveness of traditional indicators, such as value added per employee or unit of output per direct labour hour, is decreasing.

Although nonfinancial performance measures are at present rapidly increasing in prominence, there are several reasons why their use is fraught with potential dangers, see [Berliner et al. 1988] and [Williams et al. 1989]. First of all, there is a need to convert these into financial terms to ensure the alignment of the operational targets for these nonfinancial measures with specific overall business objectives and financial goals for ROI and cash flow. Secondly, nonfinancial measures will invariably carry less weight than financial ones unless we are able to express their financial impact in a meaningful and consistent manner, i.e., we must understand their impact. Thirdly, the failure to assess the true costs associated with holding stock[16] and to allocate these costs to individual products is a key weakness of present cost accounting systems. In as much as the costs of holding stock is a non-issue in accounting, this discipline has been unable to provide an incisive analysis of the benefits of stock reduction and the just-in-time concept; the analysis has been left to the engineering discipline, which "mildly disparages" the financial aspects; "[t]he gurus of the business schools simply take their cue from the engineers. [Williams et al 1989, p. 93]"

The design of a just-in-time environment involves decisions, e.g. those concerning vertical and horizontal product segmentation, which need individual product cost measurements. These, like the make-or-buy decision, are long-run decisions. Most costs must then be taken as variable. Kaplan [ibid.] points out that standard cost systems can seriously distort real products costs due to the difficulty of allocating fixed and sunk costs—that amount to a steadily increasing share of overall costs—and the erroneous inclusion of idle capacity. Cooper et al. [1988] explain how profit margins on high-volume items can be overestimated.[17]

---

[16]See table 7.3a in §7.2.5 for an estimate of the true cost associated with holding stock in the industrial case investigated. Williams et al. [1989] quote comparable figures for other industries. Interest charges on typically amount to less than one third of the true cost of holding stock. For a further discussion of the financial consequences of holding stock, see section §5.8

[17]On the basis of my limited understanding of CIBA–GEIGY's accounting procedure for standard cost calculation, I believe that the kind of gross distortions discussed by Cooper and Kaplan are less likely to occur. One need not speculate that Cooper and Kaplan are dealing with a phenomenon that is more pronounced in the U.S. In fact, CIBA–GEIGY's procedure captures some of the major ideas and benefits of activity-based accounting, which is now propagated in the literature on cost management [Berliner et al. 1988]. But to my knowledge, no attempt is made at CIBA–GEIGY to allocate the total cost of holding stock, including the overhead generated by the logistics function, to individual products. The same applies to the costs of changeovers.

Kaplan [1986] also poses the question whether investments in new, more flexible, production technology “must be justified by faith alone.” Asford et al. [1988, p. 641], conclude that the alleged bias of traditional investment-appraisal procedures is not inherent but due to their application, e.g., too high a discount rate. Kaplan would agree. Intangible components such as increased flexibility, shorter lead and throughput times can for the most part be quantified—but not easily, since they also affect market share—and thus be brought into the decision. The proper evaluation of long-term benefits and a multi-faceted approach will eliminate the bias towards short-term, incremental investments resulting from the “division of labour”. It is clear that these kind of appraisals present significant practical difficulties and are fraught with additional uncertainty. Noteworthy is in this regard the widespread failure to apply these appraisals to commonplace investments in stocks.

2.7 Insight from Mathematical Models

> ... [M]ost traditional OR is focused on the properties and management of stable processes. Without assumptions about the long-term regularity of a process, it is difficult to formulate simple policies and test their impact on performance measures, much less to identify an optimal policy. This desire for simplicity and tractability is walling operations researchers off from what this study [discussed above] suggests are some important issues that must be dealt with by an operations manager.
>
> This same understandable but dysfunctional concern with tractable problems causes operations researchers to be too willing to accept the structure of a given situation, as well as the values of most of its parameters, as given. Their job is then reduced to optimizing (or simulating) within this structure. [Hayes et al. 1985, pp. 12-13]

As will be shown in this section, operations researchers have recently started to tackle the challenge posed by Hayes et al.

In traditional manufacturing environments, production managers strive to obtain high utilization of the available equipment capacity to ensure an appropriate return on investment. Disproportionally high inventory levels typically serve to meet this goal. Inventory, however, can also been seen as tied-up capacity, see for instance the conceptual paper on production control systems of Bertrand et al. [1986, p. 13]. The extent of rush orders and rescheduling, and the demand for better forecasts and budgets in evidence in most companies today make it abundantly clear that the return on investment in inventory may be poor, at least by the standards for investments in equipment.

A prominent effect of the successful introduction of just-in-time manufacturing is a substantial reduction of the total assets of a company. This reduction is accompanied by a change in the composition of the balance sheet [Wildemann 1986b, p. 4]. By investing in additional capacity, particularly in smaller and more flexible equipment, or alternatively, in reduced changeover times and costs, a disproportionally larger amount of capital tied up in stocks is freed. Thus additional working capital become available. The research presented in the subsequent chapters attempt to substantiate these claims in the context of the chemical-pharmaceutical industry.

The tradeoff between investments in capacity and reduced changeover times is a central issue in the context of just-in-time manufacturing. It is not altogether surprising that this tradeoff tends to be ignored in industrial practice since the traditional investment procedure is triggered at a time when bottlenecks protrude from the surface. At such a point in time capacity and its costs naturally turn into the dominant decision criteria. Flexibility then only plays a secondary role.

Operations researchers have investigated and drawn the attention to a simple phenomenon that appears to provide an after-the-fact justification for the Japanese investments in reduced changeover times. They show why these investments of effort and money can be more advantageous than investments in additional capacity, particularly in large or fast equipment.

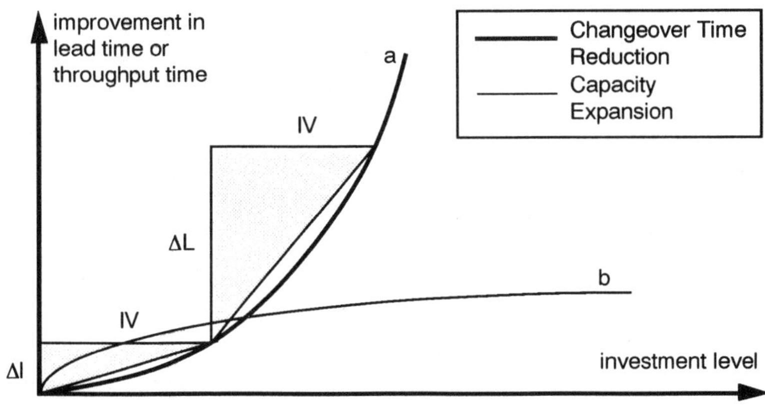

Figure 2.2: The tradeoff between tradional investments in additional capacity—faster equipment—and investments in reduced changeover times—more flexible equipment. Investments in reduced changeover times (curve **a**) show increasing marginal returns: Doubling the initial investment **IV** gives an improvement in the lead time or, alternatively, throughput time, of value **ΔL**, substantially larger than the initial return **ΔI**. The opposite holds for investments in equipment (curve **b**). Given the point in time at which investment decisions are typically made, it is important to note that the higher the utilization of the equipment, the steeper is the slope of **b**.

Marginal returns on capital invested in additional equipment, like most other investments, are decreasing. Zangwill [1987] and Porteus [1985] use the well-known formula for the Economic Order Quantity[18] (EOQ)—which has been used since Harris [1915], who introduced it, and Wilson [1934], who popularized it, to amortize setup costs—to show that under the strong assumptions of this exceedingly simple model margins on investments in setup time reduction are

[18]The economic order quantity is calculated as $\sqrt{(2Kd) / h}$, where ´K´ is the setup cost; ´d´ the demand and ´h´ the holding cost.

increasing. Of course, sophisticated and complex methods for the lot or order sizing problem have been developed. It is unlikely that a similar mathematical and convincing analysis can be provided. However, Zangwill was able to obtain similar results for the dynamic lot size model, which relaxes the assumptions of stationary demand and costs in the EOQ model.[19]

Figure 2.2 graphically displays the basic effects of investments in additional capacity and reduced changeover time on lead time or throughput time. For the sake of exposition, the two curves have been kept simple. Discrete or step functions would be more realistic. The curves imply a linear relationship between investment level and change in changeover time and capacity expansion. As the changeover time approaches zero, this assumption will certainly not hold. Of course, modern machines may be faster and more flexible.

Porteus and Zangwill have studied one of the major given parameters in the classical inventory control model. Under common intuition, large investments in setup cost (and time) reduction yield decreasing marginal returns because smaller changes in setup cost produce even smaller reductions in overall costs. This erroneous intuition about investments in setup cost reduction may, according to Zangwill, explain why this issue has mainly been ignored. It seems Japanese managers have intuitively understood the importance of slashing setup costs and times, typically by an order of magnitude. Porteus [1985] also explicitly models the costs of the investments, and the influence of the sales rate.

The EOQ model only accounts for reduced setup and holding costs. It ignores the effects of lot and campaign sizes on safety stocks, lead times, quality, flexibility, effective capacity and labour utilization, and does not take into consideration sequence-dependent changeover times, multi-level production and capacity constraints. It merely examines the tradeoff between inventory holding costs and capacity loss. As was pointed out earlier, these comments apply only to a lesser extent to modern lot and campaign sizing methods and research. However, in a recent review of this work, considering algorithmic and computational complexity as well as current practice, Bahl et al. [1987] conclude, "...the realities of plant environments ... are the Achilles heel of lot-sizing research." The analysis of the application of a more sophisticated dynamic lot sizing method (Silver-Meal) in the industrial case investigated as part of the research presented in this thesis—see chapters 6 and 7—confirms this. The list of research directions in [ibid.] focuses on the "soft spot of the field," namely, multi-level lot sizing problems with resource constraints—"which, paradoxically are the most prevalent in practice." The authors do not fail to point out the benefits of reducing changeover times and costs. They note in particular that many decisions problems are simplified.

[19]Zangwill shows with an example that in the dynamic lot size model inventory levels do not necessarily decrease when setup costs are reduced.

Fixed setup costs are problematic in their own way:

> ... [T]here is often no real setup cost in the sense of cash flows being affected. Rather, the setup cost is only a surrogate for the violation of capacity constraints .... Thus, the idea of a fixed setup cost, independent of the solution, can be misleading because it is often a consequence of the solution. When real setup costs exist due to say, material losses, they should be distinguished from the opportunity costs of lost production capacity [Karmarkar 1987, p. 409].

Karmarkar argues that the effect on capacity utilization is best captured by the lead time of a productive unit. As he points out, lead times themselves have a pervasive impact on performance [p. 410]:

- larger lead times lead to proportionally larger work-in-process inventory
- safety stocks grow more than proportionally with lead times
- long lead times entail long planning horizons, increasing the risk of schedule changes
- larger lead times lead to an increased loss of information—see the concept of induced learning discussed below
- coordination (scheduling) becomes more difficult, as variability increases with lead times
- lead time is an important strategic dimension—see the discussion of the work of Rosenfield et al. above

Karmarkar concludes, "... the lack of analysis of the relationship between batch sizing and lead times is somewhat surprising." Forrester, in his exemplary work on industrial dynamics [1961, *nota bene*], already examined the relation of lead times and instability in production-distribution systems with respect to unexpected changes in demand. However, as discussed in §3.6.2, in Forrester's work, lead time is an input parameter. For a short rehash of this particular issue and the importance of time-based competition in general, see Stalk [1988]. For a more general discussion of Forrester's work see [Augusto et al. 1980].

Exploiting the idea that when a production unit goes out of a control an entire lot will be sub-standard, Porteus [1986] examines the relationship between, setup costs reduction, lot sizing and quality.

The mathematical models of Karmarkar, Porteus and Zangwill are adding valuable insight into just-in-time. But these models need extending to multi-item and multi-level environments. This is an exceedingly difficult task, since the limits of mathematical tractability are reached all too soon. Simulation, which explicitly models and structures the logical relationships and interactions in a system, is an effective tool for constructing comprehensive models. A simulation model also provides a fertile framework for testing lot sizing methods and sequencing rules. The next section discusses a prime example of the use of simulation. In conclusion, it is safe to put forward the hypothesis that mathematical models tend to underestimate the benefits of reduced changeover times by a large degree.

2.8 Shaping the Manufacturing Environment

The most comprehensive and thorough quantitative analysis of just-in-time manufacturing has been carried out by a research team at Ohio State University with the assistance of an industrial panel of plant managers of a major manufacturing company, see [Krajewski et al. 1987; Ritzman et al. 1984]. Their analysis lends support to the currently available statistical evidence, see [Hayes et al. 1985] discussed above, and the claims of productivity improvements made by proponents of just-in-time. Moreover, it provides insight. The strength of the analysis stems from the complexity of the environments investigated. Simplifying assumptions, commonly imposed by a conventional mathematical analysis, are few in comparison.

To determine which factors shape the manufacturing environment, Krajewski et al. constructed a large-scale and detailed simulation model capable of representing diverse, discrete lot-sized environments. In cooperation with the panel, they identified thirty six factors and grouped these into seven clusters:

- customer influence - demand variability, make-to-stock vs. make-to-order
- vendor influence - quality and reliability
- buffer mechanisms - capacity slack, safety stock and safety lead time
- product structure - shape, depth and commonality
- facility design - routing pattern and length of routes
- process - scrap rate, equipment failures, worker flexibility
- inventory - accuracy, lot-sizing policy, setup times.

For each of these clusters low, medium and high settings were specified. Using three different manufacturing control systems—MRP, ROP[20] and kanban—, they then evaluated the environments with respect to performance measures reflecting labour productivity, inventory levels, and service levels.

The most surprising conclusion drawn on the basis of the experiments is that the control system used appears to be less important than the factors shaping the environment. All systems perform poorly with unfavourable settings of the factors. Factors with the greatest impact on performance are lot sizing in combination with setup times; scrap rate (i.e. quality level); worker flexibility, and in combination with large lot sizes, equipment failures, capacity slack, safety stock and service policy (i.e. make-to-stock vs. make-to-order). These factors are typically included in discussions on the implementation requirements of just-in-time.

Poor vendor performance proved to be much less detrimental than is usually claimed. This would support Walleigh's [1986] recommendation on implementation

[20]ROP – Re-Order Point review is a simple pull system with several variants which places an order when the stock level drops below the re-order point. The re-order point stock level is the sum of the required safety stock and the stock required to cover the demand during the lead time of the product. The length of the review period must also be taken into account

strategy: "[a]sking suppliers to make daily deliveries is a common mistake of managers who focus on the inventory-reduction benefits of JIT. Ultimately this is the right thing to do, but it is the wrong place to start. If manufacturing executives recognize JIT as a problem-solving techniques rather than an inventory-reduction plan, the proper starting point will be clearer [p. 38]." The result is all the more noteworthy in view of the large number of publications on just-in-time purchasing of raw materials, for examples see [Lee et al. 1985; O'Neal 1987; Schonberger et al. 1983a]. The cause is probably related to the depth of the product structure in the investigated environments and "the efficiency of integer multiple lot sizes in multi-echelon production inventory systems."[21] The danger of extending experience with (or for that matter analysis of) systems with "shallow" product structures to more complex ones becomes apparent.

Vendor-supplier relations in just-in-time settings have come under heavy criticism. The critics, who adopt a moral tone for the occasion, claim with some justification, that large just-in-time manufacturers exploit their power by squeezing the most out of their suppliers. The fact is, however, that vendor-supplier relations are not, as usual, adversarial. Long-term, cooperative agreements with a few suppliers are characteristic. Du Pont's use of consignment inventories at GM's in Detroit [Winton 1985] is not exactly a brilliant solution to the demands placed on a just-in-time supplier.

Krajewski et al. did not obtain conclusive evidence on the influence of product structure and facility design. These aspects, they feel, require further attention. For a comparison in the context of MRP, see Baker et al. [1986] on the effect of commonality on safety stocks and Benton [1985] on product structure complexity and the performance of lot sizing heuristics.

Markedly absent from the work of Krajewski et al. are cost-based factors and measures. The exclusion of costs amounts to one major limitation, especially in the light of the work of Rosenfield et al. [1985], discussed above. Product margins (sales price minus variable costs) are obviously of interest. Equally relevant is the structure of the value-added chain—that is, the ratio of value-added and total throughput time at each stage of the logistics chain.

No mention[22] is made of the impact of a widely dispersed distribution network typical for multinationals. It is not clear, whether Krajewski et al. simply neglected to investigate the tail of the chain or whether this is due to a restriction of the simulator. Using a much simpler simulation model, Bookbinder et al. [1986] analyze this aspect. Focusing on distribution may make sense because it is not uncommon that much more than half of the capital tied up in stocks is in finished goods. This applies to all multinationals with central production facilities.

Although, the experiments do show that the consequences of poor quality are much less disruptive when lot sizes are small, the model apparently doesn't account for the potentially positive effect of small lot sizes on quality. An important

---

[21] Chakravarty et al. [1985] conducted a series of experiments with a systems dynamics model to confirm that integer multiple lot sizes perform significantly better.

[22] Porteus [1986], mentioned earlier, examines a different and simpler aspect of the interaction of lot sizes and quality.

claim made by proponents of just-in-time is that by reducing inventory levels, which will cause some disruption at the outset, problems and their causes are exposed and corrected sooner.[23] The learning curve is steeper. Incorporating such a positive feedback spiral[24] in a model, adds further complexity. The concept of induced learning, as opposed to autonomous learning, is examined in [Suri et al. 1986] using a simple analytic model. The authors conclude that the magnitude of the benefits of reducing inventories corresponds to observations of real systems if in fact a positive relationship between disruption and learning exists. "... [C]onservative learning rates and assumptions ... still yield results that make a strong case for JIT [p. 303]." It is precisely this kind of second order effect that would support the hypothesis put forward in this chapter that the overall benefits of reducing setup times are underestimated by mathematical models.

2.9 Just-in-Time and Simplicity: An Avenue for further Research

An observer of just-in-time manufacturing environments might boldly argue that the drive towards simplicity is the heart of it all. Chaos and the associated organizational confusion are by all accounts prevalent features of complex operations. Most organizations are aware of the potentially debilitating effects of complexity and pay at least lip-service to the KISS[25] principle. However, the notion of complexity is not well-understood and the economic value of simplicity is especially difficult to assess. The tendency in our society in general and in our industrial organizations in particular has been to counter the symptoms of organizational complexity with the institutionalization of central power and control mechanisms. The role of the development of all-encompassing commercial E.D.P. systems needs to be seen in this light. Mowshowitz [1976, chapter 12] writes:

> The appeal to social complexity as an evolutionary principle which necessitates the growth of central power is a modern equivalent of the theory of the divine rights of kings. ... [p. 228.]
>
> ... Naturally, the entire discussion would be somewhat incomplete if it did not suggest future directions. The computer coupled with the methods of operations research and their progeny are seen to be likely candidates for handling organized complexity. These developments, then, come to be linked with the world's salvation in the future. ... [p. 231]

---

[23]This issue is discussed at length in Schonberger's [1984b] "Just-in-time production – The quality dividend" He writes, "[i]t should be clear that a quality program can have limited success if production lots are large." and "Ohno [Toyota's vice president and the man who introduced Kanban] saw that buffer stock keeps production moving but at the same time covers up problems. ... When a problem is solved a little more buffer stock is removed, which triggers more problem solving. The short-term pains are worth the long-term gains [p. 23]."

[24]The idea is that by reducing stock levels, problems are exposed and turned into opportunities which can then be exploited – see Hall [1983, p. 13] for the famous analogy of water flow to material flow in production. These two steps can be applied repeatedly, thus creating a spiral of constant productivity improvements.

[25]KISS – Keep it simple, stupid.

> As we have indicated repeatedly, the persuasive character of information systems in government and industry derives from their ability to mitigate the effects of disorganized complexity. ... [p. 240]

Some of the effects of complexity are playfully illustrated in a simple manufacturing game conceived by Wildemann for use in his seminars. His students form a team that is to assemble pyramids with built-in pharaohs using Lego blocks. Naturally, the market demands different sizes and colours in this game. Quality problems and setup times are also mimicked. Two production control concepts are simulated: An MRP-like system with large lot sizes and a central push policy on the one hand, and a kanban-like system with smaller lot sizes and a strict pull policy on the other. As the MRP-like system starts to operate full-steam and attempts to respond to erratic demand fluctuations, the general level of confusions rises with the stock piles at the different stages. Human mistakes result and go unnoticed until much later. Predictably, the kanban-like system works like a charm. The realism of this game need not be discussed. The game serves educational purposes only. However, one issue that tends to be ignored while reduced stock levels and throughput times are discussed is that the difference in performance must in part be attributed to simplicity and the absence of confusion. In the kanban-like system there is no sign of hectic. The productive units are permanently in tune with the big picture. The global effects of local acts are immediately transparent. In addition, imbalances between the stages are clearly visible: some productive units will be idle some of the time.

Returning to reality after this short excursion, academics and practitioners alike are confronted with the observations of Cole [1985]:

> Yet many discussions focus on the new technology's [EDP] intrinsic characteristics and how they affect the shape, scope, and depth of information and pay little attention to how this revolution affects organizational performance. The boosters of the new technology sometimes fail to consider the impediments to effective decision making that complex information systems can erect .... [p. 100]

> ... [F]inance and accounting departments, two main generators for the demand for information, accounted for 8% to 10% of total salaried employees in the U.S. companies but for only 2% in one of the major Japanese auto manufacturers. [p. 102]

> ... More important ... is to point out the tremendous stress the Japanese place on finding ways to simplify the manufacturing process. The just-in-time system is a good example of this. [p. 104]

Simplicity and its consequences are aspects of just-in-time environments that cannot easily be captured by formal models. Again, this means that traditional scientific research on the subject will tend to underestimate the benefits of just-in-time.

Warner [1987], in an article provocatively entitled "Information Technology as a Competitive Burden," addresses the coordinating function of information technology in organizations. Referring to other research, he notes that if inventory is to be regarded as waste, then information-processing capacity serving the same dubious function is also waste. One obvious but often ignored idea is to reduce the need for information processing in the first place and to use the scarce resources required for it where most leverage can be obtained.

2.10 Implications for Operations Research

Before turning to methodological issues, it appears appropriate to summarize some implications for operations research. As discussed at length, operations research will need to take a fresh look at the role of reduced setup times and costs. Furthermore, since in many environments these cannot be reduced to negligible values, further research on lot and campaign sizing will continue to be valuable for practitioners, also in just-in-time environments. The comment of Fleischmann [1987]:

> ... JIT ist also kein Planungssystem, sondern macht, grob gesagt, die Produktionsbedingungen so einfach, dass eine Planung, und insbesondere OR-Verfahren, auf der kurzfristigen Ebene überflüssig werden. [p. 351]

needs to be interpreted with care.

The second implication is that simulation modelling will increase in prominence, since it is the most appropriate tool for dealing with several problems that crop up when designing and evaluating a just-in-time manufacturing system. For example, the balancing of production lines or cellular manufacturing units is an issue that requires proportionally more attention since, in general, the throughput of a system suffers when operating under the pull principle. Several researchers quoted in this thesis, including also Wildemann, have stressed the importance of simulation modeling.

3 An Overall Approach for Assessing Just-in-Time

how have you sped?
archaic English

3.1 Introduction and Outline

This chapter lays the foundation for the two complementary methods that are described and discussed in detail in the two subsequent chapters. It first revisits the central question of the economics of speed. Some general observations about the overall business process, its performance measures and driving factors, as well as the role of modeling then precede the actual introduction of the methods making up the overall approach. This introduction focuses on the general aspects of these methods and how they fit together. This chapter closes with a comparative analysis of these methods and a discussion of the merits and limitations of the overall approach.

3.2 Quod Erat Demonstrandum

The resounding "QED" at the end of an hour-long academic lecture will on more than one occasion have left the uninitiated with the question "which was the thing to be proved or shown?" Before delving into the overall approach, I would like to review what this thesis sets out to show. The objective of the research presented in this thesis is certainly not to prove some kind of general statement about the impact of the just-in-time concept. It merely is to develop a comparative framework of performance measurement for assessing its impact in specific industrial cases. This framework must embody an adequate representation of the context. It must address the pre-conditions under which the application of the concept may be desirable and successful. I make no apologies to the reader who feels that this kind of underlying framework simply is a reflection of the trendy relativistic thinking that has been popularized by the New Age movement.

When it comes to assessing the impact of the just-in-time concept, the central issue, as the title of this thesis expresses, is the economics of speed, i.e. how to translate measures of speed into financial terms. The Concise Oxford Dictionary of English gives as one of the possible meanings of speed the "rate of progress or motion, rate of change of distance with time." In the case of manufacturing, progress amounts to nothing but added value. In this narrow but valuable interpretation, speed is the rate at which a manufacturing system adds value, i.e. the ratio of value-added time to the accumulated flow time per product.

Interestingly enough, an archaic meaning of "speed" and "to speed", given in the Concise Oxford Dictionary of English, equates speed with success and prosperity The quoted examples of its archaic use are: "how have you sped?" and "God speed you." To speed means to be or make prosperous, to succeed, to give success to. Given the sluggishness of present manufacturing systems, it is perhaps appropriate that this meaning has been sinking into oblivion. Be this as it may, it does nicely lead back to the original question: what is the economics of speed, or to paraphrase, in what circumstances does speed lead to speed?

There are several important comments to add about the notion of speed at this point. If one needs to be driving a heavily loaded motorized vehicle across the center of Amsterdam, dropping of "deliverables" at various points along the way, then the average speed will depend as much on the ability of the vehicle to adjust to the flow of the traffic, i.e. its ability to accelerate and slow down rapidly, as on the exact destination, route taken and the general traffic conditions. Similarly in manufacturing, there is a difference between velocity and acceleration, but one is not independent of the other. A car salesman or car fetish will, therefore, at the first opportunity point out in how many seconds say the velocity of 100 km/hour is reached. The comparable notion of acceleration for expressing the ability of a manufacturing system to respond to changing conditions, e.g. demand fluctuations, is rather elusive and does not have a prominent place when measuring performance. There is mounting evidence that the ability to change gears will increasingly be the feature to watch.

As with any analogy, this particular one also has its weak points. Fortunately, its limitation, which was hinted at by noting the impact of the general traffic conditions, serves to address a significant change in the way of thinking about speed. The layout and the planning and control procedures that comprise the environment in which the production equipment operates are at present receiving more and more management attention. This change stems, among other things, from numerous empirical observations of a single phenomenon made during the past decade in altogether different industries, see the compendium of Wildemann [1986a]. The time required for those activities that would cause a deterioration of a product's attributes if not performed, i.e. the value-added time, is a small percentage of the total time the product spends in the system, i.e. the total flow time. The issue, to be revisited in this thesis, is that the speed of the value-added activities at the different stages of the manufacturing process do not in their own set the overall pace. The actual case in the pharmaceutical industry that is subsequently investigated is no exception. Seen in this light, the shift in focus towards eliminating or reducing non-value-added activities can no longer come as a surprise.

The features of modern equipment, e.g. automated changeovers, are directed at this task. Many authors, recently Drucker [1990, p. 97], have noted the difficulties that plant personnel have encountered in justifying such investments. These difficulties, they attribute to the pitfalls and drawbacks of traditional cost accounting practices. The inputs to investment appraisals provided by these practices have tended to stack the cards against such investments, which, as noted, "must then be justified by faith alone." An interesting case concerning automation in quality control is addressed in the chapters dealing with the investigated case in this thesis. If, as American authors argue, cost accounting systems have to be revamped, then an underlying theory of manufacturing must be in place. Such a theory needs to capture the economics of speed by translating the different measures of speed into financial terms. Without it, these systems will be on weak footing.

3.3 Relevant Factors

We naturally view an industrial or business enterprise as a system composed of many diverse and interrelated variables. Besides the external factors that govern the performance of the system, there are those factors that are subject to and the consequence of managerial decisions. The decision about what classifies as a relevant factor and what as a performance measure implicitly entails a mental model of the system. The effective and efficient allocation of available resources requires an understanding of the cause and effect relationships operating in a system. Sound quantitative statements about the change in output in relation to a change in several inputs are difficult to make since they require an adequate model of the complex interplay of the various components of the system. It is not uncommon, therefore, that decisions are taken on the basis of over-simplified models, that ignore, for example, secondary and accumulative effects.

The importance of models and their underlying theories can hardly be understated. Once models have established their usefulness, they tend to have a pervasive and long-term impact on decision making. What is relevant often depends on what models previous generations adopted. The inertia that successful models build up—think of the invested effort and accrued benefits—puts a break on our ability to recognize and respond to changing environments. As Beer has said: "If it works it is out-of-date." A Kuhnian paradigm change is itself a slow and painful process. Moreover, it is concomitant with crisis. Whether there has ever been a unified and comprehensive theory of manufacturing is debatable. Taylorism hardly qualifies. That a renowned author such as Drucker [1990] can speak of "the emerging theory of manufacturing" may possibly delude a few North-American managers into believing that their operations will regain their competitive edge. But certainly it should raise the eyebrows of most critical observers. I cannot fail to get the impression that the need for another catchy title in the HBR plays as much a role as the need for a new theory of manufacturing. Be this as it may, a short discussion on the nature on the role of formal modeling, see §3.5, is more than justified,

Treatises on relevant factors and performance measurement generally do not fail to point out that what is relevant depends on the time horizon of the decisions under consideration. Since the costs of operating a fully-automated warehouse are largely independent of throughput and fill rate, day-to-day operational decisions about lot and campaign sizes should exclude the fixed costs of warehousing. The upshot of this point of view is all too predictable. The uneasy question remaining is whether this kind of reasoning, which is technically sound, leads to short-term decisions that are undesirable in the medium and long term. Critics of the conventional school argue that at least in some cases incremental costs, e.g. the costs of creating additional warehouse space, should be used.

The nature of the central question addressed in this thesis demands what may at first appear as an unorthodox approach in the sense that the analysis involves a mixture of short- and long-term decisions. Care must be exercised when separating short- and long-term decisions. One characteristic of the just-in-time concept is that operational policies are, or at least ought to be, linked with the more general manufacturing policies and investment decisions. One consequence is that for the sake of the present analysis—this should be no surprise—fixed costs are considered to be variable.

The investigated controllable factors or, better, the decision variables can broadly be categorized into four segments. Clearly, a decision in one segment can typically not be taken independently of decisions in any of the other segments. The complexity of decision making is to a large extent the result of the interdependence of these segments.

The first set of decisions concerns the kind of *equipment and information processing technology* used. This assumes the chemical-pharmaceutical production processes themselves as given. A second set concerns the *methods and procedures* to be put in place for operating the equipment and systems. A third set concerns the concepts and practices for the *planning and operational control* of the manufacturing system as a whole. This covers the design of the layout of the factory in conjunction with the material and information flows and the concepts for controlling these flows, e.g. stock and order policies. A fourth set concerns the *organization*, in particular, the functional structure establishing the breakdown of responsibilities. See §7.2.2 for a detailed description.

3.4 Conversion Processes and Performance Measures

By all accounts, making a profit will continue to be the primary objective of industrial and business organizations. However, most organizations have come to recognize that they will have to manage a multi-dimensional portfolio of objectives in order to ensure their profits and existence in the long-run. The focus of the present research remains on the conventional primary objective. On occasion, I will note an impact on environmental and social questions.

Financial performance should, as others have convincingly argued, not solely be based on profit, but on the return on capital invested in the resources required to make the profit in the first place. This thesis takes this measure as the starting point, while noting that profit or net contribution is the most prominent measure when it comes to day-to-day business decisions. Profit is, or, at least, is perceived to be, more tangible than assets. Not all of the resources required for the conversion process are considered an asset for the sake of accounting and performance measurement. Information and data stored on E.D.P. systems, know-how and expertise of people working in the organization are not included. I might add, parenthetically, that an increasing share of management attention will focus on precisely these intangibles. However, since it is already difficult enough to assess and re-assess the value of equipment and materials, it is no surprise that in everyday business the focus is on simple profit. This is also characteristic of many classical operations research models.

A further noteworthy difficulty is that current assets are subject to considerable fluctuation over time, while the measurement of these assets is performed at a key-date. The consequence is not only that the measurement taken may differ from the average value over a given period, but also that the measurement process itself is likely to amplify these fluctuations and to distort any underlying trend.

The broad range of derived performance measures in place in large organizations is a often reflection of the hierarchical structure of these and the obvious need that each unit is accountable for the performance—and the measurement thereof—that it can directly influence by its activities. In organizations with a matrix structure, a hotchpot of partially conflicting measures is the natural but undesirable result. Examples of performance measures driving the organization as whole into the wrong direction are not hard to find. Eilon's work *The Art of Reckoning: Analysis of Performance Criteria*[26] [1984], in particular the introductory chapters, serve to bring the necessary structure in what he and Gold have termed the network of productivity relationships. The network stresses the interdependencies of the various productivity ratios in use.

Eilon uses the nodes and arcs in his network flow diagram, see figure 3.1 below, to categorize the kind of performance analysis that may be pursued. Eilon is careful to point out that although each node and arc in the network can be considered in its own right, decision makers must consider the interactions with any other element in the network. An expanded version of the network is presented in §3.4.2.

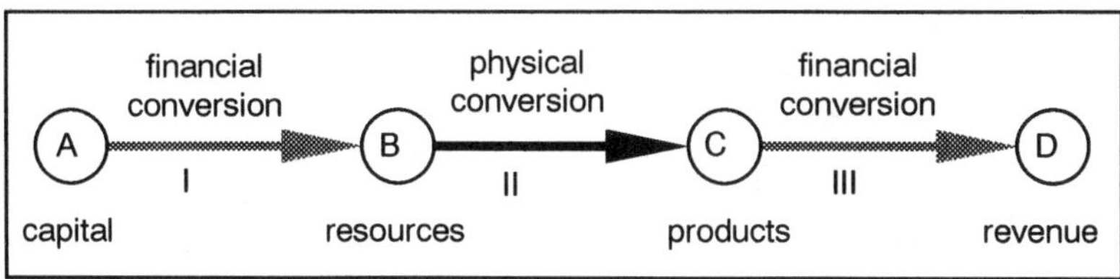

Figure 3.1: Input-output conversions after Eilon [1984]

The *nodes* focus attention on the balance and mix of the internal elements:

A: capital financing; balance between equity and foreign capital
B: resource investment; balance between equipment, labour and materials
C: product management; balance of product mix
D: cash management; balance of revenues in a multi-national (transfer prices!)

The *arcs* in the network focus attention on the conversion processes and their efficiency:

I: purchasing; via the price mechanism capital is turned into physical inputs
II: production; physical inputs are turned into physical outputs
III: sales; via the price mechanism physical output is turned into cash

[26] I owe the reference to Eilon's work to Prof. F. Rosenkranz. The reader who is familiar with this work will note the extent to which it has influenced the design and application of QED.

Just-in-time falls under the general heading of production and operations management. In other words, nodes B and C and arc II are of primary interest. The efficiency of the two financial conversion processes, largely dictated by market forces, is of secondary interest . The topic is clearly beyond the scope of this thesis. Nevertheless, it plays a role. The reason is twofold. The mixture of resources used to manufacture the desired product mix will vary in kind and in composition depending on the manufacturing concept and strategy to be put in operation. This implies that the input as well as the outputs of the physical conversion process must be put in financial terms for a meaningful comparison. The second reason is less apparent because two important elements, namely information flows and time, that are pertinent to the subject of just-in-time will tend to go unnoticed in the above network flow diagram.

Besides production and operations management, the activities and the resources required to accomplish the physical conversion process also encompass those belonging to logistics or, to use the modern term, supply chain management. This entails, furthermore, that the notion of product include not only the physical properties relevant to its application, but also the dimension of delivery service. The nonfinancial indicators related to this dimension, such as lead time and throughput time, still beg the financial question. This closes the circle and returns us to the economics of speed.

The translation of indicators of speed into bottom-line financial measures is the central issue in this thesis. In order to assess the economics of speed, the analysis needs to insert a missing link in the performance measurement framework: what links quantitative but nonfinancial measures such as inventory coverage, lead times and throughput times, on the one hand, and financial measures such as the performance factor, on the other hand? Refer back to §2.6 on cost accounting issues. It is not surprising that this leads to a new series of derived measures.

3.5 On Modeling

Given the role modeling plays in the methodological framework introduced in the following sections of this chapter, it is appropriate to review the nature and the significance of this activity and some of the characteristics of the tools that have developed since the discipline of operations research, which rightly or wrongly claims this activity as its domain and intellectual property, came into existence. In the context of this thesis, it is interesting to note that the historical development of operations research and logistics are intimately linked to each other. The early application of operations research techniques to the complex logistics problems brought about by the efforts of the Allied Forces during World War II have been well publicized. The Concise Oxford Dictionary reminds us of this origin: "logistics – [the] art of moving, lodging, and supplying troops and equipment."

Modeling is certainly not a new human activity. Progress, or at least the history of mankind, cannot be detached from our ability to understand and interpret the world around us. This ability critically depends on the quality of the mental models of our collective experience. Under the influence of developments in artificial intelligence, it is now generally recognized and stated that knowledge representation is at the heart of this activity. The need to share knowledge, i.e. communication, tends to receive less attention. In fact, the need for rigor often means that the knowledge expressed in terms of certain kinds of modeling languages is accessible to an exclusive group of insiders.

Modeling is a purpose-driven activity. How well a model satisfies a given purpose therefore defines its quality. Seen from this angle, the simplicity of models is not a virtue in itself, but an issue of practical application and insight gained. Simplicity, and complexity for that matter, are elusive concepts. The degree of success in communicating a model is a good measure of a model's simplicity. The presence of extraneous constructs in models has been tabu ever since Occam's razor, which perhaps helped to raise simplicity to an aesthetic principle, regardless of pragmatics. In passing, one cannot fail to note that a very large share of the modeling activity is aimed at man-made systems.

Kreutzer [1986, pp. 2-4] decomposes modeling into four distinct phases. The first of these identifies a real-world system, where Kreutzer defines a system to be "a collection of objects, their relationships and behaviour relevant to a set of purposes." The second phase establishes a representation of this system in which its aspects are "bound into structures of some larger mental framework of beliefs, assumptions and theories." In the third phase, the problem solver draws on this theory to design a corresponding conceptual model, which, of necessity, is always a simplification of the system under investigation. Kreutzer is careful enough to point out that different theories yield different models. The borderline between a system representation and a conceptual model has tended to become blurred since unified theories are hard to come by in many disciplines except for the natural sciences. Not surprisingly, less philosophical authors no longer draw this distinction. The fourth phase, which has become most prominent since the advent of electronic calculating engines, covers the conversion of the conceptual model into a computer program suitable for experimentation. The four components of the modeling process thus are: systems, theories, models and programs.

The mechanistic analysis under consideration defines systems (and models) in terms of a few meta-concepts. An *entity* is an object of interest in the system. An *attribute* is a property of an entity. Attributes take on values, which need not necessarily be numeric. The *state* of a system at a particular point in time is determined by the values of the attributes of the relevant entities in the system. An *event* is a set of simultaneous state changes. An *activity* is the conceptual closure of a time-consuming action performed by an entity and triggered by a set of conditions on the values of attributes of other entities. A *process* is a sequence of nested activities involving the same entity. If the modeling language is restricted to mathematical equations, the terminology changes: entities turn into variables with a level as the single numerical attribute; activities into flows; and events into changes in the levels of variables and the rate of flows.[27]

---

[27]This attempt to map the terminology of the meta-views is unsatisfactory because of the difference in the treatment of time.

3.5.1 Models Classified

The kind of symbolic models that are of interest in the context of this thesis are often descriptive. Descriptive models do not prescribe a course of action. In other words, the analyst cannot use these kinds of models to deduce an optimal solution strategy. Descriptive models generally lack a unified underlying theory. Analytical models, on the other hand, tend to be based on some strong theory, which, however, requires simplifying assumptions about the interactions in the real-world system. These assumptions either restrict the domain of application of analytical models or, worse, put a question mark on the validity of their application. The EOQ model, discussed previously, is a prime example of such an analytical model. Analytical models are usually put in mathematical terms, for example, a set of simultaneous equations which are solved to obtain an optimal solution. [Hax et al. 1984] contains a broad range of examples of applications of mathematical programming models to production and inventory management problems. Included are formulations in terms of the well-known linear and non-linear programming problems as well as integer and mixed-integer programming problems. Finding optimal and in some cases feasible solutions for the latter class of problems is exceedingly difficult. Much research effort has therefore been invested in heuristics and approximative solution methods. The availability of appropriate solution methods is a key factor for analytical models. A prime example are the mathematical formulations used in corporate modeling, see Rosenkranz [1979], for which analytical solutions exist only in special and usually uninteresting cases: "Unfortunately, analytical solutions are only of minor importance in practical corporate modeling work and in most cases numerical analysis, especially simulation, is used to determine the output variables of the model [ibid, p. 70]." Descriptive models, on the other hand, are simulation models by their very nature, not by the lack of analytical solution techniques.

The following characteristics serve to classify simulation models:

- If the element of time is not explicitly represented, then a model is *static*. A model is *dynamic,* if its state or behaviour is time dependent.
- If state changes occur only at a discrete set of points in time then a model is *discrete*. A model is *continuous,* if its state changes occur continuously with time. In a continuous model, the simulation clock advances with fixed increments. The smaller these time slices are set, the more continuous the model becomes. Strictly speaking, such models are quasi-continuous.[28] Alternatively, the simulation clock advances with irregular increments by jumping to the time of the next event, i.e. state change. In this case, the term discrete-event model is appropriate. Whether a system is simulated with a discrete or continuous model depends very much on its purpose. The analogous classification of systems according this characterization is

---

[28]The view of Rosenkranz [1979, pp. 55-59] may appear to differ from the one presented here, see for example [Banks 1984, p. 7] and [Kreutzer 1986, p.31]. His survey of the literature on corporate modelling revealed that only systems dynamics models [Forrester 1961] are truly continuous.

mainly dependent on our mental models of these systems rather than their inherent properties. The analysis of an inventory and distribution system, which is usually viewed as a discrete system, may well be performed with the aid of a continuous model. In cases where there is a choice, the continuous view will typically be preferred, if a high degree of aggregation with low-resolution of a complex system is desirable. Continuous models are also appropriate for studying relatively simple systems at a high level of detail. In such cases, changes are smooth. As Kreutzer [1986, p. 31] points out, discrete models lie in between these two extremes. Models may also be combined discrete-continuous. The mechanism for combining discrete and continuous simulation techniques is well-understood and implemented in commercial simulation languages.

• If a model does not contain pseudo-random variables, which can be described by probability distributions, then it is *deterministic* and otherwise *stochastic*. The outcome of deterministic models is in principle predictable. The outcome of stochastic models are at best estimates of the observed variables.

• If a model does not depend on the values of external (exogenous) variables, it is *closed* and otherwise *open*. In a closed model, changes in the variables are generated solely by their interactions. Understanding these interactions is then the key objective. Whether a model is open or closed is, however, a question of degree. Forrester [1961] has propagated a style of closed modeling that permits exogenous variables only to the extent that they serve "as excitation of the internal responses of the system" and are "entirely independent of the resulting response within the system." To have any explanatory power, a model must account for at least some internal interactions, i.e. the causes of behaviour must be captured endogenously by the structure of the model. The modeler's decision about the boundary between the system and its environment is an important and related issue.

• Two further characteristics of simulation models refer to their time-dependent behaviour. A model, or system, is *stable* if the effects of disturbances decline and disappear, returning the model to its original state. Otherwise it is *unstable*. In industrial systems, fluctuations tend to be constrained by bounds on resources. If a repetitive behaviour pattern establishes itself, then a model has reached a *steady-state* condition. During a period of growth the state of the model is *transient*.

• Traditionally, discrete-event simulation models have been classified according to the implementation style imposed on the analyst. The continuing discussion surrounding this typology stands a good chance of becoming obsolete, since the constructs available in some modern modeling systems have moved up a conceptual level.

3.5.2 Activities in the Modeling Process

Simulation modeling is an experimental and explorative technique. The analyst uses a model to evaluate alternative solutions with respect to a multiple-criterion objective function. Generally, the search for better solutions is an informal process. The intuition of the analyst and the insight obtained into the dynamics of the model by experimentation guide this search. Similarly, model design and implementation, are crafts. How well the analyst performs these tasks depends on the skill with which the analyst handles his or her tools. A comparison of academic texts on simulation modeling, see for example [Banks et al. 1984b], shows that there is a consensus on which activities are critical components of the process itself. The key steps in this process are:

- problem formulation and system identification
- model design
- data collection and parameter estimation
- model implementation
  - program design
  - program coding
- program verification
- model validation
- generation of alternatives—occasionally forgotten
- experimentation
  - experimental design
  - simulation runs
  - performance measurement and analysis
- formulation and implementation of recommended policies

The modeling process as described here is by no means strictly sequential. It is or should be an iterative process. The degree to which this is the case in practice is largely dependent on the tools available for supporting the different steps of the process. Implied is that the major purpose of the model is to provide accurate numerical predictions. However, during the past decade the emphasis has been shifting towards gaining insight into complex systems. Visualization and interaction have become important items on the agenda of simulation modeling techniques. As I have argued [Vaessen 1989], the major advances in simulation modeling stem from these interrelated areas and have lead to a resurgence of interest in this technique, which now goes under the heading of Visual Interactive Simulation Modeling. This technique has a beneficial impact on the modeling process as whole and is changing the way the individual activities are carried out. Its net effect, as observed in practice, has been to improve the chances of successful implementation, see [ibid, pp. 240-241] and §4.3 for the mechanisms playing a role. However, the activities as identified here will stay in place.

3.5.3 Drawbacks of Simulation Modeling

A cursory review of the standard texts on the subject will reveal some thorny disadvantages of simulation modeling:

• Simulation, in particular discrete-event simulation, is computationally expensive, not only because a single experiment requires a substantial amount of time to run to completion on a computer, but mainly because a large number of lengthy experimental observations may be required to get reliable and statistically acceptable results. The improving cost-performance ratio of computer hardware has merely ameliorated this problem.

• Simulation models are designed to answer questions of the type 'what if' and ideally 'what if and why'. Discrete-event simulations cannot answer questions of the type 'what to do to achieve'. This restriction does not apply to simulation models in general, see [Rosenkranz 1979, pp. 37-38].

• The construction of simulation models requires expertise in very different areas. Analysts capable of implementing a model in the form of a computer program are often not familiar enough with the appropriate techniques for statistical analysis and experimental design, and *vice versa*. The same applies to the holder of the knowledge about the application domain. Since each separate task also requires due time and effort, the turnaround time of the overall modeling process tends to be long. The development of new tools supporting the process as a whole and in particular those tools speaking the language of the problem owner are bridging the gap between the possible and the practical. ProfiSEE, see §3.6.1 and chapter 4, is one example of such a tool.

• The temptation to include unnecessary details in the model, and, thereby, to forego the opportunity to come to an analytic solution, is considerable. In general, however, it is difficult to determine *a priori* what an unnecessary detail is. Only experimentation may tell. An iterative approach starting off with a rough-cut analysis could be more effective. The key components driving the performance of model, as indicated by a sensitivity analysis, can subsequently be modeled in more detail. The reverse process of collapsing a set of detailed components into a single aggregated entity is not accomplished automatically with a key-stroke.

• Our ability to come to terms with complexity appears to remain strictly limited in the face of the challenging problems facing us. The availability and use of sophisticated tools for thought, which many modeling systems certainly are, may seduce the analyst into dropping the kind of intellectual modesty that ought to belong to a code of ethics of the profession. The door of intuition will stay open for those disliking formal models.

3.5.4 Advantages and Benefits of Simulation Modeling

These drawbacks of simulation modeling contrast with a set of clear-cut advantages and benefits:

• The generality of simulation modeling permits its application to a broad range of problems. In comparison with analytical models, the numerical solution techniques available for simulation modeling impose few assumptions on the analyst.

• The solution techniques are generally easier understand than the mathematical methods for analytical models. Moreover, the tools for simulation modeling most often hide the solution technique from the analyst employing the tool. An intuitive understanding of the built-in simulation engine usually suffices.

• In many instances, simulation models are re-usable. Of course, this depends on the quality of the initial modeling effort and the kind of assumptions made.

• Simulation is ideally suited to multi-faceted modeling. Different kinds of aspects of a real-world system and their interactions can, in principle, be modeled and investigated. Multiple-criterion objectives are the rule rather than the exception.

• Simulation models can typically cope much more easily with incomplete or inadequate input data than analytical models. In fact, through sensitivity analysis it becomes possible to focus the time and effort expended on data collection on the most critical segments of the input data.

• Simulation models can be combined with optimization techniques. In fact, modeling languages, taken as an intelligent front-end for an optimization package that translates an application-oriented specification into a method-oriented specification, overcome a significant weakness of optimization techniques. The importance of modeling languages will increase, see [Geoffrion 1987] for an example. The same applies to the combination of simulation and optimization. A specific example, which should clarify the kind of synergies we can expect to result, is presented in §4.12.

3.5.5 Purposes of Simulation Modeling

This section on simulation modeling ends with a summary of the characteristic purposes of simulation modeling:

• The primary purpose of simulations is to suggest possible improvements of an existing complex system by enabling the study of such a system without experiments intervening with its day-to-day operation.

• Simulation modeling may also be appropriate for the design of an entirely new system.[29] Between this latter purpose and former there is continuum.

• Simulations may serve to verify and validate structurally simpler models, especially analytical models, and their assumptions.

• Simulations may serve a pedagogical function. In particular, when designed and implemented to be run as a game with several participating players, simulation is a valuable training vehicle. For instance, the author's experience indicates that the seemingly simple concepts of the kanban method of shop floor control are often only partially understood. Apparently, the numerous written explanations have tended to trigger the reader's nodding prematurely. A graphical and animated model serves to explain the mechanics of such a concept. Moreover, if the results of an analysis are counter-intuitive, then a mathematical proof or a black-box model will do little to alleviate the lack of confidence of the model user.

---

[29] Validation is problematic in this case. Strictly speaking, there is no such thing as the validity of a model of a non-existing system—it is face validity at best.

3.6 General Methodological Framework

The general framework for assessing the impact of the application of the just-in-time concept introduced in this chapter is nothing but a straightforward extension of a conventional framework such as the one presented by Eilon. A revised version of Eilon's expansion of the network flow discussed in §3.3, see figure 3.2 below, shows the direction the analysis has to take. As mentioned, it is of paramount importance that the analysis cover logistics. Therefore, we must also understand the role of information flows since these flows in end-effect trigger the material flows and set the speed of the system as a whole. To come to a deeper understanding of these flows and processes, we need to engage in the activity of modeling and build an instrument for analysis.

The demands placed upon an instrument that provides the desired performance analysis while taking into account *all* the relevant factors and interactions discussed are enormous. Its complexity is such that, for the foreseeable future, we can deem any attempt to construct it an exercise in futility. The practical relevance of the issue calls for a pragmatic approach.

The next sub-sections sketch the two components of one such an approach. The first component zooms in on the physical conversion process as delimited by the gray zone in figure 3.2. The second component zooms out just enough to cover the efficiency of the financial conversion processes as an input. The view still includes the physical conversion process; manufacturing and logistics remain in the center. But it is of necessity much coarser. Both components of the overall approach rely on constructing a model for analyzing the performance of the conversion processes.

Although this approach reduces the complexity of the task to a considerable extent, the analysis will still have to employ a vertical and horizontal segmentation of the business to restrict the scope of the models. In practice, there will be a reasonable choice of a segment with a limited degree of interaction with those excluded. The inherent risk is, of course, that we fail to recognize certain opportunities—economies of scope, so to speak.

What is required of these models? Gaining insight into the interrelationships between the different factors is key. The models should establish which factors are the most sensitive to a change in input and assumptions. In addition, it is important to know the relative magnitude of each factor in relation to the whole and to the others. Given the state of the art, it is premature to introduce goal seeking or some form of optimization technology into these models. It is inappropriate to fit these models to the solutions methods presently available. We should only consider the application of optimization technology after an adequate representation of the real-world system as shown figure 3.2 is available in the form of a high-level model. Current research in the application of optimization technology is taking precisely this point of view. The selection and application of methods from a database of possible methods should be based on their properties and the knowledge about the problem. This knowledge derives from the model representing the real-world system.

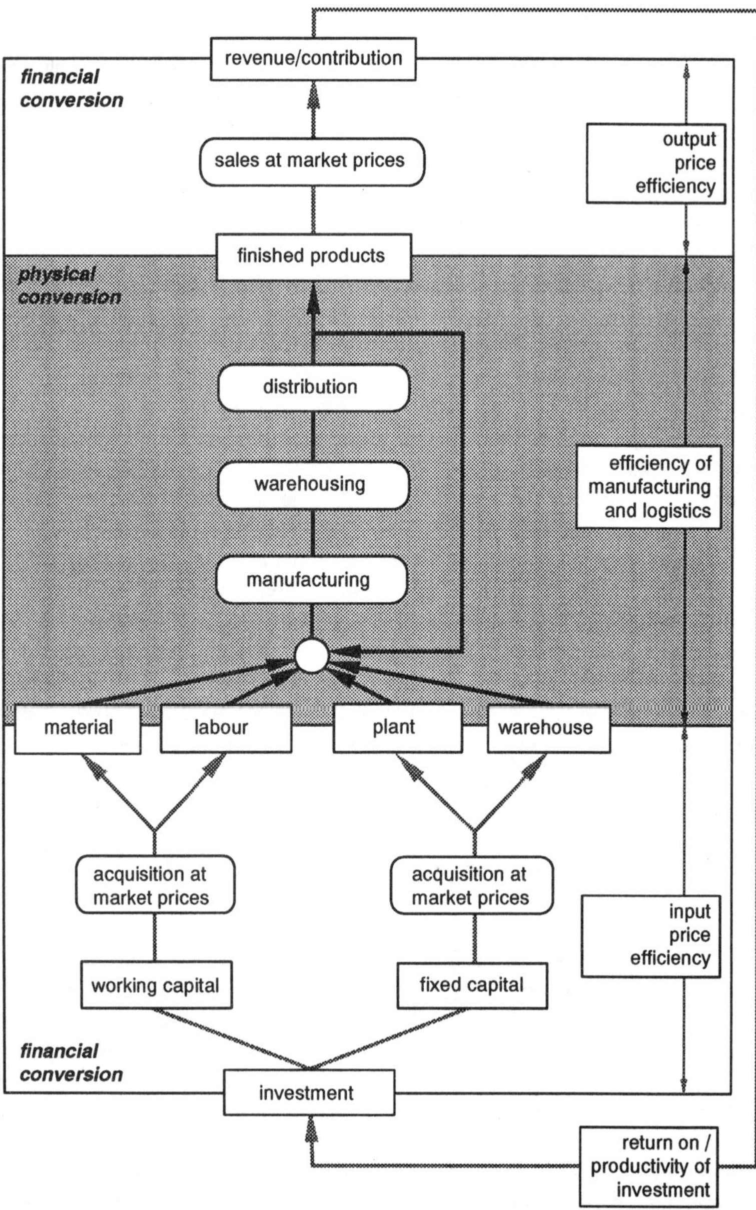

Figure 3.2: Efficiency measures for the conversion processes, after Eilon [1984]. ProfiSEE focuses on the efficiency of the physical conversion process, and should cover warehousing and distribution besides manufacturing. QED translates the efficiency of the physical conversion process into financial terms without, however, analyzing the efficiency of the two financial conversion processes. Performance measures—input -output ratios—naturally arise.

How are these two methods to complement each other and how are they to function in the context of investment analysis? The basic idea of the overall approach, shown in figure 3.3, is to provide a conventional investment analysis with sound inputs that take the economics of speed into account. The first step of this approach consists of a rough-cut financial analysis. The results of this step may subsequently form the starting point for a detailed evaluation with a simulation model—route Ia. If the analysis establishes enough confidence in the results of the first step, then this second step may come after an investment decision has been taken—route III—or be skipped altogether. In the latter case, the rough-cut results flow directly into the investment analysis—route Ib. The results of a detailed simulation, combined with the rough-cut financial results of the first step, may flow into the the investment analysis—route IIa—or, alternatively, lead to a review of the rough-cut analysis with revised assumptions—route IIb.

This elaborate procedure requires some justification. It needs no saying that the quality of a capital investment appraisal stands or falls with the quality of its inputs. Much of the criticism directed towards investment appraisals concerns not the elements of this methods but rather the inputs to it. It is a common joke by now to ask a person responsible for preparing an investment proposal which method was employed for setting the inputs to meet the cut-off criteria. Supposedly, software is available to run the conventional methods in reverse.

The approach presented here takes the conventional instruments 'as is' and concentrates on the preparatory steps. For a discussion of what a conventional investment appraisal ought to entail see, for example, [Singhvi 1979]. The available instruments focus predominantly on the short-term financial benefits of the investment using ROI, NPV, etc. as key pieces of information. As discussed in the two previous chapters, the importance of nonfinancial measures in cost accounting is increasing. This also applies to investment analysis. The literature on the subject now advocates the use of multiple-criteria decision models that take nonfinancial quantitative atrributes and purely qualitative attributes of the solutions and alternatives into account. See, for example, [Berliner et al. 1988, pp 186-197]. As will be argued in §5.8, it is important that the analysis takes account of all the consequences of holding inventory, especially the delay in income.

The benefit of the approach is simple. Early-on in the process, we establish and assess the expected results; and identify the key assumptions, the external factors and the decisions which determine these results. The effort invested in the first step can and should be relatively modest. The elapsed time will be correspondingly short. Secondly, this initial effort will throw off additional payoffs if it is used to focus the effort invested in the second step. Knowledge of the sensitivities will help the analyst decide which elements of the system should be subjected to a more detailed analysis and which key assumptions need further questioning. Moreover, it may be possible to restrict a detailed evaluation of the system to a few of its components. All in all, better and faster decisions result.

The third set of benefits of the application of the proposed approach comes into play after a decision to invest has been taken. A detailed simulation model as developed with ProfiSEE forms the first base for the implementation phase. This style of simulation modeling provides more than just a blue-print for a factory layout. It embodies the different aspects concerning process design and operational control as well. Furthermore, as the implementation phase progresses an enlarged project team will benefit from a model that documents the previous decisions. New team members thus share the insight gained earlier on.

One final point addresses the post-implementation review, which has on the whole received relatively little attention. It is clear that an audit should only be performed after enough time has elapsed to give the system a chance to reach a steady-state level of efficiency. Typically, several factors, especially external factors affecting the two financial conversion processes discussed earlier, will have changed by this time. This makes it difficult to assess variations in the projected returns of the project. It limits the value of a post-implementation review for subsequent decision making and corrective action. The original model can serve as a yardstick. By adjusting the model parameters for the changes in the different factors, we can estimate the relative influence of these changes. A clearer picture of the causes of deviation from the projected returns should emerge.

A rough-cut analysis as introduced in the next section should start off with a careful analysis of the existing manufacturing system, assess the resources required for producing a given product mix, explore a range of alternatives concepts and policies, determine the sensitivity to external factors, key assumptions, and major decision variables, and culminate with the selection of a few prime alternatives.

The complexity of the rough-cut model on which the analysis is based will vary from case to case. Important is that the modeling process takes account of financial factors as soon as possible.

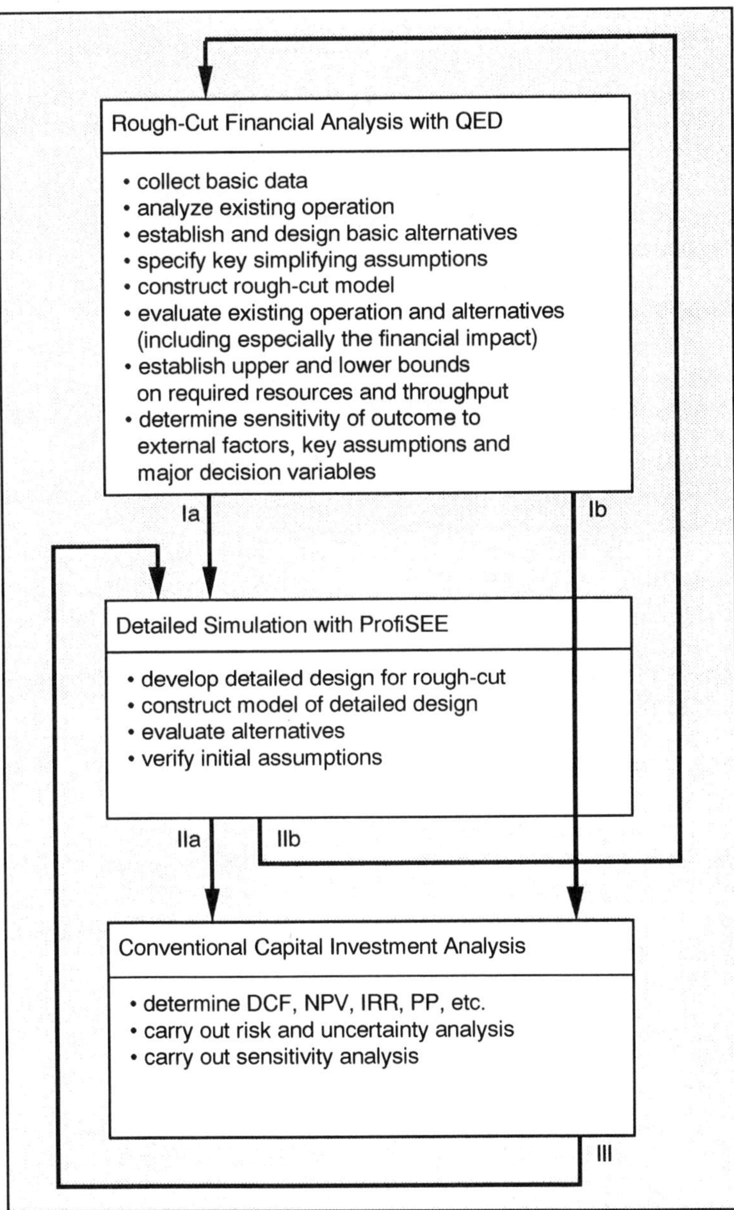

Figure 3.3: Overall approach for assessing the impact of the just-in-time concept. The basic idea is to provide a conventional capital investment analysis with sound financial inputs. As indicated, the overall approach is an iterative one. A detailed simulation with ProfiSEE may be carried out after the investment decision has been taken or, depending on the sensitivity of the results of the rough-cut analysis, be skipped altogether.

3.6.1 Detailed Evaluation with Visual Interactive Simulation Modeling

Visual Interactive Simulation Modeling (VISM) is highly suited to the analysis of instances of the physical conversion process that was discussed in the previous sections. This operations research technique, as implemented in ProfiSEE, has a number of outstanding characteristics that make a detailed evaluation of the just-in-time concept a worthwhile effort, meaning that it can be done well and quickly. The central aim of VISM is to provide transparent simulation models that display their underlying logic and behaviour in an intuitive fashion while at the same time permitting a high degree of interaction with the model builder and user. This is a tall order. ProfiSEE builds upon the classical and widely used discrete-event simulation technique, which forms the conceptual basis of a series of commercial systems. A discussion of the development of ProfiSEE and the motivation and goals behind it can be found in [Vaessen 1989]. The characteristic aspects of ProfiSEE, its functionality and underlying concepts are reviewed in the next chapter.

ProfiSEE grew out of a specific application of VISM for a dyestuff synthesis and standardization plant in which the focus was on the supply of raw materials and intermediate products to tightly coupled, zero-wait processes in a chemical production line. However, its present functionality is general enough to construct, for example, a highly transparent model of a classical kanban operation, which is characterized by loosely coupled processes, buffer zones and signal carriers to trigger and control the material flows, see chapter 4 for details on this example.

Although ProfiSEE is currently used in circa a dozen different projects at CIBA–GEIGY, it is in its present form best considered as a prototype system. A commercial implementation and release are presently under consideration. In addition a number of significant enhancements of the basic functionality are underway. However, ProfiSEE is not, and was never intended to be, a general-purpose simulator. Rather, it is an instrument that captures the generic entities of simulation models of production and logistics systems in the chemical-pharmaceutical industry. This entails that it is applicable to the broad range of problems that confront the analyst in this industry.

ProfiSEE provides the necessary entities and mechanisms for representing the different elements and processes involved in the conversion of physical inputs to the desired physical outputs. These abstractions are general enough to allow the modeler to decide about the degree of detail to introduce in the model. ProfiSEE offers three basic abstractions for representing resources: equipment for carrying out a sequence of tasks in batch and semi-continuous mode; facilities for storing or buffering intermediate products and supplying raw materials; and manpower and other auxiliary resources similar in behaviour to manpower. Naturally, the availability of these resources, their groupings and inter-connections can also be specified. In stark contrast with comparable simulation tools such as SIMFACTORY and XCELL+ [Conway et al. 1987], the specification of the processes using these resources is entirely separate from the specification of the resources. This also applies to the component that specifies when these production processes are to become active and how much production is planned. The reasons for these design decisions lie in the multi-purpose nature of the equipment and production lines in chemical-pharmaceutical plants and will be discussed at some length.

We best view ProfiSEE as a graphical programming language with which to express different kinds of operational concepts and policies for converting raw materials and intermediate products into finished products using various kinds of machines, production processes and manpower. An integral part of the system is a facility that provides performance measures for evaluating the efficiency of the conversion process as a whole. Given the application domain of ProfiSEE, these measurements include service level, throughput time, stock and WIP levels, besides the customary measurements such as utilization, cycle time and throughput.

What kinds of questions does this language permit? Some examples will have to suffice:

- in which cases is throughput increased by having more than one device for processing alternating batches of a production step in a multi-stage process?
- or, if possible, is it better to split this batch at this stage into two parts that then are processed in parallel?
- how much WIP buffer space is needed to absorb 80% of the fluctuations in processing times in a multi-stage process and where is this best located?
- when is it advantageous to pool sets of devices and when is it better to create independent production lines?
- what is a good allocation of the product mix to these lines?
- where should a production process with too many intermediate stages be de-coupled?
- where is the bottleneck stage in multi-stage process with feedback cycles and how is its cycle time reduced?
- what is the effect of limiting the amount of WIP on throughput and throughput time?
- when is manpower the limiting resource?
- what is the impact of introducing an extra shift for cleaning up?

Which of the above questions does ProfiSEE answer? It doesn't; it merely helps its user find the answer. The approach ProfiSEE imposes upon its user, assumes that the user has at least a rough idea about the basic operating policies and alternatives under investigation, and the kind and quantity of resources required to produce the desired product mix and volume. Finding an acceptable solution to a design problem or improvements of an existing operation is very much an iterative process. ProfiSEE guides and supportes this process. This is where the immediate response to interactive changes comes into play. The quality of the response in the form of output that avoids and prevents the ubiquitous data cemeteries, to use the contemporary German expression, is equally important.

3.6.2 Rough-cut Financial Assessment and Sensitivity Analysis

A structurally simpler model, dubbed QED for "Quick *et* Dirty," "Quite Easily Done" and "Quod Erat Demonstrandum" performs the financial analysis forming the core of this thesis. This financial model, however, does take into account a much broader range of decisions and contexts and lends itself to sensitivity analysis. The approach taken by QED is very different from the one introduced in the previous section. Given the context and decision variables of interest, QED first estimates the resources required to reach the desired sales volume and then puts the efficiency of the overall conversion process in monetary terms. The efficiency of the two financial conversion processes—purchasing and sales—is taken as a given factor. But clearly, the cost of raw materials, equipment and labour has a major influence on the outcome and is taken into account.

QED permits the investigation of the sensitivity of the performance measures with respect to a number of input variables. Thus, it lends insight into the impact of these variables. In addition, the relative monetary weight of the different elements composing the total cost function comes to light.

The major purpose of QED is to compare a classical operation with one using elements of the just-in-time concept. As it stands, QED is a special-purpose model; a number of its assumptions relate specifically to the model case that will be discussed and analyzed subsequently. The treatment of the construction of this model in chapter 5 makes it clear that the approach itself can be applied much more widely. The actual implementation is therefore much less important than the process used to construct it. This is also one of the reasons for the choice of a simple electronic spreadsheet as the implementation tool. The goal, at least at this stage, is not to develop a full-fledged decision support system or corporate model.

A comparison of the analysis of the manufacturing system underlying QED with early work in this field carried out by Forrester [1961] is most instructive. It has recently become popular again to quote Forrester's famous work on industrial dynamics to illustrate the pervasive impact of lead time on the responsiveness of a manufacturing system. The central concept of lead time is a measure of the time a system requires to respond appropriately to an order. It is defined and analyzed in chapter 5. If the analysis underlying QED is at all correct or if there is a modern theory of inventory and production management, then one of the basic concepts related to lead time, embedded in Forrester's model of a production-distribution system, is in fact deeply flawed. One could easily wonder whether Forrester's new fans have actually read the pertinent sections of his work. Forrester himself is careful to point out that "[t]he equations are akin to a verbal description of the situation. They are correct if our perception of the system is correct. They are wrong to the extent that we wrongly interpret the organization which is being described." [p. 141].

Forrester's model posits that the delay in responding to an order depends on the aggregated inventory level with respect to some desired inventory level. The higher the inventory level is, the faster the response. This seems plausible enough. It is clear that some kind of relationship exists. The question is in which direction this relationship goes. As the construction of QED in chapter 5 shows, the general relationship goes in fact in the opposite direction. The delay referred to by Forrester is but one element making up the lead time for responding to an order at any particular stage of the system. The lead time for responding to an order at a particular stage determines the inventory level at that stage, which in turn makes up one element adding to the lead time for the subsequent stage. In all fairness, Forrester's perception is not wrong, it is merely a gross over-simplification.

The above comment may at first strike one as subtle nitpicking. Irrespective of its academic merit, there is a solid pragmatic argument that underscores its importance. In order to improve the responsiveness of a system, the individuals in the organization in question must first come to understand what elements make up lead time and how lead time at the different stages affects the system's performance. Inventory is a symptom rather than a cause. Simply reducing the inventory levels will, at worst, only decrease the service levels or, at best, expose the problems that are the cause of the inventory in the first place. It boils down to the question whether we best view inventory as an asset or as a liability. What is best depends on the strategic intent of the organization.

The development and early verification of the logic of a rough-cut model and its system boundaries is a worthwhile, preliminary investment that pays off when implementing a detailed model. The kind of conceptual issue discussed above is a good example of one that we need to settle at the outset. The technicalities of the implementation requirements of a detailed model may bury basic questions concerning the soundness of the model and overall concept.

3.7 Comparing the Strengths and Weaknesses of the two Methods

The two modeling methods that make up the overall approach are complementary. Where ProfiSEE has its weaknesses, QED has its strengths, and *vice versa*. To conclude the description of the overall approach, we summarize the advantages and limitations of visual interactive simulation modeling in comparison with a rough-cut financial analysis as implemented in QED:

- QED lends itself to sensitivity analysis; with ProfiSEE, the extent to which the analyst can carry out a sensitivity analysis is severely restricted
- QED evaluates radically different alternatives with the same basic model; with ProfiSEE the alternatives require the implementation of different models
- QED evaluates alternative solutions in financial terms; ProfiSEE does not
- ProfiSEE is capable of assessing the impact of the different concepts on resource requirements, throughput and throughput time at the shop-floor level; QED ignores the impact of the more detailed aspects at this level on performance
- ProfiSEE models show the direction as well as the shape that the implementation of the modeled concepts might take; models developed in the style of QED leave many design questions unanswered

3.8 Limitations of the Overall Approach

The direction taken by the overall approach sketched in this chapter entails a number of severe limitations. These result from the nature and focus of the two methods used as part of the overall approach. Other, less fundamental limitations stem from the implementation of the two methods.The subsequent chapters dicuss these.

Although the overall approach needs to be based on an analysis of the present situation of an actual system, this thesis almost entirely ignores the difficulties associated with the introduction of a radically different concept into an existing operation. This thesis does as if starting from square one is always a viable option. My experience to date indicates that starting from square one may not be as undesirable as it may first appear to be. With the benefit of hindsight, it may well be a short cut in many a case. The implementation issues are typically thorny. The human element is a major factor determining the ability of an organization to adapt to changing requirements and to adopt new concepts. An organization's stability, or to avoid the euphemism, its inherent resistance to change clearly hampers its speed of learning. It is precisely the human factor that this thesis does not address. The methods employed conveniently ignore the 'soft' facts. See §8.3 for a further, but brief, discussion of implementation issues.

A second general category of ignored facts covers those falling under the heading of competitive and market analysis. The manufacturing system under investigation does not operate in a vacuum. The relative position of competitors will have an impact on market share and demand patterns. At the opposite end of the supply chain, relationships with suppliers are becoming increasingly important. The overall approach put forward for assessing the financial impact of the just-in-time concept is inward-looking. Care must therefore be excercised to ensure that the decisions taken align with the manufacturing strategy, which itself has to be consistent with the overall business and marketing strategy of the organization. As discussed already in §2.4 and §2.6, this is the reason why besides the basic financial performance measures, nonfinancial but quantitative measures of the quality of response to market requirements are important, and increasingly so.

4 The Role of ProfiSEE: A Workbench for Visual Interactive Simulation Modeling in the chemical-pharmaceutical Industry

4.1 Introduction and Outline

> ... Almost all complex multi-process production systems are unbalanced. In a Western factory with a push through production system, the build up of buffer stocks prevents idle men and machines (at considerable financial cost). In a Japanese factory with a pull through production system and zero stocks, all the machines must run at the pace of the slowest machine on the line: stocks are kept low by shutting down the faster machines or running them on extended cycle times. The problem of imbalance can be alleviated by designing a more balanced line; that, no doubt is why the Japanese spend so much time on building and modifying their capital equipment in-house. But the problem will not go away. [Williams et al 1990, p. 101]

Williams et al. put their finger on an element of the just-in-time concept that has received a remarkably small share of attention in the literature on the subject. This seems surprising since it has been widely recognized by now that just-in-time is more than a simple stock reduction programme. The pull principle and short cleanup and setup times do not in their own guarantee low levels of work-in-process and short throughput times. One further prerequisite is a well-balanced production line. Line balancing, as will be discussed in this chapter, is a particularly complex and painstaking issue in the chemical-pharmaceutical industry. The degree of imbalance of a production line is strongly indicative of the efficiency of the overall physical conversion process, as defined in figures 3.1 and 3.2. The case study presented in chapter 6 shows that this issue badly needs attention. The degree of imbalance of the steps in the production process, regardless the measure used, is so severe that it has served as an argument against the feasibility of the just-in-time concept. As Williams et al. note, line balancing ought to be part of a continual productivity improvement process. The problem of imbalance once solved will re-surface sooner or later.

The reason that this chapter on ProfiSEE emphasizes the issue of line balancing is that this tool not only helps to evaluate the benefits of balancing a production process but also shows how we may achieve this balance. This does not apply, for example, to the reduction of cleanup and setup times. This latter activity requires different methods altogether. ProfiSEE will of course show how important it is.

The main goal of this chapter is to show what role ProfiSEE, as a workbench for Visual Interactive Simulation Modeling (VISM) in the chemical-pharmaceutical industry, has to play in evaluating the potential impact of the just-in-time concept. As noted, the analysis that ProfiSEE permits is restricted to nonfinancial measures. However, the different results coming out of such a quantitative analysis can provide the starting point for a sound financial analysis.

The introductory section on VISM contained in chapter 3 listed a number of questions that ProfiSEE and a detailed simulation study can answer in general. In order to meet the goal of this chapter, it is first of all necessary to classify and characterize the issues brought up by these questions and to show how they relate to the subject of just-in-time manufacturing. The characterization of the nature of facilities design in the chemical-pharmaceutical industry, as presented in §4.2, fulfills this need. A review of the concepts and principles underlying the tool, designed to address the multi-faceted problems posed in the industry, complements this characterization.

In order to show *what* role ProfiSEE plays, it is also necessary to describe *how* it plays this role and, specifically, *how* it addresses the issues. The core of this chapter therefore contains a compact description of its pertinent characteristics and its functional components. To the extent that its structural components directly influence its functional components, and in particular possible extensions of these, they are explained in the text. On the whole, implementation issues are conveniently ignored. It needs to be stressed, however, that Smalltalk-80, see [Goldberg 1983] for a description of this object-oriented programming environment, has had a major impact on the development of ProfiSEE. In fact, it is difficult to imagine how ProfiSEE could have been implemented without this software development methodology given the available resources.

ProfiSEE is embedded in a comprehensive information analysis and management tool called The Analyst, which itself is written entirely in Smalltalk-80. The hub of The Analyst is the information centre, which organizes, links and helps finding data items and different kinds of documents. Available are integrated tools employing a uniform graphical interface for a series of common tasks: text and image processing facilities, programmable forms for constructing highly structured documents, an electronic spreadsheet, a simple database, business graphics, on-line maps and a terminal emulator. The hypermedia facility of The Analyst plays a central role in managing the experimentation process. In a sense, ProfiSEE is an extension of this system. It adds several graphical documents to The Analyst.

In over a dozen substantial projects at CIBA–GEIGY, the operations research department has extensively used and tested ProfiSEE's functionality and its logic. A classification and brief review of these projects is found in §4.10, towards the end of this chapter. Where noted, the description of the functionality anticipates some extensions and enhancements that are presently underway or planned for the immediate future. The current status of the development of an additional and fully integrated component for Visual Interactive Production Scheduling (VIPS) is sketched in a separate section.

4.2 The Nature of Facilities Design in the Batch Processing Industry

The introductory section on ProfiSEE posed a number of unstructured questions that broadly speaking fall under the heading of facilities design. The purpose of this section is, first of all, to classify the issues with particular reference to the chemical-pharmaceutical industry and the just-in-time concept, and, secondly, to discuss the motivation behind the application of simulation modeling in this area.

Facilities design is primarily the domain of industrial engineering. Its major objectives, for a discussion see Apple's [1977] comprehensive[30] work on the topic, are to:

- create a flow of materials that facilitates the manufacturing process
- eliminate unnecessary materials handling
- maintain flexibility of arrangement and of operation
- ensure a high turnover of work-in-process
- ensure the cost-effective utilization of equipment and manpower
- make economical use of the building space and infrastructure
- ensure environmental safety

These objectives amplify that facilities design covers more than the arrangement of the layout of the equipment. As Apple [ibid, p. 4] writes, "the overall objective of facilities design is to get the inputs ... into, through and out of each facility in the shortest time practicable, at acceptable cost. In industrial terms, the shorter the amount of time a piece of material spends in the plant, the less opportunity it has to collect labor and overhead charges." This statement already reflects one of the tenets of modern manufacturing and the just-in-time concept, which is to aim at eliminating all non-valued activities, see, for example [Berliner 1988, pp. 3-6]. It is not surprising that Apple [ibid, p. 5] recognizes that, "the flow of material usually represents the backbone of a productive facility, and should be very carefully planned and not allowed to grow or develop into an unwieldy octopus of confused traffic patterns." There is a significant link between the speed at which material flows through the facility and the unit cost of production. The cost-effective utilization of capacity achieved by balancing processes—see the following discussion—is not in conflict with the just-in-time concept, on the contrary, it is an integral element of it.

Facilities design is sometimes given a narrow interpretation which takes a macro view of a manufacturing system. Hax et al. [1984, pp. 13-68] treat it as "the problem of determining the number, sizes and locations of the facilities that a firm needs in order to serve its markets" with the goal of minimizing "the total cost of transportation within the system, and the cost of setting up and operating the facilities." Facilities include warehouses, distribution centres and plant. The solution must also specify the optimal flow of materials and information. The facility layout problem, on the other hand, represents the micro view [ibid, p. 16].

The issues concerning the design and operation of plants in the chemical-pharmaceutical industry have a number of distinguishing features, which can largely be attributed to the characteristics of batch process technology. A batch is the unit operation performed on a device or piece of equipment, e.g. a reactor. The term machine is not in favour in the chemical industry. The volume of the equipment items constrains the maximum batch size, which are measured by units of volume or weight. A campaign is a sequence of consecutive batches. The equivalent term

---

[30] Apple's work is comprehensive in the sense that it covers all the different topics. However, virtually no mention is made of the specific problems in the process industry.

in the machining industry is lot. Optimal batch and campaign (lot) sizing are entirely different issues.

For economical reasons, the application of continuous process technology in the chemical-pharmaceutical industry has not fulfilled the expectations that chemical engineers once placed on it. As Rippin [1983, p. 137] writes, "[i]n the early days of chemical engineering in the 1950s students might well have gained the impression that the ultimate mission of the chemical engineer was to transform old-fashioned batch processes into modern continuous ones." Pharmaceuticals and specialty chemicals will continue to be produced in a single- or multi-purpose batch plants. To improve the performance in terms of yield and quality, automated process control systems are gradually replacing manually operated batch processes. This applies in particular also to the taking and analysis of samples.

The spectrum of multi-stage batch production ranges from intermittent to quasi-continuous systems. An intermittent batch production system shares some of the characteristics of a job shop in the machining industry. Similarly, a batch production line, or quasi-continuous batch production system[31], shares some of the characteristics of an assembly line in the automobile industry. A job shop consists of a set of machines and a set of jobs, each with operations to be performed on these machines. In a flow shop, the jobs consist of strictly sequenced operations. The subject is covered extensively in the literature [Hax et al. 1984]. It is convenient to separate operational job scheduling from the design of the facility and the processes. Many of the common assumptions, see [ibid, p. 266] and §4.12 on production scheduling, are violated by multi-stage batch processes. For example, consecutive operations on devices can or even must overlap due to technological constraints or process characteristics. The line balancing problem, which arises in production and assembly lines, must be addressed in intermittent batch production systems as well, since for the duration of a campaign at least some of the operations on the different devices are tightly coupled. To put it differently, campaigns establish short-lived production lines. It is best to avoid the terms job shop and job shop scheduling in this context. Some of the differences between the two cases are illustrated in figure 4.1a.

Intermittent production systems such as the job shop are typically process-oriented. The focus is on capacity utilization and throughput at the individual work centers. Since work centers are de-coupled in a job shop, WIP absorbs some of the detrimental effects of imbalanced capacities and processes. In contrast, quasi-continuous production systems are flow-oriented. The focus shifts to the throughput of the entire production line and the production throughput time. There is much less emphasis on the utilization of the individual work centers.

[31]Continuous batch production system would be an unfortunate term, since it might be confused with a production line using continuous process technology.

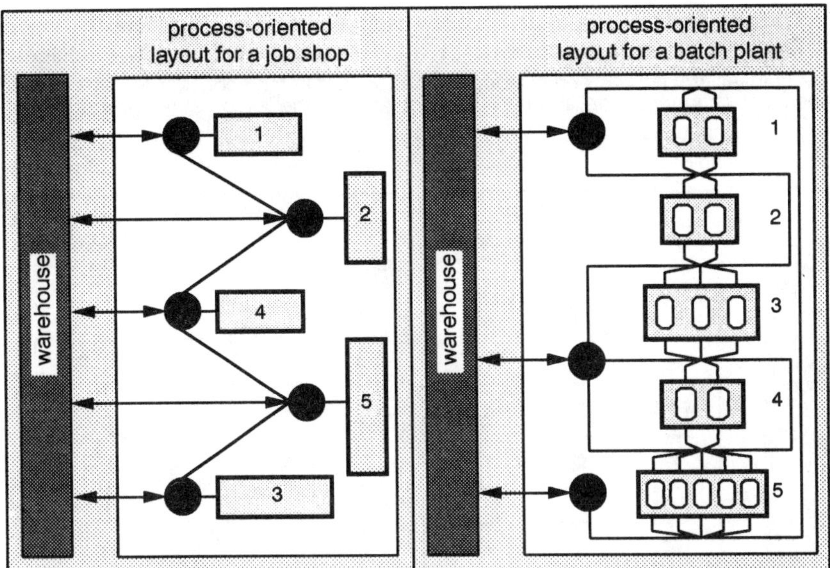

Figure 4.1a: Intermittent production systems–two cases. There are significant differences between a traditional job shop and a process-oriented batch plant. In a job shop the operations (or stages) of a job, performed at the work centres numbered 1 through 5, are de-coupled. WIP can stay on the factory floor or be moved to the warehouse. In a chemical batch plant process stages can or must overlap. As part of the changeover procedure the piping has to be re-arranged in a process-oriented layout. It stays fixed for the duration of a campaign, thus creating a temporary production line. Capacity balancing is relatively straightforward in a job shop. This does not hold for a chemical batch plant: multi-product line balancing is an essential activity for ensuring the cost-effective use of equipment. In some batch plants the work centres can be put in a sequence, as indicated by the numbering in the figure. (This is the distinguishing feature of a flow shop). However, adherence to this sequence may not be strict. Few of the assumptions of job shop scheduling apply to the scheduling campaigns in a batch plant. Scheduling, however, is difficult in either of the two cases. The operation in the chemical-pharmaceutical industry closest to a job shop is the fabrication and packaging of different dosage forms of active substances. It suffers all of its drawbacks. See chapter 6 for a description of an actual case.

Product volume and demand variability permitting, it is economic to establish independent production lines. It may be possible to segment the product mix into product families of technologically similar products in such a way that each line achieves an acceptable level of utilization. This concept, termed group technology, has been slow in taking a foothold in the chemical industry. A mixed strategy may be appropriate: one for high-volume products and one for low-volume products. In either case, if the changeover cost of shifting a line from one family member to another is non-negligible, then a changeover reduction programme is a must. The combination of the segmentation of an intermittent system into independent lines and the reduction of changeover costs to achieve the full benefits of a quasi-continuous, flow-oriented system for low- and medium volume products is a key element of the just-in-time concept. Flexible equipment and well-designed changeover procedures and methods allow the just-in-time concept to eat the cake and have it. The transition of a traditional process-oriented layout to product- or flow-oriented layout is illustrated by the difference between figure 4.1a and 4.1b.

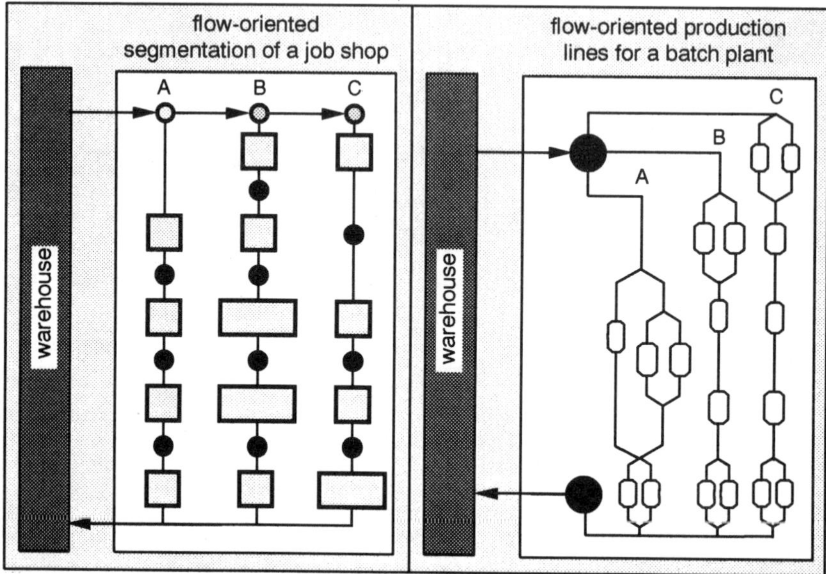

Figure 4.1b: Quasi-continuous production systems–two cases. If the volume of the products or product families are sufficiently high and their demand relatively stable for a suitably long period, it is lucrative to establish assembly or production lines, Henry Ford being one of the grand masters. With some success the chemical industry has adopted and adapted the concepts of group technology for assigning families of technologically related products to independent lines in order to reap some of the benefits of continuous production systems.

Assuming that the chemical processes for the products have been developed, knowledge of three different system components, which have already been identified, is central to the design and operation of a batch plant:

- 'software' – the characteristics of the chemical processes, i.e. the activities that need to be carried out to convert raw materials into intermediates and finished products; their sequence and resource requirements
- human resources and 'hardware'– the people; the equipment, buffer facilities, their connections, and other, auxiliary resources, including their operating hours, that are available for carrying out the activities
- market requirements – the projected independent demand and its pattern for the finished products and the load generated on the plant for the duration of the planning period

task subject	objective criteria	outcomes	characteristics
single process	• conversion rate per unit of time	• yield and process time	• modelling of physical/chemical processes
a single multi-stage process	• conversion rate per unit of time	• balanced process • common cycle time	• number/size of equipment items unconstrained
multi-stage processes in a single-product plant	• effective utilization of all resources • throughput time	• facility design • production sequence	• typically multi-purpose equipment
multi-stage processes in a multi-product plant	• effective utilization of all resources • throughput time	• facility design • production schedule	• products run in parallel • multi-purpose equipment

Table 4.1: Tasks arising in the design and operation of batch chemical plants, ordered by increasing complexity and scope of the tasks. This categorization follows Rippin's [1983] paper on the application of simulation in the chemical industry. The first task requires predominantly continuous simulation models. The nature of the subsequent tasks requires discrete-event simulation models or mathematical models with discrete variables.

In an extensive review paper on the application of simulation for the design and operation of batch chemical plants, Rippin [ibid, p. 138] discusses the series of increasingly complex tasks that arise, see table 4.1 and figure 4.2. The first of these consists of the optimization of the performance of processes that are carried out in a single batch reactor. This is the traditional domain of production chemists and chemical engineers. The modeling issues are comparable to those for continuous systems. The problems that need solving are especially difficult when the batches are non-homogeneous and when it is difficult to measure the presence of intermediates that should play a role according to the logic of the chemistry of the process. The aim of this task is to understand and optimize the time-based conversion profile for different kinds of chemical reactions subject to varying operating conditions, e.g. temperature, which will generally be changing over time. The development of stable and efficient numerical methods for solving highly constrained systems of equations applicable to these so-called flow-sheeting problems has given this area a major impetus. The commercial success of large and expensive computer software such as ASPEN PLUS™ serves as evidence.

The subsequent task consists of the optimization of a coupled multi-stage process. The output of the previous task, which will be the process time and the yield of processes running on a single reactor, can be viewed, albeit simplistically, as the input for the design of a multi-stage process. One of the aims is to balance the process and find the best common cycle time for all stages. The cycle time is the time between two successive batches, which includes, besides the time for the actual conversion process, the changeover, the loading and unloading of the reactor. Assuming a linear sequence of tightly-coupled operations and a simple objective function which maximizes the conversion rate of input into output materials per unit of time, Rippin [ibid, pp. 148-150] develops a procedure for calculating the best common cycle time, which turns out to be longer than the maximum cycle time of the individual stages.[32] The optimization of the individual stages leads to sub-optimal solutions. If additional factors are relevant, or if the maximum cycle time of the individual stages is widely different from the rest—see the discussion below—then it may be appropriate to use two or more devices for this slow stage.

The more general cases encountered in practice are much too complex to be subjected to and solved by an optimization procedure. Typically, the sequence of operations is not strictly sequential. For example, the integration of feedback loops for recycling environmentally problematic solvents is becoming more and more common. Scheduled shutdowns, daily or weekly, present a further difficulty. For example, if the period during which labour is available, e.g. 8 hours per day, is not an integer multiple of the cycle time of a process requiring supervision or manual intervention, then forced idle time will be the consequence. Are the intermediate stages stable enough so that they can be left overnight? If the processes are not tightly-coupled, i.e. intermediate buffering is allowed either in a vessel or in barrels on pallets, then the constraint of integer multiples for cycle times no longer applies. In some cases, drying or mandatory quality inspection require intermediate buffering. Finally, process times and yields can often not be treated as constants and need to be modeled by probability distributions. If manual operations are still in place, the necessary data on which to base the model input variables is not available or of poor quality.

The third task consists of the optimal design and operation of a single-product batch plant. The separate activities of the overall multi-stage process must be assigned to individual equipment units of a certain size and running under suitable conditions. If the process is poorly balanced—as is commonly the case—a simple, 1-to-1 allocation would waste the necessary resources. In other words, to obtain an efficient conversion process, it is necessary to resolve the mismatch of the cycle times of the individual stages. Other aspects, such as materials handling and the costs of the different kinds of equipment, will be relevant factors as well. In the case of a single-product plant, the volume factor does not add further complexity to the design process. Of course, we need to project the impact of a scale-up of the batches sizes on the different activities.

---

[32]A further, implicit assumption of Rippin's is that the size of a reactor is not a constraint and, moreover, that it does not affect the conversion process. However, controlling the temperature and ensuring a homogeneous mix of the reactants is much more difficult to achieve in a large reactor than in a small one.

The central issue is to balance the overall process. Subject to a variety of technical constraints, several kinds of options or their combination need to be taken into consideration, for a comparison see Rippin [ibid] but not [Hax et al. 1984, pp. 359-380][33]:

- merge the sequence of activities of consecutive stages into a single stage
- use several equipment units in parallel
- interrupt the chain of tasks by merging consecutive pairs of batches
- de-couple the chain of tasks by inserting a buffer

Each of these options is analyzed and discussed in the subsequent set of figures at the end of this section and the associated explanatory text.[34] The purpose of the discussion is to show that even in a simple case such as the one discussed below, it not possible or, at best, not very helpful to make any general kind of statement of the performance of these alternatives without taking the specific characteristics of the chemical processes and the activities into account. The conclusion to be drawn is that the merits of each case must be analyzed individually with the help of simulation modeling.

The availability of an appropriate tool combined with the knowledge and intuition of an experienced industrial or chemical engineer becomes of paramount importance if further aspects are relevant. Some such aspects have already been mentioned. Those aspects that are commonly encountered in industrial practice comprise:

- variability in process time, yield and quality
- availability of labour and other, auxiliary resources
- multiple, possibly parallel inputs and outputs for a single reaction stage
- feedback loops in a multi-stage process structure
- instable intermediates with a maximum delay until further processing
- inclusion or exclusion of certain operations for some batches of a campaign
- combination with continuous or semi-continuous processes
- health and safety procedures and regulations
- extremely long sequences of stages

A systematic discussion would require a separate section for each of these aspects. A brief characterization will have to suffice.

[33]The 21 pages on line balancing in this text and presumably some of the literature quoted are of little relevance in this context: the objective of the methods discussed is to find the number of devices, all devices being equal, that minimize the imbalance. Two assumptions are violated: specific devices may be needed to perform a particular operation, i.e. devices are not all equal, and some pairs of operations are incompatible.

[34]The specific explanations are not reiterated in the body of the text. The figures 4.3.1 through 4.3.6 and the explanatory text are intended to be self-contained.

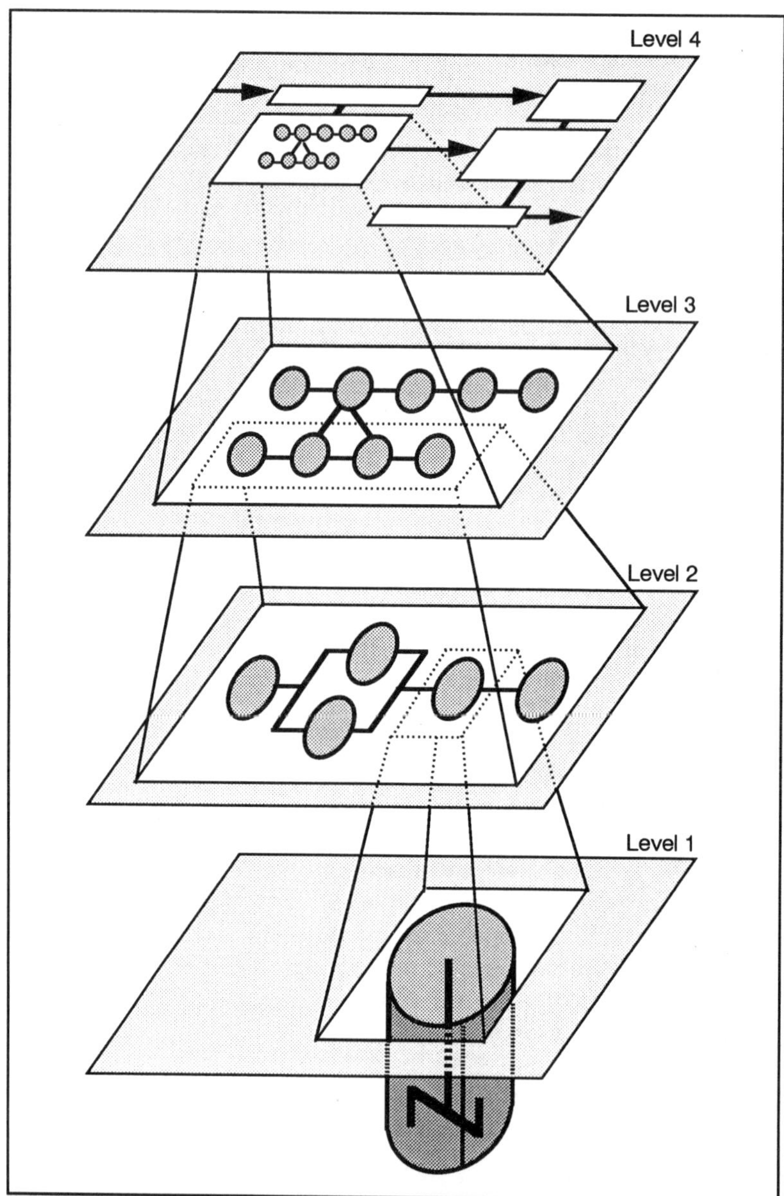

Figure 4.2: The levels at which tasks arise in the design and operation of batch chemical plant—a graphical view. Level 1: Single chemical process step in one reactor. Level 2: Multi-stage process(es) in a single-product or multi-purpose plant. Level 3: Multi-purpose, multi-product plant. Level 4: Multi-plant production complex, including warehouses. Compare this figure with the task descriptions in table 4.1.

The impact of variability is manifold. First of all, it is worth noting that the extent of the variability can be quite substantial: for example, process times ranging from ±50% of the average value are not an exception. Fluctuating process times worsen the throughput rate and the throughput time. Again, the detrimental effects deserve to be assessed on a case-by-case basis.

The general characteristics of the overall production process may lead the analyst to expect correlation and auto-correlation in the variability of different processes. Unfortunately, in the face of missing and inadequate data, the analyst is forced to adopt a pragmatic approach. This often means that the phenomena fail to receive due attention.

In some instances, additional equipment is required to absorb these fluctuations. For example, to counter the effects of varying batch quality in dyestuff production, a follow-up process, which mixes different batches, may be essential for achieving a set standard. In the extreme, re-processing is called for. Also, some dosage forms in pharmaceutical production need to be 'aged' until quality tests show that the product meets the standard on the release rate of its active ingredient.

Requirements for labour and auxiliary resources are not simply an additional cost factor. The impact of shifts and weekends, which has already been noted, is particularly difficult to estimate with pencil and paper. For instance, does an extra shift increase the average weekly throughput by a proportional amount? Moreover, capacity constraints apply to these resources, which are typically shared by several activities. If three people have been assigned to a multi-stage process with half a dozen activities that require their attention or intervention, chances are that conflicts arise. In general, these factors add additional delays and variability to the process.

A simple, linear process is a rare occurrence. Two or more stages running in tandem on different reactors may feed another stage. The transfers of these stages into the reactor performing the subsequent stage may be sequential, or, depending on the nature of the process, simultaneous. A stage may first release a solvent in which the reaction took place and then release its main product. Needless to say, the analysis of the cycle time quickly turns into a laborious, error-prone task.

Production processes containing feedback loops complicate this task. This may occur because an activity has to be carried out several times or because the recycling of solvents is an integrated part of the process. The feedback cycle may run over a number of intermediate stages. Treating the feedback loop as a black box, i.e. as a single process, in a model may therefore not be a viable alternative.

If intermediates are instable for a very short period, computer controlled operations can employ a special feedback mechanism. The stage consuming the instable intermediate has to signal the preceding stage that it can ensure further processing without any delay. The preceding stage waits with its final processing step until it receives this signal. The decision where in the chain of activities to place these coordinating points requires, among other things, an understanding of the variability of the process times.

Feedback mechanisms generally impose special conditions on the activities of the processes. In much the same way that a pump needs to be primed to get started, certain activities are in- or excluded on the first or last batch of a campaign. If campaign sizes are short, this aspect is best not ignored.

Batch processes are often coupled or integrated with a semi-continuous or continuous process. Distillation columns and certain kinds of mills are typical examples of semi-continuous equipment. The special property of semi-continuous processes is that input and output will overlap for a certain period of time. A spray-dryer used for the standardization of dyestuffs is an example of a continuous—and complex—piece of equipment. Spray-dryers are necessarily de-coupled from the preceding batch process by one or more feeder tanks to ensure a continuous and uninterrupted supply.

Health and safety regulations and requirements impose restrictions on the available options as well as precautionary measures on the design and operation of a plant. For example, an automated materials handling facility may mainly be of interest because it reduces or eliminates the exposure of workers to hazardous chemicals and less because it improves the throughput rate. The trend towards partially or fully automated operations, as evidenced by the shortage of more highly-qualified personnel, pervades the industry.

A final aspect concerns relatively low-volume products with very many intermediate stages, peptide production in the pharmaceutical industry being a prime example. The use of dedicated equipment is prohibitively expensive in such situations. The chain of tasks must necessarily be broken down into separate segments sharing the same multi-purpose equipment groups. The overall throughput time, including the storage time of the intermediates, for the production of the active substance may extend over 12 months. Laying down the production sequence which balances the goals set for utilization, overal throughput times and level output is an important additional element of operating such a plant. The issues encountered here a very similar to those encountered in multi-product batch plants, to be discussed next.

The fourth and final task consists of the design and operation of a multi-product plant. The simpler case is a plant producing only a single product at a time. Then, the different products run in sequence. If several products are produced in parallel, possibly sharing equipment, production scheduling plays a major role in operating the plant. Up and till now the discussion focused solely on the time dimension of equipment utilization. In a multi-product batch plant, the space or volume dimension of equipment utilization requires attention as well, since the relative sizes of the batches will likely be different for each product. Moreover, some products will need additional equipment. Thus the question of a suitable mix of products is relevant also.

Rippin's [ibid, pp. 151-153] mathematical model for optimizing the size of the equipment deserves some critical comments. First of all, the model excludes the different options for balancing processes from consideration. Secondly, it assumes that the size scalar and the cycle time for each process stage are constant. Rippin [ibid] notes that "[t]his assumption can usually be relaxed at the cost of some additional iterative calculations in the algorithms" for solving the model formulation. Unfortunately, the cycle time for a stage will, depending on the type of process, vary in different ways with the batch size. Using a suitable transformation in the variables the model is turned into optimization problem with a non-linear objective function that minimizes the total equipment cost and a linear inequality constraint limiting the total time required to produce the desired quantities. Rippin [ibid] does point out that only discrete sizes of the equipment items will be commercially available. The model is therefore a notoriously difficult non-linear integer programming problem. This problem need not have any feasible solutions as formulated, since the equipment sizes available for the different tasks may be incompatible. This means that some of the balancing options discussed earlier, in particular the splitting of batches to run on parallel equipment items as shown in figures 4.3.4a and 4.3.4b, will need to taken into consideration for this reason alone.[35] A production chemist having the time to ponder this kind of problem formulation might possibly get the distinct impression that it serves strictly educational purposes. Here too, there is a gaping practicality gap facing the practitioner wanting to apply operations research methods. Extending the formulation to the case of parallel products makes matters worse. The simulation modeling approach as advocated in the next section, even though it is in essence a trial-and-error method, is proving to be more helpful. It can express the multi-faceted nature of the problem and exploit the knowledge and experience of a production chemist or chemical engineer familiar with the processes and the operation.

The more complex case of the fourth task is a plant capable of producing several products at the same time. In this case, the complexity of batch plant scheduling presents itself to the fullest extent. Besides the sizes and sequence of the campaigns, the plant scheduler must also determine which combinations of campaigns are best run in parallel given the available resources and possible production (routing) variants. The scheduling problem is difficult enough in an existing plant where the resource constraints are assumed to be fixed. It becomes still more difficult if design considerations, e.g. capacity expansion and segmentation, play a role. For a good overview of the current status of solution methodologies for solving this problem see [Musier et al. 1990]. A promising approach, that abides by the guidelines put forward in [ibid], is discussed in §4.12.

The most complex case of the fourth task is multi-plant system. International supply points with long inter-plant transportation lead times, complex product routes, stand-alone materials management systems for individual plants are all characteristic for the chemical-pharmaceutical industry. Given the nature of the planning problems posed in a multi-plant system, a hierarchical decomposition into simpler sub-problems is unavoidable. At this level, the potential strengths of the MRP II can come into play. In practice, progress has been slow in coming. Besides a component for rough-cut capacity planning, the sucessful application of MRP II in the batch processing industry will also require a detailed plant scheduling component for creating feasible realizations of the master production schedule.

---

[35]The critique of the kind of approaches discussed by Rippin could have been extended by addressing the implicit assumptions embedded in the objective function. The gist of my case should be clear.

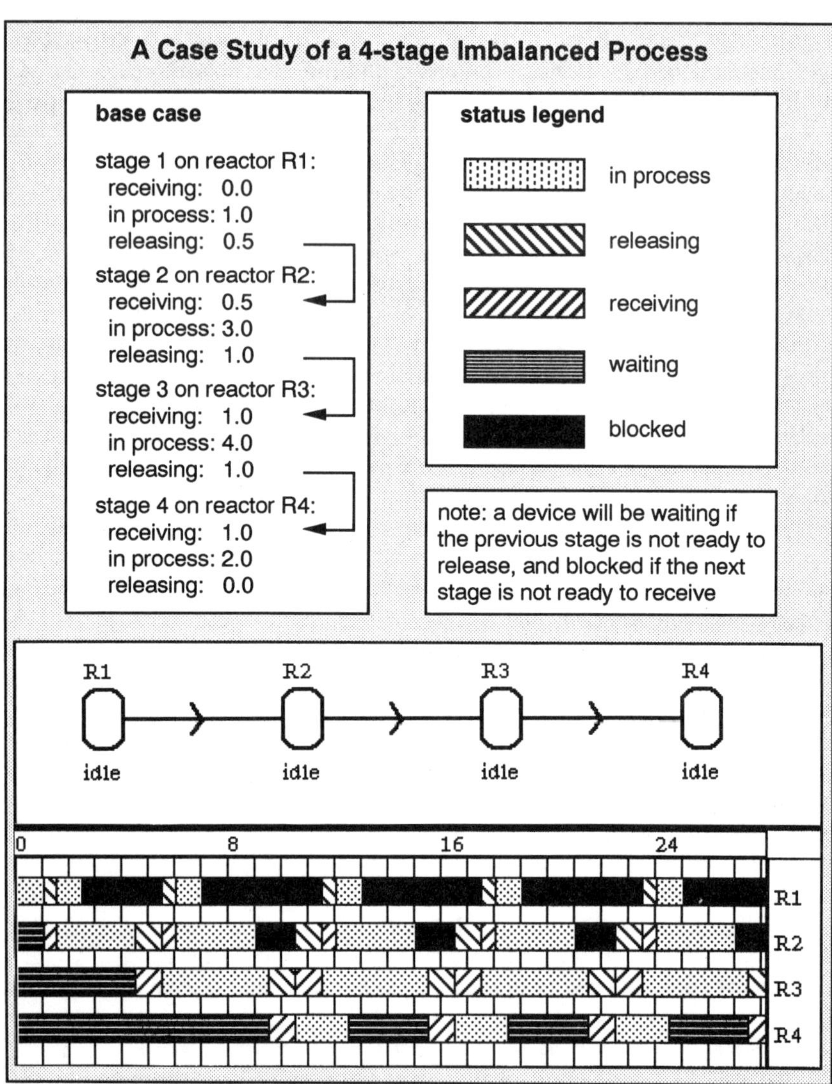

Figure 4.3.1a: Base case description of a 4-stage, imbalanced process. See also 4.3.1b. Each stage receives material from the previous stage, processes it, and then releases the intermediate to the next stage. The flowcharts show the change in status of the four reactors as batch after batch is processed. Time is measured in hours. Stage 3 determines the cycle time of this process. It is 6 hours. Note also the 'start-up' phenomenon: The fourth stage doesn't start before the ninth hour. The third, and last batch shown, is completed after 24.5 hours. The time required for loading the raw materials and discharging the finished product is ignored in this example. The subsequent figures—4.3.2 through 4.3.6—explore different ways of balancing this process. The chemistry of the processes determines which of these possibilities need to be considered in practice. How ProfiSEE is used to create these figures is discussed in the subsequent sections of this chapter.

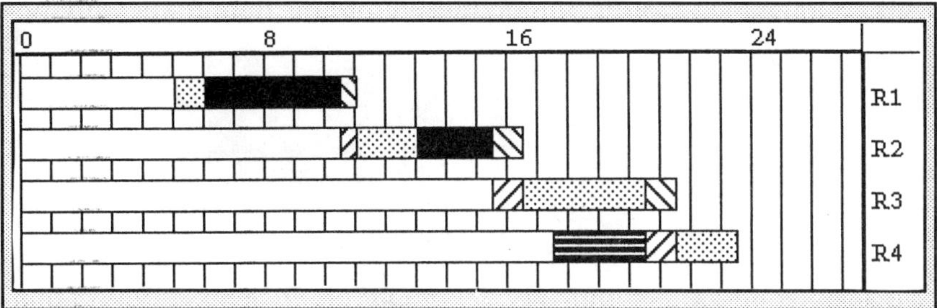

Figure 4.3.1b: The same process as the base case, except for one detail. The third batch has been selected from the campaign. The difference with the base is that the processing time on R2 is only 2 instead of 3 hours. This has the effect that the third batch can be started one hour earlier. Although the cycle time is unchanged, the throughput time of the entire campaign will be one hour shorter. If the campaign size is small, this may be significant.

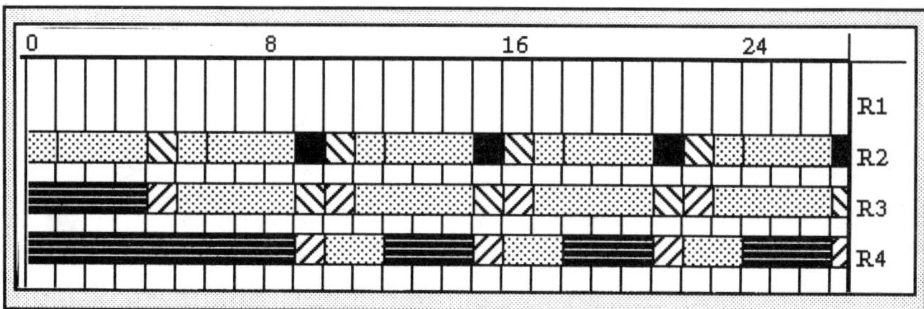

Figure 4.3.2: Merge chemically compatible tasks. The first and perhaps most obvious opportunity exists if some of the shorter stages can be combined. In the case shown, stages 1 and 2 are both performed on R2. Only three reactors are then required for producing the product. R1 is superfluous. The cycle time, however, remains at 6 hours. A similar approach can be used if several parallel stages feed into the second stage. The relative total costs of the reactors have little impact on the merits of this alternative. However, this is certainly not true for the cases subsequently discussed.

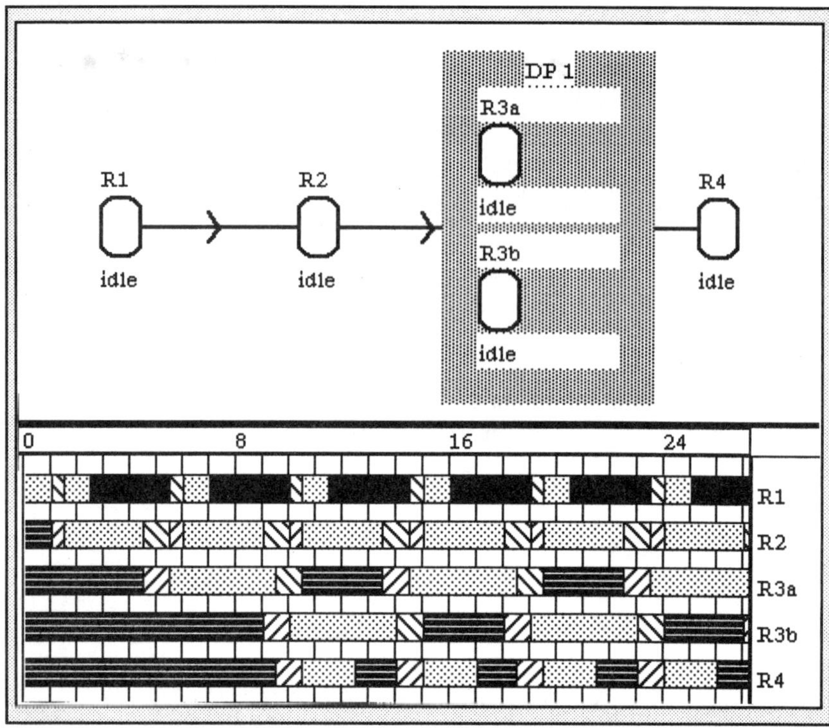

Figure 4.3.3a: Use parallel equipment for the bottleneck stage by alternating consecutive batches. In this case, an additional reactor is used for the third stage. The batches for the third stage alternate on the reactors in the pool containing R3a and R3b. The cycle time is reduced by 1.5 hours to 4.5 hours. Stage 2 on R2 is now the bottleneck stage. The result is disappointing because the time required for stage 2 was not much less than the original cycle time. Note that R3a and R3b operate 'out-of-phase'.

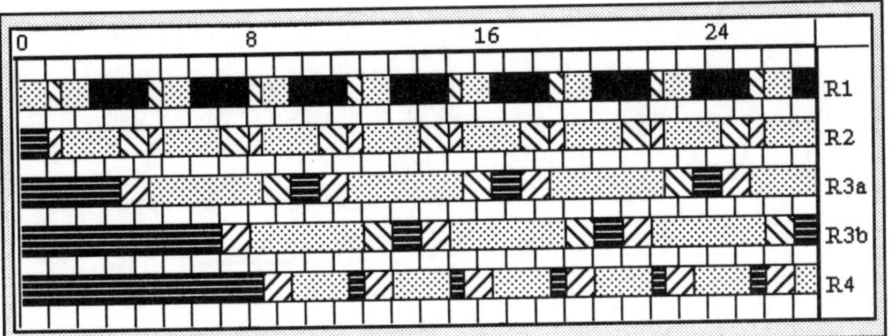

Figure 4.3.3b: Use parallel equipment for the bottleneck stage by alternating consecutive batches. In this case, the process time for stage 2 is assumed to be only 2 hours instead of 3, otherwise it is identical to the one discussed in 4.3.3a. The original cycle time of 6 hours is then nearly cut in half. The benefits of an additional reactor will depend on the overall time required for the bottleneck stage in relation to the overall time required for the next longest stage. The kind of configuration shown here is commonly found in chemical production plants. In multi-product plants, pools may contain several more reactors. The decision on whether to use 2 or 3 reactors in parallel may depend on which other products compete for the reactors in the pool.

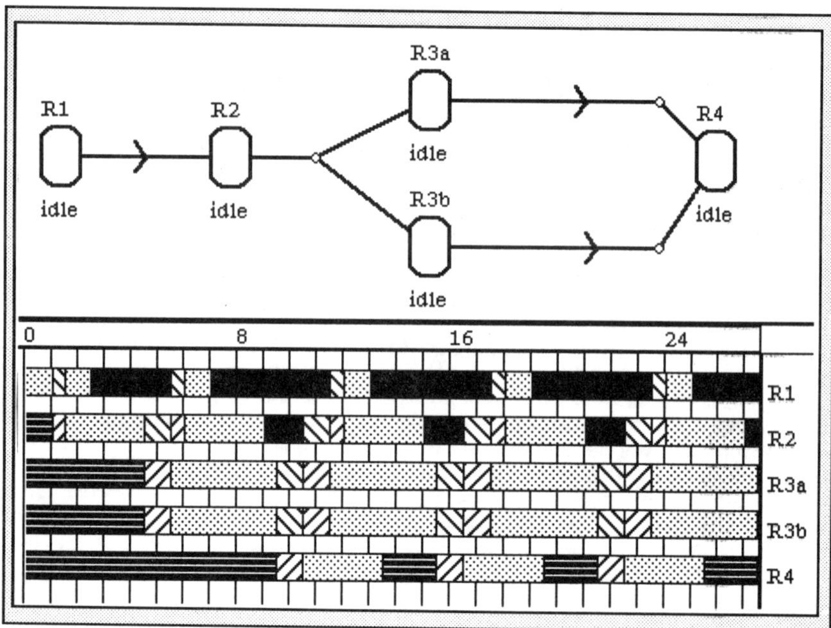

Figure 4.3.4a: Use parallel equipment by splitting batches. In this case the intermediate batches coming from R2 are split into two equal parts. R2 releases simultaneously to R3a and R3b. R4 receives the intermediates coming from the third stage. The cycle time remains unchanged unless some further assumptions are made, see the case discussed in 4.3.4b. Nevertheless, this alternative may be of interest if the size of the reactors is critical. In pharmaceutical production, governmental GMP regulations may prohibit this kind of alternative. Note that R3a and R3b operate 'in-phase'.

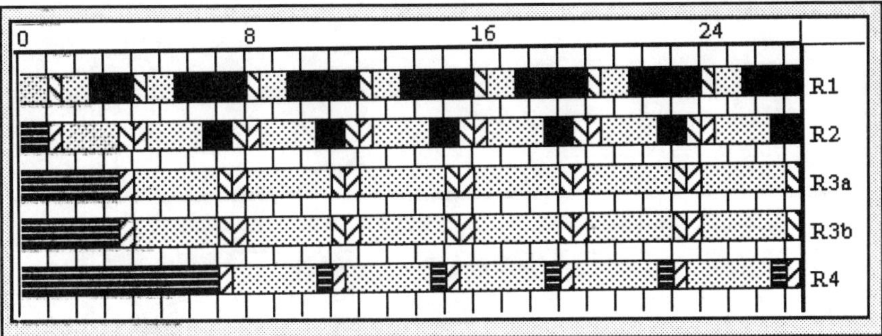

Figure 4.3.4b: Use parallel equipment by splitting batches. Assuming that the transfer times to and from R3a and R3b are cut in half and that the process time for stage 3 is reduced from 3 to 2 hours, the original cycle time of 6 hours is reduced to 4 hours. In addition R3a and R3b can be smaller than R3. In this case—compare it with 4.3.3b—reducing the process time of stage 2 by 1 hour has no effect. The assumption made about the reduction in process time on stage 3 is strongly dependent on the nature of the chemical process. The time required for an additional activity such as quality control, being independent of the batch size, can not be reduced. In fact, the number of quality samples to be analyzed would double. It is noteworthy that in this particular case, as opposed to the one discussed in 4.3.3, any variability in the process time for stage 3 will increase the cycle time.

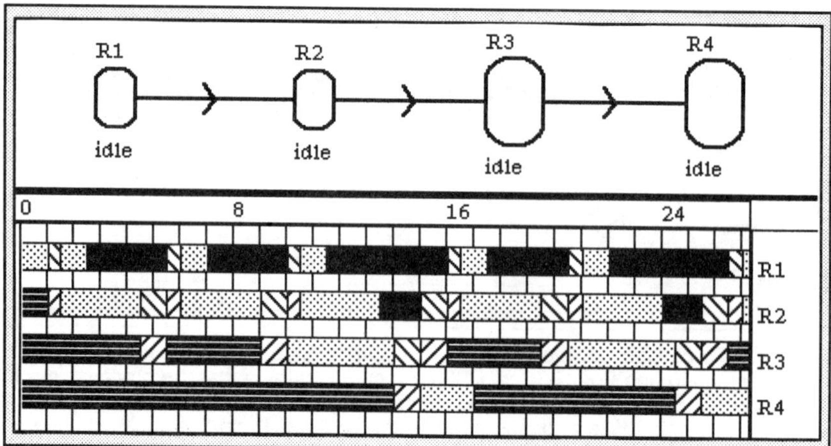

Figure 4.3.5a: Interrupt the chain of tasks by merging pairs of consecutive batches in a large reactor. In this case pairs of consecutive batches are transferred to R3. Processing starts after 2 batches have been received. This alternative results in a marginal improvement of the cycle time—two batches every 11.5 hours. The process time for stage 3 is assumed to stay at 4 hours. If in fact it increases, the cycle time will be worse than that of the base case. Clearly, other reasons are required to justify this configuration. Usually it is used in combination with a holding tank to de-couple the first two stages from the last two, as shown in 4.3.6. In this configuration, batch integrity is lost.

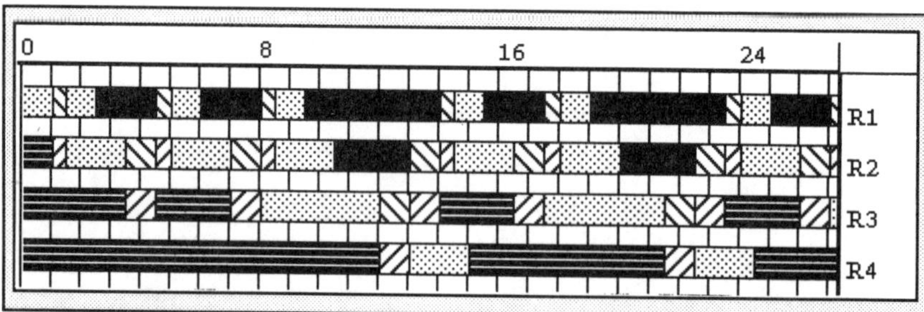

Figure 4.3.5b: Interrupt the chain of tasks by merging pairs of consecutive batches in a large reactor. The cycle time of the configuration shown in 4.3.5a is reduced from 11.5 to 9.5 hours for two batches if the process time on stage 2 is decreased by 1 hour. To be realistic, the process times for R3 and R4 would need to be examined. If cooling or heating is required, these times will be longer for the larger batches. As noted in 4.3.3b as well, the time required for the second longest stage in relation to the cycle time determines the effectiveness of the configuration.

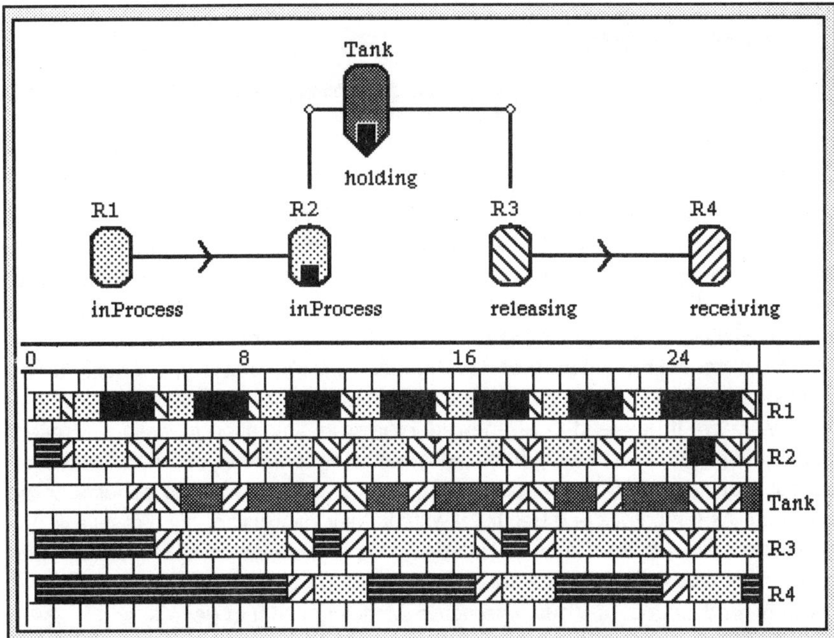

Figure 4.3.6a: De-couple the chain of tasks with a holding tank. In this case, the intermediate coming from stage 2 is transferred to a holding tank which releases its contents to stage 3. The gray shading in the flowchart of the holding tank represents the time during which the contents of the tank is not changed. By de-coupling the first two stages from the last two, more effective use is made of R1 and R2. However, if the holding tank cannot receive and release simultaneously, the cycle time of the last two stages can be worse than the original 6 hours. The flowcharts show this effect. One of the advantages of this configuration is that the batch sizes for the two segments are no longer coupled, i.e. the batch size of stage 3 doesn't need to be an integer multiple of stage 2.

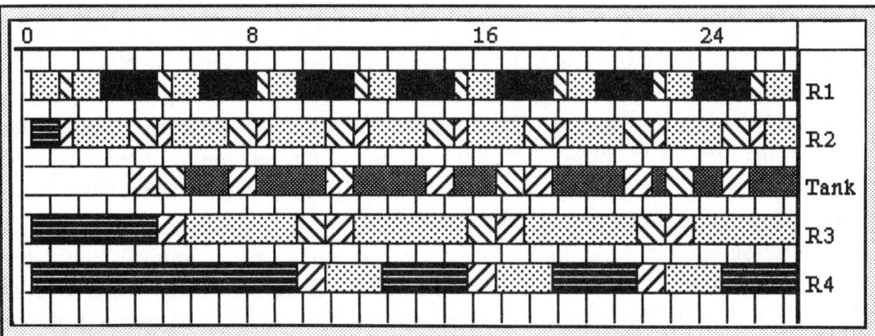

Figure 4.3.6b: De-couple the chain of tasks with a holding tank. This case is identical to the one discussed in 4.3.6a, except that the holding tank can receive and release simultaneously. Note that this happens only once, at from hour 11 to hour 12. The cycle time of the last two stage is equal to its original value. R3 no longer has to wait for the transfer of the intermediate from the holding tank.

4.3 The Role of VISM

"Are you trying to turn serious work into a video game?
Yes, but this one is more fun and enlightening than most"
from the minutes of a meeting

ProfiSEE is a realization of the major principles of VISM. The role of VISM is sufficiently important to warrant a brief review of the general work on the topic [Bell 1985], [Bell et al 1987] and on ProfiSEE [Vaessen 1989]. The introduction of the concept of VISM in the seventies and the ensuing development of packages such as SEE-WHY and OPTIK easily classifies as the most important advance in simulation modeling since the development of general purpose simulation languages such as GPSS. The importance of this advance has been recognized in industry, where it has lead to a renewed interest in simulation modeling. A recent survey [Kirkpatrick et al. 1989] of the still small user community on the construction and application of VISM addresses the numerous claims about the benefits of the technique. As Kirkpatrick and Bell [ibid] write in their conclusion, "[t]he results of this survey present a bullish view of VI[S]M." The experience of CIBA–GEIGY with ProfiSEE as reported in this chapter and [Vaessen 1989] is no different.

The overriding goal of Visual Interactive Modeling (VIM) in general and VISM in particular[36] is to improve the chances of successful implementation of the results or recommendations generated by projects employing operations research techniques. The application of VISM affects several of the activities in the modeling process as well as the 'pros and cons' of simulation modeling—see §3.5. As implemented in ProfiSEE, VISM shortens the turnaround time of operations research projects, which by itself is a critical success factor for successful implementation. Several other factors are at work. The driver of these factors, see figure 4.3, is the insight and understanding obtained by analyst and client into the dynamics of the model and the underlying real-world system under different conditions, which is the major direct benefit of VISM. The survey of Kirkpatrick and Bell [1989] supports the claims that VISM leads to improvements in the areas of model validation, client understanding and involvement, and better decisions. Also mentioned in [ibid] is "the incorporation of qualitative dimensions into modeling, and modeling complex systems." This requires some further clarification, unless the issue of multi-faceted modeling is meant. In terms of the key performance measure "[s]eventy-four percent of the respondents felt that their recommendations were implemented more often when VIM was used [ibid, p. 77]."

The interrelations of the different factors, which are shown in figure 4.3, deserve more attention than they have received in the literature on VISM, because they reinforce each other. For example, Kirkpatrick and Bell [ibid, p. 77] report that in a majority of the cases client involvement led to a re-definition of the problem, i.e. the

---

[36]The survey of Kirkpatrick and Bell [1989, p. 73] reveals that over 90% of VIM is in fact VISM. I speculate that the reasons for the use of VIM also determine the choice of discrete-event simulation as a modelling technique.

applicability of the original model was questionable, and that a different, and presumably better, solution was arrived at because of the use of VISM. The client, however, will only participate in the modeling process if the model is meaningful to the client, i.e. the client must have gained an understanding of its dynamics. Both factors have a direct, positive influence on assessing a model's validity and applicability. Moreover, client involvement itself directly or indirectly affects several other factors that are, in turn, also affected by a better understanding of the model.

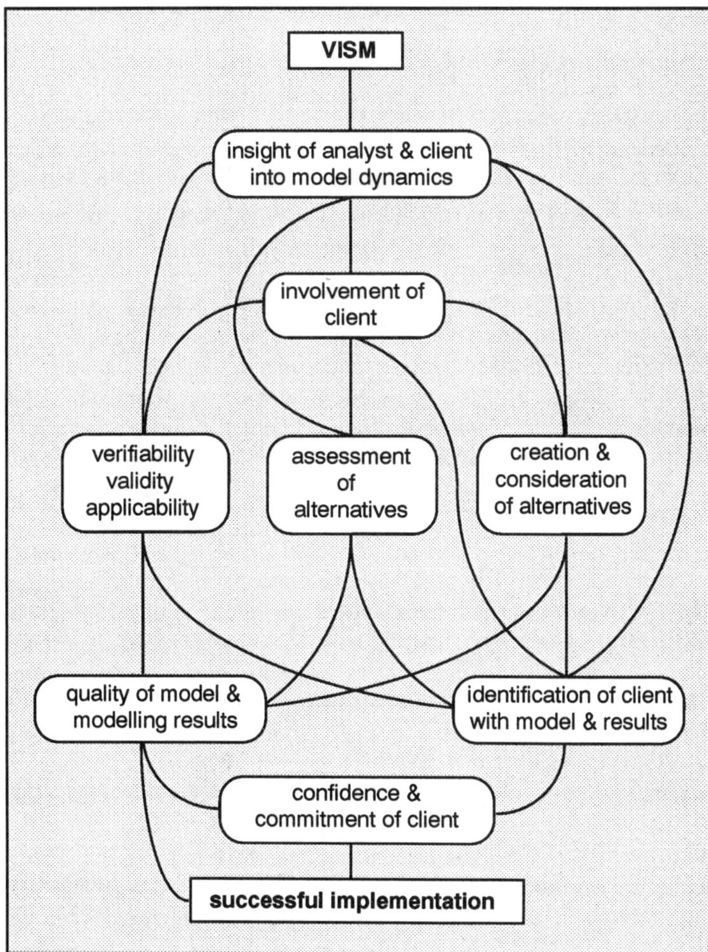

Figure 4.3: VISM improves the chances for successful implementation, adapted from Vaessen [1989]. The lines, all directed downwards, represent the relation 'has-a-positive-influence-on'. Insight and understanding into the model dynamics, which is the key driver for successful implementation, has a positive impact on several reinforcing factors. VISM clearly affects several activities in the modeling process.

Client involvement may not restrict itself to the interaction between the model builder and a single client. In more complex applications, an interdisciplinary project team may participate in the modeling process. VISM then serves as a vehicle for communication between departments with conflicting interests and objectives. It may help to bring these conflicts to the surface and establish a common view of the issues at hand. In large organizations such as CIBA–GEIGY this generally turns out to be a relevant factor. It gets additional weight in the context of the just-in-time concept, which, as noted, strives to resolve the conflicts between purchasing, production and logistics.

The work of Kirkpatrick and Bell [1989], although of value, permits few definite conclusions. The sample size of the survey is far too small[37] and the respondents include model builders only, excluded are the clients. Fortunately, the managerially driven increase in the use of VISM indicates that the success of VISM is not solely in the eye of the beholder. Further empirical research will no doubt be forthcoming.

To provide insight and understanding into the dynamics of a model, two features are essential:

- The model—including its inputs and outputs—should be visualized in an intuitive graphical fashion. Since the state of the model changes with time, animation must be provided in conjunction with a graphical display. But, an animated visual display of a factory layout is by itself not adequate. Time-based displays of the model's state variables and summary performance statistics should complement the animated display of the layout. Clearly, an analyst can hardly determine and assess the cycle time and balance of a multi-stage batch process without these supporting displays.
- The model should be interactive. As Bell and O'Keefe [1987] have pointed out, VISM without the 'I' is no more than animation and differs little from the traditional approach. The analyst obtains a good deal of the insight by observing the model's performance under different and varying conditions. An animated graphical display of a factory layout will show problematic and unexpected conditions. However, without interaction it may still not be possible to determine the causes. Clearly, interaction requires more than being able to start, stop and step through a model. In tools for VISM based on conventional programming languages, which are not inherently interactive, the model builder needs to pre-program interaction. This severely limites the degree of interaction.

What counts as a well-designed visual and interactive model still is and possibly will remain an open issue. The textbook on the art of visual interactive simulation modeling hasn't yet been written. At present, developments are strongly technology-driven. ProfiSEE exploits the most significant of these opportunities, notably: inexpensive workstations with fast processors and large disks; pixel graphics on large, high-resolution bit-mapped displays; and uniform and extensible

---

[37]The number of respondents is not cited in the text. Adding the number of respondents in table 4 [ibid, p. 75] gives a sample size of 37.

user-interfaces providing overlapping windows, pop-up menus and mouse-oriented control.

4.4 Overview of Design and Functionality

Throughout the development of ProfiSEE the guideline has been to promote intuitive and natural models by maintaining a one-to-one correspondence between the model's components and their counterparts in the relevant real-world system under investigation. ProfiSEE is a workbench—an environment—that initially wets and subsequently increases the user's appetite for first describing a problem, and then for discovering, exploring and evaluating alternative solution strategies. In this context, the following specific goals were set:

- display the underlying logic of simulation models using animated graphical displays
- provide a high degree of interaction that creates a tightly coupled feedback loop between input and output
- simplify the specification of the input components of the model; represent and manipulate these graphically
- extract high quality results, including traditional statistics, from the experiments
- reduce the time and effort required to develop meaningful simulation models
- manage the experimentation tasks

ProfiSEE makes a significant step in the direction of graphical programming, albeit for a narrow domain of application. ProfiSEE is not and was never intended to be a general-purpose simulation system. This restriction has made it possible to reduce the time and effort required to develop simulation models. The standardized set of concepts contained in ProfiSEE allow the model builder to go about his or her task without being hampered by cumbersome technical details, but only as long as the problem domain falls under the umbrella of batch-oriented processes as described in §4.2.

ProfiSEE's three basic input components are graphical descriptions of the physical (or logical) layout of a manufacturing system, the conversion processes and flows that can occur in a system, and the rough-cut production plan specifying the quantities and due dates of the products to be produced, thus driving the start-up of activities in this system. A production chemist will naturally think of and refer to the description of the conversion processes and flows as a product recipe or bill of materials. A planner will think of and refer to a production plan as a gantt chart containing campaigns. Once put together by the simulator, these components literally turn into a dynamic representation of the manufacturing system in action. Part and parcel of ProfiSEE are a number of basic instruments that measure the status and performance of specific aspects of the entities in the system under investigation over time. Facilities for more aggregated statistics, e.g. integrated over time, are also available.

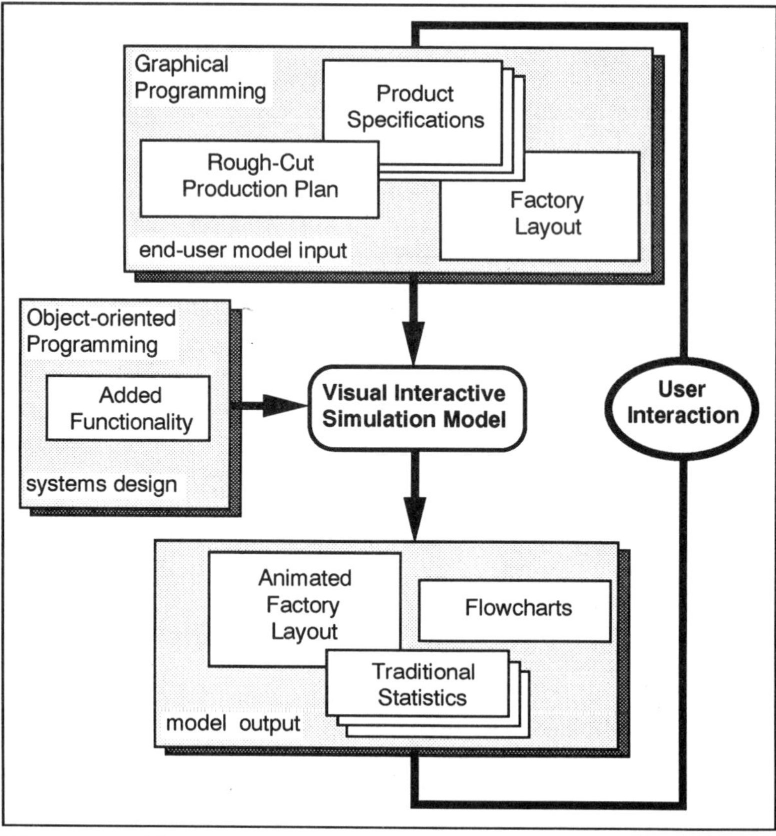

Figure 4.4: The three major components of ProfiSEE are graphical documents. These allow the end-user to develop simulation models of a broad range of manufacturing systems in the chemical-pharmaceutical industry in a natural and intuitive fashion. Experimental modeling with ProfiSEE is in essence an interactive and iterative process. ProfiSEE creates a tight feedback loop by immediately and simultaneously providing animated, graphical displays of the factory in operation and time-based performance statistics. A systems analyst can, if necessary, extend the basic functionality of ProfiSEE by taking advantage of the object-oriented programming paradigm.

The elements of the interactive feedback process supported by ProfiSEE are displayed in figure 4.4. Section 4.12 on VIPS describes an extended version that incorporates an additional cycle for detailed production scheduling in the overall process. To specify a complete model, the end-user graphically programs the relevant characteristics of real-world system using the three basic components of ProfiSEE. In most cases, the functionality of ProfiSEE will be adequate to express these characteristics in a natural and intuitive fashion. If the functionality is not powerful enough to cover the desired behaviour, then a systems or operations research analyst possessing the necessary knowledge of the specific design concepts of ProfiSEE and the more general lower level simulation constructs it uses can with a modest amount of effort enhance or extend the existing functionality. Through its application in diverse projects, ProfiSEE has matured to the extent that the bulk of the modeling process in the chemical-pharmaceutical industry has been reduced to graphical programming, thus eliminating the intervention of a specialist. Once the end-user has created a first-cut model, the simulation engine of ProfiSEE will 'run' or execute it.

Running a simulation is equivalent to performing an experiment. As time proceeds, the simulator schedules the campaigns entered into the production plan—a master production schedule in terms of MRP II terminology—to run in the selected layout. For each campaign, the associated description of the production processes, i.e. the product recipe, is interpreted and assigned to a set of entities in the layout that can perform the necessary activities and that are available at the time the campaign is scheduled. ProfiSEE is in a sense a laboratory. The model builder or its user watches the experiment as the simulation proceeds and may at any time intervene or extract, as a background task, performance measurements. See the example of a small factory in figure 4.5 that shows the use of plotters.

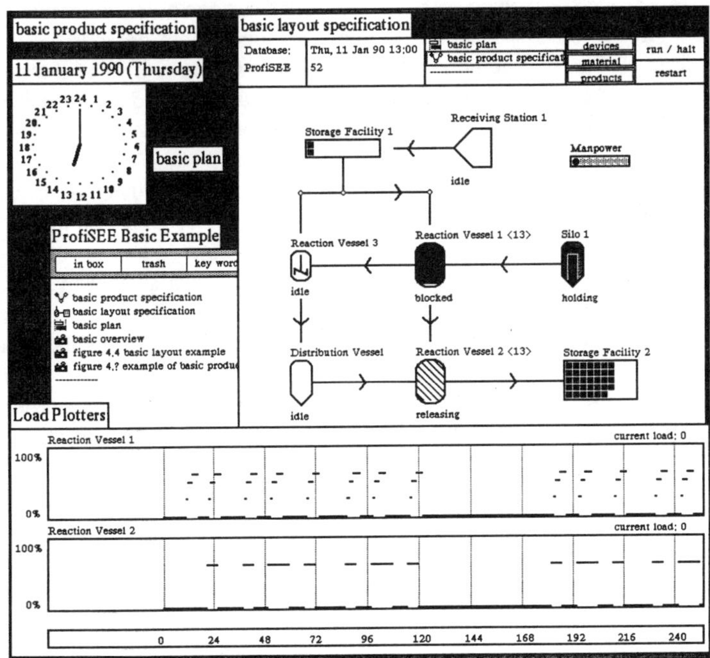

Figure 4.5: An overview of a simple experiment. The top-right window shows a small factory in operation. The bottom-right window displays time-based plots of the load ('how full') of the two devices in use. See figure 4.6 for a description of the basic layout specification shown.

The initial runs will quickly reveal the kind of errors and inconsistencies in the model description that in the traditional style of modeling are typically discovered much later in the process. The chances of making the simpler kind of programming mistakes and erroneous input are greatly reduced by graphical programming. All in all, the experimental part of the process, including the evaluation of alternative designs, can begin early, since model verification has become much less cumbersome.

In subsequent runs, the model user will observe the factory in operation, monitor the performance statistics, spot a specific problem, and then interrupt the simulation to restart the experiment under different conditions. The insight thus obtained may lead the user to change elements of the model's components and to compare the performance of this alternative with the previous designs. Eventually, the process will converge on one or more prime alternative designs. Subsequent steps will focus on refining, validating and analyzing the performance of these alternatives.

The design and implementation of ProfiSEE extends Smalltalk-80's framework for discrete-event simulation, see [Goldberg 1983, pp. 417-540] for a lengthy discussion. This framework, which follows the process-oriented style of Simula-67, performs the coordination and synchronization of the activities of the simulated objects. In Smalltalk-80, objects[38] pass messages to each other to coordinate their actions. However, at critical moments some objects cannot proceed to carry out their actions without first getting access to resources unavailable at the moment. The standard system classes *Process*, *Semaphore* and *SharedQueue*. provide the essential synchronization mechanisms. These abstractions will be familiar to designers of simulation systems. The class *Simulation* maintains a simulated clock and a queue of future events, sorted by their time. Time advances in variable increments as events on this queue are processed. The class *Simulation* also manages resources and schedules the arrival of new instances of the class *SimulationObject*—the second major class in Smalltalk-80's simulation framework. *SimulationObject* describes the properties of the different kinds of objects that have tasks to carry out. It provides a set of methods in terms of which its subclasses can describe their tasks. The basic abstractions for constructing simulation models, to be discussed in the next section, are all subclasses of *SimulationObject*. As shown in the class hierarchy depicted in figure 4.5, there are several intermediate layers of abstraction.

The strength of ProfiSEE lies in its ability to hide these implementation details of the simulation framework from the casual user. A basic understanding of this framework is required only if functionality is to be added. To the end-user, the classes at the leaves of the hierarchy are of interest. These allow the modeler to

---

[38]In Smalltalk-80, literally everything is an object. An *object* consists of attributes—private memory—and behaviour—the set of tasks or operations it can perform. Every object is an *instance* of a class. A *class* describes the form of its instances' attributes and the way its instances perform their tasks. The tasks that objects can perform are called *methods*. A *message* is a request to one object of another object to perform a method. Smalltalk-80 is based entirely on these few concepts. Building the right classes and subclasses, which inherit and refine the properties of their superclass, is the art of abstraction. Thus programming in Smalltalk-80 is best viewed as a way of modeling, a way of communicating.

capture the behaviour and properties of the entities in the real-world system of interest.

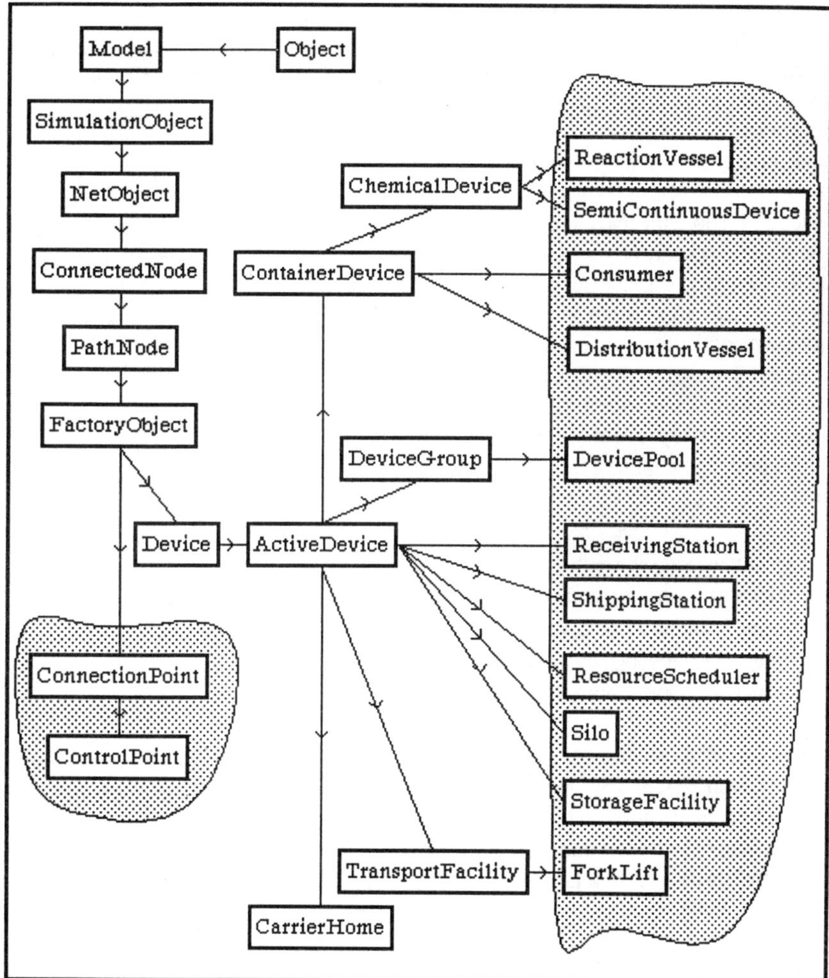

Figure 4.6: The class hierarchy for *FactoryObject*. The basic abstractions of ProfiSEE are subclasses that inherit their properties and behaviour from the classes *SimulationObject* and *FactoryObject*, with several intermediate levels of abstraction. ProfiSEE hides the implementation details. Of interest to the end-user are the classes at the leaves of this tree.

4.5 Layout Specification

The layout specification is a graphical document that contains a representation of the layout of the physical and logical parts of a manufacturing system—typically, this is a factory or a part of a factory. The layout is depicted as a directed graph that describes the components of the system and their interconnections. The nodes in the graph model the entities in the real-world system and their directed connections reflect the flow of information and materials that is permitted. To create a layout, the user opens a new graphical document, selects the desired entities from a pop-up menu, places these in the layout, and gives each one its name and parameter values.[39] The user then joins the entities with directed connections. ProfiSEE uses the display mechanisms of Smalltalk-80 and The Analyst to provide a partial view, called window, on this document. The window is 'scrollable' in both directions, so that the user can create and inspect large layouts. The user can move and place nodes at any desired position within the view, and give connections the desired shape by using the mouse as a pointing and dragging device. A series of standardized icons, some of which are commonly used by chemical engineers, can be selected to represent the different entities.

Several basic abstractions are available for modeling the following kinds of entities:

- production equipment
- auxiliary resources required by processes running on other equipment
- buffer facilities to hold WIP and de-couple production processes
- materials handling and transportation facilities
- consumers and markets

The available abstractions are general enough to model a broad range of cases in the batch-processing industry to a varying degree of detail. Each different abstraction is in itself relatively simple and easily understood. Observing and gaining insight into their interplay is at the heart of the exercise.

A simple example of a layout specification is shown in figure 4.7. The associated product specification is shown and discussed in the next section. The example intends to give only a first impression of how the different abstractions that will be described subsequently might fit together to form a working simulation model.

---

39 Underlying the graphical representation is a structured text file with an associated syntax. It is therefore possible to generate layout (and product) specifications using another interface or to generate these with a program that extracts and imports the necessary information from a central database. This feature is essential for integrating ProfiSEE with existing materials management systems. See section 4.12. The syntax is designed to ensure upwards compatibility. See § 4.13 for a few examples of the looks of the user-interface.

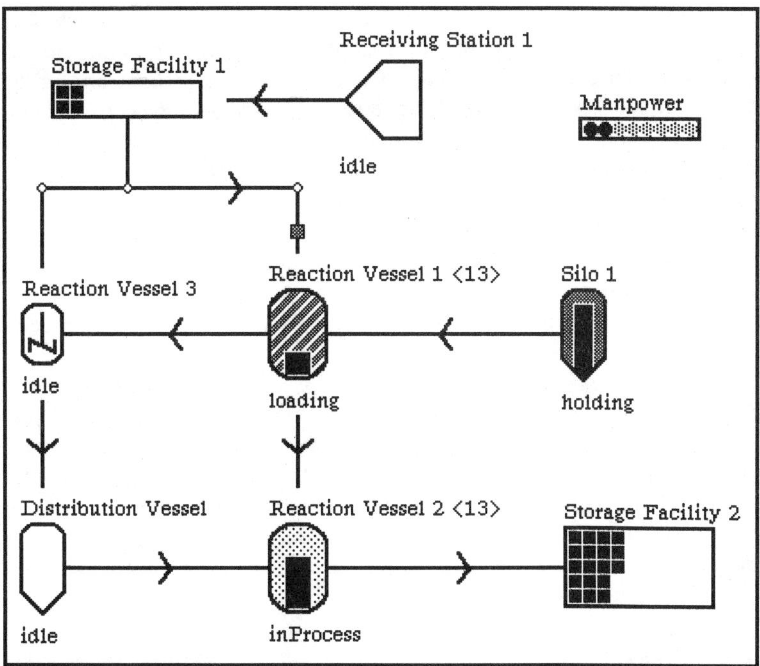

Figure 4.7: A snapshot of simple example of a basic layout specification in operation. Raw material on pallets enters the factory via **Receiving Station 1** at regular intervals and waits at **Storage Facility 1** to be loaded into **Reaction Vessel 1**. This device has already loaded some material, as indicated by the black bar in the middle of the device icon that represents the load, and is presently loading additional material, as indicated by the material on the pallet that is about to enter the reactor and the status text and pattern. **Silo 1** supplies a second kind of raw material directly to **Reaction Vessel 1. Reaction Vessel 2** is in the process of performing the second stage in this two-stage production process. It is taking the intermediate product from **Reaction Vessel 1** and has already completed a number of successive batches, as indicated by the material that has been delivered to **Storage Facility 2**. The two other devices in the factory are idle. Two of the eight workers in the auxiliary resource **Manpower** are busy.

The remainder of this section describes the standard abstractions available in ProfiSEE. Each one of these descriptions consists of a brief statement of the function of the abstraction, its parameters and, if applicable, its dynamic behaviour. In combination with the next two sections, this section should indicate the scope of the present functionality of ProfiSEE and show how the abstractions could serve to model manufacturing systems in the chemical-pharmaceutical industry.[40]

[40]The sections are far too brief to provide a complete description of ProfiSEE. Since a reference manual will not be available for some time, the descriptions of the different abstractions are somewhat lengthier than I would have liked them to be.

Connection

Flow Control

A *connection* connects two entities in a layout. A *connection* may represent a pipe, which is the case, for example, if a liquid is pumped from one reactor to another, or a pathway along which transportation devices move to transport the materials that the carry. This is the case, if the connection is drawn between buffer facilities. A series of *connections* and buffer facilities may form a path from one device to another.

The primary function of *connections* is to express which device routes come into question for producing a multi-stage product. *Connections* are static entities without a state and dynamic behaviour. If a pipe or a pump is a critical resource, the modeler may choose to model these items explicitly with a *SemiContinuousDevice*, see below.

Each *connection* has four parameters.[41] A *connection* has a measure of *distance* <integer> or length, which can be used for calculating the time required for transportation and selecting the shortest routing. A *connection* has a *line style* <feature combination>, e.g. 'thick & dotted' or 'dashed', to give the modeler the option to clarify its purpose. For example, is it used for information flows or material flows? Furthermore, connection may be *bi-directional* <boolean>, display its direction with an arrow—*arrow visible* <boolean>—and inhibit the animated display of material movement—*animation visible* <boolean>.

ReactionVessel

Chemical Processing

The basic entity for modeling batch processes is *ReactionVessel*. It usually represents a single device or reactor. If the analyst so desires, it can also be used to represent an entire production line. It repeatedly carries out a sequence of tasks. These tasks consist of consuming inputs, which may be material or information, processing these inputs, and releasing outputs, which again may be material or information. The detailed specification of these tasks and the sequence in which they are to be performed belongs to the product specification. In other words, which tasks a reactor carries out depends on the stage of the product specification that is assigned to it. Each of these tasks may take a certain amount of time and require different auxiliary resources for their duration.

Although *ReactionVessel*, as the term indicates, mainly serves to model chemical processes, it is sufficiently general to model objects that process information. A typical application is a logic unit that coordinates other processes.

At any time during a simulation, a device modeled by a *ReactionVessel* will be in a well-defined state. If the required inputs or auxiliary resources, described below, are not available at the point in time the device is ready to proceed to the next step, then its status will turn to 'waiting' until all items become available. Similarly, if a device is ready to deliver its outputs after it has completed a conversion process and no other entity is ready to consume its outputs, then its status will turn to

---

[41] Parameter values of an entity are edited by invoking the corresponding pop-up menu option or "double clicking" the entity and entering are changing the values in the query box that pops up on the display. Alternatively, parameters can be edited via a spreadsheet interface.

'blocked' until they are consumed. Besides being 'waiting' and 'blocked', a device may be 'loading' or 'receiving' inputs, 'releasing' outputs and 'inProcess' of converting inputs to outputs. Between a repetitive sequence of tasks, i.e. a campaign, or possibly between a sequence of tasks, i.e. a batch, the device may require a changeover to be performed. If this is to occur before the conversion process, the status is 'minorSetup' or 'majorSetup' and, if afterwards, the status is 'cleaning'.

It should be emphasized at this point already that the states 'blocked' and 'waiting' are a result of interaction with other entities in the model. The amount of 'blocked' and 'waiting' time is a reflection of how well the system is performing. It is an outcome of the simulation and not specified as an input by the model user. If the times required for consuming, processing, and releasing are constant, then it is in principle possible to calculate the amount of dead time for a range of isolated multi-stage processes without carrying out a simulation. However, it is non-trivial to generalize such a calculation. Simulation turns out to provide a general mechanism for this computation. See also the previous discussion on line balancing in §4.2. In addition, simulation can account for the stochastic nature of these activities.

The task performed by a simulation—to reformulate it—amounts to calculating the relative starting time of each stage in the multi-stage process and the process cycle time[42] and also needs to be performed for detailed production scheduling.

The status of a device is augmented by its contents, which is a represented by a set of units and the amount for each unit. The class *ReactionVessel* does not perform any logical consistency checks. These are typically application specific and can, if explicit rules are available, be implemented by creating a sub-class of *ReactionVessel*. The main use of contents is to represent the load of a device.

parameter	**type of value**	**purpose**
name	<character string>	description
icon name	<icon name>	visualization
attributes	<list of character strings>	process assignment
logging enabled	<boolean>	statistics collection
maximum contents	<integer amount of unit>	resource requirements
default major setup time	<duration>	time requirement
default minor setup time	<duration>	time requirement
default cleanup time	<duration>	time requirement
resource for major setup	<resource class>°	resource requirements
resource for minor setup	<resource class>°	resource requirements
resource for cleanup	<resource class>°	resource requirements

Table 4.2: Parameters for *ReactionVessel*.

[42]The term cycle time as used in the process industry is per definition the time between two consecutive batches in a tightly coupled multi-stage process. It is determined by the stage in the process that forms the bottleneck and sets the throughput per unit of time. By using a buffer facility to de-couple a multi-stage process the de-coupled stages can operate at different cycle times.

A *ReactionVessel* has a set of parameters, see table 4.2, which can conveniently be edited by the modeler. Every *ReactionVessel* has a *name* <character string> and an *icon* <icon name>, which are both displayed in the layout. *Icons* can be selected from a standard set. Neither the *name* nor the *icon* affect the function of the device. The *attributes* <list of character strings>, e.g. 'steel, cooled, segment liquids', of a *ReactionVessel* are used during the simulation to select the right type of device to use for producing a product. See §4.7 on the mapping of product specifications onto a layout. Sub-classes can use *attributes* for additional purposes. The *maximum contents* <integer amount of a unit> is specified by the kind of unit and the amount of this unit, e.g. '50 kg'. In addition, the modeler has the option to specify the default hours of *setup* and *cleaning time* <duration[43]> and the manpower, or other auxiliary resources, required during the changeover, see the subsequent description of *AuxiliaryResource*.

Each ReactionVessel has a set of *WorkPlans*. The class *WorkPlan* is a central concept for the simulation functionality of ProfiSEE. However, it is not visible to the casual user of the system. At any one time, only a single *WorkPlan* will be active. A *WorkPlan* describes the sequence of activities that a device carries out for a particular product stage and batch. It is repeated for the number of batches of the campaign. A *WorkPlan* is best viewed as a programme containing instructions that the device is capable of executing. The instructions executed by a device make use of the synchronization and coordination mechanisms provided by the lower level simulation framework. Once a *WorkPlan* has signalled that its sequence of activities has been finished or that it allows the device to switch to another process stage, the device selects another *WorkPlan* to start or complete processing. By setting the *selection rule* <rule name>, the modeler determines the order in which *WorkPlans* are processed. The selection may be based on the time the *WorkPlan* was assigned to the device, on a priority assigned by the user to the process stage, or on the total processing time of the stage.

DevicePool — ***Device Sharing & Control***

A set of devices may be collected in a *DevicePool*. Connections are then drawn to the *DevicePool* instead of to the individual devices. The selection of the device to use for a stage of a production process is not taken at the time at which the campaign was scheduled to enter the system but at the time this stage can become active. In addition, a stage may use two or more devices in a *DevicePool* in parallel. As discussed in §4.2 of this chapter, this technique is commonly employed in cases where the overall length of the process stage is long relative to the other stages in the production process. Two devices process alternating batches in order to achieve a more balanced overall process.

If several process stages of different products are assigned to a pool with too few devices to run all stages simultaneously, then these stages will have to wait for their

[43] All durations are probability distributions. If the duration is constant, the class ConstantProbability-Distribution is used which simply returns the constant value every time a sample is drawn. Each distribution requires a seed for the random number generator it uses.

turn and may switch device from batch to batch. The modeler has to specify whether the switching is permitted and what penalty is incurred in terms of changeover time.

The parameters *name* and *attribute* of *DevicePool* are identical to those of *ReactionVessel*. The parameter *selection rule* is slightly different. A *DevicePool*, like a *ReactionVessel*, has a set of *WorkPlans* and assigns these to devices as they become available on the basis of the *selection rule*. Normally, transfers between devices in the same *DevicePool* are not allowed. The parameter *self connected* <boolean> specifies whether the devices in a *DevicePool* are connected to each other. These connections are never drawn on the display for the obvious reason.

SemiContinuousDevice **Chemical Processing**

A straightforward and useful variant of the basic *ReactionVessel* is the abstraction *SemiContinuousDevice*. A *ReactionVessel* carries out its tasks in strictly sequential order. In general, however, a variety of tasks can be carried out in parallel on a specific device class. This is where *SemiContinuousDevice* fits in. A modeler can abuse the power of ProfiSEE and use an artificial construct to generate the desired behaviour on a *ReactionVessel*. However, 'clever' modeling quickly leads to black-box models, which is what ProfiSEE tries to avoid in the first place. It violates the principle of maintaining a one-to-one correspondence of model to modeled system. This principle is a central one in VISM.

The most difficult aspect of the general case of simultaneous tasks—one requiring careful thought and some ingenuity on part of the system designer—is the representation in the product specification, see the next section. Once the desired behaviour can specified naturally and concisely, it is not difficult to extend the class *ReactionVessel* such that it performs any selected set of tasks in parallel.

A special case of parallel tasks concerns processes on a device that starts to produce output before it has completed consuming all of its inputs. After an initial *delay* <duration>, input and output will overlap for a certain length of time. *SemiContinuousDevice* captures this special case. This entity is useful for modeling band filters and certain kinds of mills. If the *delay* between input or output is nearly or exactly zero, then a *SemiContinuousDevice* behaves essentially like a pump or a pipe. A batch production line, see below, viewed has a single, aggregated entity may also display similar behaviour.

The function of the parameters *name*, *icon*, *attributes* and *maximum contents* of *SemiContinuousDevice* is identical to those of *ReactionVessel*. The parameter *delay*, which characterizes this device, specifies how much time passes before output is generated. Sub-classes of this device could calculate the delay on the basis of the *maximum contents*, making the parameter *delay* superfluous.

BatchProductionLine[44] ***Multi-stage Processing***

For the sake of developing a rough-cut capacity plan, it is desirable to take an aggregated perspective of a manufacturing site. A detailed model of a production facility including all the different equipment items would then be inappropriate. In

[44]This abstraction still needs to be implemented.

such a situation, the abstraction *BatchProductionLine* is useful. It should capture the behaviour of a linear sequence of *ReactionVessels*. Its characteristic parameter is the *number of devices* <integer> in sequence. A *BatchProductionLine* successively runs different multi-stage batch processes. It releases its output intermittently. The processes are characterized by the number of stages, the relative starting time of each stage, and the common cycle time. Since these multi-stage processes may overlap, two or more campaigns may be active simultaneously.

The use of a single *ReactionVessel* or *SemiContinuousDevice* for modeling a multi-stage process would ignore the throughput time of the production process. In a few circumstances this approximation may be acceptable. From a technical point of view, a *BatchProductionLine* combines the features of a *ReactionVessel* and a *SemiContinuousDevice*.

StorageFacility — *Buffering & De-coupling*

A *StorageFacility* is one of two kinds of buffer facilities available in ProfiSEE. It can store different raw materials, intermediates and finished products. It serves as a model for entities such as warehouses, floor space and drying rooms. Space in a *StorageFacility* is occupied by carriers of storage media. The standard carrier in ProfiSEE is a pallet. Examples of storage media are barrels, drums and big bags. *ReactionVessels*, *SemiContinousDevices* and *BatchProductionLines*, can release material directly to a *StorageFacility*. When a certain quantity of material is discharged from these chemical devices, ProfiSEE calculates how many pallets will be required on the basis of the parameters of the carrier and storage media used. If not enough space is available, then the device wanting to release the material will be blocked. Similarly, when these chemical devices require a certain quantity of a material, the number of pallets is calculated. If the material hasn't yet arrived, the device will be waiting.

Raw materials enter a *StorageFacility* via a *ReceivingStation*. Finished products may leave a *StorageFacility* via a *Consumer* or a *ShippingStation*, see below.

StorageFacilities are connected to each other via *ControlPoints*. *TransportationUnits* transport materials from one *ControlPoint* to another, see below. If *TransportationUnits* are absent between *ControlPoints*, then transportation is assumed to be an unlimited resource and no transportation delays can result. Material is transported to the destination from where it will be processed further. It will be waiting, if the *TransportationUnits* serving the *ControlPoints* are not available and blocked if the *StorageFacility* to or via which it is transported is full. It is possible to specify a minimum duration that material will spend in a *StorageFacility*.

The function of the parameters *name* and *attributes* is identical to those of *ReactionVessel*. The parameter *capacity* <integer> specifies the capacity of the *StorageFacility* in terms of carrier spaces. *Width* <integer> is used to specify the shape of the *StorageFacility* on the display; it doesn't affect its functionality.

DistributionVessel ***Buffering & De-coupling***

A *DistributionVessel* is the second kind of buffer facility available in ProfiSEE. The major difference with *StorageFacility* is that it can contain only a single product at any one time. After cleaning, the product that is held in the vessel may be switched. A shortage of space or material may, respectively, cause blocking or waiting time on other devices.

A *DistributionVessel* is typically used to model a holding tank that de-couples a multi-stage batch process with liquid phases only, i.e. the intermediate is pumped to and from the *DistributionVessel.* Another example for its application are large buffer tanks which collect different bio-degradable wastes that are processed in a waste treatment facility.

The function of the parameters *name*, *icon*, *attributes* and *maximum contents* is identical to those of *ReactionVessel*. The parameter *simultaneous* <boolean> specifies whether input and output can occur at the same time.

Silo ***Raw Material Storage & Supply***

A *Silo* is a more restrictive case of *DistributionVessel*. It holds a single raw material ("educt") which is pumped via pipes to different chemical devices. It receives its input from an external source. Different processes may share a *Silo*. It is typically used to model tanks or silos which contain raw materials that are used in large quantities or that represent a safety or health hazard. Silos and tanks used in this way reduce the amount of materials handling.

The function of the parameters *name*, *icon*, *attributes* and *maximum contents* of *Silo* is identical to those of *ReactionVessel*. The parameters *educt ID* <educt reference> identifies the raw material contained in the Silo. The parameter *refilling time* <duration> specifies the duration of the reloading of the Silo, *refilling cycle time* <duration> specifies the duration between the reloading. The parameter *simultaneous* <boolean> specifies whether input and output can occur at the same time, i.e. can the *Silo* deliver to two devices or deliver and reload simultaneously.

AuxiliaryResource ***Resource Use & Control***

An *AuxiliaryResource* is a versatile modeling entity. Nearly all activities on process stages, including changeovers, may require the availability of one or more different *AuxiliaryResources* for the duration of the activity. Using a simple construct in the product specification, it is also possible to acquire an *AuxiliaryResource* for a set of activities spanning several process stages. Each *AuxiliaryResource* has a fixed amount of identical units for the duration of a simulation period. The modeler can, of course, change the number at any time. These units are non-consumable: an activity using an *AuxiliaryResource* will release the units required upon completion The availability of an *AuxiliaryResource* may be restricted to a certain time of the day and week.

Graphically, an *AuxiliaryResource* is represented by a rectangle containing circles; one for each unit available. The colour of an additional circle changes from light gray to black if a process acquires a unit and *vice versa*. If the units are off-duty, they are not shown in the rectangle.

The most common use of *AuxiliaryResource* is for modeling labour requirements. But, it may equally well be used for modeling special apparatus and instruments that belong to the infrastructure of the factory. It is also useful for implementing a range of logical restrictions on model processes. For example, safety regulations may prohibit that silos located in the vicinity of each other are reloaded at the same time. An *AuxiliaryResource* with a single unit will ensure in a transparent fashion that the model adheres to this constraint.

The function of the parameters *name, icon, attributes* and of *AuxiliaryResource* is identical to those of *ReactionVessel.* The parameters *class* <character string> and *amount* <integer> specify the kind and quantity of the *AuxiliaryResource* to be made available in the model. There is no restriction on *class*; it is a label that needs to be consistent with its usage in the product specifications. The parameter *shift* <shift-period> describes the time of day during which the resource is available; *weekend* <weekend-period> describes the time of the week during which the resource is *not* available. The parameter *overtime allowed* <boolean> specifies whether the use of the resource can extended beyond the end of the shift or into the weekend to complete the operation for which the resource was required. The terminology reflects the use of *AuxiliaryResource* for labour requirements.

TransportationUnit **Materials Handling & Transportation**

TransportationUnits are useful if the modeler chooses to investigate materials handling and transportation in more detail. A *TransportationUnit* can represent the behaviour of system entities such as forklifts and automated guided vehicles (AGV). It should be stressed at the outset that in many cases material flows can be analyzed adequately without the use of this abstraction. On the whole, materials handling and transportation systems in the chemical-pharmaceutical industry are comparatively simple. In comparison with other industries, the costs of sophisticated automated systems are harder to justify. The focus is on reducing the amount of handling and transportation required. A further factor playing a role is that the processing times on the chemical devices are relatively long compared to transportation times required even by conventional systems, i.e. the speed of a materials handling system has a small impact on production throughput times.

The present implementation of *TransportationUnit* is exceedingly simple. A *TransportationUnit* is capable of moving between two *ControlPoints* to pick up and drop off a number of carriers. The groundwork for a more comprehensive treatment of materials handling and transportation facilities has been laid in ProfiSEE. In conjunction with *ControlPoints,* this groundwork provides the functionality for covering a broad range of applications. Each carrier has a *home base* <ControlPoint reference>. It has the *capacity* <integer> for holding and transporting carriers from, to and via *ControlPoints.* If it has a *fixed route* <list of ControlPoints>, it will repeatedly visit the *ControlPoints* along its route. It returns to its home base if no requests for transportation are open. *ControlPoints* and routes may be served by more than one *TransportationUnit.* Instead of a fixed route, a *TransportationUnit* may have a *routing strategy* <strategy name>. An example rule: a *TransportationUnit* will stay at the *ControlPoint* where it last dropped off material and serve a request for transportation only if it is the *TransportationUnit* closest to the *ControlPoint* issuing the request.

The state of a *TransportationUnit* is characterized by its current load and location and the activity its is performing, i.e. 'idle', 'loading', 'unloading', 'moving' and possibly 'blocked'.

The design of materials handling and transportation systems and the detailed modeling of such systems quickly escalate into overly complex tasks. As noted, the requirements imposed by applications in the chemical-pharmaceutical industry are modest in comparison with other industries, where operations share the characteristics of job shops and processing times are measured in seconds or minutes. For a sophisticated treatment of materials handling and transportation systems like XCELL+ [Conway et al. 1987, pp. 66-82] are more suitable.

ControlPoint **_Materials Handling & Transportation_**

As noted, *StorageFacilities* are connected to each other via *ControlPoints* and *TransportationUnits* transport materials from one *ControlPoint* to another. Used in conjunction with the functionality of *TransportationUnits* as outlined above, *ControlPoints* provide ample modeling functionality for designing materials handling and transportation systems.

A *ControlPoint* has a *request strategy* <strategy name> which affects the behaviour of *TransportationUnits*. Examples of such strategies are:

- default – place a request when materials arrive
- opportunistic – grab hold of a passing *TransportationUnit* with no task assigned
- aggressive – place a standing request for a *TransportationUnit*

This basic functionality suffices for the modeling of the use of forklifts on the factory floor and AGV's operating between a central warehouse and production plants. A simple as it is, considerable care must be taken to avoid configurations that lead to deadlocks.

ReceivingStation **_Raw Material Supply_**

Raw materials enter the system via a *ReceivingStation* at intermittent intervals. A *ReceivingStation* must be connected to the *StorageFacility* where the raw material is to be stored. Its purpose is to model a receiving area. The functionality of a *ReceivingStation* is simple; it is mainly required for collecting statistical data.

The function of the parameters *name* and *attributes* is identical to those of *ReactionVessel*.

ShippingStation **_Finished Product Delivery_**

Finished products leave the system via a *ShippingStation*. A *ShippingStation* is the logical counterpart of a *ReceivingStation*. A *ShippingStation* must be connected to the *StorageFacility* where the finished product is stored. Its purpose is to model a shipping area. The functionality of a *ShippingStation* is required for collecting statistical data and reducing the build-up entities in the system that are no longer of interest.

The function of the parameters *name* and *attributes* is identical to those of *ReactionVessel*. The parameter *default shipment cycle time* <duration> specifies the default time between two successive shipments.

Consumer **_Market Demand_**

The abstraction *Consumer* generates a process that places orders for finished products stored in a *StorageFacility*. An inter-arrival time distribution serves to describe the order arrival process, see *ConsumerStage*. A *Consumer* has a *grace period* <duration>, which specifies the length of time a customer is willing to wait for an order to be filled. If the order is not filled within this period, the business is lost. As much as inter-arrival time is a parameter of *ConsumerStage*, the parameter *grace period* should really be assigned to *ConsumerStage* as well, see the next section. The state of a *Consumer* is characterized by the number of backorders.

Consumer is an important entity for measuring the responsiveness of a manufacturing system to fluctuating market demand. Typical performance measures that are the percentage of orders that can be served from stock, the percentage of lost business, order delivery times and, of course, the average number of backorders.

4.6 Product Specification

The product specification—short for the process specification of a product—is a graphical document that contains a representation of the stages of the process and the operations performed at each stage. The description of the stages and operations includes their sequence, the kind and quantities of inputs and outputs, the durations of the operations, and the resource requirements.

The use of graphical techniques for describing material flow patterns and multi-stage processes is not uncommon, but not by far as prevalent as the use of graphical diagrams for representing layouts. Apple [1977, p. 122] divides the techniques for analyzing material flows into two categories:

> *Conventional*—which have been in use for many years, are relatively easy to use, are primarily graphical, and are, on the whole the best tools for their intended purposes.[45]
>
> *Quantitative*—which make use of more sophisticated mathematical and statistical methods, and are commonly classified as *operations research* techniques, frequently making use of the computer to carry out the complex calculations necessary.

> ... many of [these conventional, graphical techniques] have been grossly underrated ... possibly because they are brushed aside as too simple, in comparison with the computerized approaches—many of which fall down for lack of data that might be available if the conventional techniques were used as preliminary data collection and analysis devices.

The main point of interest is, of course, that ProfiSEE has merged the two approaches. The product and layout specifications are used for "conventional" purposes as much as quantitative purposes. The borderline between them has become blurred.

Apple's observation that a graphical representation is a valuable first step in the analysis process is most pertinent in industrial practice. It coincides with the experience gained with the application of ProfiSEE. The use of these kinds of graphical specifications structures the analysis process and puts the initial focus on the input data requirements and quality. Many projects, which should never have gotten off the ground, fail at too late a stage in the analysis process for lack of adequate input data. It is reasonable to conclude that the combination of the two approaches is a synergistic one.

ProfiSEE provides a number of building blocks for describing product specifications. The user constructs product specifications in a similar way as layout specifications. The basic abstractions are used for describing the different stages in

---

[45] Apple [ibid, pp.122-154] discusses ten "more common" techniques. The one that is closest to the product specification in ProfiSEE in the *operation process chart*, which adds additional information about the operations to the *assembly chart*. The concept of *operation process chart* is well over forty years old, as the reference in Apple [ibid] indicates.

a multi-stage process. There is a natural correspondence between these abstractions and those used for modeling facilities and equipment items.

A simple example of a product specification is shown in figure 4.8. It is the product specification that was used to bring the factory shown in figure 4.7 into operation. Again, the example intends to give a first impression of how the different abstractions that will be described subsequently might be joined together to form a product specification.

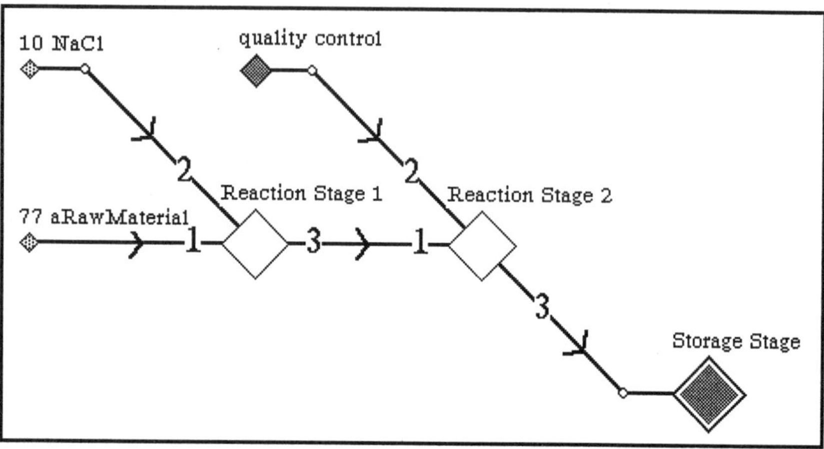

Figure 4.8: A simple example of the process specification of a product. **Reaction Stage 1** takes **aRawMaterial** and then **NaCl** to process these. **Reaction Stage 2** takes the output from the previous stage and processes the product further. Before the finished product is stored, it is subjected to a quality control check. The numbering of the connections indicates the sequence in which the operations are to be performed. Additional information is hidden in the connections and diamonds.

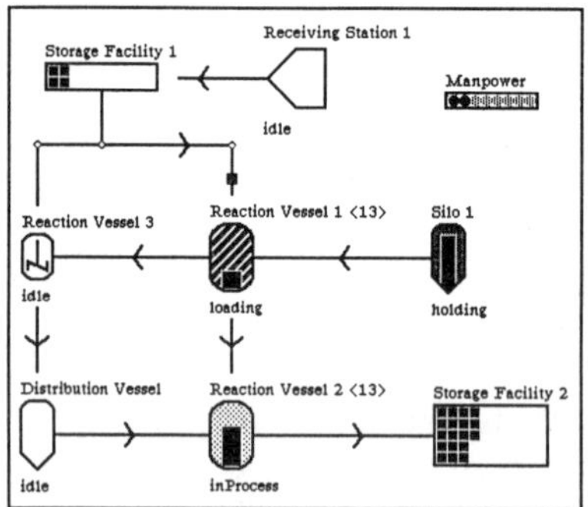

This product specification was assigned to the layout shown in figure 4.7, which is shown again to demonstrate how the two components fit together. **Reaction Stage 1** maps to **Reaction Vessel 1**, **Reaction Stage 2** to **Reaction Vessel 2**, and **Storage Stage** to **Storage Facility 2**. Note that there are no alternatives. In most cases, however, the assignment will be much more difficult. The modeler has to exploit the attributes of entities to restrict the number of alternatives, see §4.7.

The remainder of this section describes the standard abstractions available for creating the process descriptions of products.

ReactionStage ***Conversion***

The abstraction *ReactionStage* corresponds to a stage or step in a multi-stage chemical process. It represents a conversion step that consumes different inputs to produce different outputs. *ReactionStage* contains the information that ensures that the stage is performed on the right kind of chemical device. It also contains additional information that is not specific to the individual operations. The information describing the actual operations is contained in the *Connections*, see the description below, that enter or leave the stage.

parameter	type of value	purpose
name	<character string>	description
possible devices	<list of device names>	device selection
required attributes	<boolean expression>	device selection
major setup time	<duration>	time requirement
minor setup time	<duration>	time requirement
cleanup time	<duration>	time requirement
resource for major setup	<resource class>°	resource requirements
resource for minor setup	<resource class>°	resource requirements
resource for cleanup	<resource class>°	resource requirements
initial contents	<integer amount of unit>	initialization
can share	<boolean>	logic control
wait for input	<**none, first, all**>	logic control
no. of parallel workplans	<integer>	logic control

Table 4.3: Parameters for *ReactionStage*.

The purpose of most parameters listed in table 4.3 will be apparent. The topics device selection and logic control require a few comments. If *possible devices* and *attributes* are not specified, then any chemical device can be used for the *ReactionStage*. *Required attributes* is a boolean expression. For example, 'PL 5 & stainless steel' or 'temperature controlled & large'. The expression is evaluated against the *attributes* of chemical devices in the layout in order to select only those with the desired features and location. *Possible devices*, as the naming indicates, further restricts the chemical devices that come into question.

The parameter *can share* specifies whether the *ReactionStage* can be performed intermittently with batches of other campaigns. *Wait for input* specifies at what point in time a chemical device is allowed to activate the *WorkPlan* for the *ReactionStage*. The use of the values **first** or **all**, to indicate that the first or all of the inputs for this ReactionStage must be available, may avoid deadlocks. Starting the process of the *ReactionStage* before any of its inputs are available will put the chemical device in a waiting status and possibly lock parts of the production system. The parameter *number of parallel workplans* specifies how many devices in a *DevicePool* can be used in parallel for this *ReactionStage*.

Connection ***Flow Control & Resource Consumption***

The abstraction *Connection* represents a flow of information or material from one stage to another. *Connections* contain the information about the different operations to be performed at a stage of a multi-stage process. There are a number of different kinds of *Connections* depending on the type of entities that they connect. This sub-section covers the case of a *Connection* between two chemical devices. The other kinds of *Connections* are simpler and have fewer parameters.[46] Any special parameters are discussed in the text. All requirements are stated in terms of the standard unit of operation for the product, which is the batch.

parameter	**type of value**	**purpose**
line style	<feature combination>	visualization
comment	<character string>	documentation
quantity per batch	<integer amount of unit>°	transfer quantities
unload time	<duration>	time requirements
resource for unloading	<resource class>°	resource requirements
load time	<duration>	time requirements
resource for loading	<resource class>°	resource requirements
process time	<duration>	time requirement
resource for processing	<resource class>°	resource requirements
transport allowed	<boolean>	route selection
storage allowed	<boolean>	route selection
index as taker	<integer>	operation sequencing
index as feeder	<integer>	operation sequencing
number of batches	<integer>	logic control
applied to batches	<**all, first, last, etc.**>	logic control

Table 4.4: Parameters for *Connection.*

The purpose of most parameters listed in table 4.4 will be apparent. Some additional comments are required. The parameter *quantity per batch* allows the modeler to specify any amount of a desired unit, or a combination of these. The use of these units in the model has to be consistent of course. Examples of possible specifications are: '10 kg', '500 gallons', '1 signal', and '1 sample'. These examples should make it clear that *Connections* cover information as well as material flows. The parameters *index as taker* and *index as feeder* specify the sequence number of the operation on the stage from, respectively, to which the flow is directed. The parameter *number of batches* specifies how many batches are combined into a single operation. This facility is used to express, for example, that the process of putting a raw material into suspension may be carried out for several batches in one operation, thereby reducing the amount of materials handling and the number of analytic samples to be analyzed. The parameter *applied to batches* specifies for

---

[46]ProfiSEE automatically selects the right kind of *Connection* when the user is creating a product specification.

which batches of a campaign the operation is to be performed. For example, in many cases involving feedbacks, it is essential that some initial operation is only carried out for the first batch or all but the first batch. The default value for this parameter is, of course, **all**. Application experience has shown that a general expression for specifying the batches to which the operation applies would simplify product specifications.

EductProvider — ***Material & Information Requirements***

The abstraction *EductProvider* is the simplest possible version of a stage. It has no inputs and only a single output. It specifies material or, possibly also, information requirements. Material requirements can be for intermediates, in which case some other production process in the model must look after the supply, or raw materials, in which case the system generates the supply at regular intervals. The facility to model the consumption of intermediates is an important feature of ProfiSEE. Input quantities are specified on *connections* to the *ReactionStage*.

parameter	**type of value**	**purpose**
educt	<educt reference>	identification
internal source	<boolean>	logic control
receive cycle time	<duration>	time requirement
no. of batches per cycle	<integer>	logic control

Table 4.5: Parameters for *EductProvider*.

If the material requirement is for an intermediate product generated by another production process, then the parameter *internal source* should have the value **true**. If a raw material is required that comes from outside the system, its value should be **false**. The third and fourth parameter specify the arrival pattern of raw materials entering the system.

Educt is not always a typical raw material. A dirty container could be the input for a cleaning process. A *ReactionVessel* adequately models a cleaning station. The use of *attributes* will ensure that no chemical process is assigned to it.

ActivityProvider — ***Time Consumption***

The abstraction *ActivityProvider* is a variant of *EductProvider*. The process it represents does not consume any inputs, but time only. The single parameter of *ActivityProvider* is its *name*. The *status* associated with this activity and the *duration* are specified on the *Connection* from the *ActivityProvider* to a *ReactionStage*, which is the only stage to which it can be connected. *ActivityProvider* might represent the taking of analytical samples from a reactor or model a process consisting of a series of steps each with a specific probability distribution for *duration*.

StorageStage — ***Buffering***

The abstraction *StorageStage* is used to specify that material will be put into or onto storage media that are placed on carriers and stored in a *StorageFacility*. This requires materials handling and in some cases transportation facilities and capacity. The parameter *required delay* <duration> specifies the minimum amount of time the material will be kept in storage. An example would be drying time. The parameter *product* <product reference> specifies the identification of the product to be stored. Consistency is essential if this *StorageStage* is a final stage and the product is an intermediate that is referred to by the *EductProvider* of another product specification. The other parameters of *StorageStage*, *name*, *possible devices* and *required attributes*, are identical in function to those of *ReactionStage*.

DistributionStage — *Buffering*

The abstraction *DistributionStage* is used to specify that material coming from a chemical device will be transferred to a *DistributionVessel*, where it will be stored for an indefinite amount of time. The parameter *product* has the same function as the one of *StorageStage*. The parameter *can share* <boolean> specifies whether source integrity has to be preserved, i.e. can batches coming from different processes be mixed. The other parameters of *DistributionStage*, *name*, *possible devices* and *required attributes*, are identical in function to those of *ReactionStage*.

ConsumerStage — *Finished Product Consumption*

The abstraction *ConsumerStage* is used to specify the consumption of finished products by the market. More generally, it removes objects from the system a certain intervals. Its parameters *name*, *possible devices* and *required attributes* are identical in function to those of *ReactionStage*. The parameter *can share* specifies whether the *Consumer* to which the stage is assigned may mix orders generated by other *ConsumerStages* also assigned to this *Consumer*. The parameter *interarrival time* <duration> specifies the time between the arrivals of two successive orders. The *Connections* from *EductProviders*—an order may have several items on the bill—to a *ConsumerStage* specify the *quantity per order* <integer amount of unit> and the *handling time* <duration>. The *quantity per order* represents a stochastic variable and should of course be a probability distribution.

In the make-to-order case a *ConsumerStage* may first generate an output to a *StorageStage*. The output represents a production order, i.e. a signal and not a physical entity, which will triggers the start of the production process Logically, this production order must be one of the first inputs of some process stage.

The use of *Consumer* and *ConsumerStage* is an important element of the investigation of the dynamics of manufacturing systems. This is particularly true for the fabrication and packaging of dosage forms in the pharmaceutical industry. Chapter 6 provides a description of such a case.

SinkProvider — *Finished Product Shipment*

The abstraction *SinkProvider* is the logical counterpart of *EductProvider*. It used to remove finished products from *StorageFacilities* if the impact of market demand and fluctuations are not of interest to the modeler. *SinkProvider* is assigned to a *ShippingStation*.

Its parameters *name, possible devices* and *required attributes* are identical in function to those of *ReactionVessel.* The parameter *shipment cycle time* <duration> specifies the time between two consecutive shipments.

General Product Parameters ***Product Information***

The product specification also has some parameters of its own. These include its name and reference number, standard campaign size, standard yield, names of the first and last stages, and its estimated cycle and production throughput times.

4.7 Mapping Product Specifications onto a Layout Specification

ProfiSEE imposes a clear separation of the specification of the layout, on the one hand, and the production processes for the products, on the other hand. As noted, this approach offers distinct advantages for the modeling and experimentation process. But it has its price. Fortunately for the user, the implementation effort of ProfiSEE has already paid the price for this conceptual clarity. Imbedded in ProfiSEE is a procedure which maps a product specification onto a layout whenever it becomes necessary to do so. The burden of this task does not lie with the modeler or model user.

From an algorithmic point of view, this component of ProfiSEE needs to determine whether the directed graph underlying the product specification is a sub-graph of the one underlying the layout specification. For every stage in the product specification, ProfiSEE must search for an assignment to an entity in the layout, subject to the constraints imposed by the connections. Several mappings of the product specification onto the layout specification may be possible. These represent alternate routes. There are no efficient algorithms for solving this problem. Some kind of explosive search procedure is unavoidable.

The onus is on the modeler to make judicious use of *attributes*, a device parameter, and *required attributes*, a stage parameter, to avoid spectacularly long computation times. In practice, this has not turned out to be an issue, even with the largest problems that have been simulated. Providing useful error messages when the mapping fails turns out to be more difficult.

The procedure contains a rudimentary facility for scoring alternate routes. If possible, it will also avoid the selection of devices that are already active or scheduled.

ProfiSEE needs to invoke the mapping procedure during a simulation experiment whenever a campaign in the production schedule is due to become active. It is also used for generating a detailed production plan, see §4.12.

An integral component of the mapping procedure is the generation of the *WorkPlans* for the devices to which the stages of a product specification have been mapped. In other words, each stage in the product specification translates into a *WorkPlan* for a device. At this point in the mapping procedure, the parameter values contained in the product specifications are also taken into account. In this way, ProfiSEE generates the specific operations to be performed by the different devices in the layout.

4.8 Rough-cut Production Plan Specification

The rough-cut production plan contains the demand requirements for a given perlod and product mix. For each product, one or more campaigns capture the required production quantities and due dates. A gantt chart with time along the horizontal axis represents the production plan in the familiar graphical form. The vertical axis is used to express which campaigns could potentially be run in parallel. For example, if the layout contains four independent production lines, then the production plan will typically have at least four rows of campaigns.

The production plan drives a simulation experiment. As simulated time proceeds, ProfiSEE activates the campaigns in the plan, attempts to map the products onto the layout and generates the *WorkPlans* that in turn activate the devices and other resources required. Different shadings of the boxes representing the campaigns are used to display the change in status of the campaigns, i.e. whether they are 'inactive', 'mapping failed', 'active' or 'completed'.

To create a production plan the user opens a graphical document, specifies the parameters of the production plan specification, and successively places campaigns in the gantt chart. The parameters of the production plan specification are the *starting date* <date> and *end date* <date> of the plan, and a *global seed* <integer> for the random number generators of all probability distributions used during an experiment. The *starting date* determines the initial value of the simulation clock.

To enter a campaign in the production plan, the user selects a product from a folder in the information center that collects the relevant documents of a model and then 'copies and pastes' the product into the plan. The system responds by asking for the parameters of the campaign to be entered. Each campaign requires the *number of batches* <integer> and a *due date interval* <date, interval width> and a seed for all the random number generators of the probability distributions used by this campaign.[47]

Campaigns can be selected and moved to any desired position on the gantt chart. The position of the campaign initially determines its planned starting and completion dates. The latter is based on on estimate of the duration of the campaign. There are two further and important ways to set the planned starting and completion times of campaigns. These fall under the heading of detailed production scheduling and will be discussed in §4.12.

After a simulation experiment has been completed the modeler can compare the actual starting and completion dates with the planned starting and completion dates to assess whether the rough-cut plan was a realistic one. Moreover, with the help of additional performance measures, it is also possible to assess whether the campaigns were scheduled so as to make efficient use of the available resources.

---

[47]The actual seed used for the random number generator of a probability distribution is a combination of the three seeds mentioned: the global seed of the production plan, the seed for the campaign and the specific seed specified as part of the distribution itself. This is an important design consideration for the experimentation process and not a mere technicality.

4.9 Instruments for Performance Measurement and Insight

An animated graphical display of the factory in operation is by itself not sufficient to support the simulation process. A simulation system needs to provide facilities for collecting statistics on the performance of the system over an observed period, both for establishing the experimental validity and evaluating alternatives. The most obvious are summary statistics which measure key indicators over a specified period. Users of traditional batch simulation systems will be familiar with these: long reports in tabular form of the minimum, maximum, mean and standard deviation of the observed variables; as well as histograms. Such average statistics focus on the long-run performance of the system. Experience with the application of ProfiSEE has proved these to be the least useful. Typically, they end up decorating the final project report. Much more critical are time-based statistics of key indicators displaying the transient behaviour of the system. These, in combination with the animated layout, provide the necessary insight for assessing overall performance and long-term results, and creating alternatives on which to base improvement actions. Moreover, particular care must be exercised when interpreting aggregated, long-run statistics for detailed models of a multi-purpose and multi-product batch process plant. The average throughput measured in batches or tonnes per month or quarter can vary by as much as 50%, depending on the product mix and the sequence in which products are processed.

ProfiSEE provides a basic set of instruments for performance measurement and gaining insight. The design and implementation is such that a Smalltalk-80 programmer can easily augmented or refine this set to meet the special requirements of an application. A key feature of the instruments is that their selection and use is not pre-programmed. The model user decides interactively which aspects of which entities in the layout are to be observed by selecting what is of interest. ProfiSEE creates a window for viewing the information. Also, the user can (re-)size, (re-)position, 'collapse,' scroll, close, and save the window contents as a picture. The most useful 'observers' show an aspect of the state of the selected objects as it changes over time. In addition, there are instruments which show the output or speed (cycle time) of a process over time. The remainder of this section briefly describes, by way of example, some instruments available in ProfiSEE.

Simulation Clock

As a trivial as it sounds, a clear display of the simulation time is a must. ProfiSEE's display also shows the date, see figure 4.5. Available for use are a 12- and 24-hour analog clock and a digital one. The clock is initialized to the starting date of the production plan selected to be run. These kinds of detailed features, of which there are many in ProfiSEE, are what make a system usable and visually meaningful. The clock supports the interpretation of other information. A user familiar with ProfiSEE will quickly see from the snapshot shown in figure 4.5, that the simulation is now in its second week; that manpower is available 24 hours per day, but not on weekends; and that 7 batches were completed in the first week.

Flowcharts

Using the same pattern for displaying the status of devices in the layout, flowcharts display the changing status of selected devices over time. Figures 4.3.1 through 4.3.6 show a series of such flowcharts of different ways of implementing a 4-stage process. Without flowcharts ProfiSEE would not have gained the popularity at CIBA–GEIGY that it now has. The reason is simple. Production chemist and chemical engineers have been drawing the same kind of flowcharts with pencil and paper—a painstaking fashion. The use of the drawing programs, that are now commonplace, just makes them look better. ProfiSEE does it quickly and accurately. it reduces the chances and scope for making mistakes and not discovering these. At the same time, it also shows the influence of numerous factors on the basic production process. The usefulness of this instrument for de-bottlenecking and line-balancing complex batch processes is unrivaled. Although 'outsiders' will have difficulties interpreting flowcharts of more complex processes, production chemists and chemical engineers find flowcharts natural to their way of thinking and quickly draw conclusions from this graphical representation that are not immediately obvious to an OR analyst.

By opening two windows with differently scaled flowcharts of the same devices, the modeler, can gain additional insight. Recently, an application of ProfiSEE in one of the industrial divisions provided an interesting example. The cycle time of a complex chemical process that was simulated converged over a period longer than its normal campaign length to its 'theoretical' value. In the day-to-day operation of the plant the campaigns would never be long enough to reach this stable value. The project team only discovered and understood the phenomenon after a 'zoom out' was made of the flowchart.

By selecting the right devices in a reasonable sequence and choosing a particular batch from the campaigns shown in a flowchart the structure of the process becomes more clear. See figure 4.3.1b. Unfortunately, this only works for processes without feedback loops.

Plotters

ProfiSEE provides a set of plotters for numerical entity attributes of the different kinds of entities used in a layout. As the name indicates, plotters plot attribute values over time. The attribute value may be an aspect of the current state of the entity, e.g. load, or some average, e.g. percentage of idle time for the duration of the observed. In the latter case, plotters display the moving average. Figure 4.5 contains an example of a load plotter. Figure 4.9 below contains an example of a resource plotter, which displays the current number of units of an *AuxiliaryResource* in use.

The different plotters are all variants of one general mechanism. The basic plotter samples values at regular intervals and draws these values on a moving strip of paper. By changing the shape and shading of the pen additional information about the status of the entity can be incorporated. See 4.9 and 4.11b. Plotters would benefit from the availability of colour. Different colours permit more compact displays and, if more than one attribute is shown, easier linking of different aspects.

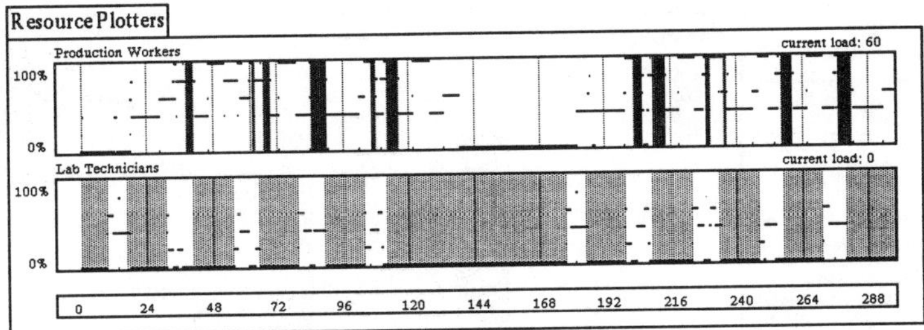

Figure 4.9: Plotters for *AuxiliaryResources.* Resource plotters display the current number of units in use. The dark gray shading in the plotter at the top shows when **Production Workers** are in short supply, i.e. some other process requesting more units than available is delayed. The light gray shading in the plotter at the bottom shows that the **Lab Technicians** are off-duty during the evening and night shifts, and weekends. The total number of **Lab Technicians** appears to be sufficient for the time period shown.

Logfile Statistics

Besides animated time-based statistics, ProfiSEE provides a facility for producing traditional after-the-fact statistics. Logically, this facility consists of two components: one for recording statistics during a simulation run and another for manipulating and presenting these in a meaningful way at some later point. The guiding idea is to make it convenient for the end-user to produce a standard set of commonly used statistics and to provide basic constructs with which more sophisticated and application specific statistics can be built. The present set of standard statistics, which is still quite rudimentary in scope in comparison with traditional simulation packages, has served the needs of most applications of ProfiSEE.

ProfiSEE contains a general mechanism for recording different kinds of events—status changes—associated with selected entities. During a simulation ProfiSEE collects the information of interest, which includes for each entry the time, the entity, the event type and some value, and writes it onto a disk logfile in a compact format for subsequent analysis. The user controls during which periods and for what entities information is gathered.

The second component provides a view onto a selected logfile, see figures 4.10a and 4.10b.[48] Using the information in the sub-views, which specifies what information is available in the logfile, the user selects the desired entities and aspects of interest and then invokes a menu selection for the desired presentation and its format. Alternatively, the user can use a further sub-view to enter an expression for evaluating and displaying the data if the standard options are inadequate. In principle, it is also possible to transfer data to an electronic spreadsheet for further analysis.

---

[48]The statistics shown in these figures are based on the Kanban example discussed in §4.11.

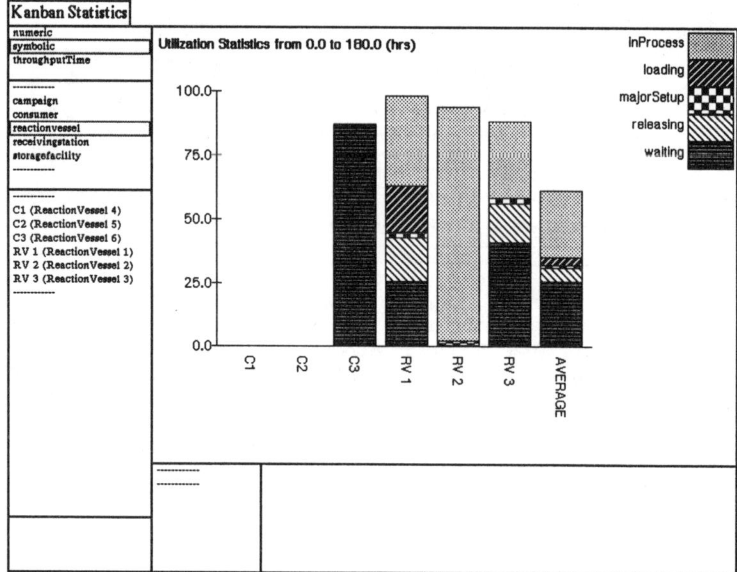

Figure 4.10a: A view on a logfile showing the utilization of the selected *ReactionVessels*. The left three sub-views allow the user to select the entities and aspects of interest. The bottom sub-view is for expressions generating non-standard statistics. See the example in §4.11.

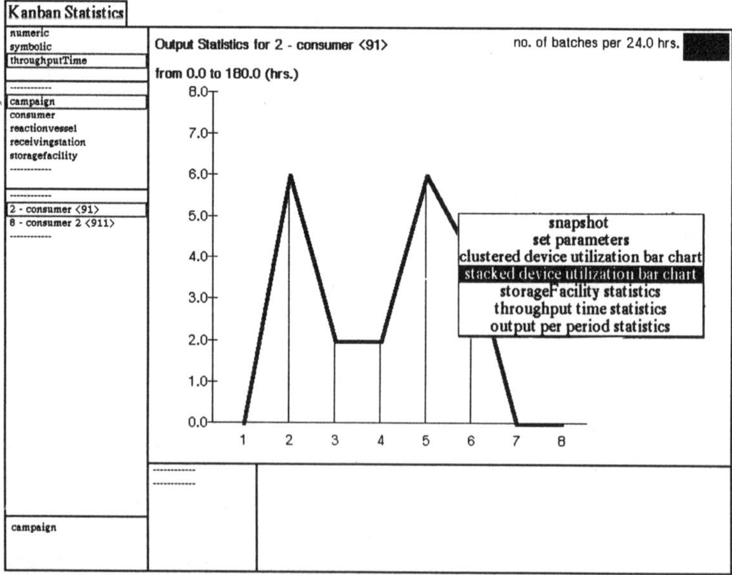

Figure 4.10b: A view on the same logfile showing the output—number of batches/orders per day—during the specified period of the selected campaign. By invoking one of the pop-up menu options, the desired presentation of the statistics is displayed.

4.10 Application Review and Critical Assessment

ProfiSEE has gained a degree of acceptance and popularity at CIBA–GEIGY that is quite unusual for an OR tool. In contrast with a number of major applications developed in the OR department in the past, which from a technical point of view were at least as sophisticated as ProfiSEE and quite successful initially, there is a good chance that its use will not peter out over the next few years. Chances will be best if its use decentralizes and if this development is actively encouraged. This means that ProfiSEE and VISM will eventually go the way of other—successful—OR methods that their users no longer recognize as such. In view of these developments, a commercial re-design and implementation is underway. Decentralization and commercialization entails a different set of tasks for OR, perhaps not wholly suited to the typical OR department. In the medium-term, it also means that the laurels for productivity improvements go to the end-users.

Since its introduction two years ago, the OR department has applied ProfiSEE in a dozen formal projects. Roughly 30 man-months of OR effort, excluding technical developments, were directly charged to the clients during this period. Tables 4.6a, 4.6b and 4.6c[49] give an overview of the main projects; excluded are small-scale projects and those that have just begun. As indicated by the data in these tables, the range of applications in terms of size, complexity and focus varies considerably. I speculate that the size as well as the complexity of these applications is greater than the typical VISM application in the batch process industry. The first column in table 4.6a—Charger WBA—provides the justification. The modeling effort and effective turnaround time required for this particular project, which now looks relatively straightforward in comparison with some of the others, would under normal circumstances be prohibitive and leave little room for successful and timely results. The simulation model was still written directly in Smalltalk-80; it served as a prototype for ProfiSEE—see [Vaessen 1989]. The speed-up in the modeling process, derived from the specialization and implementation concept of ProfiSEE, has, among other things, eliminated the laborious design of screen layouts by specialists. The speed-up has been a key factor for its successful application.

Several of the projects listed in table 4.6 have on their own thrown off tangible benefits that easily exceed the total hardware, software and software development costs of ProfiSEE of ca. 0.5 MSfr. by an order of magnitude. Typical benefits are increased throughput for products in short supply achieved by cycle time reductions and line balancing. In two of the projects, potential cycle time improvements ranging from 25% to 40% turned out to be possible without major investments in new equipment. Since cycle times are directly coupled with production throughput times and campaign lengths, these improvements have also increased the speed and flexibility of the manufacturing process. Although the efficient use of resources is the primary focus of a large number of these projects, the impact on throughput time of basic chemical processes is starting to receive more attention.

---

[49]Besides hard figures, this table contains some judgement from my point of view as an OR analyst. See the following page for an explanation of the terms used.

For proper interpretation of the data in table 4.6 a number of the terms used require some additional explanation:

Project Process

OR effort required includes the writing of interim and final reports. Roughly 50% should be added to the MW—man week—figures if the software development time is allocated to the individual projects. The fee structure of the OR department reflects that this is not done. *Effective turnaround time* is the time between the date of the initial project proposal and the submission and approval of the final report or the presentation of the final results and recommendations in the absence of a formal report. *User involvement & commitment* indicates the level of interaction with the user project team: 'good' means regular reviews and discussions of progress made, and active—pull rather than push—project management by the user; 'excellent' means that the user interactively developed solutions and tested alternatives rather than the OR department providing or testing the new ideas. *Results accepted* reflects whether the client accepted and understood the results, and followed up on the recommendations. It does not assess whether the recommendations have been implemented at this point in time. In a number of cases, the term implementation would not be applicable to start with.

Factory Layout

No. of entities indicates the total number of objects in the principal layout, excluding connections. *Complexity* expresses my judgement of the level of complexity of the material and information flows. It captures more than the density of the connections between the objects. The terms used for describing *structure of layout* are discussed in §4.2 and §7.3.2.

Product Specifications

No. of product classes indicates how many different types of products are produced in the system investigated, counting only the final product level. If *no. of production stages*, see below is equal to 1, then the ratio between *no. of product specifications* and *no. of product classes* indicates the diversity of the products. *Ø no. of levels per product* indicates the average number stages in the critical path of the product specifications. *Ø no. of stages per product* indicates the average total number of stages in a product specification. The ratio of the two, in combination with *feedback & recycling* and *special features used,* indicates the complexity of the product specifications.

Rough-cut Production Plan

No. of production stages indicates the number of major intermediates in the production process as indicated by the link of one product specification into another. *Complexity* indicates whether campaign scheduling or sequencing needs to take account of the effects on resource utilization or conflicting resource requirements that can lead to deadlocks

	Charger WBA	Delta USA	Line 13 WBA	JIT in WST
Application Area & Objectives				
division	dyestuffs	dyestuffs	dyestuffs	pharma
new or existing facility	existing	new	re-design	new
size of investment	n / a	> 30 MSfr.	n / a	> 40 MSfr.
type of process	chemical	chemical	chemical	packaging
focus of objectives & type of benefits	balancing; materials handling	balancing; throughput; resources	throughput supply continuity	speed; resources; design
Project Process				
rough-cut model employed	no	no	yes	yes
quality & availabilty of data	ok	good	good	good
new features required	prototype	initially no	yes	no
OR effort required	40 MW	12 MW	8 MW	4 MW
effective turnaround time	12 months	3 months	4 months	2 months
user involvement & commitment	good	good	excellent	ok
results accepted	mainly	yes	yes	partially
report available	yes	yes	yes	yes
Factory Layout				
no. of entities	> 40	> 40	> 20	56
no. of entity types	4	4	2	4
complexity	medium	medium	medium	medium
structure of layout	lines	process	line	pools
shifts relevant	no	no	no	yes
Product Specifications				
no. of product specifications	5	15	6	24
no. of product classes	1	5	2	7
Ø no. of levels per product	6	6	5	6
Ø no. of stages per product	6	8	10	10
feedback & recycling	no	no	no	no
special features used	n / a	initially no	yes	yes
stochastic input elements	yes	no	yes	no
Rough-cut Production Plan				
no. of campaigns in RCP	12	inessential	not used	40
planning horizon	1 month	inessential	not used	3 months
no. of production stages	1	1	1	1
complexity	low	n / a	n / a	high
detailed scheduling beneficial	no	yes	no	yes

Table 4.6a: Evaluation matrix of ProfiSEE projects carried out at CIBA–GEIGY.

EFI Spain	Tinuvin MM BSG	Pigments WMO	Lanasol WBA	Irganox WSH	Irganox BRD
pharma	works	pigments	dyestuffs	additives	additives
new	mixed	existing	existing	existing	existing
> 50 MSfr.	n / a	n / a	n / a	n / a	< 1 MSfr.
packaging	mat'l flow	chemical	chemical	chemical	chemical
speed; resources; design	flow; feasibility study	balancing; throughput	throughput	impact of shifts; throughput	balancing; throughput
no	no	no	no	no	no
ok	poor	good	poor	good	good
no	yes	no	no	yes	no
36 MW	3 MW	2 MW +	4 MW	2 MW	6 MW
12 months	3 months	6 months	10 months	3 months	5 months
good	poor	n / a	very poor	good	excellent
yes	partially	yes	no results	yes	yes
yes, 2	no	user report	no	yes	yes
> 70	44	15	20	8	32
4	5	2	3	3	7
medium	medium	low	low	low	high
lines	lines	process	simple	simple	process
yes	yes	no	no	yes	no
26	2 (x 8)	3	2	1	6 variants
9	1	1	1	1	1
8	2	6	4	6	9
8	3	8	8	6	9
yes	yes	yes	no	no	yes
no	no	no	no	no	yes
no	no	no	no	yes	yes
100	300	not used	not used	not used	inessential
6x1 month	3 months	not used	not used	not used	inessential
1	8	1	1	1	2
low	medium	n / a	n / a	n / a	n / a
no	yes	no	no	no	no

Table 4.6b: Project evaluation matrix continued.

	H-Acid WBA	Peptides WBA	TKZ Japan	C-Lenses CV
Application Area & Objectives				
division	dyestuffs	pharma	dyestuffs	ciba vision
new or existing facility	existing	new	new	existing
size of investment	n / a	> 50 MSFr.	> 10 MSfr.	n / a
type of process	chemical	chemical	chemical	production
focus of objectives & type of benefits	supply continuity; design;	resources; design	design check; throughput	speed & service level
Project Process				
rough-cut model employed	no	yes	no	no
quality & availabilty of data	ok	acceptable	ok	poor
new features required	no	yes	yes	yes
OR effort required	8 MW	32 MW	1 MW	1 MW
effective turnaround time	4 months	10 months	1 month	n / a
user involvement & commitment	ok	good	good	poor
results accepted	yes	yes	yes	no results
report available	yes	yes	user report	no
Factory Layout				
no. of entities	6	35	6	20
no. of entity types	2	5	4	5
complexity	low	high	low	high
structure of layout	line	process	simple	line
shifts relevant	yes	no	yes	yes
Product Specifications				
no. of product specifications	1	80	4	1
no. of product classes	1	2	2	1
Ø no. of levels per product	5	7	4	1
Ø no. of stages per product	5	10	4	2
feedback & recycling	no	no	no	yes
special features used	yes	yes	no	no
stochastic input elements	yes	no	no	yes
Rough-cut Production Plan				
no. of campaigns in RCP	not used	250	2	inessential
planning horizon	not used	12 months	3 months	inessential
no. of production stages	1	**35**	1	2
complexity	n / a	medium	low	n / a
detailed scheduling beneficial	no	yes	no	no

Table 4.6c: Project evaluation matrix continued.

The information provided in table 4.6, which should largely speak for itself, focuses on what has been accomplished. However, a number of additional comments are in order that indicate the weaknesses of detailed simulation studies of the kind performed by systems like ProfiSEE. Refer to chapter 3 for a more general discussion.

No major alternatives were investigated with ProfiSEE in the cases of the projects involving the design of a new facility. This of course puts some question marks behind the assessment of the design. As recent events have—once again—confirmed, the sensitivity of the design with respect to volume changes would have been a worthwhile aspect of the analysis. Apparently, the *overall* effort is still too large to permit or stimulate a broader study of alternatives and scenarios. There are two reasons. First, ProfiSEE doesn't lend itself well to sensitivity analysis. Second, ProfiSEE has drastically reduced the OR content of the overall effort; but, data collection and preparation, although improving, still appear to be in their infancy. In my estimate, the OR content now amounts to less than 30% of the overall effort required for the detailed simulation analysis of a new facility.

A further observed weakness in the overall appraisal process is that the results of the simulation studies did not directly link into the formal financial analysis. The various excuses, which reflect upon the process and its organization as much as anything else, could possibly be circumvented by a preliminary rough-cut financial analysis, as suggested in chapter 3. This approach would ensure that financial data is incorporated at an early stage. The availability of an electronic spreadsheet in ProfiSEE and the facility to link data items from various sources, although it requires familiarity with the use of the constructs offered by The Analyst, support the recommended approach more than adequately.

Although the marks given in table 4.6 for data quality and availability are generally high, there is a particular area of concern about the data on process variability and equipment breakdowns. Critics of VISM have noted the neglect of this aspect by VISM models. At least for the applications reported here this neglect is not so much a result of the technique. In nearly all of the applications there is no sound data, if any, on which to base an adequate treatment of the detrimental effects of variability. In those applications where variability was known to play role, largely fictitious probability distributions were adopted to assess the extent of the impact and motivate further data collection. But this only applies to existing facilities with computer controlled operations, which just happen to have less variability. Thus, precisely in those cases where this data would be must useful it is missing. A compounding factor is that in tightly-coupled (chemical) processes the detrimental impact of process variability increases as the process balance improves. It becomes a limiting factor.

4.11 Some Examples

Instead of a full-length description of one the industrial applications reviewed in §4.10, this section presents two non-trivial examples that should allow the reader to judge the claims made in this chapter about the benefits of ProfiSEE and VISM.

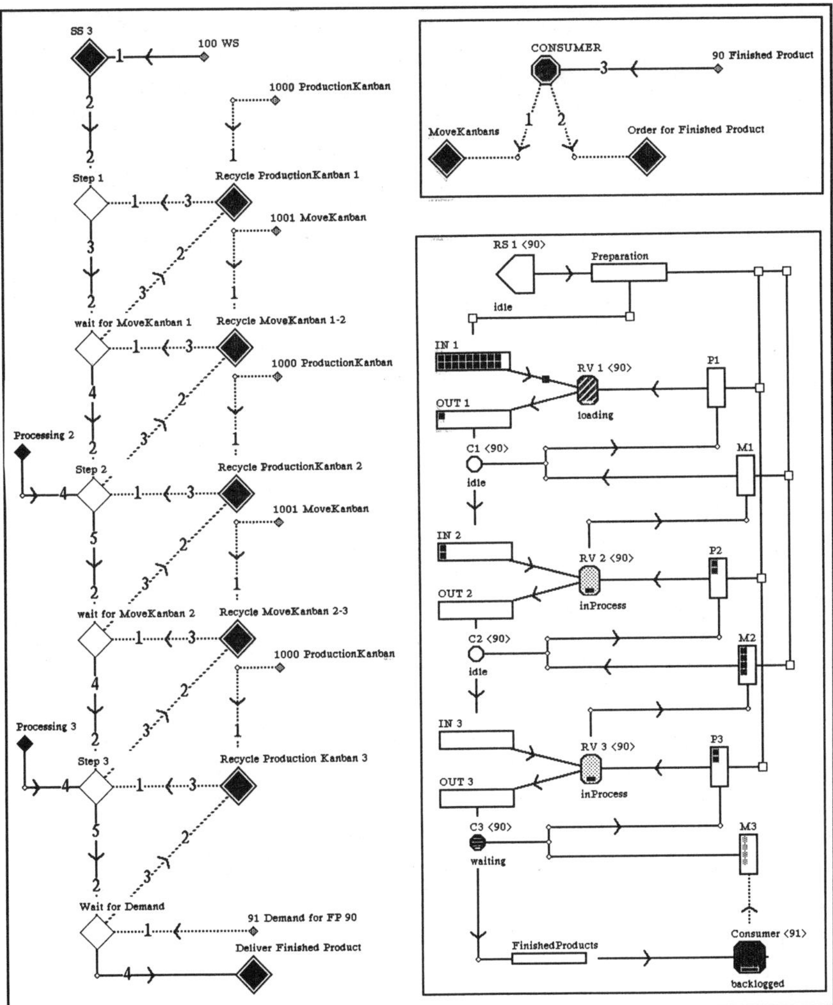

Figure 4.11a: The logic of kanban for a simple three stage process: on the left the product specification of the process; on the top right the product specification of consumer demand; on the bottom right a snapshot of the layout.

In the context of this thesis, there could hardly be a more appropriate example of ProfiSEE than the modeling of the kanban concept for controlling material flow. This particular example also illustrates the versatility and flexibility of ProfiSEE. Although the application of the kanban concept to tightly-coupled chemical process has little merit, there are a number of areas where its basic logic should come into play.

In the kanban system information flows pull material through the production units. Information typically flows in the opposite direction of material. Using kanban cards as clearly visible information carriers, down-stream processes signal up-stream processes to proceed with the next activity. No kanban card means no activity. There are two kinds of physical activities: basic production steps and transportation; and two kinds of kanban cards: production kanbans and move kanbans.

The dashed lines in the product specification of the process represent information flows. As indicated by the input numbers on the connections, the consumption of the kanban card always takes place first. The kanban card is recycled again as soon as the next step in the process can begin. The first input on the kanban recycling stages is the introduction of the kanban cards into the system; this only applies to the first batch of course. The number of kanban cards introduced determines the level of WIP. The key to understanding the overall flow of information and material lies in the numbering on the connections.

As an example, *ReactionStage* **Step 2** in the product specification, which models the second basic production step and is mapped to **RV2** in the layout, translates into the following sequence of tasks:

- wait for a production kanban from *StorageFacility* **P2**
- pull in the required material from *StorageFacility* **IN 2**
- return the move kanban to *StorageFacility* **M1** so that the next item can be moved from *StorageFacility* **OUT 1** to **IN 2**
- perform the basic physical production process
- release the intermediate product to *StorageFacility* **OUT 2**, where it waits until moved to the next process stage.

The WIP build-up before **RV 1** occurs because the product specification for the process does not extend the pull-logic to the supply of raw material, which is obviously necessary: **Step 1** does not include the information feedback that pulls raw material into the system. It is pushed into the buffers.

The sequence of tasks carried out by the *ReactionStage* **Wait for MoveKanban2**, which is mapped to **C2**, is almost identical to **Step 2**: The movement of material from **OUT 2** to **IN 3** replaces the physical production process. **C2** waits for a move kanban on **M2** and returns a production kanban to **P2** Technically, **C2** is also *ReactionVessel*.

The product specification of consumer demand ties into the two loose ends at the bottom of the product specification for the process, thereby closing the feedback cycle. The *ConsumerStage* **CONSUMER** in the product specification is mapped to *Consumer* **Consumer** in the layout. It translates into the following tasks:

- introduce an initial and fixed number of move kanbans that control the level of safety stock in *StorageFacility* **FinishedProducts**
- place an order, i.e. put a move kanban on **M3**
- fill the order from **FinishedProducts**

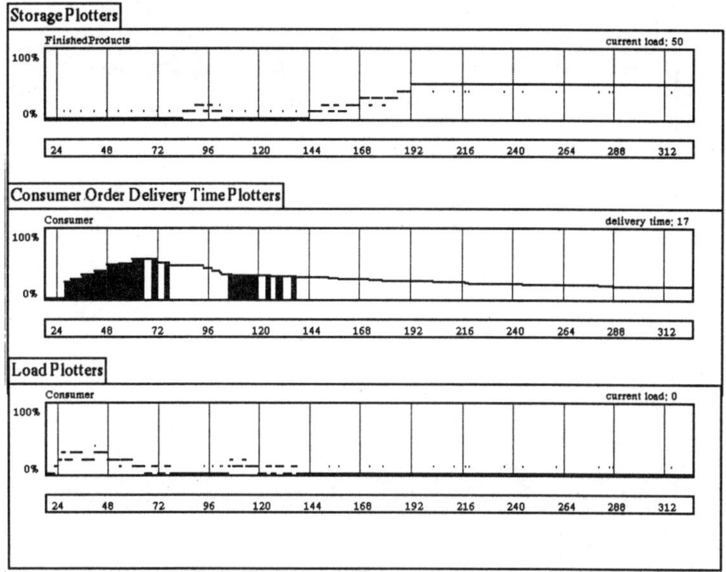

Figure 4.11b: Performance plotters for the kanban example: at the top, the stock level in 'Finished Products'; in the middle, the average order delivery time for customer orders; at the bottom, the number of backorders, i.e. open orders. If there are backorders, then the area under the delivery time plot is shaded—a visual detail. Demand tapers off after the first week. The average order delivery time steadily improves and backorders disappear. But note that the finished product level does not increase beyond the level specified by the number of kanban cards.

Why turn a simple three stage manufacturing process into such an intricate system specification? To begin with, the shop floor control rules that plant personnel have to obey by are in fact quite simple. Without strict adherence to these rules, hectic operations and plenty of WIP are the all too predictable results. This holds in particular in case of the pool concept—see §7.3.2. Different products will be competing for the same resource pools and storage space. To avoid conflicts and to ensure smooth operations in a push system, detailed scheduling and re-scheduling require continual attention and care. As discussed in §2.9, games serve to make this difference between pull and push apparent. ProfiSEE can play an educational role also. By watching the simulation and stepping through the process steps the student of the concept gains insight. Once the concept has been digested, the example can be extended to model realistic configurations for investigating the relationships between WIP level, throughput, throughput time and service level.

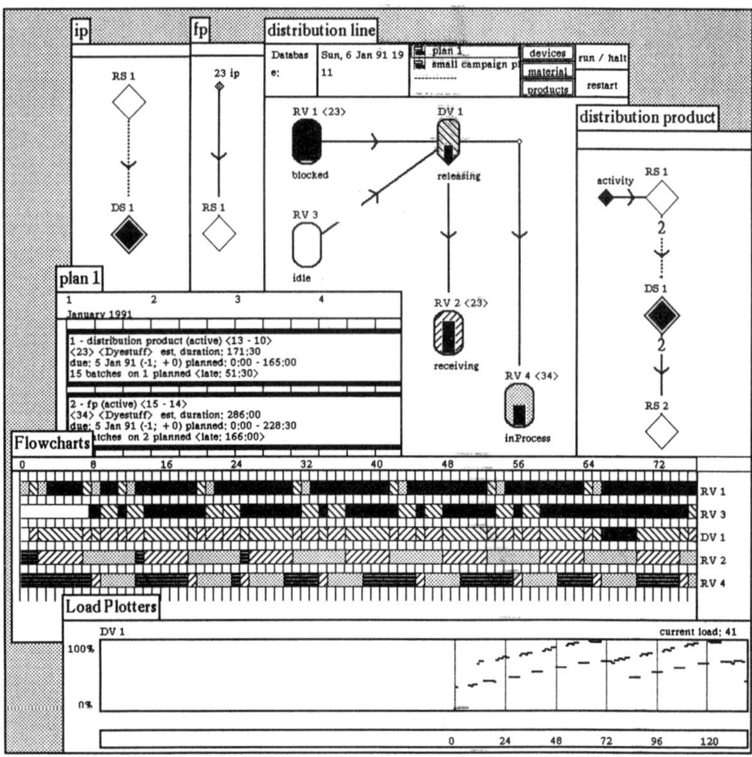

Figure 4.12a: The use of a shared *DistributionVessel*—the case of non-simultaneous input and output.

The next small-scale example to be discussed in some detail shows the use of a *DistributionVessel.* It investigates the effects of allowing simultaneous inputs and outputs to a *DistributionVessel.* The basic ingredients of the example are:

- **distribution line** – a factory layout with two *ReactionVessels*, **RV 1** and **RV 3**, that feed into *DistributionVessel* **DV 1**, and two further *ReactionVessels*, **RV 2** and **RV 4**, that are fed from **DV 1**
- **ip** – a product specification for an intermediate product with one *ReactionStage* and a *DistributionStage* that stores the intermediate product in **DV 1**
- **fp** – a product specification for a finished product with one *ReactionStage* that simply takes the intermediate product **ip** from **DV 1**
- **distribution product** – a product specification with two *ReactionStages* and a *DistributionStage* in the between; this is an alternative way of specifying the logic of **ip** and **fp**; the difference is that the production campaigns for **ip** and **fp** are separate.
- **plan 1** – contains a campaign for each of the three products, and runs them at the same time

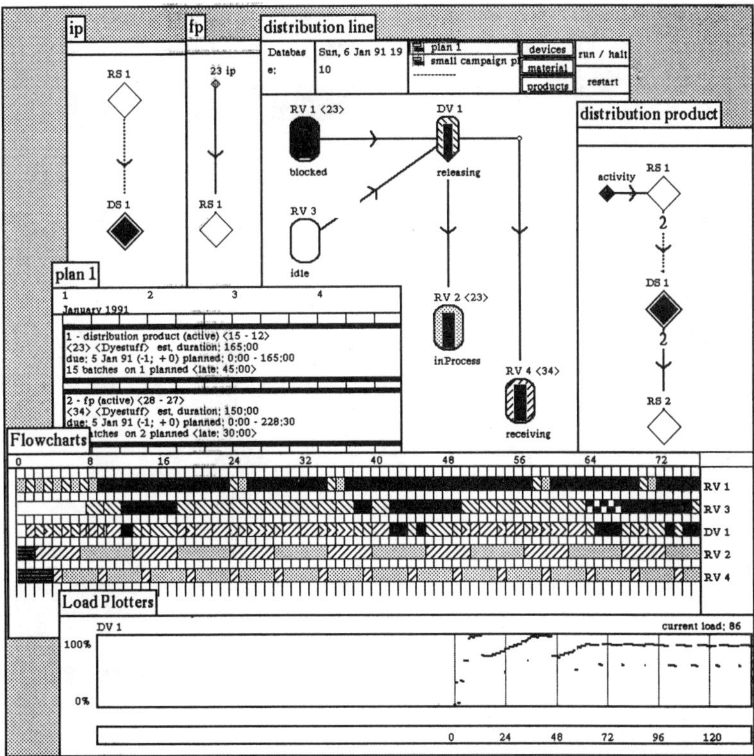

Figure 4.12b: The use of a shared *DistributionVessel*—the case of simultaneous input and output.

The parameter *simultaneous* <boolean> of *DistributionVessel* **DV 1** determines the difference between the cases shown in figures 4.12a and 4.12b. In case 4.12a simultaneous inputs and outputs are not allowed; in case 4.12b they are. All other parameter values, including quantities and processing times, are identical. The effects on the overall process are shown by the flowcharts for the devices in the layout and the load plotter for **DV 1**. As expected, the throughput as measured by the number of batches completed in the first 72 hours of operation is significantly higher in the simultaneous case. The load plotter shows that the capacity of **DV 1** prevents **RV 1** from delivering its batches more frequently. **RV 1** is blocked—black in the flowchart—most of the time. At the time the snapshot of the layout was taken, see figure 4.12b, **RV 1** happens to be blocked for that reason. In figure 4.12a it is blocked because **DV 1** is busy releasing the intermediate to **RV 2**.

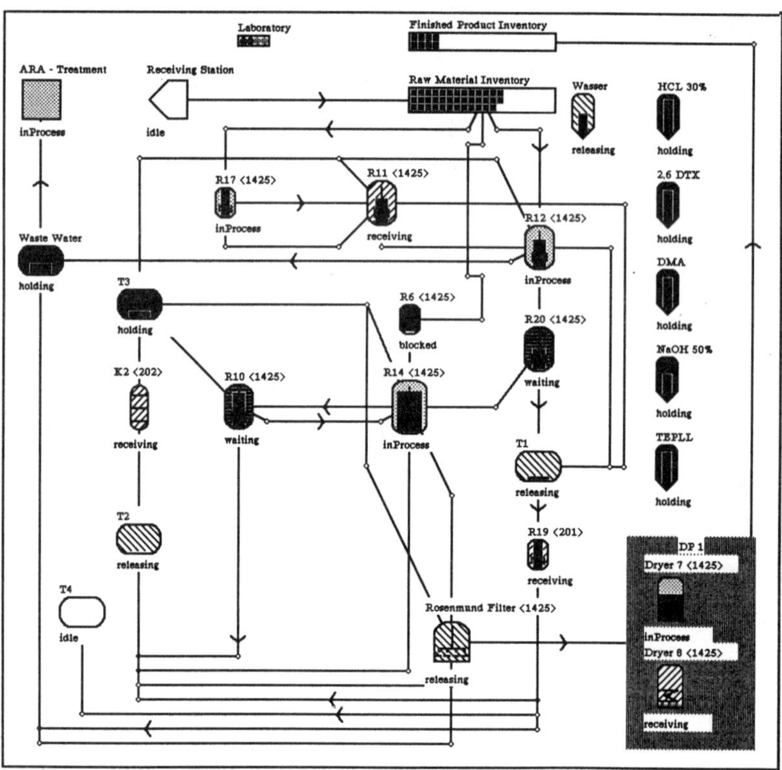

Figure 4.13: A classic example of a tightly coupled batch process, including several feedback loops for recycling inorganic solvents. It is a slightly modified version of a layout for one of the industrial applications reviewed in §4.10.

Figure 4.13 shows a snapshot of a factory layout, producing a single multi-stage product, for one of the more complex industrial applications of ProfiSEE. The layout includes:

- *DevicePool*, **DP1**, with *ReactionVessels*, **Dryer 7** and **8**, operating in parallel.
- *DistributionVessels*, **T1** through **T4**
- *ReactionVessels*, **R11** through **R20**, for basic chemical processes
- *Silos*, for the supply of raw materials
- *StorageFacilities* for the storage of raw materials and finished products
- *AuxiliaryResource*, **Laboratory**, for the analysis of samples

The associated product specification of the chemical process is considerably more intricate than the layout itself. Thanks to the client involvement fostered by ProfiSEE, the development and evaluation of successive alternatives led within a short time to a potential improvement in throughput of 60%, requiring only a relatively small investment in additional equipment, and additional flexibility.

4.12 Visual Interactive Production Scheduling

"Although scheduling algorithms have been the focus of study for many years with simple models, optimization of complex factory models is in its infancy."

[Musier and Evans 1990]

Just-in-time reduces this complexity.

A fan of the concept

The importance of detailed production scheduling in batch process industry has been widely recognized. What is a schedule? The gantt chart, a well-known and widely–used graphical representation of a schedule, captures its essential elements:

- the set of devices in the plant to be scheduled
- a series of time slots covering the planning period for each device
- the assignments of the production processes fulfilling the demand requirements to the available time slots

Different kinds of constraints come into play when the production planner tries to develop a feasible schedule. What's a good schedule is a question of multiple, and conflicting, objective criteria.

The problem is *complex* because of a variety of characteristics of the batch process industry which have been discussed in §4.2. To summarize the major ones:

- individual process stages may be assigned to alternative devices, possibly in parallel
- individual devices typically are multi-purpose
- the placement of the different stages of one product must take the characteristics of the process and devices into account
- changeover times depend on the sequence of the campaigns

The problem is *important* because effective scheduling will

- make better use of the available capacity
- increase the flexibility of the plant
- increase conformance to the desired as well as the promised due dates

Detailed production scheduling should be seen in the larger context of the MRP II concept. In a multi-plant and multi-level environment, the MRP II system generates a rough-cut plan of demand requirements for the next planning period for each individual plant. Since MRP II systems are generally not capable of producing a detailed schedule, it is up to the planning staff in the plant to assess whether the rough-cut plan is feasible and to specify or confirm the due dates for the individual campaigns. Detailed production scheduling classifies as the missing link in the MRP II process. The VIPS-VISM concept of ProfiSEE is intended to close the gap.

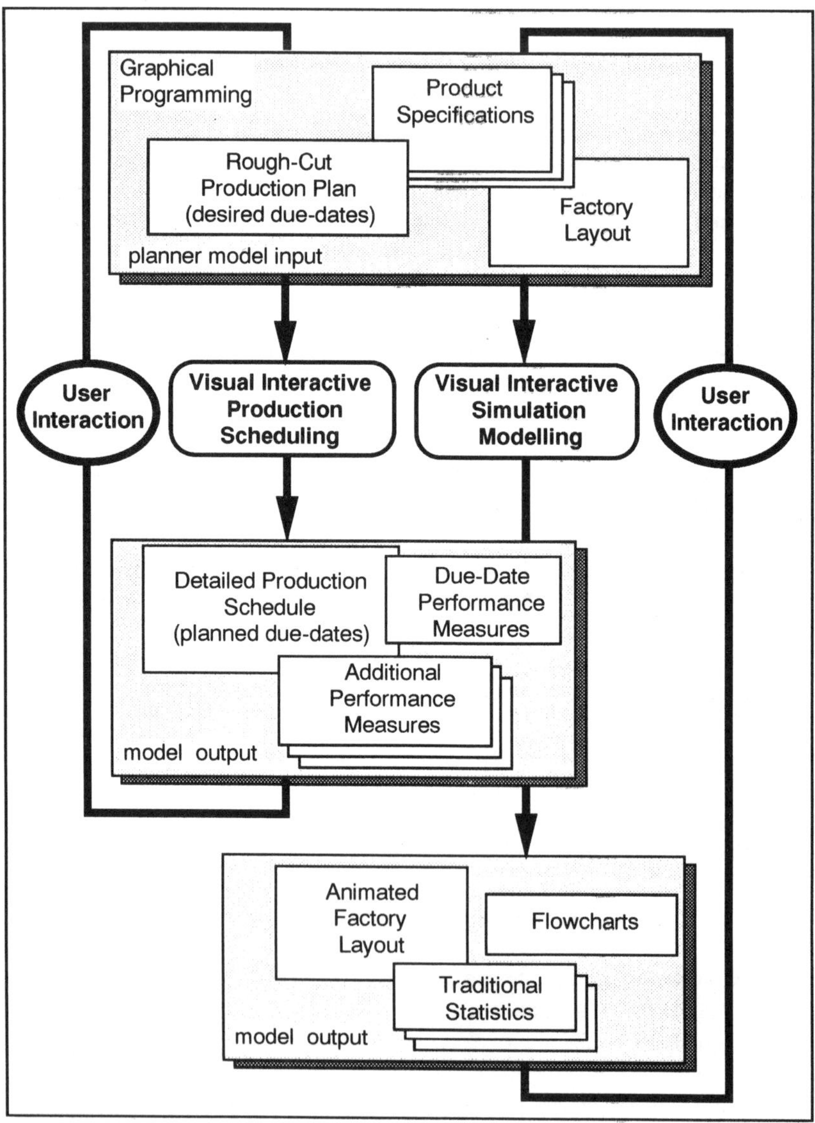

Figure 4.14: The VIPS-VISM concept of ProfiSEE. On the basis of the same factory model, the planner develops a detailed schedule and then simulates it.

In a simplistic way, simulation can serve to generate a detailed production schedule. This applies to ProfiSEE also. During a simulation run the campaigns in the rough-cut production plan can record the effective times of the processes and the devices on which they ran. The idea is not new. Swann [1986] describes the use of VSIM techniques for scheduling at ICI PLC. This particular use of simulation is little more than a trial-and-error method. Clearly, there is a need to expand the facilities. In fact, the absence of a scheduling component also hampers simulation studies. Table 4.6. indicates that several simulation studies carried out with ProfiSEE would have benefitted from the availability of such a component.

A recent extension of ProfiSEE is an integrated component for scheduling. The approach taken is Visual Interactive Production Scheduling (VIPS), a variation on the principle themes of VISM. The extension of VISM to VIPS is a very natural one. Furthermore, the combination of VIPS with VISM, which has received little attention up and till recently, offers several advantages which may prove critical for the successful introduction and application of the concept. The concept is illustrated in figure 4.14.

The first step and a key element of effective scheduling is to construct a sufficiently accurate model of the factory and the production processes, and to specify the demand requirements and raw material availability. The scheduling component then derives a variety of constraints from the underlying object-oriented model of the system in order to exploit these in a constraint-directed search for feasible placements of the campaigns. See [Fox et al. 1984] on this concept. Besides material availability, these constraints must in principle also cover manpower and equipment capacity and availability, storage and buffer space capacity, process characteristics and precedence rules. Furthermore, scheduler preferences need to guide the search for solutions. At present ProfiSEE uses a commonly used two-stage heuristic:

- order the campaigns by some suitable criterion
- find a feasible placement for the campaigns in the remaining slots in the detailed production schedule

Several variations of this basic procedure are possible. For instance, the campaigns that haven't yet been placed could be re-ordered after each placement. Of course, this only makes sense if the campaign placement changes the ordering. Typical examples of sorting criteria use the capacity requirements of the campaign and the projected load on the resources, which can be estimated on the basis of the desired due dates. The idea is to schedule campaigns with place a high load on bottleneck devices first. A further refinement takes account of the load pattern over time.

Similarly, there are different possible campaign placement strategies. To place a campaign ProfiSEE must first determine the 'shape' of the campaign, i.e. the relative starting times of the process stages and their length. A virtual simulation that creates a flowchart for the campaign provides the information. The shape of a campaign is best thought of as a puzzle piece that is partially stretchable. If the process is tightly coupled, the puzzle piece is largely fixed. Unfortunately, there may be more than one puzzle piece to consider. The placement of the puzzle piece in the puzzle—the remaining time slots in the schedule—then relies on a constraint-directed search procedure. Its is obvious that a combinatorial explosion of possibilities occurs at this point.

The planner has complete control over the selection of the top-level strategies and the sequencing of the placements of the campaigns, and can retract the placement of any campaign in the detailed production schedule. If this were not the case, the term VIPS[50] would be a misnomer.

The present capabilities of ProfiSEE are rather rudimentary. The focus has been on doing a few simple things well and to provide further instruments for measuring the quality of a detailed planned with respect to several different criteria. A major one is the comparison of desired due date with scheduled dates. Any changes in the detailed plan, which the planner makes by moving the puzzle piece to a different location, are immediately reflected in the performance statistics. In this visual and interactive fashion, the planning tool supports and exploits the skills and experience of the planner.

The properties of ProfiSEE as sketched here satisfy a number of the system requirements for interactive scheduling that are put forward and discussed by Musier and Evans [1990] in a good review article of scheduling in the batch process industry. See [Gröflin et al 1989] on a good scheduling system in use at Sandoz.

Given the complexity of the scheduling problem, it is unreasonable to expect that the scheduling shell will ever take care of all the intricacies and constraints. The ability to simulate and test a detailed schedule immediately after it has been generated, as shown in figure 4.14, is a major advantage. By letting the simulation shell take care of the least important, but possibly tricky, aspects, the task of developing an effective scheduling shell hopefully becomes a more realistic and manageable one.

As much as a detailed production scheduling tools provide the missing link of MRP II systems, these tools cannot be expected to function effectively as a stand-alone effort of a plant scheduler. Systems integration and the supply of reliable data are key areas of concern which will bring unresolved data management issues to the fore. Some of the plant and process data required for detailed scheduling is either not available or only in a highly aggregated form on the central materials management systems. This throws up the thorny question where this detailed should be kept and how consistency is to be guaranteed. The exchange of information between central and decentral systems is merely a technical problem. As mentioned, the design of ProfiSEE ensures that product specifications and demand requirements down-loaded from a central database can be incorporated. An open question is how detailed or aggregated factory models should be.

---

[50]The planner remains in the centre of the process. ProfiSEE doesn't replace the natural intelligence of the planner by an artificially intelligent system. The acronym VIPS could, therefore, just as well stand for Very Important Production Scheduler.

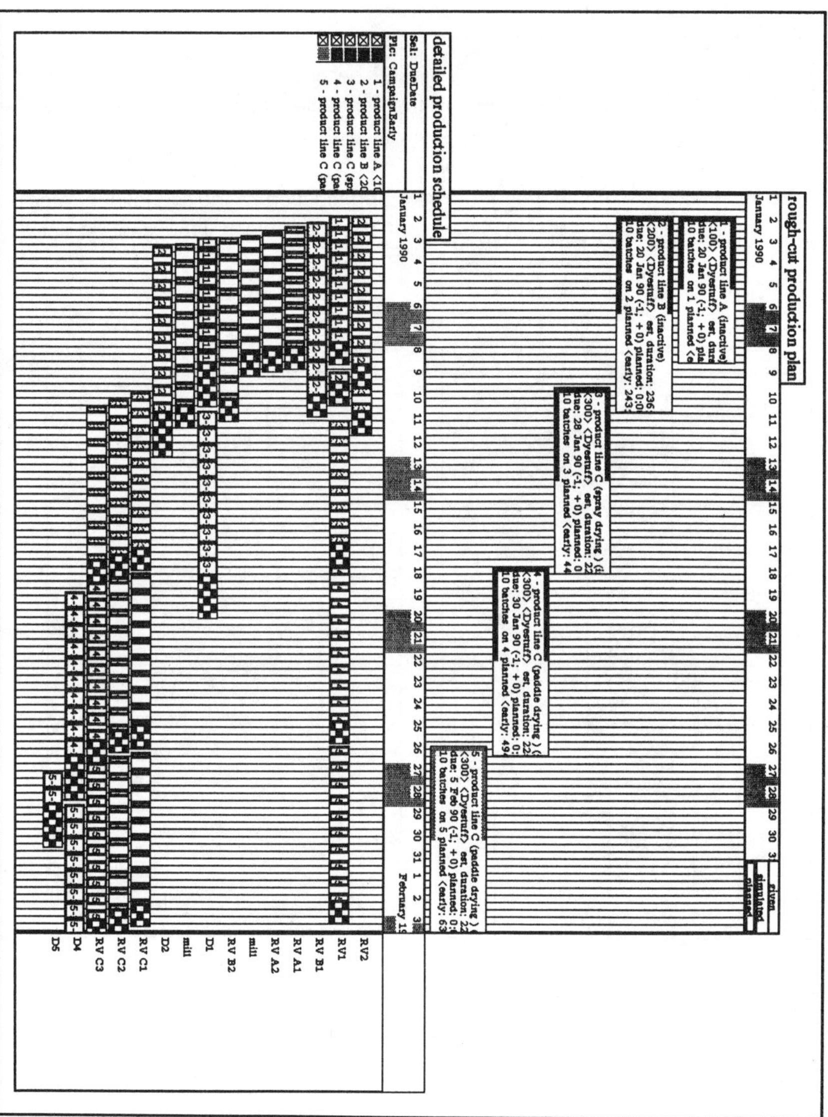

Figure 4.15a: Example of a rough-cut production plan and a detailed production schedule—zoom out. At the top, the rough-cut production plan; at the bottom, the associated detailed production schedule. The campaigns in the rough-cut plan can be displayed on the basis of given (desired), simulated or scheduled due dates. In the example shown, they are based on the scheduled due dates. This means that they match with the detailed production schedule. The detailed schedule shows the placement of the batches of the campaigns on the individual devices. The checkered shading indicates the cleanup time between the campaigns.

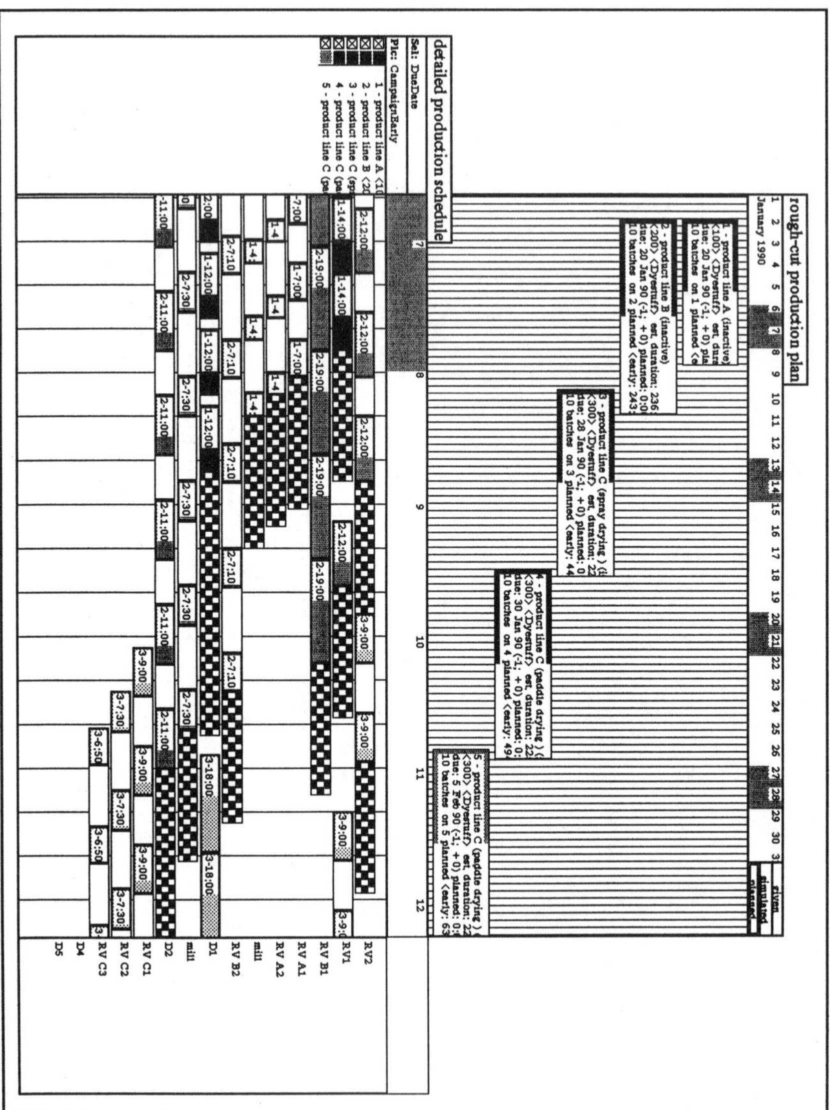

Figure 4.15b: Example of a rough-cut production plan and a detailed production schedule–zoom in. The scale has been changed to focus in on the second week.

This section has sketched the present status of ProfiSEE for detailed scheduling of resources in a single chemical batch plant. Further developments and, as mentioned, a re-design and -implementation are in the planning phase. In closing, it should be mentioned that the same approach is applicable to the planning problem at the next higher and more aggregated level of a multi-plant supply chain.

4.13 Elements of the User Interface

No amount of description will provide an adequate overview of the interactive interface of ProfiSEE. Two examples of its elements will have to suffice to give the reader a flavour of its looks.

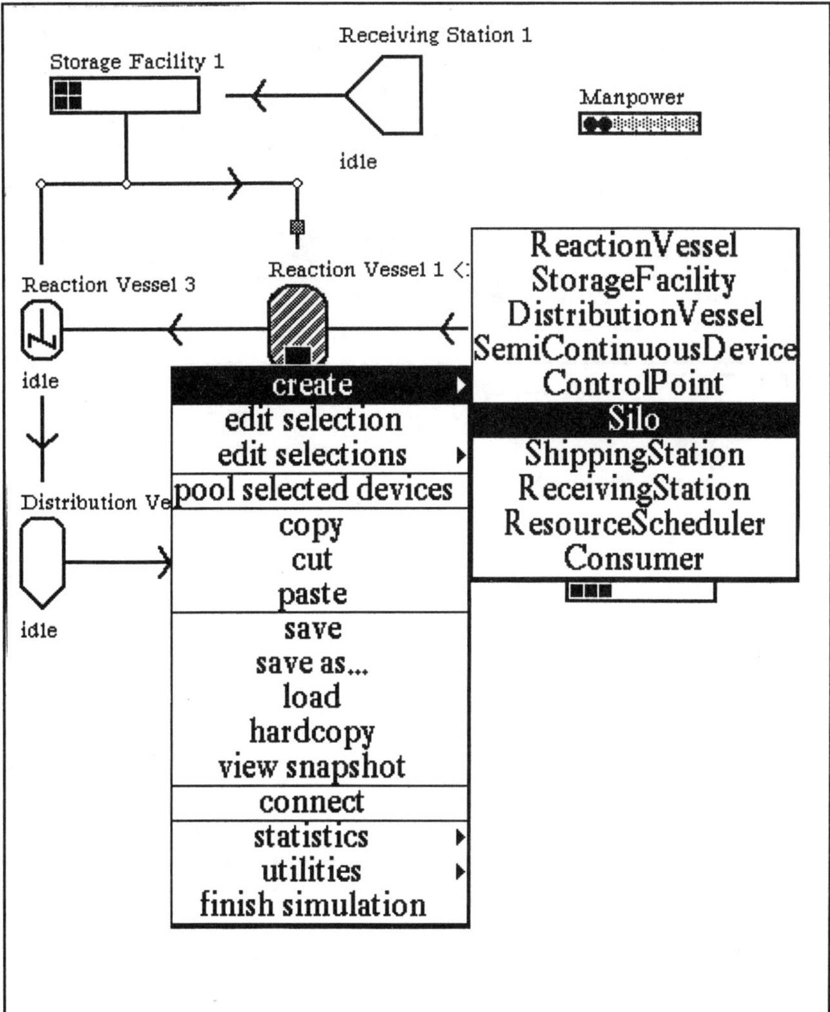

Figure 4.16a: Elements of the user interface: the pop-up menu for the layout specification. The product specification and rough-cut production plan specifications have similar menus. But each one has its specific options. Simulation control—start, stop and step—is provided by buttons on the top of the window.

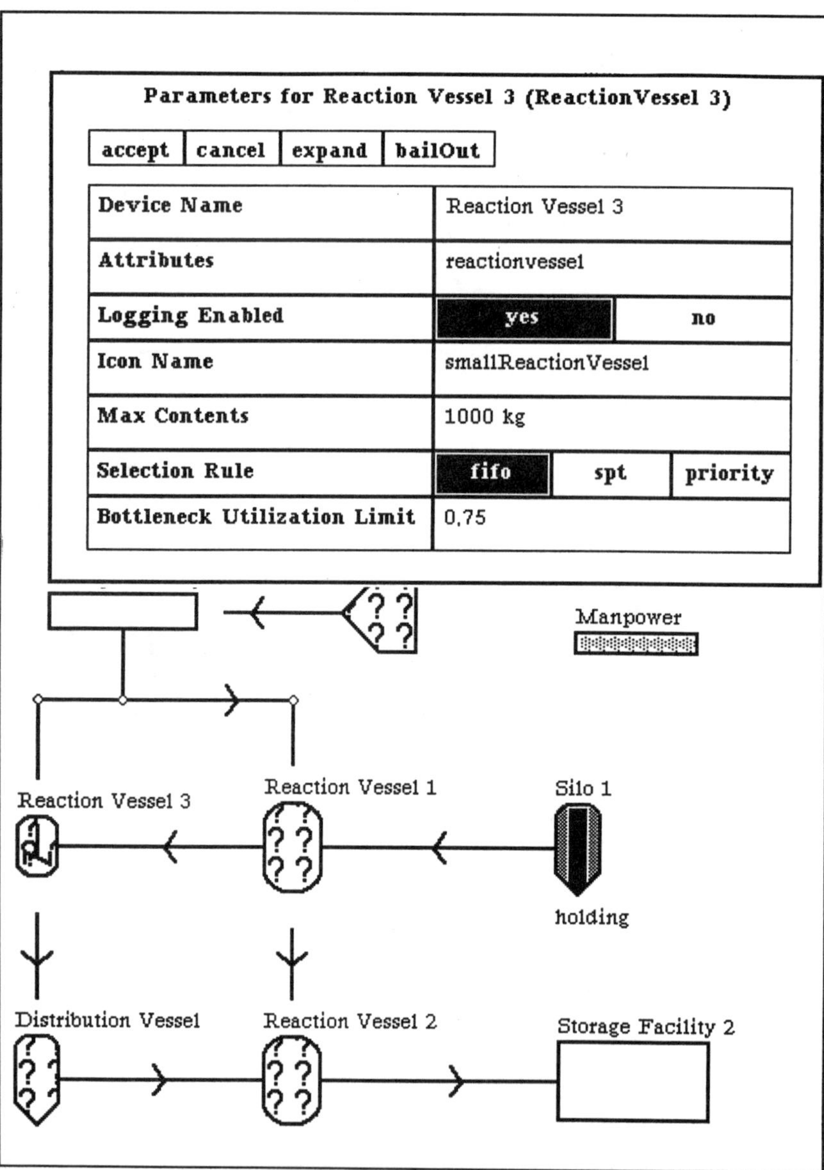

Figure 4.16b: Elements of the user interface: A query-box for specifying the parameters of a *ReactionVessel*. The parameters of entities in a product, layout and rough-cut production plan specification can conveniently be edited via query-boxes or, alternatively, via a speadsheet which contains selected parameters for selected entities. The spreadsheet also provides a compact overview of all the entities in a specification and can also be used for further calculations.

5 The Role of QED: A Spreadsheet for a Rough-cut Financial Assessment and Sensitivity Analysis

5.1 Introduction and Outline

The previous chapters discussed what role a rough-cut financial analysis has to play in a broader framework for assessing the impact of the just-in-time concept in comparison with a detailed simulation analysis. This chapter describes how this financial analysis is to be carried out. It focuses on the structure and logic of the QED model which performs the analysis and how to construct such a model, without, however, delving into the implementation details. In the process, we gain a deeper understanding of the interactions between the various elements of the manufacturing and logistics system.

The underlying concept and top-level structure of QED is applicable to a broad range of cases. The implementation of the low-level aspects must obviously take account of the specifics of the real-world system under investigation. We need to adapt it from case to case. The actual implementation is, therefore, not a general-purpose solution. Technically, QED is an electronic spreadsheet. The specific structure, scope and parameter values of QED are not presented until chapter 7; they folow the description in chapter 6 of the industrial case from which QED draws its empirical substance.

The model itself has purposely been kept as simple as possible. In particular, it avoids the application of sophisticated mathematical techniques, which would have been questionable to begin with. At least in this case, however, simplicity does not imply that QED ignores the multi-faceted nature of the problem. On the contrary, the model addresses the various aspects of the system that a sound business perspective demands. In addition, it accounts for several significant secondary effects of the basic decision variables on the performance factors.

The factor time is a major player in the network of relationships of the system. QED therefore carefully assesses its impact. Nevertheless, the model as implemented is static and not dynamic. In other words, it does not represent the changing states of the system over time resulting from, for instance, changes in demand. The effects of demand variability and volatility are explicitly specified. Putting it differently, QED models time implicitly.

Central to the modeling of time are the concepts of production throughput time, lead time and flow time. Section 5.5 defines, clarifies and distinguishes these key concepts, shows what role they play and how QED calculates their values. The major point put forward is that lead times and lead time variability determine, among other factors, stock levels; not *vice versa,* as discussions about stock reduction programmes commonly state or assume. Stocks are a symptom of the lack of speed, reliability and flexibility, not the cause.

The overall structure of the model and the interrelationships between its different components and variables are described in terms of 'mobile' diagrams in a strictly top-down fashion. These diagrams are there to help the reader assess the scope and logic of the model. They explain which decision variables and which exogenous variables determine the overall performance of the manufacturing system to be modeled. They show which endogenous variables play a central role, and clarify which input variables and relationships the model considers to be relevant. Where necessary, the text provides, explaines and justifies the important formulas.

Section 5.8, which is a provocative one, focuses on QED's treatment of the time value of money. It emphasizes the importance of capturing the cost of capital for showing the difference between a traditional capacity-focused manufacturing system and a 'modern'[51] time-focused manufacturing system.

The final section assesses the aspects that are lost in QED. As will be explained, these aspects concern areas where time-focused manufacturing brings further advantages. On the whole, therefore, it is safe to conclude that QED's assessment of the full benefits of speed is conservative.

5.2 Overview of Model Scope and Design

QED performs an analysis which assesses how a manufacturing and logistics system converts financial inflows to financial outflows. The conversions that take place are obviously not only financial ones. An organization obtains labour, material, equipment, and other resources to produce and distribute finished goods in what typically involves a series of intermediate steps. Figure 3.2, which is a modified version of one used by Eilon [1984] to introduce the concept of efficiency, shows what kinds of performance measures naturally arise. In this context, the very general and hence popular notion of productivity is measured by the ratio of input to output. The overall performance is the return, a financial output, on total investment in assets, a financial input. This financial indicator will be termed the performance factor, an abbreviation for supply chain performance factor, or simply PF.

In order to calculate the performance factor of a manufacturing and distribution system, QED determines the resources required to produce a selected product mix and volume. The basic outputs and the areas of input are depicted in figure 5.1. Given a range of non-controllable factors and the characteristics of the production processes, QED calculates the effects of the choice of operational concept and equipment technology on the total asset base and net contribution.

For example, QED could answer the conventional question whether a more expensive, somewhat faster packaging machine requiring less labour per machine hour would improve the return on total investment in assets. In the context of the issues faced in modern manufacturing, this is not only a particularly uninteresting question, but also the wrong question to ask in the first place. In this case, the customary phrase "all other things being equal" is typically not appropriate since the setup or cleaning time of this machine could well be different. QED, therefore, also answers the more interesting and relevant variation of the original question: What is the advantage of a more expensive, somewhat slower machine requiring less labour per machine hour and virtually no time to setup and clean?

---

[51]Henry Ford was time conscious in his day already.

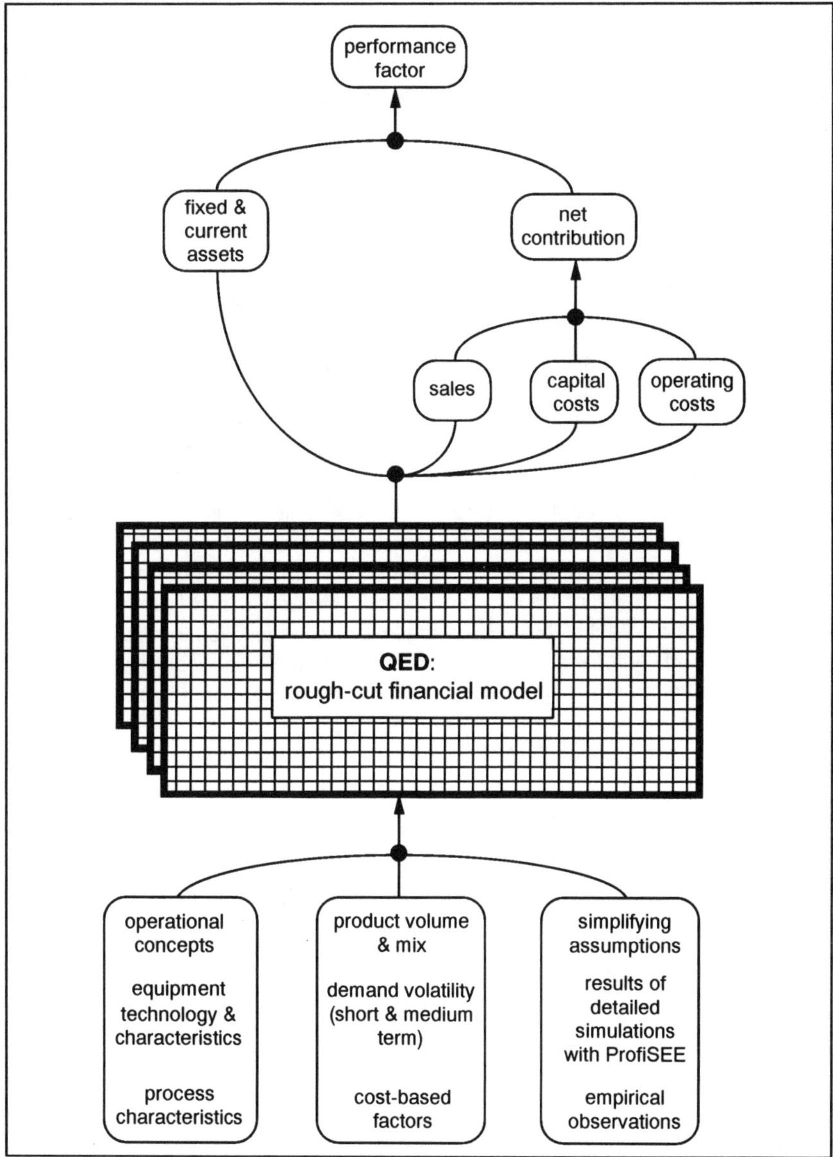

Figure 5.1: The basic concept of QED—Quick&Dirty. QED is a rough-cut financial model that converts a variety of inputs into common financial performance indicators. Technically, QED is implemented as an electronic spreadsheet.

The basic decision variables that distinguish the just-in-time concept from a classical *modus operandi* are listed and classified in the table shown in figure 7.2. In addition, there are other decision variables subject to managerial action that are not listed in this table. An important one that will subsequently be discussed is the number of shifts that the factory is to operate. This illustrates that managerial decisions encompass a broad range of areas and activities in the supply chain. Moreover, various cost-based factors have an effect. The major categories according to which the primary decisions can be classified are:

- equipment characteristics—a technological issue,
- methods and procedures on the factory floor and in administrative areas
- organizational issues, e.g. division of labour, assignment of responsibilities
- operational planning and control

The decision variables in these categories primarily drive the output of QED. What may look very simple on paper is in practice fraught with difficulties. Returning to the subject of the complexity of organizations, touched upon in §2.9, it is worthwhile to consider at this point the currently prevailing organizational structures. These are such that the middle management decisions referred to above are not usually the domain of a single individual. This should explain that even if the insight and answers provided by a model such as QED establish a preferred and clear course of action, an actual implementation may never come about without the active involvement of upper management. Moreover, middle management is well aware of the potential threat to its present position entailed in a restructuring of the organization. Any further investigation of implementation issues would benefit from addressing the questions generated by the structure of organizations.

QED also takes account of exogenous variables. The distinguishing feature is that management has relatively little or no control over these variables. These exogenous variables and the market forces that dominate them nevertheless demand a substantial share of managerial attention. The following aspects are explicitly represented in QED:

- product mix and volume
- demand variability and volatility, i.e. short- and medium-term fluctuations
- cost-based and cost-related factors
- sales prices

Cost-based factors determine how financial inputs are converted into physical inputs. The present analysis does not address the efficiency of this financial conversion process, although it is important and to some extent also relevant.[52] QED uses the following cost-based factors as inputs:

- cost of materials and energy
- cost of labour
- cost of equipment, infrastructure, building and land

52 The topic of purchasing lot sizes and quantity rebates, covered in the OR literature, is an example.

- depreciation period
- cost of capital, i.e. interest rate
- customs duties
- transportation costs

These cost-based factors in combination with sales prices, which determine how physical outputs are converted into financial outputs, allow the model to determine the performance factor.

Exogenous variables may to some degree or other also be decision variables. Consider, for example, the sales volume. The total world-wide volume is indeed given, but how much to produce and where is not. The issue referred to is an important one for multi-national companies and centers around the location of international supply and distribution points. The location of facilities is an obvious strategic decision that must take into account the anticipated world-wide sales volume, its geographic composition, economies of scale, and the difference in costs factors for materials, labour and equipment. In addition, the transportation costs and customs duties incurred may differ significantly. §7.2 briefly revisits the issue.

5.3 Return on Total Assets

The performance factor is a measurement of the return on total assets employed. It is the ratio of net contribution to total assets. The more obvious abbreviation ROA is not used, to make it clear that QED excludes both assets and costs that would normally be included in the ROA calculation. QED assumes that these are not affected by the decisions under consideration. Futhermore, to emphasize the difference between ROA and the closely related measure of return on investment (ROI), the performance factor includes a constant multiplier. This conforms with current practice at CIBA–GEIGY. The performance factor as used by QED is strictly speaking a supply chain performance factor; it is more restrictive about what items are included than the performance factor of a strategic business unit.

The well-known Du Pont formula breaks this prime ratio down into two factors, which again are ratios:

- return on sales, i.e. contribution divided by sales
- asset turnover, i.e. sales divided by total assets

This breakdown serves here to stress what will be obvious to a student of business economics. It is unsatisfactory to restrict attention to the return on sales since it is only one side of the coin. This holds in particular for the present topic. The experimental results in chapter 7, which compare a traditional manufacturing system with a time-focused alternative, confirm this observation: the difference between the two cases becomes much more visible if we take the asset base into account as well.

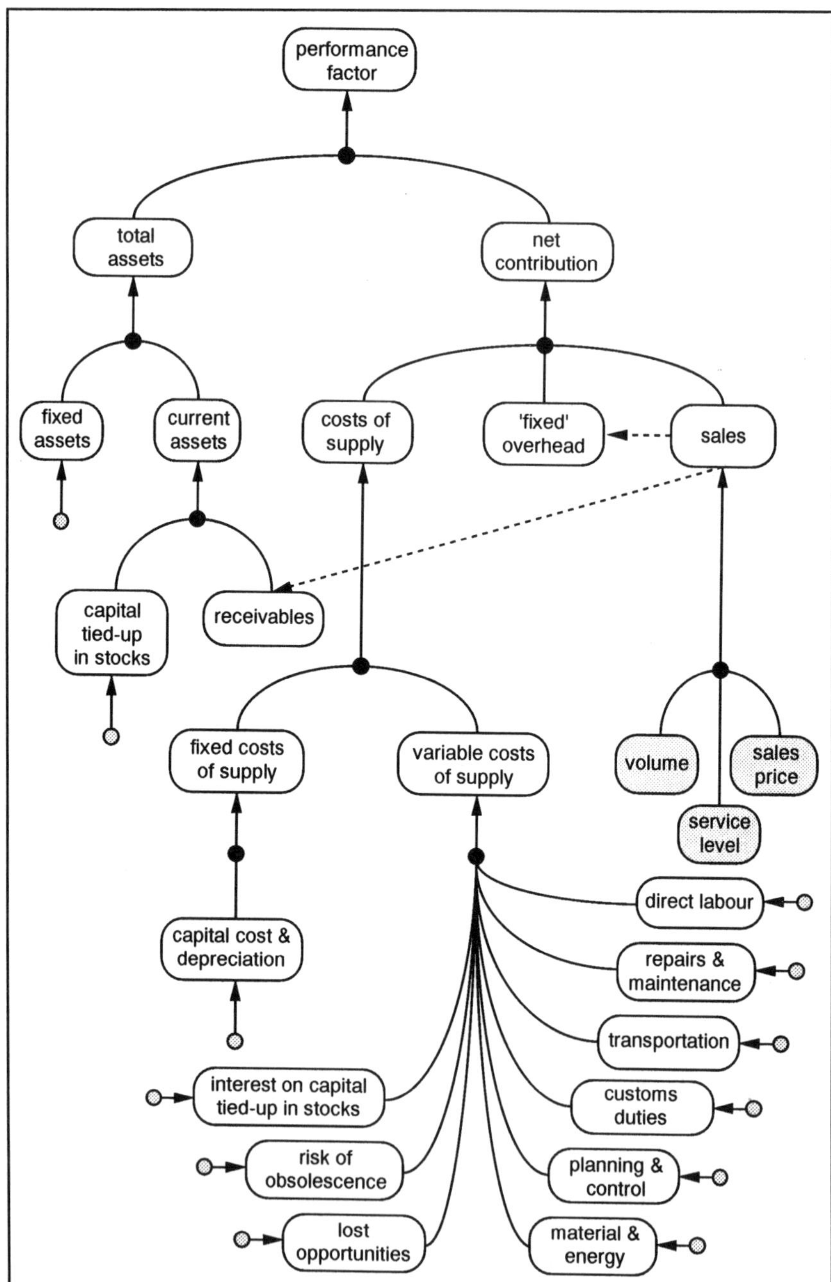

Figure 5.2a: Mobile diagram for the performance factor. The shaded variables are inputs to QED. The performance factor, total assets and cost of supply—purchasing, production and logistics costs—will be used as the prime financial indicators.

As mentioned, the overwhelming share of the operations research literature on optimal campaign and lot sizing techniques ignores asset turnover. One notable exception can be found in [Pack 1989]. See §7.3.1 for a discussion of the experimental results obtained with QED on campaign sizing and its effect on costs in contrast with its effect on the performance factor.

The logic and the top-level formulas that QED uses to determine the performance factor are depicted in figure 5.2a and 5.2b, respectively. These are largely self-explanatory. However, a few comments are still in order. QED bases all calculations on *average* revenues and costs for one year. Fixed assets are, therefore, valued at half their current purchase cost, which is a customary approximation for the average value over the useful economic life.

$$\textbf{performance factor} = \frac{\textbf{net contribution}}{\left(\textbf{fixed assets} / 2\right) + \textbf{current assets}} \times 10$$

net contribution = gross revenue – cost of supply – 'fixed' overhead

current assets = capital tied up in stocks + receivables

receivables = 20% of gross revenue

'fixed' overhead = 30% of gross revenue

Figure 5.2b: Formulas for calculating the performance factor.

Receivables have been included in the current assets so as not to distort the performance factor more than necessary. QED expresses receivables in terms of a fixed number of months of sales. A radical advocate of the just-in-time concept would posit a relationship between the number of months of receivables and the service level. The argument is simple. If suppliers deliver orders rapidly and on-time, customers may feel obliged to pay sooner. The inclusion of such a speculative relationship would, depending, of course, on its strength, significantly change the performance factor in favour of a manufacturing and distribution system geared up for speed and flexibility, especially if one additionally takes the interest charge on receivables into account. This relationship would benefit from an empirical investigation, which is well beyond the scope of this thesis. It's worth noting that receivables are valued at sales prices. Just before the goods are sold, they are still valued at TPC or at CIBA–GEIGY at VPC—a quantum leap. Paradoxically, a 'clever' manager could increase his or her incentive bonus by shifting receivables into stocks through the creation of consignment stocks at major customers.

To calculate the net contribution, QED subtracts from sales, besides the usual costs of supplying the customer, a 'fixed' block of overhead for marketing and sales support, as well as R&D. This overhead is also calculated as a percentage of sales.

Lost business opportunities and the risk of obsolescence are two items in the mobile diagram for the performance factor that deserve particular attention. Both items have largely been ignored up and till recently in the financial analysis of the just-in-time concept and, as will be shown, can make a significant contribution to the economics of speed.

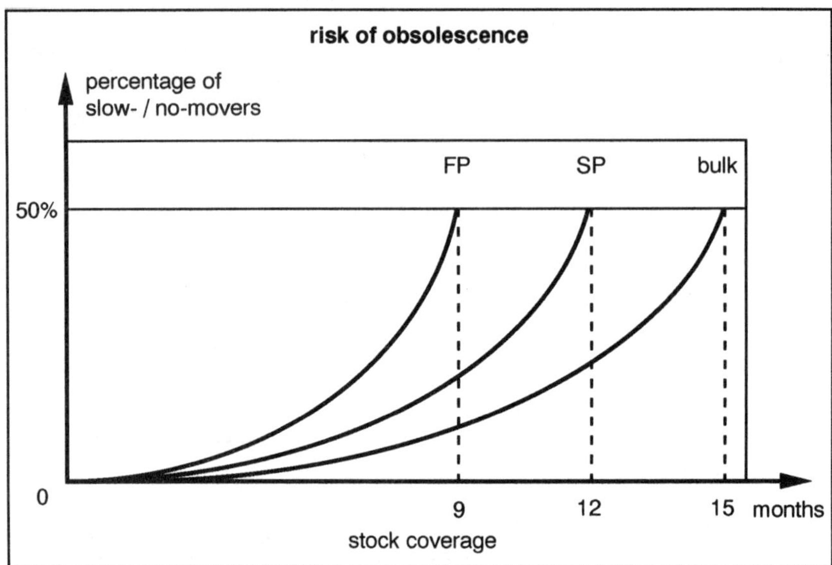

Figure 5.3a: The risk of obsolescence. Fully- and semi-packaged products have a higher risk percentage of slow- and no-movers than bulk products for the same stock level, measured in terms of demand coverage.

Slow- and no-movers costs are a consequence of the risk of obsolescence. Due to demand volatility there is a risk that stocks become obsolete. As shown in figure 5.3a, the percentage of slow- and no-movers that are kept in stock and that need to be disposed of at the end of a regular review period depends on the product stage and the stock level in relation to the demand. The more specific the product stage, the higher is the risk of obsolescence. The actual percentage depends on the medium-term demand volatility, see figure 5.4 for a comparison.

The only relevant cost from the point of view of cost accounting are charges for disposal costs and extra handling. These are small in relation to the value of pharmaceutical products. Incineration costs are currently quoted at circa 2'000 Sfr. per metric tonne. But what is the true cost of incineration? It is becoming increasingly difficult to obtain permission to build an incineration plant. CIBA–GEIGY is going through this process at the time of writing and is faced with opposition from the community at large. If one views waste disposal as part of the supply chain—which ought to be case—and recognizes that incineration capacity may be a limiting resource, if it is not so already, then its true costs are very substantial, albeit not quantifiable. I might add that in the actual case investigated there is some reason to believe that obsolete stock is being built up at a faster rate than that it is being disposed of from the warehouse.

Assuming that there is little or no surplus of manufacturing resources, the true total costs of slow- and no-movers are significantly higher. Resources, including in particular those in chemical production, were wasted on making the wrong product and could have been used instead for making a saleable product. Since it is not possible to assess these opportunity costs, QED uses TPC values as the basis for an approximation. QED does not assess the *additional* inventory holding costs that in practice accumulate until the point in time that these slow- and no-movers are classified as such. No reliable figures are available on what share of the stocks slow- and no-movers accounted for. As an aside, two of the semi-packaged products included in the investigation concern an active substance that was unexpectedly withdrawn from the market.

percentage of slow- and no-movers — psm

$$psm_{stage} = \min\left(a_{stage} \cdot coverage^{2}_{stage} ; 1\right) \cdot 100\%$$

stage is one of the product stages FP, SP or bulk

$a_{FP} = 0.0062$

$a_{SP} = 0.0035$

$a_{bulk} = 0.0022$

$$\text{slow- and no-mover cost}_{stage} = psm_{stage} \cdot tc_{stage}$$

where 'tc' is the tied-up capital at TPC
for the product stage

Figure 5.3b: Formula for the risk of obsolescence.

QED calculates slow- and no-mover costs by estimating the slow-mover percentage for every item in stock and multiplying this with the amount of tied-up capital in stock for this stock item. The slow-mover percentage is a function of the stock coverage, which is an endogenous variable, and the demand volatility, which is an exogenous variable representing medium-term fluctuations. The formula, described in figure 5.3b, poses a quadratic relationship between the stock coverage measured in months of demand. The constant factors have been set such that at 9, 12 and 15 months of coverage for fully-packaged, semi-packaged and bulk products, respectively, the probability reaches 50%. This results in realistic[53] slow- and no-mover costs for the actual model case investigated. This empirical input is likely to be conservative for two reasons. There is the occasional opportunity for 'disposing' of slow-movers in other ways. Secondly, the point in time

[53] The *opinions* of those interviewed on this issue vary considerably. As mentioned, no hard and reliable figures are available. This is a point worth noting in its own right.

at which write-offs are activated to reflect changes in the balance sheet and the profit and loss statement is partially discretionary. As a consequence a certain amount of smoothing is bound to occur.

Lost business opportunities result from the inability of the system as whole to respond to unforeseen demand, large tenders being a case in point. Typically, there is also a non-quantifiable image loss associated with losing large tenders. Moreover, the longer the lead times are, the more additional hectic and re-planning results. QED distinguishes between the regular loss of sales that results from setting the safety stock at a level to reach a desired level of customer service, which will be discussed in the next section, and lost business opportunities. Common measures of actual customer service level usually exclude the latter.

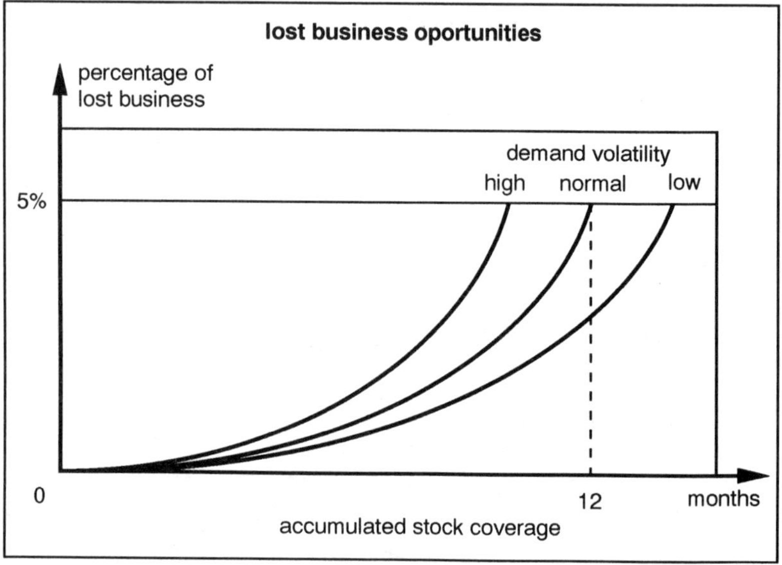

Figure 5.4a: Lost business opportunities.

The costs of lost business opportunities are estimated in a similar way as the cost of slow- and no-movers. QED estimates the percentage of lost business per finished product and multiplies this by the profit margin of this product and its sales volume. As shown in figure 5.4a, the percentage of lost business is a function of the accumulated demand coverage for the three stock levels of the product and the medium-term demand volatility. The formula, described in figure 5.4b, makes the reasonable assumption that the accumulated stock coverage is an accurate indicator of speed and flexibility. See §5.5 for the justification. Of course, the accumulated lead time would serve the same purpose. The relationship is again assumed to be quadratic. The constant factor in the formula is set such that the percentage reaches 5% at 12 months of accumulated demand coverage. It is a realistic value for the actual model case investigated. But again, the same observation must be made: no hard empirical figures are available. Knowing the speed and flexibility of the central manufacturing and distribution system, a group company may fail to pass on the information about a business opportunity such as a large tender if it thinks it cannot meet the delivery dates required by the customer. Penalty clauses for late deliveries will shy a product manager away from taking the risk.

percentage of lost business — plb

$$plb = 0.035 \cdot \left(\sum coverage_{stage}\right)^2$$

coverage is accumulated for FP, SP and bulk

'cost' of lost business = plb • pc • volume

where 'pc' is the product contribution, i.e. the difference between sales price and TPC

Figure 5.4b: Formula for percentage of lost business.

5.4 Current Assets

A major driver of the performance factor are current assets. As noted, QED uses a short-cut to calculate receivables. The mobile diagram in figure 5.5a shows how QED calculates the amount of tied-up capital in stocks, which is a major component of the current assets that is of interest. QED takes the modern view stock and especially safety stock, i.e. safety stock reflects the amount of slack in the manufacturing and distribution system. The safety stock formula used, see the explanation below, is essentially descriptive, not prescriptive in the sense that it attempts to set an optimal safety stock level. In the same way QED uses the *value* of the product, either VPC or TPC, to calculate the tied-up capital in stocks, it uses the *number of units per pallet* for each individual product, e.g. 100'000 tables or 10'000 blister packs per pallet, to calculate the required amount of warehouse space. Stocks not only consume current assets but also fixed assets—which should best be termed consequential assets. A secondary and accumulative effect is the impact of the total stock holding costs on TPC. More examples are in the offing.

Since the mobile diagram is deceptively simple, a number of explanatory comments are in order. First of all, the diagram reflects the more complicated make-to-stock case and can be pruned for the make-to-order case.[54] The logic of the stock calculations applies to finished products and intermediates at each stage of the manufacturing and distribution system.

---

[54]In the make-to-order case safety stock is merely a misnomer for WIP and driven by the throughput time. The space required by WIP is estimated separately, see figure 5.7a.

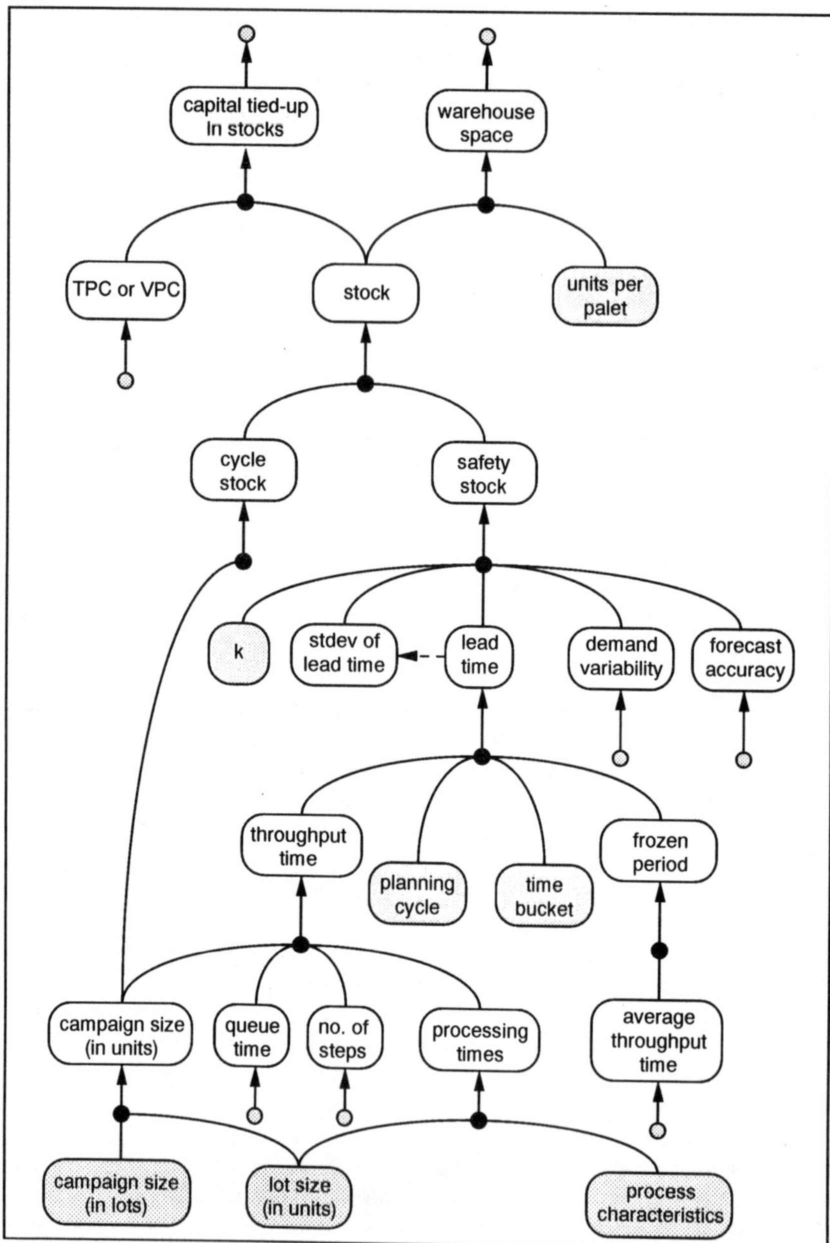

Figure 5.5a: Stock level, capital tied-up in stocks and in warehouse space. Lead time is a central concept. It ties together a series of lower-level factors and has itself a major impact on stock levels and forecast accuracy. The links fail to show that campaign sizes influence the demand variability at the up-stream production stage. Queue time includes, among other items, changeover time.

The mobile diagram shows that campaign and lot sizes not only affect the cycle stock level but also the safety stock level. Given the decomposition of inventory—generally, more than half is safety stock—one might think it all the more surprising that most campaign and lot sizing methods ignore the latter effect.

Demand variability is an interesting case because it is a function of the campaign or order sizes of the next stage in the production process. Large campaign sizes increase demand variability and hence safety stock levels. In a similar way, the associated longer lead times have a tendency to amplify demand fluctuations. The resulting home-made distortions of primary demand, which are symptomatic in environments with long lead times, will have a significant secondary effect on stock levels and perceived capacity bottlenecks. Unfortunately, QED cannot account for this effect. This would require a more sophisticated technique that explicitly models time, e.g. systems dynamics.

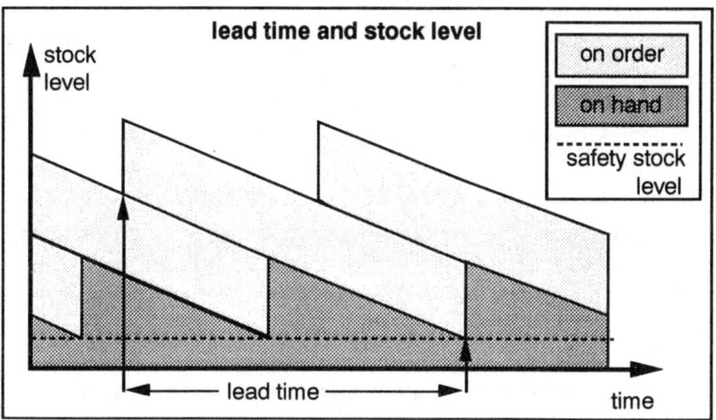

Figure 5.6a: Lead time and stock level.

The safety stock level is estimated on the basis of the perceived demand variability during the lead time, which itself is also subject to variation. The formula used by QED is given in figure 5.6b, see [Williams 1984] and [Fincke et al. 1989]. If demand and lead time are constant, then no safety stock is required in principle.

The forecasting component any materials mangement should employ serves to reduce the effects of demand variability. If forecasts are entirely accurate, then safety stocks have to account for lead time fluctuations only. It is not uncommon, however, that the forecast error is larger than the demand variability. In such cases, we best discard the existing procedures in favour of using a simple moving average as a predictor. In QED, the average value and standard deviation of the order size and frequency determine the demand and its variability. QED uses the factor *forecast accuracy* as a multiplier for demand variability. *Forecast accuracy* takes on the value 0.0 if the forecasts are entirely accurate; and values greater than 1.0 if the forecasts distort the demand fluctuations. As noted above, the forecast quality improves with shorter planning horizons. The longer the lead times, the farther into the future the production planner has to look and the less predictable the demand.

prescribing the safety stock level

$$SS = k \cdot Var(fedlt)^{1/2}$$

Var (fedlt) is the variance of the forecast error during the lead time

$$= k \cdot f(l, d)^{1/2}$$

$$= k \cdot \left(\left(Var(d) \cdot E(l) \right) + \left(E^2(d) \cdot Var(l) \right) \right)^{1/2}$$

d = demand
l = lead time
k = suitable constant

E (x) is the expected value of x;
Var (x) is the variance of x

Figure 5.6b: Prescribing the safety stock level or describing the surplus stock level. Refer also to §7.3.4.

The factor *k* is a multiplier for setting the safety stock level, which in special instances has a definite interpretation. It is set so as to achieve a desired level of service—a measure of the ability to serve orders for ex-stock products from stock. It grows to infinity as the desired customer service level approaches 100%. Typically, it takes on values between 1.0 and 2.5. At intermediate stages, QED uses *k* to represent the amount of surplus stock or slack in the system. It is an adjustment or fudge factor so to speak that covers up the poor performance of the system.

Lead time and lead time variability reflect the speed and reliability of the manufacturing process. Lead time does not affect cycle stocks. As shown in figures 5.6a and 5.6b, lead time and lead time variability[55] determine the safety stock level in combination with the demand variability. Lead time itself comprises, on the one hand, of a component associated with the planning of the necessary productive activities and, on the other hand, a component associated with the elapsed time required for performing these productive activities, called the throughput time. QED takes the standard deviation of the lead time to be a fixed percentage of the lead time, i.e. lead time variability improves as lead times come down.

The production throughput time of a campaign is computed by the taking the maximum processing time per lot of all the processing steps, which is an estimate of the product's cycle time, and multiplying this by the sum of the number of lots and steps minus 1. If the overall process is well-balanced, there will be little WIP, and waiting and dead time between the process steps. The queue time, which covers several factors that may cause a delay of the actual start of a campaign, must be included in the overall throughput time. Note that the average throughput time over all products determines the length of the frozen period. This is a measure of the flexibility of the system. It represents the time period within which no more changes can be made to the production schedule. The next section attempts to clarify and differentiate the notions of cycle time, throughput time and lead time.

[55]Lead time variability is the reason that the popular formula which takes the square root of the mean square forecast error times the lead time is less appropriate. It ignores the variability. The formula used by QED has the further advantage that demand variability can be separated into the variability of the size and frequency of orders. See chapter 7 for further details.

5.5 Cycle Time, Throughput Time, Lead Time and Flow Time

"For every day of lead time reduction
your company takes out one day's worth of inventory!"

adapted from the broadway pandemonium
"Scoops and Light Brands Deployed"

The introductory quotation reflects some of the imprecise thinking about the abstract notion of lead time that purveyors of the MRP II concept occasionally serve to an obliging audience as the best current thinking in manufacturing practice. The previous sections have used the notions of cycle time, throughput time, lead time without emphasizing the difference between these. Occasionally, some of these notions are equated. The APICS dictionary, for example, defines cycle time and throughput time to be synonymous. As explained in chapter 4, in the batch process industry, the cycle time determines the production throughput time in combination with the size of the campaign. The overall throughput time for a production stage contains queue time over and above the basic production throughput time of the value-added process. Throughput time—*Durchlaufzeit* in German—is in turn one element of lead time, as shown in figure 5.5a. Lead time—*Wiederbeschaffungszeit* in German—is the most complex notion. The previous discussion failed to clarify and define the term. The following definition of lead time is put forward to stress that the basic, usually physical activity, which makes up the most obvious component of lead time, is embedded in information processing activities:

> *The lead time for fulfilling a requirement is the span of time from the time the need for fulfilling this requirement first arises to the time that its actual fulfillment is recognized. Thus, if inventory must be replenished at a certain date, the lead time specifies how far in advance this replenishment order must be generated.*

For any activity planned by a materials management system, these two key dates required for calculating the lead time and its variability can (and should) be recorded. The lead time as defined here is sometimes called the planning lead time to avoid any confusion with throughput time. To understand and assess the lead time for a particular activity, it is necessary to address the issues that determine how far in advance a requirement for this activity must be generated:

- What is the planning frequency? Once a requirement is generated, it must first wait until the next planning round. If the planning is performed monthly, this waiting time will range from 1 day to a full month with an expected value of half a month.
- What is the planning accuracy? The length of the so-called time bucket for specifying the requirement date is part of the lead time. If the time bucket is, for example, a weekly one and the requirement is for the first day of the week, the

requirement may end up being fulfilled at the end of the week, nearly a week too late; and *vice versa*. The typical response is to plan all requirements for the previous week.

• How flexible is the system as a whole? Experience has shown that it necessary to introduce time fences in a production schedule. In fact, the use of time fences is a major innovation of the MRP II concept. The first part of the schedule up to the first time fence is frozen to ensure sufficient stability in production. The length of the frozen period is a policy decision. However, it should reflect the flexibility of production. As shown in figure 5.5a, QED uses the average production throughput time to set the frozen period. The shorter the production runs, the more flexible the system is. The length of the frozen period is part of the lead time.

• How long does the basic, physical activity take and how reliable is it? The most obvious component of lead time is the production throughput time, which includes queue time, changeover time, basic processing time and move time. Variability in the production throughput time due to missing materials, breakdowns, variable yield or bottlenecks, to mention the main examples, leads to non-conformance to the schedule, and hence additional variability in the lead time.

• To what extent do the lead times times of successive stages in a multi-stage manufacturing process overlap? In an integrated materials management system, MRP II being the prime example, the planning process for the different stages is designed to overlap. This effectively reduces lead times. Integrated planning of a multi-stage production system is, of course, one of the strengths of the MRP II.

• How soon is the actual fulfillment of the requirement recognized? The lack of synchronization or integration of different compenents of a planning system, see for example §6.3.3, may build additional delays into the lead time. Material will be available physically, but the system that generated the original requirement isn't able to use it until it has received the information.

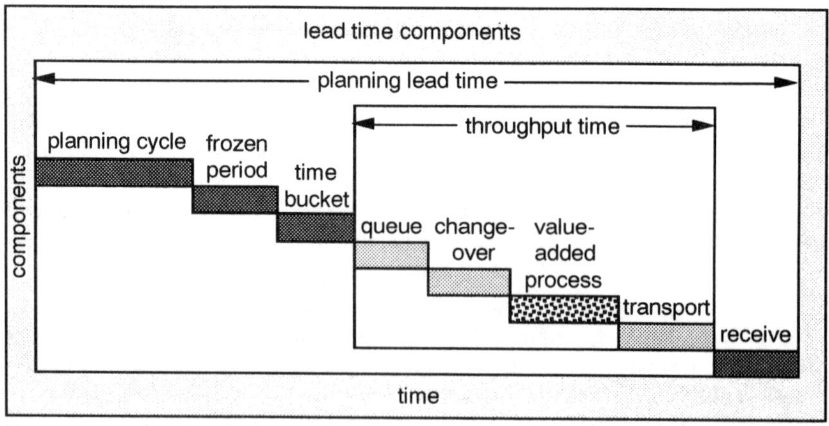

Figure 5.6c: Planning lead time. Not all components of lead time are activities. The logic shown in the diagram assumes 100% data accuracy. Inaccurate inventory records and bills of material have a detrimental effect on lead time variability.

The concept of flow time focuses on the physical flow of material through the manufacturing system and its total duration from supplier to customer. It is a much more intuitive concept than lead time. Lead time and its variability have a pervasive impact on the performance of a manufacturing system. But these notions focus on the individual stages of the supply chain. Flow time promotes a cross-functional view of the supply chain. It captures the combined impact of the following factors over all stages of the supply chain:

- lead time and lead time variability
- forecast error, including bias
- synchronization and integration of planning activities

The flow time for a product or product family is measured by accumulating:

- the longest flow time of its intermediate products
- the throughput time for the production process
- the inventory coverage for this product stage
- the flow time of a raw material is simply equal to its inventory coverage.

In other words, we compute the critical path. See figure 5.6d for an illustration. In most manufacturing systems flow time is largely made up of stock time. The term 'stock & go-go time' would therefore be at least as appropriate.

Alternatively, the flow time of a product can be measured by tagging the raw materials with the entry date as they enter the supply chain, passing these tags onto the intermediate products, taking the oldest tag attached to the final product at the point the customer receives it, and comparing the delivery date with this entry date. This is precisely what a lot tracing facility of an MRP II system should be capable of doing. In the pharmaceutical industry such a facility is of course mandatory.

The difference between the concepts of flow time and (accumulated) lead time returns us to the introductory quotation. If the forecast accuracy is poor, which it will be if lead times are long, then a one day reduction in lead time will most likely reduce inventory coverage by more than one day. As actual lead times become shorter and more predictable these benefits start to diminish. Putting it differently, if lead times are long and variable, then the flow time will be longer than the accumulated lead times, and *vice versa*. If lead times are short, then the flow time may in fact be smaller than the accumulated lead times and approach the total processing time. The key to understanding this lies in the function of safety stock.

In a hypothetical case in which the planning lead time is one year, including one week for production throughput time, and the variability of the lead time and demand are negligible, the flow time need not be any longer than the production throughput time. There will be no stocks except for WIP, as long as production is scheduled *and* completed just in time for the finished product to fulfill the demand.

This sections concludes with hierarchy of time-based measures that have been discussed with the associated elements of the supply chain:

- cycle time — production of a single batch of a campaign in a production line
- production throughput time — production of a campaign in a production line
- overall throughput time — production of a campaign in a multi-purpose plant
- lead time — planning and production of a campaign in a multi-purpose plant
- flow time — supply chain of a multi-stage system

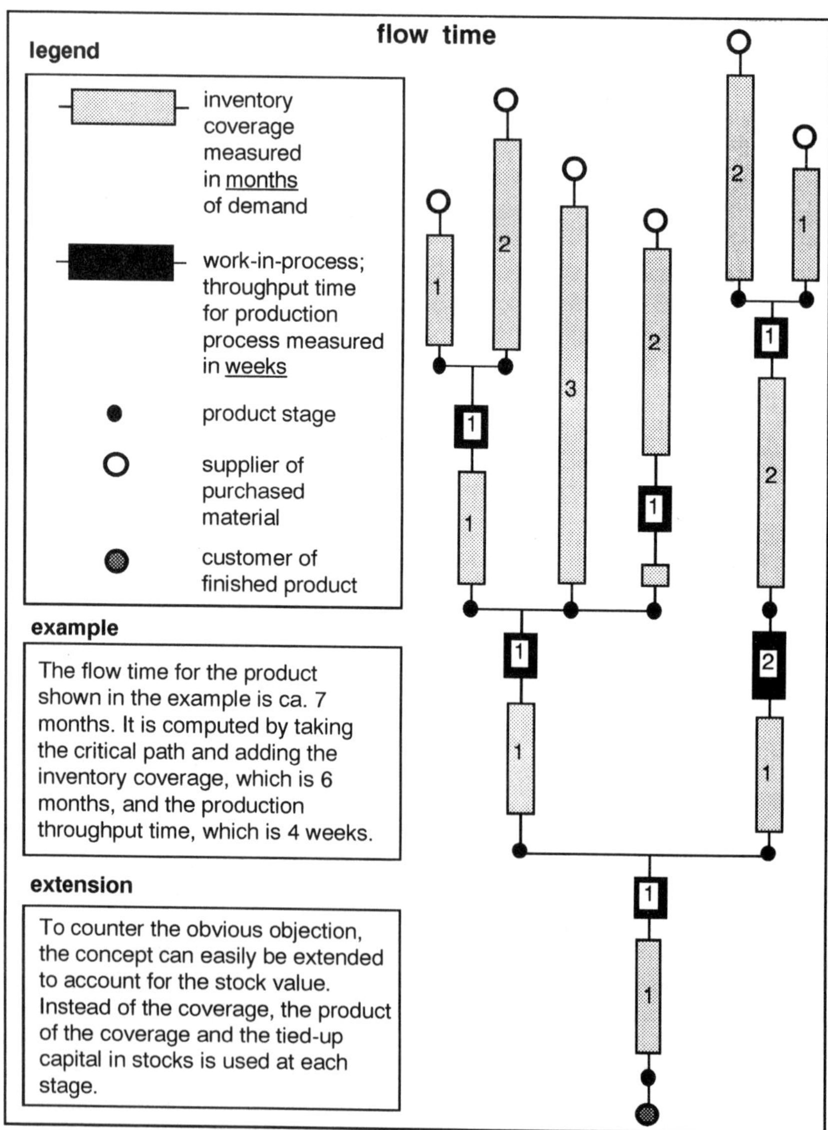

Figure 5.6d: The concept of flow time. See Goldratt [1987] on the extension.

5.6 Fixed Assets, Capital Costs and Depreciation

The mobile diagram in figure 5.7a shows how QED bases its calculation of fixed assets, capital costs and depreciation on an estimate of the required equipment capacity, see the next section for a description of the calculation for resource requirements. Fixed assets comprise four elements:

- equipment
- infrastructure
- building
- land

Given the equipment required and the space necessary to operate the equipment, QED calculates the investment in land, the building and the equipment itself. The infrastructure investment is derived directly from the equipment, as can be seen from the mobile diagram. Infrastructure covers a variety of auxiliary and often quite expensive equipment items such as high-precision scales for weighing large quantities. Using the write-off period or, as it is also called depreciation period, and the interest rate, QED calculates the annuity. This is the average annual depreciation and capital cost of the investment over the write-off period. The length of the write-off period will depend on the kind of element and equipment. It typically takes on values between 5 and 30 years. As mentioned, the write-off period and the interest rate are two exogenous variables; they obviously have a major impact on the performance factor.

QED applies this simple concept to all stages and elements of the manufacturing and distribution system falling within the scope of the present investigation. In the investigated case these stages and elements are:

- fabrication of bulk products
- semi-finished packaging
- fully-finished packaging
- floor space required for WIP—this is calculated separately, and subsequently added to each of the above three items
- quality control of bulk products
- warehousing at all intermediate stages and in the group companies

A number of comments are in order. Firstly, QED allocates capital costs and depreciation to the TPC values of products on the basis of actual capacity consumption. This applies in particular to the cost of warehousing. Secondly, in a factory operating with an additional shift, the 'value-added' per product will be lower, since the hourly equipment rate is less. Given that inventory is valued at TPC, this means that the tied-up capital in stock, and the interest charges, will also be lower, in other words, not only the fixed assets, and the associated capital and depreciation costs. It should be stressed that TPC values are mainly used for the sake of valuing inventory. This is shown clearly in figure 7.1.

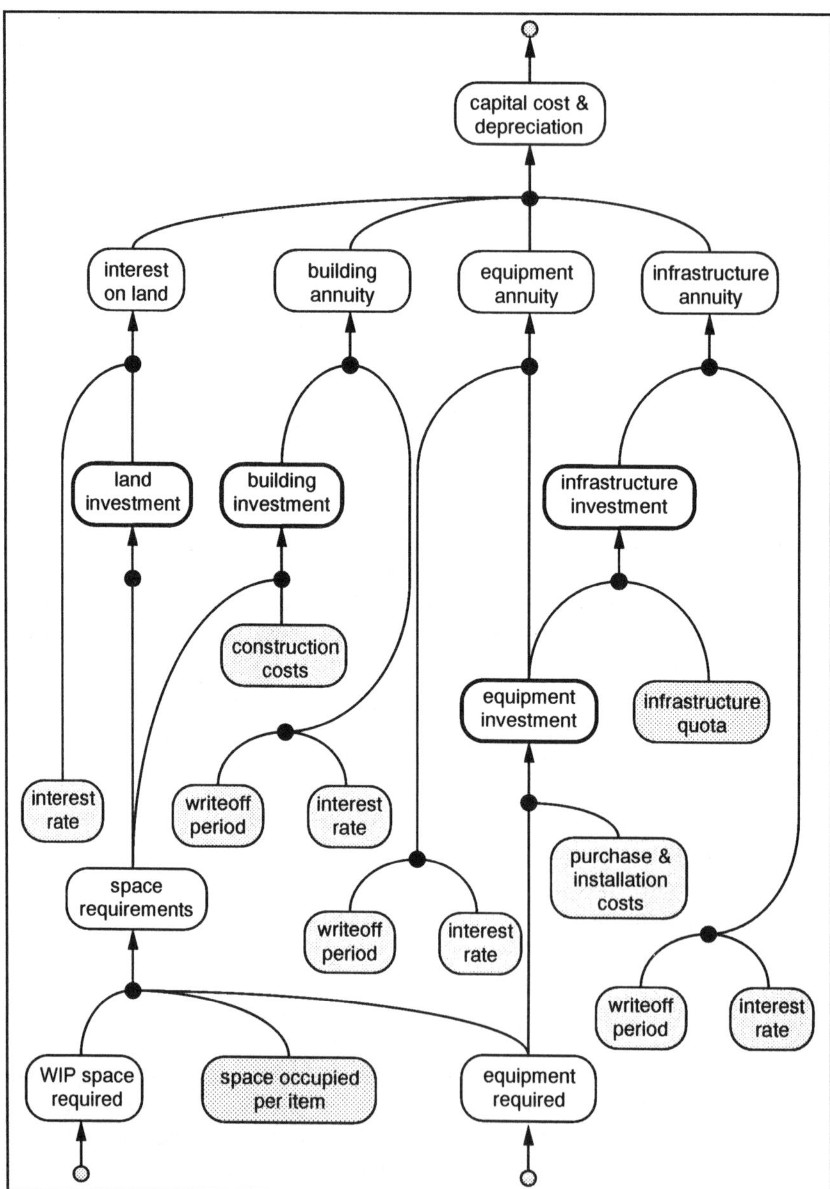

Figure 5.7a: Mobile diagram for the capital costs and depreciation of fixed assets. The investment in land, buildings, infrastructure and equipment enters into the calculation of the performance factor—see figure 5.2a.

If we use QED for comparing an existing operation with a new one, then we must exercise considerable care. How is the old equipment to be valued? Several possible answers spring to mind:

- cost of replacement
- cost at the time of acquisition minus depreciation for every year thereafter
- as above plus a correction for the inflation rate

It hardly needs saying that the outcome of the comparison will depend upon the answer chosen. In addition, the answer ought to be consistent with the value for the remaining economic life of the equipment.

A comparable question applies to the cost of warehouse space. What is the cost of creating a new warehouse or additional warehouse space? Here the same comments apply that were made earlier about the true cost of disposing of slow-movers. The political costs are substantial and increasing. In addition, time delays until the start of construction nearly always play a role.

5.7 Labour and Equipment Capacity Requirements

To understand how QED calculates labour and equipment requirements, it necessary to make a clear distinction between the concepts of campaign and lot. In other industries, these can (and tend to) be used interchangeably. As discussed in chapter 4, this is entirely inappropriate in the chemical-pharmaceutical industry. A campaign is made up of a series of batches or lots. Generally, lots come about because of the presence of a batch-type processing step. The maximum amount produced at one such a step is strictly limited by the volume of the reaction vessel. The processing time for a batch-type step does not increase linearly with the amount to be processed; it is largely independent of it. For pharmaceuticals, health and safety regulations stipulate that each lot receive a unique identification. Therefore, lots usually do not get merged in subsequent steps. The bill of materials, i.e., the product recipe, is specified per lot. The lot size is typically specified in kg, number of tablets or number of packs; the campaign size, on the other hand, is specified in terms of the number of lots.

As a consequence, the terms utilization and flexibility, restricting the latter for the moment to cleaning and changeover times of equipment, need to be used carefully. Utilization has two dimensions: traditional time utilization—"what was the average amount of dead and idle time in relation to the total time available or used?"—and volume utilization—"how full was the reaction vessel on average?" Obviously, both factors affect throughput. Lot sizes have a direct impact on volume utilization, whereas campaign sizes do not. Flexibility, on the other hand, is a characteristic of equipment that applies to a change of lot as much as to a change of campaign.

Clearly, there is a double price to pay for small lot sizes. A smaller machine rarely costs correspondingly less, see p. 249 in §7.3.2. Its production cost per unit of time and hence also per unit of output will be higher. To assess the overall economic impact of small lot sizes, which is just one element of the just-in-time concept, any serious analysis must necessarily take the impact on lead times into account. The resolution of the conflict arising between throughput time and throughput may lie in introducing variable lot sizes. The idea of having two or three lot sizes for the same product will not be welcomed with open arms in a manufacturing environment that is already suffering from the consequences of having a multiplicity of product variants. §7.3.2 explores this topic.

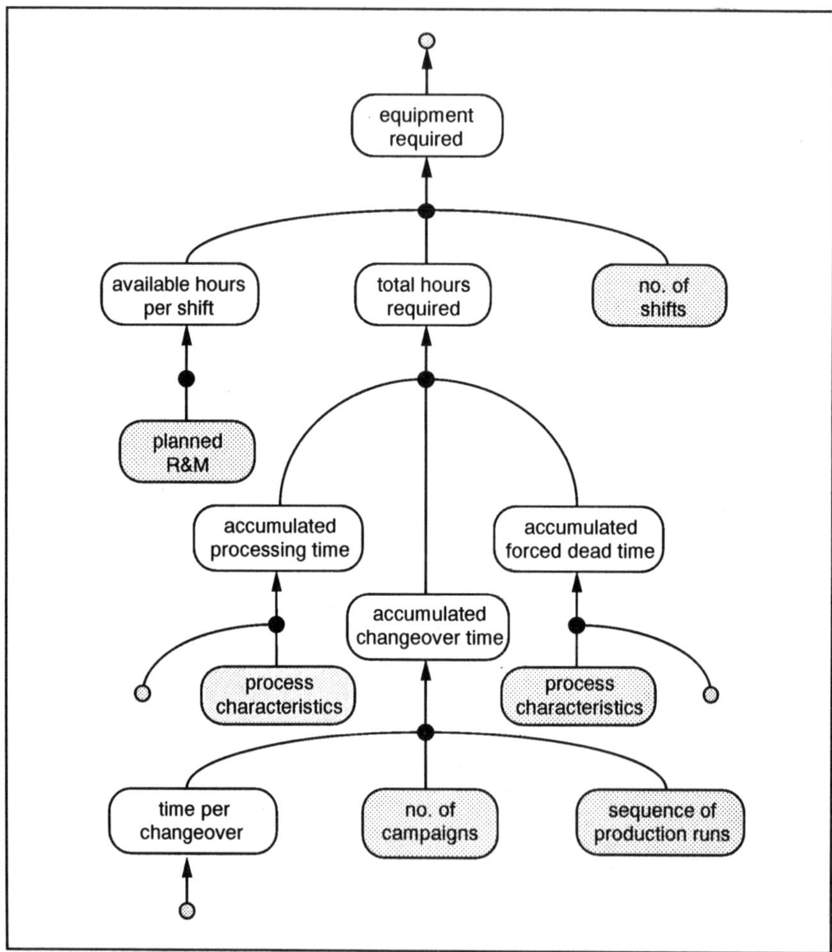

Figure 5.7b: Mobile diagram for the number of equipment items required.

In a classical operation, WIP stock ameliorates the detrimental effects of imbalanced processing times or, putting it differently, a large amount of WIP stock gives a clear signal to start balancing the overall process. In a pure just-in-time operation using the kanban concept, the number of 'move' and 'production' kanbans would restrict the amount of WIP stock. If the throughput is not to suffer, we must improve the process by achieving a better balance of the separate steps. As it stands, QED assumes that maximal throughput is achieved at the expense of WIP. QED also ignores the fact that additional WIP is required to cover fluctuating processing times. The amount of WIP is estimated to be directly proportional to the product of the campaign size and the overall throughput time. Thus, WIP is a quadratic function of the campaign size.

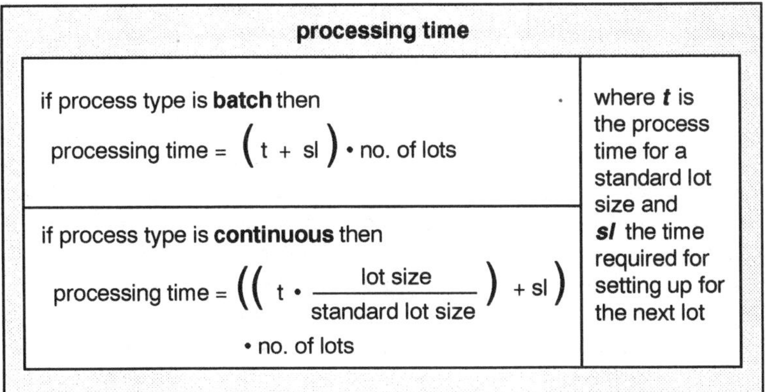

Figure 5.7c: Accumulated processing time for a single process step.

The formula for the accumulated processing time is given in figure 5.7c. The processing time is specified as the time required to process a lot of a standard size; the labour requirements are specified as the number of people required during the process. QED multiplies this value with the processing time to get the labour hours required. Given the number of campaigns, derived from the campaign sizes and the total yearly volume corrected for yield losses, QED calculates the total amount of setup and cleaning time. This requires the cleaning as well as the minor and major setup time per machine. The calculation for the labour hours required for setups and changeovers is the same as above. The sum of these components gives the total equipment and labours hours required. Given the number of shifts the factory is to operate and the planned available hours of the equipment, QED calculates the capacity requirements for each step in the production process. This is done across the board or for each vertical segment, i.e., each independent production line.

As it stands, QED ignores the impact of the utilization level on the throughput time. It is easy, however, to extend QED and capture this impact by linking utilization level and queue time, see figure 5.5a. The specific inputs for the available hours per shift in the application of QED described in chapter 7 are quite conservative. The bottleneck work centers can, therefore, absorb additional hours to avoid overly long queue times.

5.8 Nippon vs Erewhon[56] – A Contrivance

There once was
an engine and then one ...

To cut it short, this modern day tale presents a not entirely innocuous comparison of two engines. The Butler Engine – Model S, conceived and operating in the Erewhonian kingdom and the Ohno Engine – Model T, operating in the Nipponian empire, are both similar and different. The Nipponians, have—for lack of creativity and inventiveness, as their Erewhonian competitors cannot fail to point out—carefully re-engineered a clone of an earlier version of the current Butler Engine. The Erewhonians continue to take pride in their engine, which they carefully continue to steep in tradition. This tradition goes back to the original Babbage Engine that was first put to use by Lady Lovelace, daughter of Lord Byron. Both engines come close to what is still known as a think tank. They produce useful concepts for a somewhat peculiar consumer market segment. Without having to go into the details of the enigmatic mechanics of these, a noted Erewhonian professor of hypothetics[57] has stumbled on the difference between the two engines. The Ohno Engine processes and structures thoughts as they are generated and focuses these on particular topics. Towards the end of a month it gathers all collections of thoughts and then packages each collection as a useful concept. The Butler Engine is, as mentioned, strikingly similar, except for the fact that its concepts are sold with an impressive name attached. These names, the engine concocts during the idle cycles which start to become available towards the end of the year, since the engine learns and becomes more efficient and effective as it produces. In their effort to eliminate waste—and what else is idle capacity—the Erewhonians have made a virtue out of a problem. Once a full list of names is available, they are sorted for easy selection and assignment to the concepts. The naming of the concepts also turns out to be useful for tracing history in the annals of the company. Unfortunately, the Erewhonian company is as weak in the area of marketing as its Nipponian competitor. Market forces could not but fail to recognize the added value of the named concepts and naturally pay the same price for both products. By the end of the year both machines start to regurgitate their old concepts and therefore have to be shut down. Further properties of these two engines are summarized in figure 5.8a.

The properties of these engines are not as far-fetched as may appear at a first glance. Some of the pertinent differences between a batch chemical process in a large reactor and a continuous process in a pipeline[58] are common to both cases.

---

[56]After Samuel Butler's famous satirical novel *Erewhon* (1872). Reprinted in *Erewhon and Erewhon Revisited*, Random House, New York, 1927.

[57]See the chapters on "The Colleges of Unreason" in Butler's *Erewhon*.

[58]Continuous chemical processes still have high changeover costs due to start-up losses and the associated waste treatment. These costs entail long campaigns in a multi-product facility.

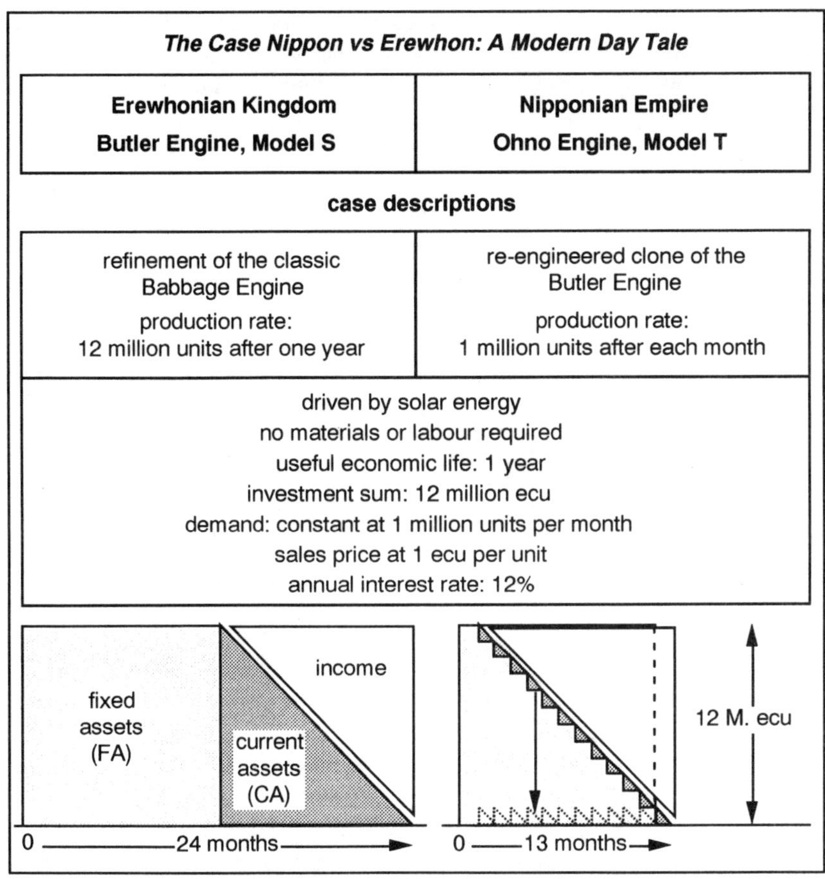

Figure 5.8a: The case "Nippon vs Erewhon" or the time value of money.

This tale, although frivolous, drives home a pivotal point about the economics of speed. In Erewhon, it is a severe crime to possess a watch or any other instrument that measures time. It is only consistent that the Erewhonians do not charge interest on borrowed or lent funds. The time value of money does not play a role. From the Erewhonian point of view, therefore, the Butler Engine is running as economically as possible. Under the point of view that capital is an important resource in its own right,[59] the economic analysis of the two cases, to be presented shortly, comes out

[59]As voiced in the international business press, the micro- and macro-economic impact of a world-wide shortage of capital, which financial analysts are presently predicting for the last decade of this century, is the source of considerable concern. At the same time that CIBA–GEIGY is making moves that will ensure better access to international capital markets, its cost accounting system pays virtually no attention to the cost of capital. The CIBA–GEIGY MIS Handbook, re-issued September 1989, states on pp. 3-9 and 3-11: "A division is not charged with any financing expenses neither as primary or secondary expenses. At the time of developing the MIS the financing of the business was defined as a corporate responsibility of Function Finance and consequently these expenses were accounted for

rather different. Of course, this difference is, as indicated by the diagram, an obvious one. The Butler Engine looks significantly worse than its re-engineered counterpart. The subsequent analysis primarily intends to justify and clarify the treatment of cost-based factors in QED. At the same time, however, it briefly lifts the lid on Pandora's box of cost accounting issues for modern manufacturing systems, only to close it again.

analysis ignoring compounded interest

net shaded areas to finance	12 x 18 x 1% = 2.16	12 x 7 x 1% = 0.84
		2.16 - 0.84 = **1.32**
depreciation	12.00	12.00
financing cost FA	12 x 12% = 1.44	12 x 12% = 1.44
CA	6 x 12% = 0.72	0.5 x 12% = 0.06
	14.16	13.50
discounted income loss	12 x 6 x 1% = 0.72	12 x 0.5 x 1% = 0.06
	14.88	13.56
		14.88 - 13.56 = **1.32**

discounted income loss = sales x flow time (months) x monthly interest rate

Figure 5.8b: Analysis of the case "Nippon vs Erewhon" ignoring compounded interest. Ignoring the time value of money, the two competitors come out the same. The standard approach that only calculates the financing costs of fixed and current assets fails to capture the full difference between the competitors. This approach also ignores cost items and areas, such as R&D, that are not allocated to standard product costs. Erewhon is analyzed in the column on the left; Nippon on the right.

The simplest way to look at the difference between the two cases is take the interest on outstanding debt minus accumulated income, which is equal to the shaded areas shown in figure 5.8a. The difference, as calculated in figure 5.8b, is 1.32 M. ecu. Alternatively, we calculate the depreciation and financing costs for fixed and current assets. This alone won't do. Starting from the time the product has been produced the Nipponian product is on the market 5.5 months earlier. The Erewhonians face a loss due to the fact that their future income is worth less in today's terms. Putting it differently, the Nipponians accumulate interest on their

---

strictly as functional expenses. Besides, in those years financing expenses were rather modest both in absolute and relative terms. In the nineteen seventies, however, rapidly accelerating inflation in many of CIBA–GEIGY's important markets and the rising cost of money made it more and more necessary to make divisional management aware of the relationship between generating contributions and the entailing financing needs. Up to now CIBA–GEIGY has dealt with this aspect not within the framework of its groupwide unified responsibility accounting but in the form of complementary statistical information for high inflation countries."

sales income. The argumentation follows the Discounted Cash Flow (DCF) concept used for the purpose of an investment analysis. The discounted income loss is a function of the flow time, which in this simple one stage production system is simply equal to the inventory coverage. If we do account for the difference in discounted income loss, we arrive at the same figure of 1.32 M. ecu. The calculations are shown in figure 5.8b. It should also be apparent that if inventories are valued at VPC, the results of the analysis are different.

cash flow analysis

	cash in	cash out	cash in	cash out
1		**12.00** 12 x 12% = 1.44	**11.00** 5.04 x 12% = 0.61	**12.00** 12 x 12% = 1.44
2	**12.00** 6 x 12% = 0.72	13.44 x 12% = 1.61	**1.00** 12.60 x 12% = 1.51	13.44 x 12% = 1.61
	12.72	15.05	14.12	15.05
		-2.33		-0.93
				2.33 - 0.93 = **1.40**

analysis including compounded interest

depreciation		12.00	12.00
financing cost	FA	12 x 12% = 1.44	12 x 12% = 1.44
	CA	6.72 x 12% = 0.81	0.56 x 12% = 0.07
discounted		14.25	13.51
income loss		12 x 6 x 1% = 0.72	12 x 0.5 x 1% = 0.06
		14.97	13.57
			14.97 - 13.57 = **1.40**

Figure 5.8c: Analysis of the case "Nippon vs Erewhon" including compounded interest. Again, discounting is required to capture the full difference between the competitors. The cash flow analysis accumulates the interest on the cash inflows and outflows—**bold** figures. As an example, in year one Nippon receives 12% interest on an average of 11/2 M.ecu for 11 out of 12 months, i.e. 121/24 or 5.04.

A proviso is in order. The approach taken by the analysis hinges on a critical assumption about depreciation. QED uses a fixed-time method with linear depreciation, commonly referred to as the straight-line method. In practice, the revaluation of fixed and current assets is performed periodically—typically annually or quarterly—and at the same time as the standard products costs are revised. Ignoring current costs adjustments, fixed assets as a function of time are a decreasing step function with a linear trend. The case "Nippon vs Erewhon

Revisited," see figure 5.8d, shows this more clearly. In other words, if fixed assets are depreciated as soon as they are consumed, then the discounting is incorrect. It would result in double counting, since the interest on the fixed assets for the Nipponian engine would already make up for the difference. The culprit is in fact the stepwise depreciation of fixed assets. This also explains why costs that need not be capitalized, e.g. material and labour costs, must be excluded from the discounting.

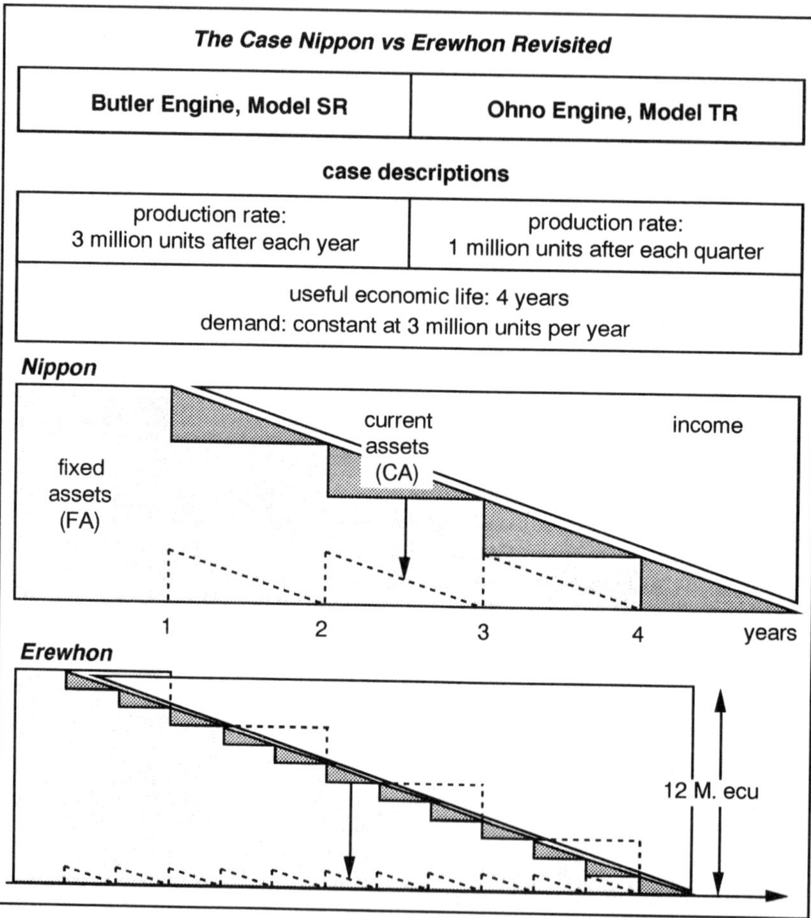

Figure 5.8d: The case "Nippon vs Erewhon Revisited." The useful economic life of the equipment has been increased to 4 years. The diagram shows that for the sake of the analysis fixed assets are being depreciated linearly at the end of each year. The calculations performed with QED use the same approach. Even for a multi-purpose facility the assumption, made explicit by the diagram, that there is a direct relationship between (average) campaign size and production lead time is especially appropriate.

It is straightforward to extend the analysis to include compounded interest. A simple cash flow analysis captures this. Alternatively, we can assess the value inventories more carefully. The previously analysis valued inventory on the basis of depreciation only. The extended analysis, as shown in figure 5.8c, uses the annuity, i.e. depreciation plus interest, to value inventory. This is exactly the way QED treats these cost-based factors. The result of this approach, as shown by the outcome of the detailed calculations, matches the one of the cash flow analysis. Ignoring the time value of money, the two cases come out the same.

The case "Nippon vs Erewhon Revisited," as shown in figure 5.8d, is more realistic. The conclusion drawn from the results of the analysis, as shown in figure 5.8e, does not change. The case makes it clear that the results hold regardless of the useful economic life of the two engines.

analysis ignoring compounded interest of revisited case

net shaded areas to finance		12 x 3 x 12% = 4.32	12 x 7 x 12% = 3.36
			4.32 - 3.36 = **0.96**
depreciation		12.00	12.00
financing cost	FA	30 x 12% = 3.60	30 x 12% = 3.60
	CA	4 x 1.5 x 12% = 0.72	4 x 0.5 x 12% = 0.24
		16.32	15.84
discounted income loss		12 x 6 x 1% = 0.72	12 x 4 x 1% = 0.24
		17.04	16.08
			17,04 - 16.08 = **0.96**

Figure 5.8e: Analysis of the case "Nippon vs Erewhon Revisited." The results show that the same conclusions can be drawn as in the original case.

In summary, what are the relevant characteristics of QED? In order to account for the economics of speed, QED needs to and does perform the following combination of operations:

- calculate the financing costs of fixed and current assets
- compound the financing costs
- value inventories at TPC
- depreciate fixed assets linearly and periodically
- discount part of the sales income as a function of flow time

The latter issue requires some final comments. The largest impact of the delay in income results from costs that are not included in the TPC but that still have to be recovered through the sales price. QED computes the performance factor (PF), see §5.3, as well as the discounted performance factor (DPF), which captures this impact. To determine DPF and the discount, which is to be subtracted from the net profit contrinution, QED takes sales income only at half its actual value, see figure 5.2b. QED assumes that 50% of the sales price accounts for activities such as marketing and R&D that cannot in practice be allocated to individual products. This is a conservative figure for the investigated case. The application of QED to this specific industrial case shows that the difference between PF and DPF ranges between 10% to 20%, depending on the sales volume.

The analysis of this provocative case admittedly needs its rough edges polished. It lacks the rigor required to support any definitive conclusions of a more general nature. It is safe to say, however, that cost systems cannot adequately assess the economics of speed, especially in the context of long-term decisions, in as far as these systems fail to:

- account for financing costs
- and apply these to all costs, not just those that can be allocated to products,
- pay due attention to effects of depreciation practice and inventory valuation

It should also be noted that the concept of discounting income using flow time has little practical merit for product costing in a multi-stage manufacturing environment. It will be difficult to avoid unacceptable distortions while keeping the complexity at a tolerable level.

Although the analysis provided here is by no means intended to be a replacement for a dynamic investment analysis, as discussed in §3.6, the results should be in line with each other. Modern investment appraisal methods do in principle account for the time value of money. Effectively, however, this is only is the case, if the projected stock levels serve as a measure of the extent to which the sales income is deferred. It is an understatement to say that investment appraisals rarely take account of this aspect. Moreover, the more obvious impact of different alternatives on inventory levels and warehouse space requirements ought to be covered as well. Surprisingly enough, this is often not adhered to in industrial practice either.

In addition, the analysis has consequences for conventional theory on optimal campaign sizing, which simply ignores the loss of income due to its discounted value. The calculations performed in figure 5.8b and 5.8c show that it is insufficient to take only the direct and and indirect costs of holding inventory. In monetary terms the impact of the inclusion of the costs of the income delay caused by long campaign sizes and high levels of inventory coverage can be expected to be quite significant. This holds especially in the pharmaceutical industry where, as mentioned, TPC typically cover much less than 50% of the sales price.

5.9 Aspects Lost

The description and justification of the logic of QED would not be complete without a brief statement of the most important limitations of this rough-cut financial model:

QED makes no attempt to assess the impact of speed, reliability and flexibility on market share. QED mainly looks at the cost side at the equation for the performance factor. As discussed in §2.4, these dimensions of the product position it in the market. More rapid and reliable service may directly increase sales and market share. Equally important benefits of reduced flow times are that new products come on the market sooner, thus capturing the important early share, and, secondly, that the effective length of the patent protection period is increased. Coming on the market sooner also raises the average selling price Concomitant with reduced flow times and lead times are shorter planning horizons. This eliminates at least some of the numerous uncertainties associated with the introduction of new products and permits a more flexible response to unexpected events.

Since QED is not and could not be applied to cover the chemical production of active substance, it is not possible to assess the quantitative impact on chemical production of shorter flow and lead times in the last part of the supply chain. But, it can be argued, for instance, that the resulting reduction in the overall planning horizon[60] will help to improve medium-term capacity planning and avoid at least some of the capacity bottlenecks that currently exist. The benefits would go well beyond those captured under the risk of obsolescence discussed in §3 of this chapter.

QED largely ignores aspects related to or concerning the qualification, skill levels and traing of personnel. These aspects are particulary interesting in combination with equipment changeovers. Has the changeover process been simplified to such an extent that specialized mechanics are no longer required and that the production line workers can be trained to carry out the job themselves?

QED conveniently ignores the thorny details and practicalities of the actual application of the just-in-time concept in an existing operation. One example suffices. The design of a suitable collection of boxes for export-packaged products and especially their dimensions is a critical and technical problem that needs solving when the processes for full-packaging and export-packaging are to be coupled. There are many dependencies that range from the dimensions of fully-packaged products to the needs of the customers and the ability of the materials management systems to handle packaging variants. QED obviously doesn't provide any solution for this problem area; however, it does address the question whether it's worthwhile to look for and find solutions.

[60]If the flow time from active chemical substance to the market is one year, then today's change in demand would already have had to be matched by a change in the production rate in chemical production one year ago to avoid a supply shortage or inventory build-up. Given that the change in demand is hardly recognized immediately and that chemical production is itself a multi-stage process, the planning horizon needs to be much longer.

6 Description and Analysis of the Empirical Research Object

"If time is money,
is just-in-time Cash-in-der-Täsch [61] ?"
after Ben Franklin and Prof. Horst Wildemann

6.1 Introduction and Outline

This chapter describes and analyzes pharmaceutical production and logistics in the parent company of CIBA–GEIGY, while concentrating on the material and information flows associated with the fabrication and packaging of solid dosage forms. The analysis evaluates the speed of the system, shows it to be sluggish, and attributes this sluggishness to the present focus on period cost reduction and high capacity utilization. The system is not geared for time-based competition. The economic assessment, which applies the overall approach for assessing the just-in-time concept presented earlier to the empirical research object, does not follow until chapter 7. This assessment covers the impact of overall order delivery times on stock levels in the group companies.

This chapter also presents a possible just-in-time strategy that will subsequently be contrasted in economic terms with the existing operation. The threefold solution concept put forward shows that the major elements of the just-in-time concept are applicable, even though there are no ready-made solutions to adopt from other industries. The special issues and conditions facing manufacturing in the parent company, addressed in §6.2, indicate the need for a manufacturing strategy focusing on speed and flexibility. But, what are the economics of a such a strategy?

6.2 Critical Success Factors in Supply Chain Management

To put the present situation of pharmaceutical production in the Stein works and the associated export and plant logistics in perspective, it is useful to review the key conditions characterizing the business environment in the pharmaceutical industry. Without discussing the underlying socioeconomic developments, we note a number of well-known trends that directly affect the profitability of this industry. Several of these curtail and constrain prices. In an effort to contain the cost explosion in health care, governments and health insurance companies are putting policies and measures into place that curtail drug prices. As a result of the developments in the EEC, industry observers are expecting market forces to bring about a further erosion in the average European selling price during the 1990's. Estimated revenue losses during this decade for any major pharmaceutical firm such as CIBA–GEIGY are on the order of magnitude of the costs of developing several new drugs. Already, generic substitutions are widespread and quickly capture large market shares once the patents on the original products have expired. This affects product prices as much as product life cycles. In addition, longer development times reduce the effective length of the patent protection period.

[61] Slang in modern day German for money in the pocket.

On the cost side of the equation, both the costs for the development and introduction of new products and the costs of producing and delivering existing products are on the rise. To take advantage of the opportunities offered by the expected liberalization and harmonization of various regulations in the EEC, companies may first have to invest in new production and distribution facilities, besides having to realign their manufacturing strategy. What often goes unnoticed is that the cost containment efforts mentioned earlier are also changing the nature of the demand. Drug consumers are shifting inventories to their suppliers by putting more weight on rapid and reliable delivery. On theoretical grounds, this must effect the demand pattern as well: volatility should increase.

Several characteristics of the industry itself play a role as well. The typical supply chain in the pharmaceutical industry is an international and entangled web of material and information flows covering many supply and distribution points. Accumulative lead times typically exceed 24 months. Although there is a trend in the direction of single-product chemical production lines, many multi-product and multi-purpose facilities remain. Due to capacity bottlenecks, the same intermediate may be produced at different locations, adding further complexity. Chemical production facilities are getting increasingly complex and expensive. In addition, the possibility of the development of alternative production methods—biotechnology—increases the uncertainty associated with capital investments in installations based on traditional process technologies. Last but not least, the product range is very broad, especially at CIBA–GEIGY with several thousand items at the finished product level. Consequently, logistics issues form a critical component of any successful manufacturing strategy.

Although it is clear that traditionally important issues such as innovation in R&D, drug efficacy, safety and quality will remain on the agenda, new issues are being added. The nature of the business is gradually changing. Rapid and reliable delivery service is an additional product dimension on which basis firms may decide to compete. This applies in particular to generics and self-medication. These specific marketing requirements, together with those for 'surplus' production capacity maintained to guarantee a flexible response to unexpected market opportunities, are putting upwards pressure on logistics and manufacturing costs, especially in traditional environments. At the same time, business analysts expect the double-sided, external squeeze on profit margins to be met by measures aimed at improving the cost-effectiveness of manufacturing operations. The disadvantageous cost structure of research-based firms in comparison with imitators accentuates the need for these improvements. Viewed from a different angle, rationalizations of manufacturing operations are to be a source of R&D funding. The potential for developing manufacturing strategies with built-in conflicts is apparent.

It is hardly bold to conclude that these changed conditions call for a re-alignment of the critical success factors to match the chosen strategy. Issues in supply chain management, particularly speed and flexibility, will increase in prominence.

6.3 Pharmaceutical Production in the Parent Company

Pharmaceutical manufacturing divides into chemical production of active substances, and the fabrication and packaging of various dosage forms. The latter two stages are generally referred to as pharmaceutical production. The term galenic production is not common. Both terms are somewhat misleading to an outsider. The manufacturing processes in these areas are of course very different.

The Stein works in the parent company is sometimes called the pharmacy of the firm. This joke captures the outstanding feature of pharmaceutical production in the parent company. In comparison with pharmaceutical production in the group companies, the product range at the finished product level is broad in absolute terms and especially in relation to the sales turnover. Since the opening of the Stein works more and more group companies with sufficiently large home markets to serve have constructed their own packaging facilities, possibly including fabrication facilities also. The outcome of this development is predictable. Today, the Stein works is not only left with the smallest markets and least attractive from a manufacturing point of view; it is also required to look after those products that cannot be manufactured economically in the group companies with their own facilities or those products for which the technical expertise to ensure quality and safety are not available locally. These conditions, coming at a time when rapid and reliable delivery and flexibility are increasing in importance, place stringent demands on performance improvements. Furthermore, the design of the facilities and operational concepts for controlling the flow of information and materials stem from a time when the requirements were substantially simpler.

The subsequent description and analysis of pharmaceutical production in the parent company is based on an evaluation of the existing situation, which was the first phase of a project, dubbed JIST, with members from the Stein works and the export logistics department participating. The project started in the fourth quarter of 1988. The results and a proposed solution concept were first presented in May of 1989. Key parts of this chapter come from a summary of the results contained in the first part of a project report written by the author. The second part of this report described the results of a simulation study of one element of the proposed threefold just-in-time strategy, performed with ProfiSEE. It is summarized in §6.4.5.

Early on, the project team decided to focus on solid dosage forms. Manufacturing in the Stein works also includes trans-dermal patches as well as liquid and semi-solid dosage forms, but these were not part of the project. The production and distribution of solid dosage forms represent a sizable share of the business and appeared to be a prime candidate for a pilot project because of its complexity.

6.3.1 Product and Process Characteristics

Solid dosage forms cover tablets, sugar and film coated tablets (also called dragees and film-dragees) and capsules. These are fabricated from active ingredients and various auxiliary or supplementary substances. At this stage, the product is in so-called bulk form. Afterwards, it is packaged. The product is put into a blister pack that typically contains ten or more bulk items of the same kind. Alternatively, the bulk product may be bottled. The blister pack is a semi-packaged form. There is an increasing trend to include country or market specific labelling already at this stage. The fully-packaged form, typically a presentation pack, contains one or more blister packs or a bottle and a leaflet containing pertinent information about the product. Clearly, this product stage is country specific. The information required to be on the leaflet and on the outside of the box, and the language it is written in will vary from country to country. Together, these properties account for the explosion of the product tree at its leaves, as illustrated in figure 6.1.

The fabrication of solid dosage forms is a multi-stage process. Granulation, the first real step (it is preceded by the dispensation of active substance), is itself a multi-step batch process. It is performed in an enclosed, air-conditioned room in order to eliminate contamination. Compression, the next stage in the process, takes granules to form either tablets or the cores for coated tables. Capsules require encapsulation instead of compression. Encapsulation and compression are semi-continuous process steps. Sugar and film coating of cores are again batch process steps and require an additional auxiliary substance. The subsequent selection and imprinting steps are semi-continuous. Figure 6.2 describes the basic alternatives for the material flow of solid dosage forms. The equipment requires a careful and possibly time consuming cleanup after each campaign. Some stages—for example, compression—require a short setup before a campaign is started.

Bulk products are stored in relatively small containers and take up little space in comparison with packaged products and packaging material.

The balance of the process times for the different stages is typically very poor. Moreover, what is the bottleneck stage depends highly on the individual product. The size of the tablet in relation to the amount of active substance is but one relevant factor. Section 7.2 contains the processing times for the different stages of the selected products. The consequence of these characteristics is that it is difficult, if not impossible, to create balanced processes for all products, while maintaining a high level of equipment utilization. See §4.2 for a discussion.

Blister packs, which consist of several layers of packaging material, vary in metric dimension, number of tablets and the type of material used. Blister packaging, and semi-finished packaging in general, is a semi-continuous process. The packaging process lends itself to high degree of automation. The processing rates of the different machines available on the market today vary substantially. The choice of equipment to invest in depends on the anticipated product mix and volume. Given a machine mix, the size of the production job and the format of the pack determine what specific packaging machine will be selected. The same comments apply to cartoning machines, which wrap one or more blister packs or a bottle, together with a leaflet, in a carton box. The setup time for packaging machines is dependent on the sequence in which production orders are processed—change of format—, the technical characteristics of the machine, the level of training and availability of personnel, as well as changeover policies and procedures.

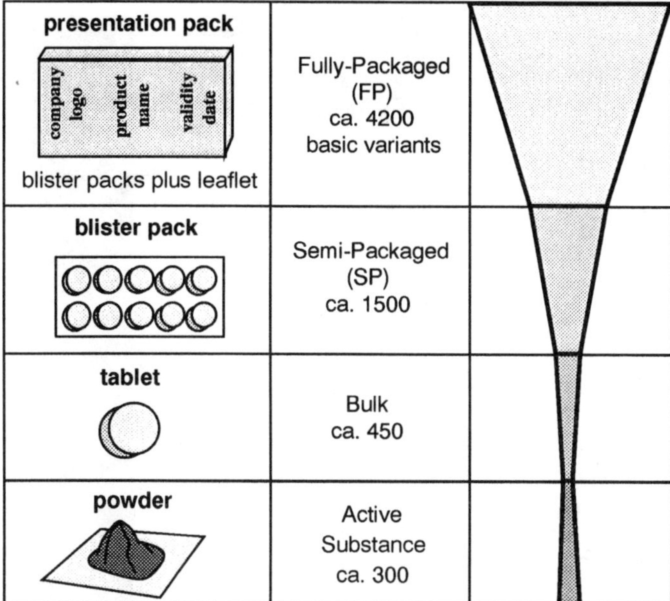

Figure 6.1: The three basic product stages of solid dosage forms.

6.3.2 Material Flows and Plant Layout

Manufacturing in the Stein works divides into fabrication and packaging, resulting in four major production stages with stocks of intermediate and finished products. Quality control, which involves a series of complex tests, is not an integrated part of the process. Generally, it precedes semi-finished packing. It is becoming more common to take the risk and to perform these stages in parallel. GMP regulations require quality control to be an independent unit in the organization.

The flow of materials for solid dosage forms is depicted in figure 6.2. Goods need to be transported in and out of the plant to one of the two warehouses. The automated warehouse will soon expand by 12'000 pallet spaces. The basement of the production building contains a manual warehouse. The total number of pallet spaces in the warehouses hovered around 40'000 during the past couple of years, with the average annual free capacity fluctuating between 5% and 20%. Active and auxiliary substances, which are outside of the scope of the project, roughly take up one quarter of the available space, while packaging materials take up nearly one third. The automated warehouse with about 26'000 pallet spaces performs about 330'000 pallet movements annually. This means that the typical pallet stays in the automated warehouse a little less than 2 months. The corresponding figure for the manual warehouse is of course higher. No figures are available that show which percentage of pallets has been taking up space in the warehouse for say more than 6 or 12 months.

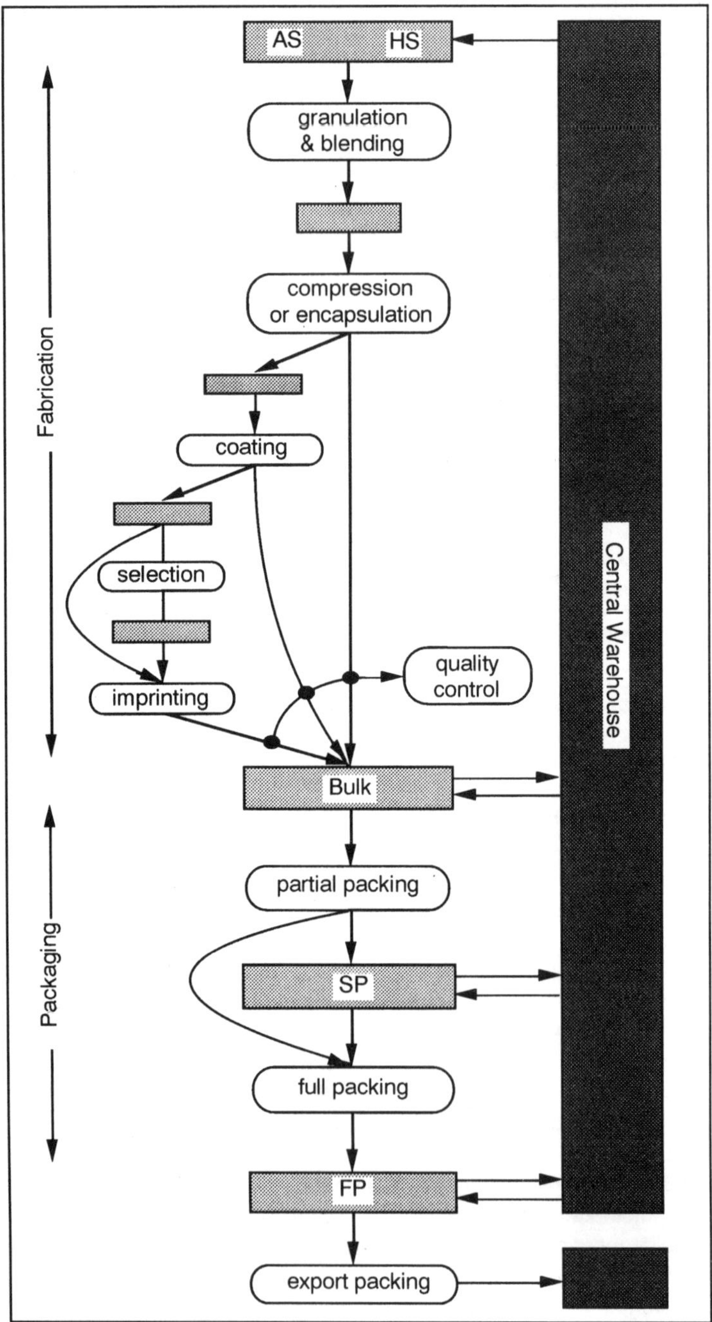

Figure 6.2: Material flow for solid dosage forms in the Stein works.

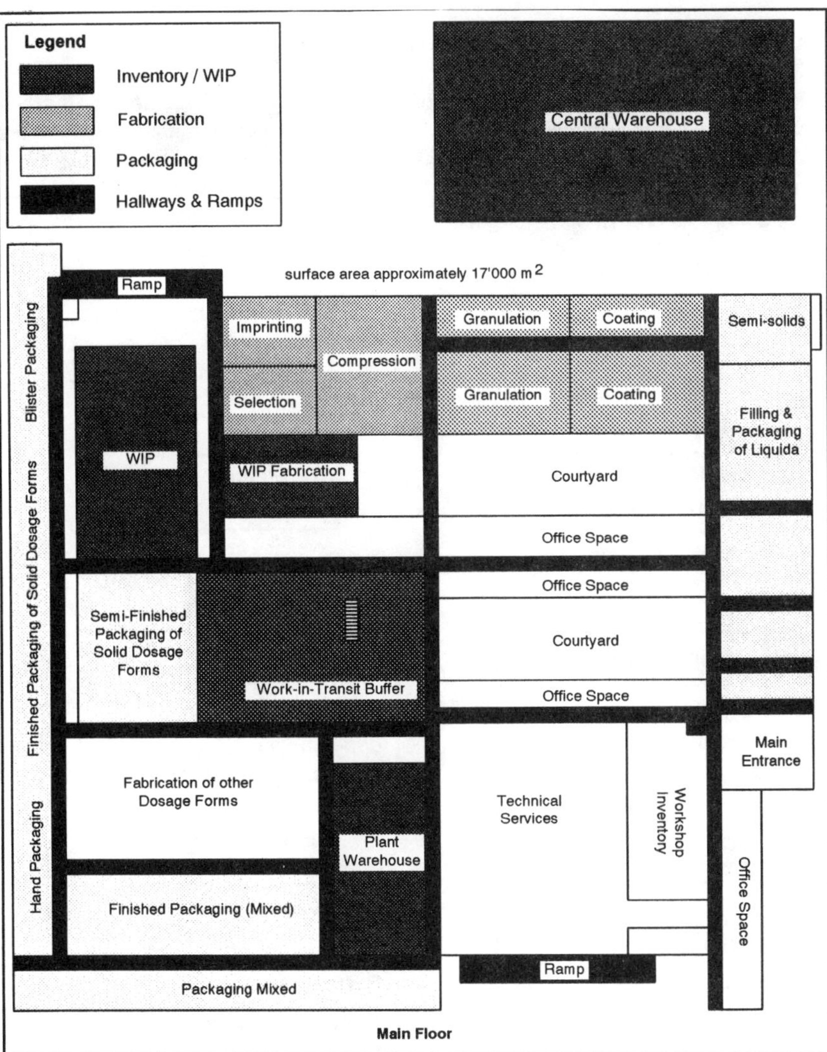

Figure 6.3: Physical Factory Layout of the Stein works. Except for the warehouse, the diagram is drawn to scale. Export packaging is performed in the same building as the central automated warehouse. A smaller manual warehouse is located in the basement of the production building. Quality control has its own building, which is not shown on the diagram. Suppose we take a red string to mark the material flow.

The traditional functional layout, see figure 6.3, and the associated structure of the organization do not align well with the flow of materials or product segments. The layout provides little or no visibility of upward and downward processes. Besides requiring space in the different production areas, work-in-process also occupies further building space as shown in the diagram of the plant layout.

6.3.3 Information Flows and Information Processing

A full description of the central system for materials management and other, associated systems controlling the flow of information and materials would require more space for detailed explanations than is justified here. The analysis will focus on the strengths and weaknesses of the overall system based on the observations made during the course of the project.[62]

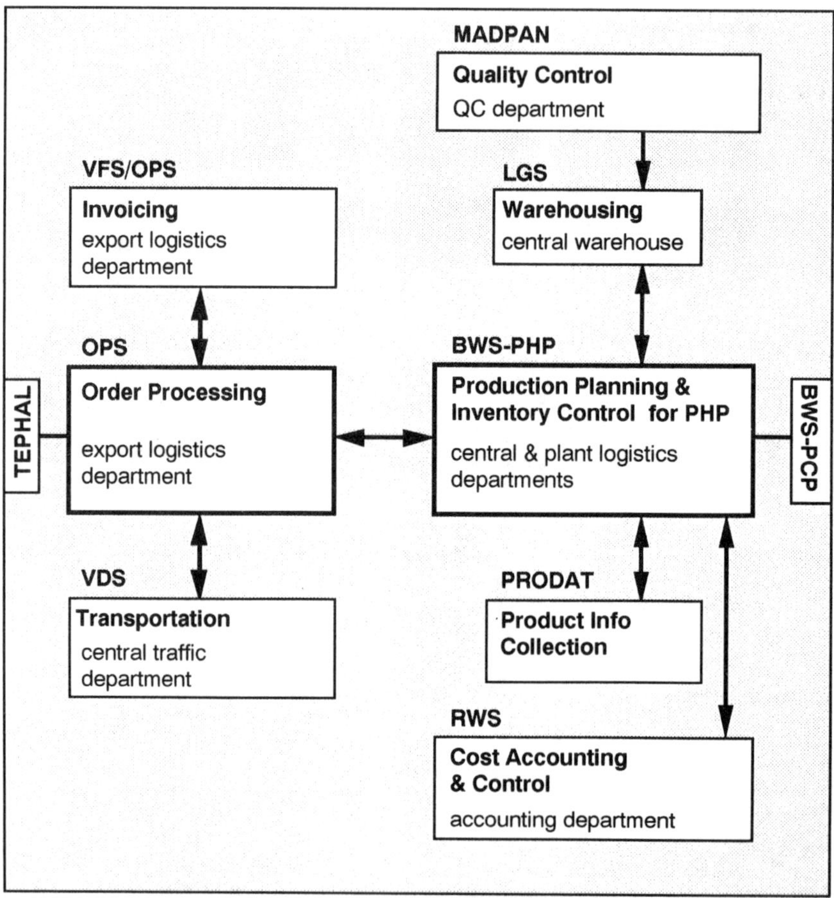

Figure 6.4: Information flows and information processing systems.

A large number of EDP systems, linked to each other by interfaces, support the different departments fulfilling logistics functions. The history of the central materials

62Not being an actual user of the systems, the author's knowledge lacks depth. My comments are, therefore, open to criticism of those more familiar with the specific features of the system.

management system goes back to 1971. It is clear that these systems and their operation collectively represent a major investment of company resources, that requires on-going maintenance and training. This investment covers the knowledge of the staff about the proper use of the planning tools as much as the technical development.

Through the telecommunications system TEPHAL, group company requirements enter the order processing system OPS. These requirements may be actual purchase orders, fixed amounts to be delivered on a due date, or budgets, estimated medium-term demand requirements for certain time intervals. Purchase orders are transferred to the materials management system for pharmaceutical production, BWS-PHP. Periodically, the system nets actual demand against the budget. The rest of the budget is passed on to BWS-PHP for a net requirements calculation. This calculation triggers purchase orders for components such as carton boxes, and production orders for intermediates or active substance if a shortage is projected. BWS-PHP transfers active substance requirements to the materials management system for chemical production, BWS-CHP. In due time, receipts of actual deliveries are transmitted back to BWS-PHP and recorded. The logic used corresponds roughly to the MRP component of the MRP II concept. It involves basic procedures such as explosion of bills of materials, lead time off-setting and requirements netting. BWS-PHP consists of a large number of sub-systems, including a facility for dynamic lot sizing and a rudimentary simulation capability.

Detailed scheduling in fabrication and packaging relies heavily on the expertise of several full-time production planners. The process is entirely manual. Large planning boards for each of the production areas aid this process by giving an overview of planned production orders and the status of work-in-process.

In response to a purchase order, BWS-PHP notifies OPS about the availability of items that are produced to stock. For items that are produced to order, BWS-PHP checks the availability of the components, including intermediates, and releases a production order if these are already available or expected to be delivered in time for production. Upon completion of a production order, the finished product returns to the warehouse, where it is stocked until needed or immediately packed for export. In the latter case, the warehousing system LGS informs the invoicing system VFS/OPS via BWS-PHP about the availability of the export packaged products and the dimensions of the shipment as soon as all items on the order bill are completed. The final step of this sequential order handling process is the arrangement of transportation capacity by the central traffic department via the transportation planning system VDS. Subsequent sections in this chapter analyze the speed of this process and present an alternative information flow concept.

The overall operation of the system requires intensive coordination between the different organizational units that jointly carry the responsibility for logistics. It appears to be functioning well enough to provide a level of service that, as it is defined, is considered to be adequate. Operations continue to be quite hectic. At times, re-scheduling is the rule rather than the exception. Tenders, which represent a small percentage of the business, could well be among the contributing culprits.

Concerns about poor demand forecasts and budgets, shortages of intermediates and packaging materials[63], and delayed transmittals of urgent production orders by the export logistics department frequently surface. In the face of these symptoms, the basic approach has been up and till now to hedge production lead times.

The strength of the overall system lies in the people operating it. On the whole, the level of knowledge, even of the more technical aspects, appears to be sufficient. However, planning staff has to overcome several significant weaknesses of the systems. Although data entry has largely been converted to on-line applications, the basic system relies on batch transactions; this applies in particular to the interfaces between the various systems. The repercussions are visible in several areas. For example, the current lead time for retrieving a packaging component from the automated central warehouse amounts to five working days, which clearly affects the production lead time for packaged products. The largest part of these five days is required for getting the request down to the computer system that controls the crane which physically retrieves the component.

The planning cycle of the materials management system has been reduced from quarterly to monthly intervals over the past years. Monthly intervals still represent a significant delay in the processing and transmittal of production requirements. A request for further increasing the planning frequency was submitted during the course of the project. However, the returns diminish, since the flexibility of the production system needs to improve at the same time.

Although the manufacturing strategy in place in the plant translates into high levels of capacity utilization, the production planning system is on the whole unaware of capacity constraints, let alone able to cope with them. Problems surface[64] at the earliest on the planning board at the detailed scheduling level, which is obviously too late to allow for a timely response. Again, the solution has been to build slack into production lead times, thus giving the scheduler a sufficiently large time frame to smooth out short-term capacity shortages.

Consistent with the focus on capacity utilization and throughput is the lack of regularly reported performance indicators measuring aspects such as conformance to production schedules (reliability), and throughput and lead times. The raw data for such indicators is available in the systems, and could be extracted and aggregated with a modest amount of effort. In general, cross-functional measures directed at improving speed and flexibility will conflict with traditional productivity measures. Today, the systems and procedures successfully hide this conflict.

6.3.4 Tied-up Capital in Stocks and Fixed Assets

The inventory figures quoted in the table 6.1 below cover the logistics chain from the delivery of active substance (AS) to the shipment of fully-packaged products (FP) packaged for export, excluded from the calculations are bulk and semi-packaged products exported directly to the group companies. The inventory

[63]Comparing this observation with the stock levels reported in the section, makes it clear that stocks do not guarantee a high level of service. See section 6.3.4 for further comments.

[64]These problems have so much become a way of life that they are no longer perceived as such.

coverage for BK, SP and FP was determined by taking the average demand and stock level for the previous period of each individual line item. The first column contains the average coverage weighted by volume; the second column contains the simple average over all products. The weighted figures turn out to be consistent with the aggregated, value-based figures computed by the stock reporting system. The non-weighted figures indicate that the inventories at the different levels may in fact be poorly balanced. A few high-volume products with little or no available stock make the standard inventory coverage figures look better than they are. An age profile of the inventories would be the more useful measure for analyzing and controlling inventory levels effectively.

It should be noted that the stock levels for active substances, which are produced by chemical production (CHP), are not under direct control of the Stein works and the export logistics department and thus beyond the scope of the project.

	Inventory Coverage (months of demand)		Tied-up Capital (M. SFr., TPC)
	weighted	non-weighted	
Active Substance (AS)	4.7		16.0
Packaging Material (PM)	5.6		3.0
Bulk (BK)	2.8	3.7	5.0
Semi-Packaged (SP)	1.8	3.1	2.4
Fully-Packaged (FP)	0.4	1.0	2.6
Export-Packaged (EP)	0.7		4.8

Table 6.1: Inventory coverage and capital tied-up in stocks.

The above estimates for tied-up capital in bulk, semi-packaged and fully-packaged products may be as much as 40% too low, since the costs for warehousing, transport, dispensation and utilities are part of overhead in the Stein works and thus not included in the total product costs. Also excluded are financing costs, see §5.8.

The estimate for the corresponding capital investment in equipment for the manufacturing of solid dosage forms is at 32 M.SFr., using current depreciated values. A comparison of this figure with the capital tied-up in stocks in the Stein works—18 M.SFr., excluding AS—that could potentially be reduced by the introduction of just-in-time concepts, makes it clear that even a drastic reduction in the stock levels does not release sufficient capital to justify the required investments in its own right.[65] Besides the obvious costs of stocks, further factors must be taken into account. In addition, the benefits of improved delivery performance in the parent company on stock levels in the group companies play a significant role. The *average* stock level in the group companies corresponds to approximately 2 months of demand. This average includes the group companies with large markets

[65]Illustrations explaining the just-in-time concept typically assume fixed assets to make up the *smallest* share of the balance sheet in a traditional operation. See, for example, [Wildemann 1988, p. 15].

to serve that have their own pharmaceutical production facilities. The estimated demand coverage of stock levels in the group companies served by the Stein works ranges between 3 and 5 months.

An analysis of the stock breakdown for the 14 bulk products going into the largest semi-packaged products shows that safety stocks make up 62% of the total amount of stocks. This number was obtained by first estimating the cycle stock level for each product and then defining the remainder of the total to be safety stock. It is somewhat misleading to refer to these stocks as safety stocks. Surplus stocks could be the more appropriate term. The cycle stock level was computed by taking one half of the average of the campaign sizes over a one year period, i.e. assuming uniform demand. Given that the planning system uses netting and time-phased demand requirements, the figure for cycle stock calculated in this way should be an over-estimate. Therefore, 62% is likely to be a conservative number.

This 'comfortable' safety cushion is the indirect result of high changeover costs and simplistic campaign size optimization techniques which ignore the effects of large campaigns on lead times and lead time variability. It is hardly necessary to use a calculator to determine that these empirical safety stock levels are several times higher than the theoretically optimal level. To put it differently, textbook safety stock formulas are not a good predictor of empirical safety stock levels. A large part of what is called safety stock is in fact surplus stock.

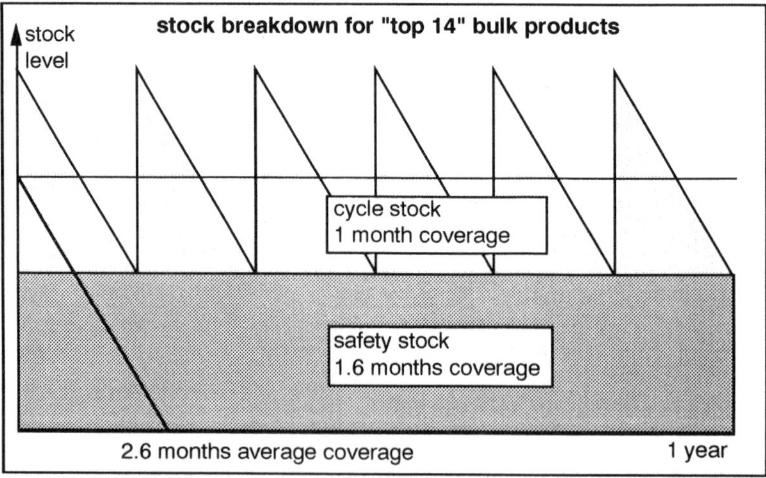

Figure 6.5: Stock breakdown into cycle and safety stock for the 14 bulk products going into the largest semi-packaged products. The average campaign covers 2 months of demand. The remaining stock serves, among other things, to cover demand uncertainties during fluctuating production lead times. However, the present safety stock level is mainly a reflection of the actual performance of policies and procedures for production planning and control.

6.3.5 Value-added Analysis and Overall Flow Time

The value-added curve, shown in figure 6.6a, presents the above figures for inventory coverage at the different levels in a different form. The x-axis marks the accumulated throughput time, or flow time, of the four different stages in pharmaceutical production. The y-axis marks the corresponding accumulated variable and period costs. See [Wildemann 1988a, pp. 177-179]. As noted, the term value-added is being abused. Excluded from the figure are the period costs and the accumulated throughput time for the chemical production of active substance.

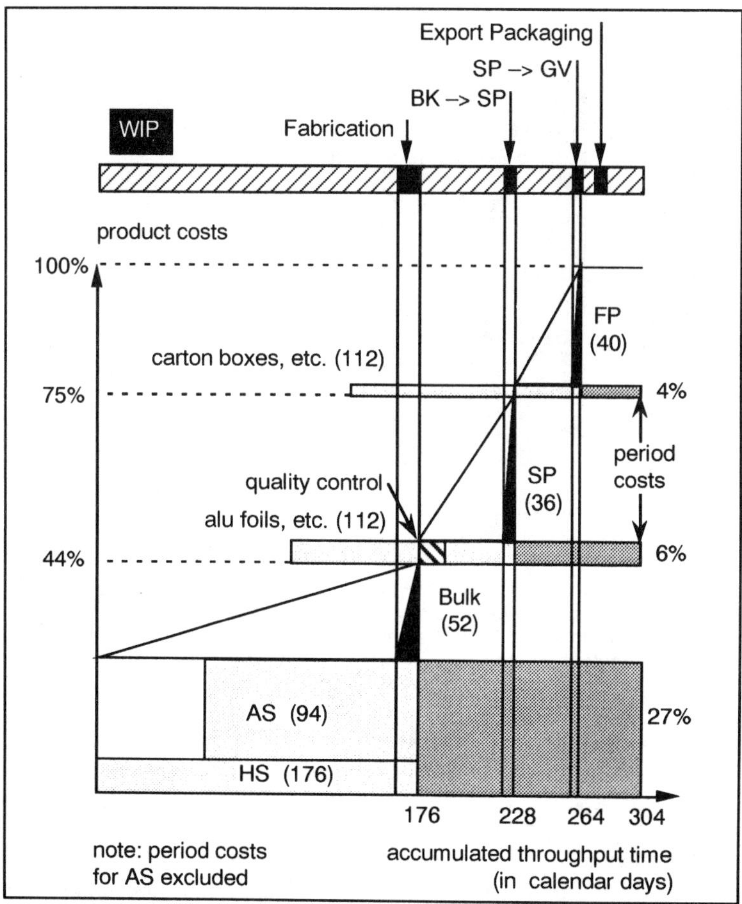

Figure 6.6a: Value-added curve for solid dosage forms covering the delivery of active substance in the Stein works to the shipment of export-packaged products. The shaded bar at the top of the diagram depicts the relation between the amount of dead time and Work-in-Process (WIP) time. Processing time is much less than 50% of WIP time. Product costs exclude those associated with holding stock.

As shown, the ratio between dead time and processing time is extremely poor. Given that processing time makes up much less than 50% of the work-in-process time shown in the figure, this ratio is worse than 20:1. Putting it provocatively, the flow of goods is stocked more than 95% of the time. Since stocks are hidden in an automated central warehouse, it tends not to be seen this way.

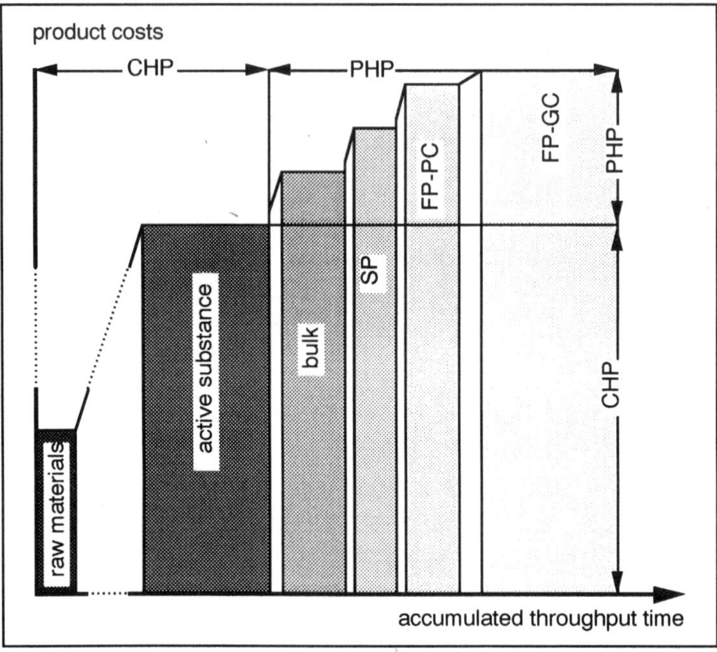

Figure 6.6b: Speculative value-added curve for the entire logistics chain of solid dosage forms. The top right-hand section corresponds to figure 6.6a with the further assumption that the small group companies served by the Stein works have an average coverage of 3 months. The shape of the lower left-hand section, which is determined by the total product costs and the accumulated throughput time in chemical production, will vary with the active substance. Compare with 6.6c.

The preliminary conclusion is that improvement efforts should aim at slashing the times during which no value is added, particularly in the last and apparently slowest part of the supply chain. This will reduce the correspondingly large non-value-added costs that are associated with holding stock. The results on p. 196 show these to be about 25% of total supply chain costs. A prime example of such non-value-added costs are those created by a sophisticated, automated materials handling system required in a traditional factory when production and order quantities are on the decrease and work-in-process clutters the production areas. Investments in larger or faster machines or traditional rationalization strategies that decrease unit production costs are becoming less effective and possibly counter-productive because they tackle the smallest segments of the logistics chain.

When it comes to revising an existing manufacturing strategy the value-added curve may provide the necessary insight. The merit of the value-added curve, which is occasionally put into question, is that it steers away from the pitfalls of these traditional cost cutting strategies by putting the focus on the overall flow of materials—as opposed to individual functions—and its speed; flexibility; and the time value of money. However, we need to know the true costs of holding inventory.

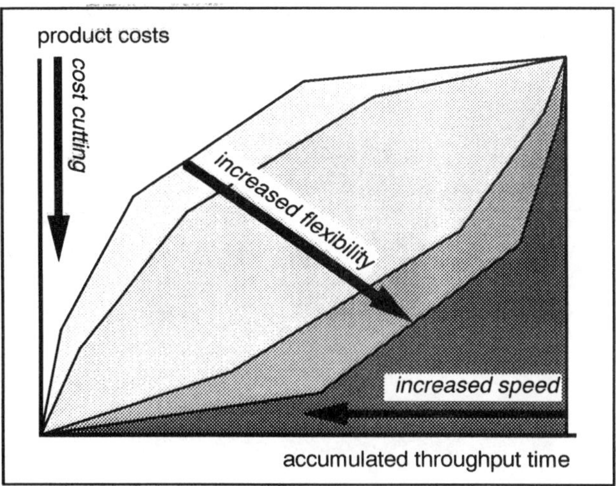

Figure 6.6c: Changing the shape of the value-added curve.

Three basic directions of a manufacturing strategy are illustrated in figure 6.6c. Reducing the accumulated throughput time is not the only way to increase flexibility. By shifting stocks to less specific product stages the ability of the overall system to respond to changes in product mix is greatly improved. Chances of lost business opportunities decrease and financing costs are lower. This strategy will typically also improve the overall speed or be combined with measures improving flexibility and throughput times at the last stages. Moreover, the strategy helps to ensure that the right product is made at the right time. Thus, more effective use is made of resources at the first stages; and product costs may decrease as well.

6.3.6 Order Delivery Times

During the course of the project, two randomly selected samples of one thousand group company orders for fully packaged products were extracted from the order processing system for analysis. The basic results obtained from the samples turned out to be nearly identical. In addition, they are highly consistent with the figures for throughput times and inventory coverage discussed above.

The analysis examines the milestone dates in the life cycle of a group company order. The average amount of time taken between the time the order is entered into the order processing system and its eventual shipment to the group company is ten calendar weeks, with a standard deviation of three weeks. Contained in these ten weeks are three weeks which pass after the orders have been packaged for export in the Stein works until eventual shipment. During this time, an invoice is prepared and the transportation arranged. The order handling activities are strictly sequential. Furthermore, it should be pointed out that an entire order (shipment) will be delayed if only one single item on an order is not produced according to schedule. Orders completed early make up part of the three weeks of lost time after export packaging. The basic results of the analysis are summarized in figure 6.7. A histogram for the order delivery times is displayed in figure 6.8.

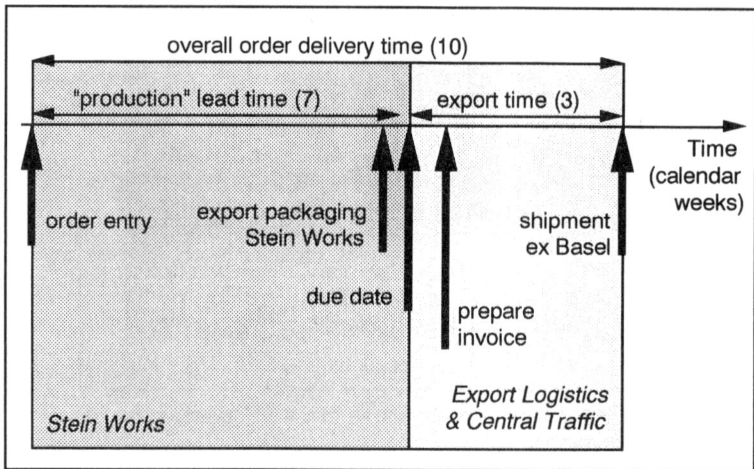

Figure 6.7: Milestones in the life-cycle of group company orders for fully-packaged products.

The current stock policy categorizes end items into whether the orders are to be delivered from stock or produced to order. Interestingly enough, the size and fluctuation of the order delivery times and the due date conformance turned out to be largely independent of this categorization. This indicates that no effective use is made of stocks at the finished product level. Performance is poor across all countries placing orders. For known reasons, the performance for a few special countries is significantly worse. A detailed examination of individual orders revealed that placing orders the last minute may not be a bad policy on the part of the group companies: the due date performance and the time until shipment for a fair number of these 'rush' orders turned out to be above average.

Taking a customer-oriented performance measure such as order delivery time provides valuable insight into the speed and flexibility of the productive system as a whole. Stock levels in the group companies are determined by these order delivery times. Safety stocks must cover the market fluctuations during these long and fluctuating order delivery times. Long planning and forecasting horizons and largely futile attempts to forecast erratic market demand accurately are noteworthy and prevalent side-effects.

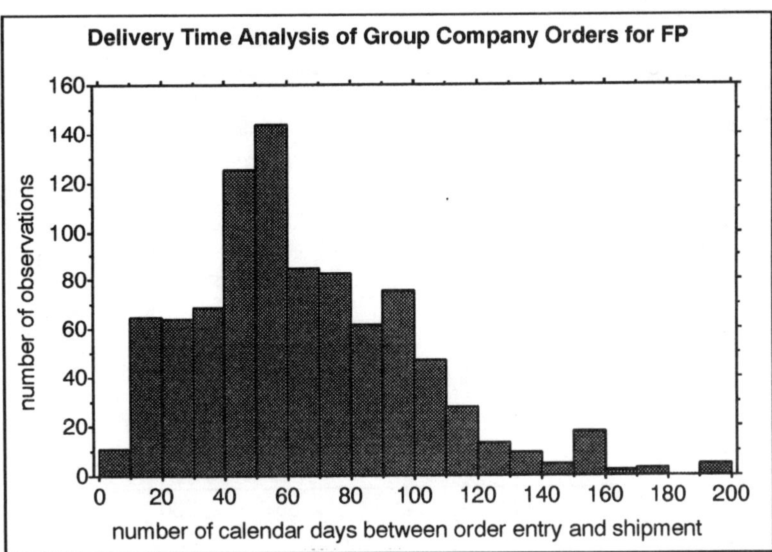

Figure 6.8: Histogram for the overall order delivery times of 1000 randomly selected orders for fully-packaged products. The average time between order entry and shipment is ca. 70 calendar days (10 weeks) with a standard deviation of ca. 20 days (3 weeks). These values also include the effects of the planning cycle in the group companies, approx. 20% of the overall time.

The planned shipment date was not available for performance analysis. Ideally, the performance analysis of a measure such as customer service level shoul use the planned and actual arrival dates at the group company or third party ordering the product. The fact that this cannot be done today, not even by an ad-hoc analysis, is indicative of the present situation.

Besides examining order delivery times, it's worthwhile to take a closer look at the due date performance of production, which can be measured. Figures 6.9a and 6.9b depict, in different ways, the conformance of the actual competition date of export packaging with the planned date. Due date performance might appear to be acceptable. Common definitions of service level with a suitably large tolerance will provide values of 95% and up.

If, however, one tightens up the tolerance and takes into account that several orders may make up a single shipment to the customer, which does not take place until all items are available, then the customer service level will be significantly worse. For example, if the service level for a single order is 96%, then the service level for shipments with 3 orders on average will only be 88.5%. In addition, the subsequent delay until the actual shipment is not only long—3 weeks as shown above—but also subject to fluctuations. A customer service level measure based on planned versus actual shipment or, better, reception of an order will consequently be even lower. This observation is consistent with the high fluctuation of order delivery times. It is of little consolation that export packaging, as shown below, is on average completed three calendar days too early.

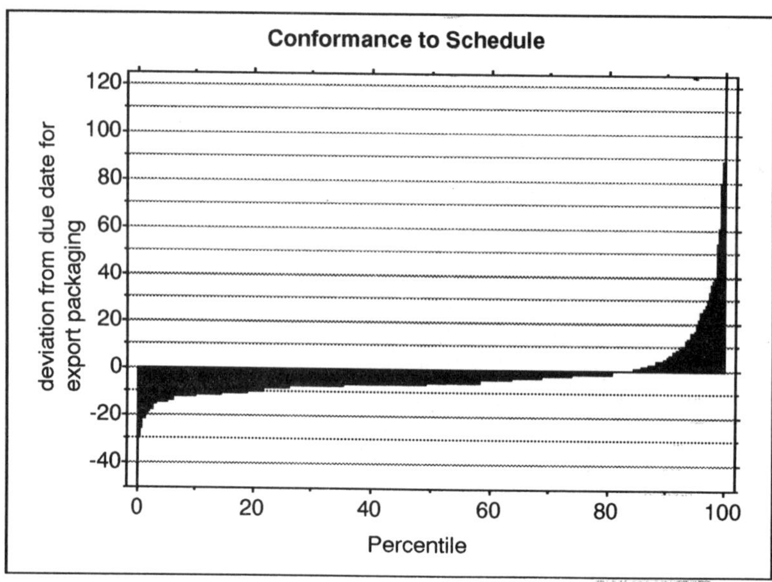

Figure 6.9a: Percentile plot for the deviation from the due date for export packaging for 1000 randomly selected orders. The plot shows that 84% of the orders are packaged for export on or before the planned due date.

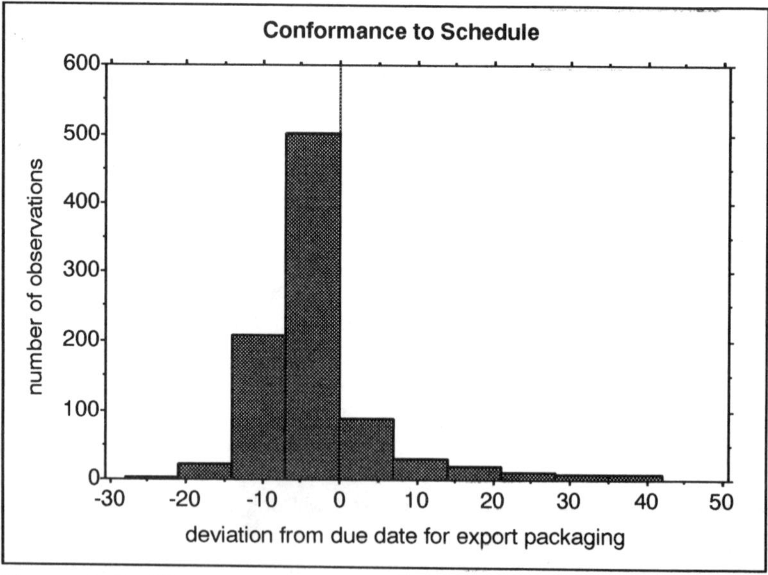

Figure 6.9b: Histogram for the deviation from the due date for export packaging for 1000 randomly selected orders. On average export packaging is completed 3 calendar days early with a standard deviation of 13 days. Note how skewed the distribution is.

6.3.7 Equipment Flexibility and Capacity Utilization

One key dimension of equipment flexibility is changeover time. The importance of reducing changeover times will increase as job sizes decrease. Due to the simple fact that there are a lot more production orders in packaging than there are campaigns in fabrication, changeover time reduction carries a different weight in the two production areas. There appears to be less opportunity for improving changeover times in fabrication: washing down a granulation room and the equipment is a straightforward manual activity. In packaging, changeover time is basically setup time; cleanup is insignificant in comparison. In case of a change of format, the changeover performed is a major setup. The amount of time will depend among other things on whether all dimensions of the pack need adjusting on the machine. A major setup almost certainly requires a technician. The changeover is a minor setup in case of a change of active ingredient—a different product but the same size of tablet or blister pack—or a mere change of production order.

Detailed data on interrupts, actual processing and changeover times is collected and recorded on a regular basis for the work centers in fabrication and packaging, see figure 6.10. The reporting concentrates on the capacity utilization of the equipment. There is no standard report that shows the average amount of time required for major and minor setups per job and work center, let alone the trend in these two values. Moreover, the data required to determine the breakdown of changeover time into different activities is not available. Analyzing this breakdown is an important first step for reducing changeover times, see for example [Hall 1983, pp. 85-111]. For instance, going through the packaging department one will regularly find a work center that is waiting for a major setup to be performed. Is this waiting time part of the changeover time? Should changeovers be scheduled and when does the changeover team take its breaks? It has been the experience of many companies that they can achieve significant reductions in changeover times by taking a closer look at the different activities making up the changeover process and improving upon the conventional procedures and organization.

In connection with changeover times, it should be mentioned that the mix of orders is sometimes very poor for work centers in packaging. Fast and expensive machines with complicated setups are also used to package relatively small orders, see figures 6.11a and 6.11b. Older and slower machines should be kept and dedicated to these small jobs. Recently, management of the packaging department came to recognize that the decision to sell off two older machines after a new and fast machine with enough capacity to cover the load had an unexpected price tag attached. A comparison of figures 6.11a and 6.11b shows that there is a policy in place that puts the smaller jobs to older machines. Unfortunately, these may not be the most flexible either.

At the time of the investigation the age of the twenty six equipment items in use for packaging solid dosage forms averaged 16 years. In comparison, the cost accounting system depreciates the equipment over ten years. The conclusion that either the useful economic is more like thirty years or the investment in new equipment is not keeping pace suggests itself. The average age of the equipment is consistent with the focus on period costs in production.

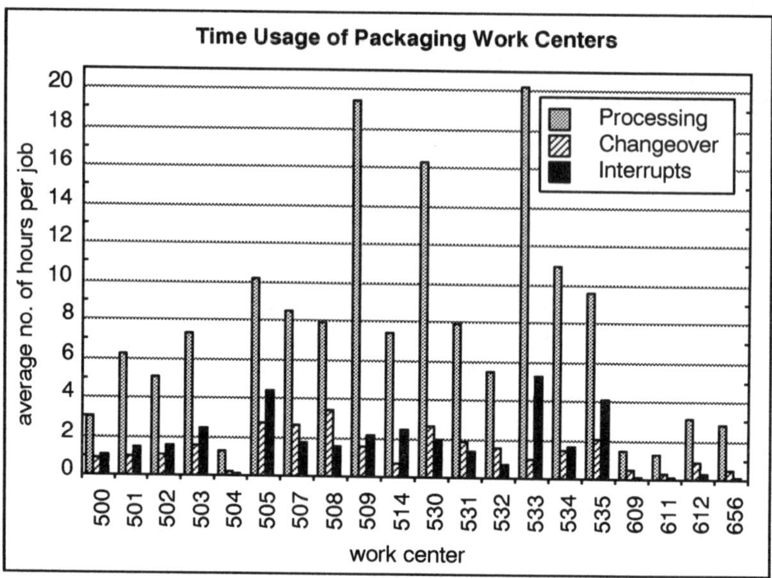

Figure 6.10: Processing and changeover times, as well as interrupts per job for packaging work centers. Changeover times are an average of the hours required for minor and major setups. As the job size, and hence the processing time, decreases changeover times will consume more of the overall available time. Some interrupts are directly related to changeovers. On average changeover time makes up 13%, while interrupts make up 16%.

A further consequence of tight control of production period costs is that utilization, at least in terms of planned available hours, is on the whole very high. This holds both for fabrication and for packaging, but not uniformly so across all work centers. High capacity utilization, as already noted, leads to longer queue times that must be built into production lead times. In addition, it means that the overall system has little or no flexibility to respond to volume changes and, to a lesser degree, to product mix changes. The lead time for packaging orders includes five working days that allow the production scheduler enough leeway to sequence production jobs in view of reducing total changeover time. Given the focus on capacity utilization, the amount of capacity wasted on interrupts, see figure 6.10, appears to be surprisingly high. An opportunity for making more of the existing capacity available is manifest.

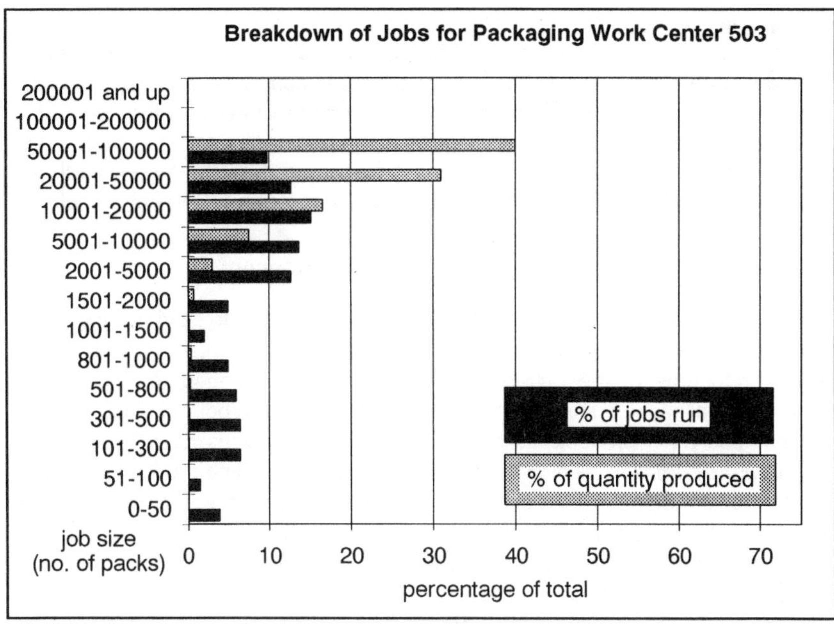

Figure 6.11a: Breakdown by job size for WC 503, acquired in 1973. Statistics for 1987: 204 jobs; 2.7 million packs; process time: 7.3 hours/job; cost 24 Sfr./ hour.

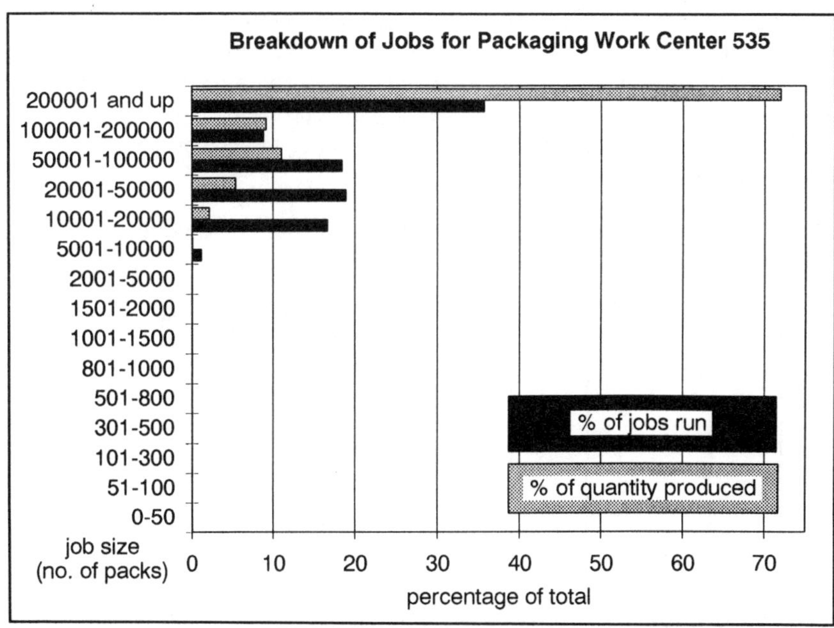

Figure 6.11b: Breakdown by job size for WC 535, acquired in 1987. Statistics for 1987: 168 jobs; 21.2 million packs; process time: 9.6 hours/job; cost 115 Sfr./hour.

The primary conclusion about the impact of the focus on capacity utilization draws on the characteristic shape of the value-added curve and the explosion of the product tree. Together with the changing market conditions and requirements, these put a question mark behind the appropriateness of the *de facto* manufacturing strategy. Additional 'surplus' capacity in packaging, providing the necessary flexibility and speed in that part of the supply chain that is closest to the market, is one element of an alternative that will be presented in the next section.

6.4 The Way Forward: A Threefold Solution Concept

Based on the analysis of the present situation with respect to solid dosage forms and the objectives set for the project, a threefold proposal containing most of the major components of the just-in-time concept was developed. The proposed segmentation eliminates stock holding at two intermediate product stages, leaving only semi-packaged products as an intermediate. Order sizes for fully-packaged products are so small in relation to bulk batch sizes that on-line production without any intermediate being held in stock is not viable. The proposed concept not only addresses manufacturing and material flows, but also the order processing by the logistics department. It excludes, however, quality control and the purchasing of packaging materials from the first phases. Three sub-projects are the result.

Both the benefits and the disadvantages of having three, simpler sub-projects were recognized at the outset. The project team felt that the risks entailed in not viewing each component as an integral part of the whole and evaluating the economics of the strategy accordingly were compensated by the benefits of simpler project management and higher chances of eventual implementation. Nevertheless, the team pointed out the need for adopting a consolidated point of view to account for the reduced stock levels in the group companies.

The final two sub-sections of this section summarize the potential impact of the strategy and the actual outcome.

6.4.1 On-line production of Semi-Packaged Products directly from Active Substance

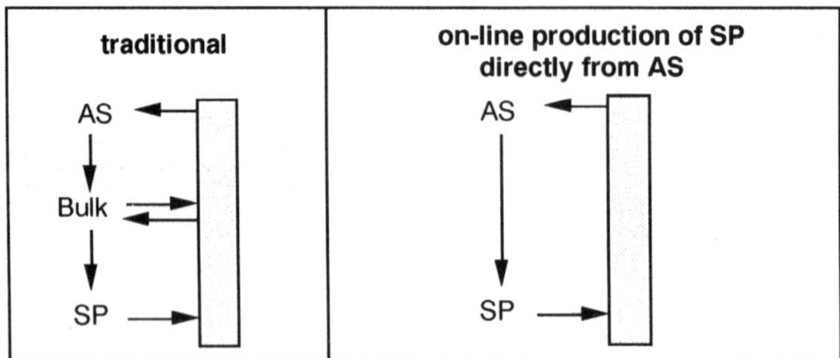

Figure 6.12a: On-line production of semi-packaged products directly from active substance without intermediate storage of bulk products.

The first sub-project, headed by the line manager directly responsible for fabrication, calls for the on-line fabrication of a selected class of semi-packaged products to be produced directly from active ingredients, as illustrated in 6.12a. The major elements of the concept are:

- apply the concept to class A semi-packaged products only
- produce classes B and C, and Bulk Export (BKX) on existing equipment
- invest in smaller equipment and reduced changeover times, especially in fabrication
- perform semi-finished packaging immediately after fabrication without putting bulk products into storage
- perform fabrication and packaging in close physical proximity
- continue to use simple materials handling and transportation
- segment the machinery and equipment into production lines if possible, use a pool concept otherwise
- produce to stock in small campaign sizes
- perform quality control in parallel with packaging
- invest in 'autonomation' in quality control to reduce setup and variable costs

It should be stressed that the wisdom of the concept hinges on the idea that it should be applied to fast movers (class A) only. Slower movers should still be produced from the bulk level and exploit the pooling effect. The idea is to obtain a very substantial improvement in the speed for 80% of the volume, resulting in a nearly equal overall improvement.

6.4.2 On-line Production of Export-Packaged Products directly from Semi-Packaged Products

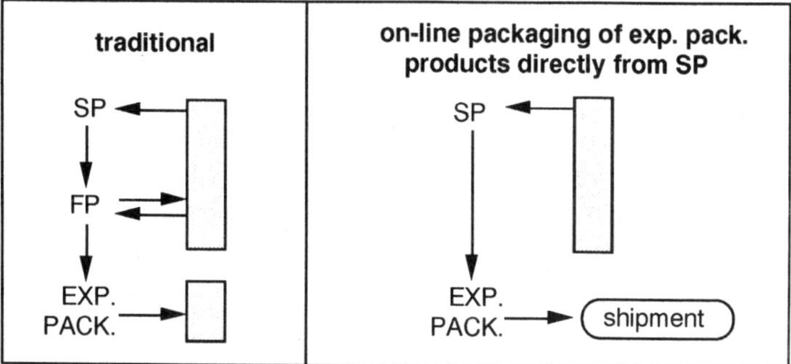

Figure 6.12b: On-line packaging of export packaged products directly from semi-packaged products without the intermediate storage of fully-packaged products; the concept is similar to the one for the on-line fabrication of semi-finished products, but significantly different in its details.

The second sub-project, headed by the manager in charge of packaging and warehousing, calls for the fabrication of export packaged products directly from the semi-packaged level, as illustrated in figure 6.12b. The basic idea of the first sub-project is applied to the final two stages in packaging: no storage of the intermediate, which in this case is a fully-packaged product. The major differences are that production is to order, not to stock, and that the selection of the products that come into question is determined by the composition of shipments. The elements of the basic concept[66] are to:

- package semi-packaged products directly for export for as large a segment of all shipments as possible
- process remaining customer orders with non-standard order sizes by unpacking export-packaged boxes and using up opened export-packaged boxes kept in stock
- standardize production order quantities to a certain minimum size or multiple thereof
- design a new collection of re-dimensioned boxes for export-packaged products with the objective of minimizing the extent of unpacking, while taking into account the standard production order quantities and the dimensions of fully-packaged products[67]
- reduce the number of line items on orders
- use partial shipments whenever a delay in shipment threatens
- invest in additional smaller and more flexible equipment
- invest in a setup reduction programme to achieve significant improvements with existing equipment
- perform export packaging immediately after fully-finished packaging
- perform export and fully-finished packaging in close physical proximity, possibly in the central warehouse
- continue to use simple materials handling and transportation
- operate the system like a flexible manufacturing system
- produce to order
- use scheduling to synchronize the completion of the export packaging of different line items on an order
- apply the concept to all dosage forms, i.e. do not restrict it to solid dosage forms; perhaps, exclude certain countries that require special order treatment in packaging and the export logistics department

It was recognized at the outset that a number of significant aspects would need to be addressed in detail to assess the feasibility of the basic concept. As it stands, the concept involves a wide range of different organizational, procedural and technical

[66]The concept as presented here is a refined version of the original concept. It reflects the additional insight obtained in the complexities of the packaging process during the second phase of the project.

[67]This is a classical and difficult OR problem. Most recently it was addressed at the joint OR conference of the German, Swiss and Austrian OR societies held in Vienna, August 1990.

issues. It hardly needs saying that the actual implementation of the two proposed concepts requires skilled project management and a major investment of human resources: only a highly-qualified and motivated interdisciplinary team can circumvent the obstacles and eventually accomplish the task.

6.4.3 Parallel Activities for Order Processing in Export Logistics

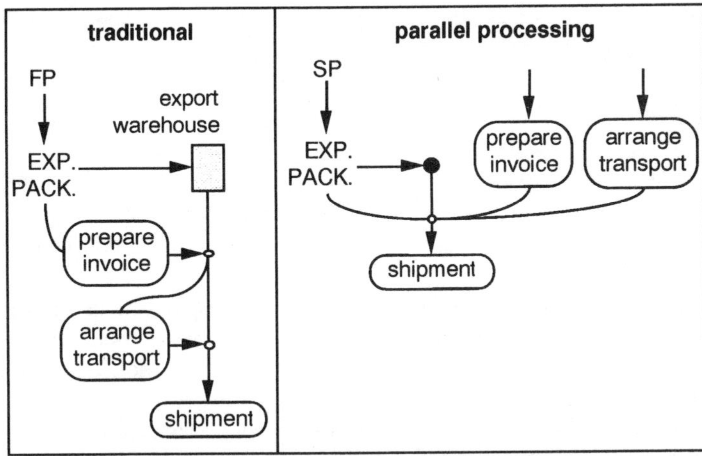

Figure 6.12c: Parallel processing in the administrative area. The basic and simple idea is to perform the order handling activities no longer sequentially but in parallel instead, thereby reducing the current time of three weeks that passes after export packaging has been completed.

The third sub-project, led by the head of the export logistics department, calls for parallel processing in the administrative area. It concerns the coordination of activities of several departments. As shown in figure 6.12c, the traditional flow of information is sequential. After export packaging has been completed, the product enters the separate export warehouse and doesn't leave it until after invoicing and transportation have been arranged. This projects aims to achieve a drastic cut in the three weeks that export packaged products presently spend in the export warehouse waiting to be shipped.

The major elements of the seemingly simple concept are to:

- carry out export packaging, invoicing and the arrangement of transportation in parallel: a group company order triggers the start of three activities
- coordinate these activities so that finished product can be shipped immediately after export packaging without storage in the export warehouse
- achieve a very high level of conformance to schedule in packaging

The alternative to this concept is to (sub-)optimize each individual activity. This sub-project easily qualifies as the "low-hanging fruit." A relatively small investment is required with which a major improvement in performance can be achieved.

6.4.4 Impact of the proposed concept

The major and perhaps most difficult preliminary task at hand centers around the assessment of the potential impact of the proposed threefold strategy. A number of direct benefits are immediately apparent:

- drastically reduced throughput and lead times
- rapid response to group company orders
- reduced inventory related costs in the parent as well as the group companies
- substantially less and simpler materials handling and transport
- less administration and simpler coordination in the area of production planning

In addition, indirect benefits should result: quality improvements, less material damage and waste, shorter planning and forecasting horizons, which will make the system as whole a less susceptible to overshoots, i.e. less nervous, in the face of medium-term demand fluctuations.

One of the consequences of realizing the proposed concept is that it may no longer be necessary to invest in an automated materials handling and transport system since the proposed concept will significantly reduce the overall volume to be moved in and out of the central warehouse. An automation project addressing this issues is already on the drawing board. Projects of this kind give an indication of the cost of maintaining the *status quo.* An important management decision is on the agenda: should a major investment be made in that part of the overall production process that does not add value to our products? Or, alternatively, is it more opportune to focus on the part which does add value and increase the responsiveness of the system, i.e. invest in smaller and more flexible equipment? These questions will resurface.

To obtain the above benefits, a number of investments are essential, particularly also in fabrication and, as the subsequent analysis revealed, in quality control. For example, granulation rooms setup to process smaller batches efficiently are required. Traditional unit production costs are likely to increase. Smaller batch sizes place an additional load on quality control and dispensation. A related and still open question concerns manpower requirements and flexibility.

Several important questions remain. These concern the economics of the proposed solution concept. First of all, what are the financial benefits? Second, how large are the required investments? Third, are the benefits large enough to justify these investments? Fourth, what is the strategic impact of a time-based productive and logistics system that is coupled more closely with the markets consuming its products? Senior plant management, including the director, expressed their justifiable concerns and skepticism about the first three questions on numerous occasions. Proving the economics was, therefore, turned into a major issue.

It is interesting to compare this observation with the results of a survey carried by Wildemann [1988b, pp. 254-277] on key problems experienced with the implementation of just-in-time concepts. Out of a total of seven potential problems the proof of the economic benefits rates second to last in importance. Resistance to change due to a lack of understanding of the issues, personnel qualifications and retraining, assessment of time and resource requirements for project planning, availability of project sponsors willing to promote the concept actively, and technical problems all rate higher in Wildemann's survey.

6.4.5 The Aftermath: An Initial Assessment

From the time that this section is being written, it is eighteen months ago that the threefold concept was first put forward. It is perhaps too early to formulate a definitive judgement on the results achieved to-date. In view of the author, the progress that was made has been slow in coming. Looking back, it is would be too easy to attribute this to the lack of applicable training and education in the basics of the just-in-time concept. Enthusiasm and what now seems an overdose of naivety on the part of the author were at the root of this failure in project management.

Notwithstanding this, the objectives of the second project phase, which were to assess the feasibility of the three sub-projects and to perform a cost-benefit analysis, have been met. This section summarizes the conclusions of the project teams and comments on the results obtained.

The detailed evaluation of the concept "on-line production of SP directly from AS," which was restricted to the twenty semi-packaged products with the largest sales volume in terms of their TPC value, representing about 60% of the total volume of solid dosage forms, lead to the following conclusions:

- given the products and mix selected, it is necessary to construct a new production building; the volume is too small to free up a significant number of equipment items, and hence also space, from the existing factory
- unit production costs are calculated to be about 50% higher with the just-in-time concept
- however, 65% of this difference in unit production costs results from the hourly rates for the new equipment, which are about twice that of comparable, but depreciated equipment in the existing factory
- the savings in directly affected inventory costs—elimination of bulk and significant reduction in SP products—, materials handling and planning & control costs cover less than a third of the additional production costs
- smaller batch sizes and shorter throughput times demanded from quality control result in a threefold increase in quality control costs under the assumption that the way of carrying out quality tests is left unchanged—see §7.3.1 for some comments on current investments in setup time reduction and 'autonomation' in quality control which have reduced the setup time for an important test from hours to less than 10 minutes

- the pool concept—see §7.3.2 for a detailed analysis—as opposed to independent lines is best for the small volume
- variable batch sizes should be taken into consideration
- a larger segment as well as a more suitable and narrower product mix must be selected to justify the anticipated investment

In consideration of the uncertainty about the anticipated changes in the overall product mix for the Stein works, resulting from a major restructuring of the European production concept for the 1990's, the project was stalled. In its recommendations, the project team stressed that the proposed project should be integrated in the overall conceptual framework for future manufacturing in the EEC.

At a present, another project team is evaluating a modified and scaled-down version of the proposed on-line concept in a different area of production. The basic idea is to eliminate storage of the intermediate by planning two consecutive product stages to be run simultaneously. The decision about which variant of the second stage to produce is left to the latest possible point in time.

A more detailed analysis carried out by the author supplied the basic quantitative input for some of the cost-benefit calculations quoted above. ProfiSEE was the obvious tool to use. The in-depth simulation study of the proposed concept showed that average production throughput times of seven calendar days can in fact be achieved, while maintaining an adequate utilization of the major work centers. As can been seen from figure 6.6a, this is roughly *ten times faster* than the time currently required by material to flow from AS to SP. The study also provided a quantitative assessment of the anticipated daily load on quality control; and the impact of shifts, in combination with the mandatory drying between some stages in fabrication, on throughput times.

The detailed simulation model consisted of the three basic input components required by ProfiSEE, as described at length in chapter 4:

- precise product specifications for each one of the selected top twenty products, see figure 6.13 for an example of one of the simplest product specifications
- a layout specification, including WIP buffers, quality control and auxiliary resources
- a representative quarterly production plan based on the small batch and campaign sizes selected and the projected quarterly demand for 1990-1994

Each one of the top twenty products selected was run independently through the factory to eliminate the effects of any interaction with other products competing for the same equipment. The flowcharts generated by these runs determined the throughput time that could theoretically be achieved. Several simulation runs of the quarterly production plan provided a realistic throughput time estimate. Because of the use of the pool concept, it turned out to be cumbersome to generate a detailed plan with no deadlocks and an acceptable number of conflicting resource requirements. Forty campaigns to shift around generate plenty of combinations. The

VIPS component of ProfiSEE now addresses precisely these conflicts. As indicated by the example product specification shown in figure 6.13, kanban-like flow control was not implemented in the simulation logic. The use of the pull concept would have significantly reduced the need for manipulating the production plan.

The general case for a detailed simulation study was argued in chapters 3 and 4; it will not be repeated here. Two specific aspects that justify the effort deserve mentioning. First, a large number of the products in the selected product mix require drying from 8 to 16 hours after some of the steps in fabrication. The degree to which drying time affects the throughput time depends on the number of shifts that the factory is to operate. A 24-hour operation will not perform as well as might be expected. Simulation helps to answer the question whether a second or third shift will bring the desired benefits. Second, simulation shows the impact of a container cleaning station on the total number of containers in circulation. Typically, the operating hours and capacity of such a station are kept low to ensure high utilization. This may be counter-productive: it increases the number of containers required. Special containers such as flo-bins are surprisingly expensive. Queues at the cleaning station may also cause interruptions of the material flow in the production process. Simulation provides the necessary visibility of such problems.

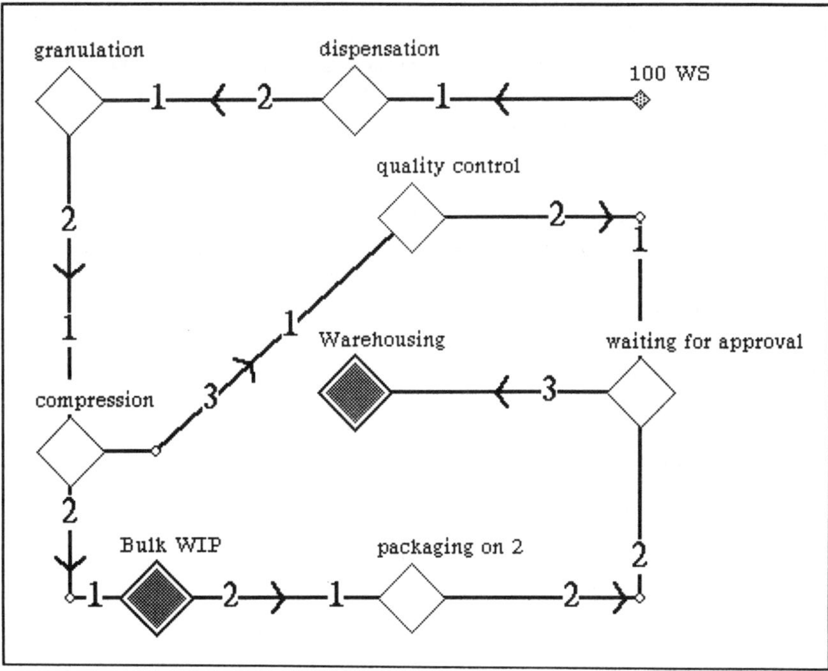

Figure 6.13: Example product specification in ProfiSEE for a Tegretol tablet, one of the simplest of the top twenty products selected for the analysis of the proposed concept. Note that the steps quality control and packaging are parallel to each other.

The detailed evaluation of the concept "on-line production of export-packaged products directly from SP" and the analysis of the composition of shipments to the group companies lead to the following quantitative results:

- class A products cover 75% of the 72 million FP boxes packed and 45% of the 19'000 orders shipped in 1989
- order sizes, either by product or by country, vary widely
- for these class A products only 11 of the 80 different boxes for export packaging are needed
- 50% of all export boxes shipped contain more than one different product
- the extra large export box currently in favor for some countries will increasingly have to be filled with padding material

In its report the project team concludes that a number of prerequisites first need to be satisfied in order to achieve a significant reduction in the overall packaging throughput time:

- the present on-line EDP systems which rely on batch transactions must be replaced by integrated 'real-time' EDP systems to reduce the time required to retrieve packaging components from currently five days to less than 24 hours
- the materials management system must the capability of planning packaging variants to cope with the different export boxes, otherwise the administrative and planning work cannot be kept at a tolerable level

Unfortunately, the project team had little incentive to go beyond the stage of recognizing and formulating the obstacles. For example, setup time reduction and the design of a new collection of export boxes, which are important and difficult issues, did not receive the amount of attention necessary for developing a constructive proposal.

The third sub-project, which focuses on the concept "parallel activities for order processing in export logistics," is most likely to deliver the expected benefits with small investment of resources and effort. Although the feasibility study also took its share of elapsed time, a detailed design for the sequencing of the numerous information and material processing activities, developed by the export logistics department in cooperation with the central traffic department, was recently tested on a small scale in practice with encouraging results. The target of shipping orders within 48 hours after export packaging is now considered to be realistic.

The positive results that can be expected to come out this sub-project lead to the observation that significant improvements can be obtained by addressing informations flows and information handling, an area where the casual observer might be inclined to have the lowest expectations. The use of electronic information processing systems and the belief in their efficiency probably lets one lose sight of the effectiveness of the information handling process.

7 QED at Work: Applying the Approach

Everything flows,
but deep rivers slowly.

7.1 Introduction and Outline

Without this chapter, this thesis would not deserve its title. It is an important chapter. By demonstrating the application of the rough-cut financial model QED, developed in chapter 5, to the industrial case, described and analyzed in chapter 6, this chapter quantifies and assesses the economics of speed. This demonstration is a purpose in itself: the application of QED helps to verify its logic.

The analysis investigates the strength of the links between, on the one hand, several low-level decision variables, which have the desirable property that they can be influenced directly by management and easily measured, and, on the other hand, high-level financial performance measures. This should to some extent rectify the shortcomings of the assessment of the just-in-time concept up and till this point, which has largely been qualitative. Of course, any quantitative analysis requires its qualitative counterpart. A clear understanding of the interplay of the different elements of a complex system is a prerequisite.

Although the experiments and their analysis cover a substantial number of very different aspects of the industrial case discussed in chapter 6, it would be more than pretentious to call it comprehensive. Broad generalizations—tempting as they may be—are unwarranted. Fortunately, several interesting conclusions that shine light on the just-in-time concept as applied in this case, can be and are drawn in the discussions following each set of experiments in this chapter. The final chapter summarizes and discusses the business implications of these conclusions and specifically their strategic impact.

To fulfill the primary purpose of this chapter, the basic data and characteristics of the empirical research object, see §6.3, and the alternative solution based on just-in-time principles, see §6.4, serve as a starting point for a comparative financial analysis. The present situation of this pharmaceutical fabrication and packaging plant, referred to as the CLASSIC case, is subjected to an in-depth comparison with its just-in-time counterpart. PURE JIT is the label for the standard and most radical just-in-time case. Also of interest are two pragmatic variants of PURE JIT. The results are particularly relevant for industrial practice, as they address the two most costly aspects of the radical variant of the concept. The experimental results are presented in §7.3. It is a lengthy one because of the numerous graphs depicting the results. Since the general focus is on the *economics* of speed, the impact of cost-based factors receives special attention in a separate sub-section.

The analysis as performed in this chapter assumes a clean sheet, i.e. the decision is simply to implement either the CLASSIC or the JIT manufacturing system. This, of course, circumvents a prime managerial dilemma: what to do if an operation of the type CLASSIC is already in place? This dilemma is addressed—not resolved—in §8.3.

The features of the model's inputs and its scope are such that the specific conclusions presented derive from a sound basis. This applies, for example, to the product and process characteristics of the case. The different scenarios cover four representative product segments in solid dosage forms and include the top 18 class A products at the semi-packaged level. The scope of the model covers distribution to the group companies as well as inventory control in the group companies. As expected, the outcome of the analysis proves this to be a crucial feature. The next section describes the specific structure, scope and parameters of the model.

7.2 Specific Structure, Scope and Parameters of the Model

This section describes in detail a specific instance—strictly speaking two instances—of the conceptual model underlying QED. It therefore revisits and reviews some of the material discussed earlier. Described in the next three sub-sections are the structure and scope of the specific application of QED, its decision variables and exogenous parameters.[68] Section 7.2.4 contains the specific input values for the two basic alternatives. QED's financial output panel for a specific set of input values is shown and described in §7.2.5.

7.2.1 Structure and Scope

The structure of QED, as implemented in an electronic spreadsheet, is summarily displayed in figure 7.1. It closely corresponds to the conceptual model described in chapter 5. The logic of this model is uniformly applied to the last three production stages—fabrication, including quality control, and two levels of packaging—in the pharmaceutical manufacturing process and the final distribution stage. The model represents the tail end of the supply chain. Its covers the fabrication of solid dosage forms from active substance to the delivery of fully-packaged products stocked in the group companies to the local customers.

QED models three relevant elements of the overall manufacturing process in less detail than the basic production and distribution stages:

- The planning process for raw material acquisition is excluded from the model. Instead, the estimated stock coverage for raw materials is an input to QED.
- Quality control of bulk products is not, as assumed by QED, a simple single stage process. It involves a series of processes and activities.
- Export packaging should in principle be treated like the other two stages in packaging. It requires its own equipment items.

[68]This distinction is as far as some model parameters is concerned an arbitrary one. For example, product volume and mix are discussed under the heading of exogenous parameters. Since certain product segments can be allocated to different international supply points, these exogenous parameters are in fact decision variables. QED lends itself to the analysis of a series of interesting questions that are posed in the context of the design and implementation of a new supply chain management concept that should take advantage of the opportunities offered by the current developments in the EEC. See §6.2.

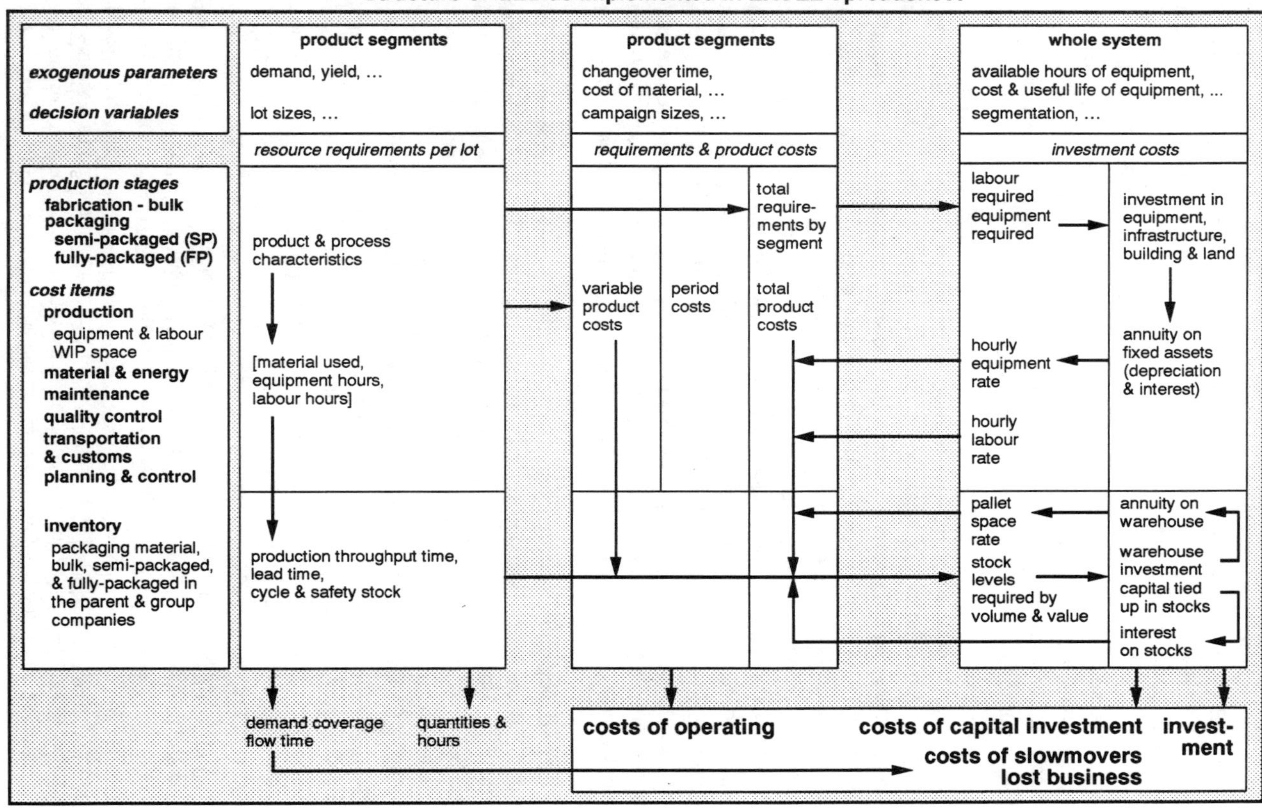

Figure 7.1: QED Structure.

As shown in figure 7.1, QED calculates for each stage and product segment the consumption of resources—manpower, materials and machines—and the required fixed assets for production. Similarly, it calculates the stock levels at each stage. To determine the amount of capital tied up in inventory, QED also needs to calculate the total product costs (TPC) for each product and level. To avoid confusion, it might have been better to use the term total manufacturing product costs. In CIBA–GEIGY's cost accounting system, for example, the values for TPC exclude a number of cost items that QED includes, in particular the cost of capital—i.e. the financing cost. The case study "Nippon vs Erewhon" has justified this approach for the sake of this kind analysis. The hourly equipment rate as calculated by QED, therefore, depends on the annuity, which covers depreciation and interest. This rate, together with the labour rate and the unit cost of materials, sets the production share of TPC.

The second share accounts for the costs that are the consequence of holding inventory. These consist of the costs of the capital investment in warehouse space, the interest on tied-up capital in inventory valued at TPC, the costs of planning and control, and, finally, materials handling and internal transportation. The final distribution stage to the group companies incurs distribution costs, which in turn, consist of the costs for external transportation (freight charges, including insurance) and customs duties.

It should be emphasized that TPC only serves to value inventory accurately and correctly. It does not determine the operating costs. The costs of the capital investment are derived directly from the fixed asset base. They are independent of the utilization of the equipment. Thus, QED avoids the pitfalls of varying degrees of absorption of fixed costs. For interest sake, QED does calculate the absorption rate.

QED assesses two further items worth mentioning here. The costs of slow- and no-movers are estimated on the basis of the slow-mover percentage, which as described in §5.3, is taken to be a quadratic function of the inventory coverage, the TPC value of the product stage, and the additional costs incurred by slow-movers. QED assesses the costs of lost business in a similar fashion. The percentage of lost business is taken as a quadratic function of the accumulated inventory coverage, i.e. flow time. For this item, QED uses the profit margin of the product to calculate the cost of lost business.

QED calculates and reports all cost on an annual basis. The cost of the capital investment in equipment therefore reflects the average annual cost over the useful economic life of the investment. It is comparable to the rental value of the investment. For the same reason, the performance factor takes fixed assets at half their acquisition cost.

In summary, QED accounts for the costs of the four M's: manpower, materials, machines and money. The time value of money is a critical element of the economics of speed. As discussed in section on the case "Nippon vs Erewhon," QED also discounts a part of the sales income in relation to the flow time, i.e. the speed at which assets and the products coming out of R&D are converted into income. As the experimental results will show, if the analysis ignores the time value of money, then the financial case for a just-in-time manufacturing system is lost. All that remains are strategic arguments pointing out the competitive advantages of more rapid and reliable delivery service. These are woolly because hard empirical data supporting these arguments and quantifying the benefits is not available.

7.2.2 Decision Variables

The basic decision variables, or areas, that distinguish the CLASSIC case from PURE JIT and its variants are listed in figure 7.2. The figure also categorizes the decision variables to show that the pertinent decisions affect a broad and varied range of activities. The standard numerical values for the decision variables in the cases CLASSIC and JIT are supplied in the tables contained in §7.2.4.

The vertical segmentation for CLASSIC and PURE JIT stem from the descriptions in §6.3 and §6.4, respectively. PURE JIT, furthermore, uses a horizontal segmentation into production lines for the four main product segments: tablets, film-dragees, dragees and capsules. If the production volume for a particular segment is sufficiently large, additional segments may be appropriate. The CLASSIC operation in the Stein works uses a pseudo segmentation in packaging to reduce the total amount of setup time. As mentioned, the plant scheduler assigns and sequences production orders with similar formats to the same work center over a period of time. QED takes this into account when it estimates the total amount of setup time in packaging.

Campaign and lot sizes are two further key decision variables. They have been discussed at length. The impact of the use variable lot sizes could be, but is not, investigated.

The investigation of equipment flexibility focuses on changeover time, which is only one aspect of flexibility. As shown by the equipment item requirements in table 7.2.2, PURE JIT would benefit from more versatile tablet core compression equipment. Two of the segments require two different equipment items. An aggrevating factor is that compression happens to be the bottleneck stage in the fabrication process. Using two machines in parallel to balance the process turns into an expensive proposition.

There is one notable exception in the experimental setup. For all JIT variants, QED takes the CLASSIC values for changeover times. A separate set of experiments investigate the impact of changeover times.

A conglomarate of decisions builds the delivery time for group company orders. Table 7.2.6 lists the specific components and values that together set the lead time for filling a group company for CLASSIC and JIT. The values for JIT assume parallel activities in the order handling process and reliable delivery times for the final packaging stage, as described in the solution concept put forward in §6.4.3.

The planning cycle is a decision variable that applies to every single planning stage in the manufacturing process. One of the aims of the just-in-time concept is, of course, to reduce their number by on-line production. To be realistic, the specific values for this parameter must reflect the flexibility of the production stages.

As mentioned, QED doesn't model quality control of bulk in detail. The decision to carry out packaging in parallel with quality control, rather then afterwards, is a further variable distinguishing CLASSIC from JIT.

decision variable	**classic**	**just-in-time**	**decision category**			
			equipment technology	**methods & procedures**	**organization**	**operational planning & control**
segmentation	functional	flow-oriented				
• horizontal	pure pool	lines or pool			√	√
• vertical	stocks at all levels	on-line where appropriate			√	√
campaign size (no. of lots)	large	small				√
lot size (kg, packs, boxes)	large	small or variable				√
equipment flexibility	low	high	√			
• campaign change	long	short	√	√		
• lot change	long	short	√	√		
order processing & delivery to GC	sequential processes	parallel processes		√	√	√
• order delivery time	7 weeks	1-2 weeks		√	√	√
lead time for packaging material acquisition	weeks	days			√	√
planning cycle	1 month	1 week, 1 day				√
quality control of bulk products	before packaging	in parallel with packaging			√	√

Figure 7.2: QED's key decision variables and categories that distinguish the alternatives CLASSIC and JIT. As noted however, all experiments use standard, i.e. high, campaign changeover times. The impact of changeover times is the subject of a separate set of experiments.

7.2.3 Exogenous Factors

Product Volume and Mix

QED determines the total demand volume for a specific fully-packaged product variant on the basis of specific values for the following three input parameters:

- total demand for all fully-packaged variants of a semi-packaged product, expressed in number of packages
- number of group companies or locations to which the product is supplied
- average number of different packaging formats at these group companies

The latter two parameters together determine the total number of variants, and hence the demand for a specific variant.

All in all, the product mix includes 18 different semi-packaged products. Three of these have been added to another semi-packaged product in the mix, since they share the same bulk product. For each one of the remaining 15 different semi-packaged products, there is a set of columns in the spreadsheet implementation of QED. As noted, PURE JIT segments this mix into the four basic categories: tablets, film-dragees, dragees and capsules.

The product mix selected is a representative sample of the solid dosage forms produced in the Stein works. Since its volume amounts to less than 60% of the current total volume for solid dosage forms, most experimental sets investigate the sensitivity of the results with respect to volume.

Cost-based Factors

QED determines the annual costs for the four M's on the basis of specific values for the cost of the following items:

- labour – hourly labour rate in SFr.
- packaging materials – SFr. per package
- active substance – SFr. per kg of bulk product
- capital – annual interest rate
- equipment, including infrastructure and building space – annuity
- floor space – annuity
- warehouse – annuity

To calculate the annuity, QED requires specific values for the total investment cost for the item, the useful economic life of the item, and the cost of capital. The total investment costs for a specific item comprise of the costs for the basic equipment item, auxiliary equipment items and building space requirements. For each one of the equipment items, QED also needs to know how much space it takes up. See tables 7.2.5a through 7.2.5c for the specific values.

The annual cost of repairs and maintenance is specified as a fixed percentage of the total investment sum.

Demand Variability and Volatility

The variability of short-term demand determines the safety stock levels at the different stages. It enters the safety stock formula as a mutliplier of the demand variance as described in §7.3.4. The demand volatility, i.e. abnormal demand variability, determines the percentage of slow- and no-movers as well as the percentage of lost business as described §5.3. In §7.3.4, demand variability is subjected to a sensitivity analysis.

Product and Process Characteristics

To characterize the manufacturing process, QED requires for each selected product and each process stage specific values for the following resource requirements:

- basic equipment type
- equipment and labour hours for production and quality control
- equipment and labour hours for per changeover
- material—active substance, intermediate and packaging material

The values are listed in tables 7.2.1 through 7.2.3.

7.2.4 QED Input Parameter Values

				SETUP			
			CLEANUP	MINOR	MAJOR	LOT	BATCH?
FABRICATION	blending	BLENDER	1.0 1.0				yes
	granulation	GRANULATOR	3.0 2.0				yes
	compression	FETTE PT 2080	6.0 2.0			0.1	no
		FETTE 3002	8.0 2.0			0.1	no
		DRYCOTA MANESTY	8.0 2.0			0.1	no
	encapsulation	ENCAPSULATOR	18.0 2.4			0.2	no
	film coating	GLATTCOTER	0.5 1.0				yes
	sugar coating	PELLEGRINI	0.5 1.0				yes
	polishing	TROMMELN	0.5 1.0				yes
	sorting	SEIDENADER	0.5 1.0			0.1	yes
	printing	HARTNETT	4.0 1.0			0.1	no
QUALITY CONTROL	quality control	LABORATORY	4.0 1.0				yes
PACKAGING	semi-finished	SERVAC PH2		1.0 2.0	4.0 2.0	0.1	no
	fully-finished	FP PACKAGER		0.5 2.0	2.0 0.5	0.1	no

Table 7.2.1: Process stages in the pharmaceutical production; equipment type selected for each stage, changeover times per campaign and lot; and process type. The upper numerical value in each cell specifies the machine time lost in hours; the lower value specifies the number of people required to perform the changeover. The final column specifies whether the stage is a batch type process or semi-continuous.

	TABLETS			FILMDRAGEES					DRAGEES				CAPSULES		
	1	2	3	4	5	6	7	8	9	10	11	12	13	14	15
BLENDER	0.7	0.7	0.7	0.7	0.7	0.7	0.7	0.7	0.7	0.7	0.7	0.7	1.0	1.0	1.8
	1.0	1.0	1.0	1.0	1.0	1.0	1.0	1.0	1.0	1.0	1.0	1.0	2.0	2.0	2.0
GRANULATOR	1.0	1.0	1.0	5.5	2.3	2.9	2.0	2.0	2.7	3.5	1.0	2.2			
	2.0	2.0	2.0	2.0	2.0	2.0	2.0	2.0	2.0	2.0	2.0	2.0			
FETTE PT 2080	2.5	3.5	4.5		3.5	4.5	4.8	3.0	3.6		11.0				
	0.2	0.2	0.2		0.2	0.3	0.3	0.3	2.0		0.2				
FETTE 3002				7.5											
				0.5											
DRYCOTA MANESTY										20.0		6.6			
										0.6		0.6			
ENCAPSULATOR													6.0	8.0	7.5
													2.0	2.0	2.0
GLATTCOTER				3.8	7.6	3.8	3.0	3.0	2.5	2.5	2.5	2.5			
				0.3	0.6	0.3	0.3	0.3	0.6	1.2	0.3	1.2			
PELLEGRINI									8.0	12.0	8.0	8.0			
									1.2	1.2	1.2	1.2			
TROMMELN									1.5	1.5	1.5	1.5			
									0.6	0.6	0.6	0.6			
SEIDENADER				2.0	0.8	4.0	2.0	2.0	2.0	11.0	14.0	3.0			
				1.0	2.0	1.0	1.0	1.0	1.0	0.5	0.4	0.3			
HARTNETT									2.5	12.0	16.0	2.5	4.5	8.0	6.0
									0.4	0.4	0.4	0.4	0.4	0.4	0.4
LABORATORY	4.0	4.0	4.0	12.0	4.0	4.0	4.0	4.0	6.3	8.0	3.0	7.0	4.0	4.0	4.0
	1.0	1.0	1.0	1.0	1.0	1.0	1.0	1.0	1.0	1.0	1.0	1.0	1.0	1.0	1.0
SERVAC PH2	225	115	115	115	225	225	115	115	115	155	225	115	115	115	60
	3.0	3.0	3.0	3.0	3.0	3.0	3.0	3.0	3.0	3.0	3.0	3.0	3.0	3.0	3.0
FP PACKAGER	250	250	250	250	250	250	250	250	250	250	250	250	250	250	250
	4.0	4.0	4.0	4.0	4.0	4.0	4.0	4.0	4.0	4.0	4.0	4.0	4.0	4.0	4.0

Table 7.2.2: Processing times per standard lot and labour content. The upper numerical value in each cell specifies the equipment time in hours; the lower value specifies the number of people required. Besides direct labour, this value includes first-level supervisory labour. QED ignores drying times between stages. The bottom two rows (for packaging equipment) form an exception. The upper value in each cell specifies the output rate: packages per minute. QED calculates the processing time per lot. In general, it should be pointed out that the individual production processes are very poorly balanced. Only a detailed simulation can assess the detrimental impact on WIP levels and resource utilization, especially in combination with drying between the process stages, changeovers and shifts.

PARAMETER VALUES FOR CLASSIC																
SEGMENT		TABLETS			FILMDRAGEES					DRAGEES				CAPSULES		
		1	2	3	4	5	6	7	8	9	10	11	12	13	14	15
BULK																
lot size (kg)	330	440	440	440	450	350	350	250	250	220	370	300	350	300	320	120
campaign size (no. of lots)	7.0	16	3	3	8	12	6	8	12	4	6	5	6	6	4	6
yield (K-units per kg)		4	2	2	2.5	5.6	3.5	3.5	1.8	1.9	7.8	20	2.5	2.1	4.2	3
loss		0.1	0.1	0.1	0.1	0.1	0.1	0.1	0.1	0.1	0.1	0.1	0.1	0.1	0.1	0.1
demand (tonnes)	132.9	21.8	4.9	7.3	23.1	7.1	7.3	7.6	9.4	5.3	6.8	3.8	11.2	7.3	3.8	6.1
no. of lots	412	50	11	17	51	20	21	30	38	24	18	13	32	24	12	51
no. of campaigns	65	3	4	6	6	2	4	4	3	6	3	3	5	4	3	9
throughput time	12.0	30	4	6	7	22	10	14	11	6	5	20	5	5	3	5
SP																
campaign size (M-units)	3.0	7.7	1.8	1.8	3	3.5	3.5	2.2	1.1	1	2.7	8.5	2	2.5	3	1
loss		0.05	0.05	0.05	0.05	0.05	0.05	0.05	0.05	0.1	0.1	0.1	0.1	0.1	0.1	0.1
demand (M-packs)	43.3	7.9	0.9	1.3	3.7	3.6	2.3	2.4	1.5	0.9	4.9	6.9	2.5	1.4	1.5	1.4
format (units per pack)		10	10	10	14	10	10	10	10	10	10	10	10	10	10	12
no. of campaigns	157	10	5	7	17	10	7	11	14	9	18	8	13	6	5	17
throughput time	5.9	8.4	4.2	4.4	5.0	4.4	4.1	5.0	3.0	2.9	4.6	9.0	4.5	5.2	6.3	3.8
FP-PC																
campaign size (K-packs)	22.4	32	32	32	16	24	24	16	16	16	16	24	16	24	24	24
loss		0.05	0.05	0.05	0.05	0.05	0.05	0.05	0.05	0.05	0.05	0.05	0.05	0.05	0.05	0.05
no. of different formats		4	4	4	4	4	4	4	4	4	4	4	4	4	4	1
indep. demand (M-boxes)	14.4	1.8	0.2	0.3	1.7	1.1	0.7	1.1	0.7	0.4	2.1	2	1.1	0.4	0.42	0.4
format (packs per box)		4	4	4	2	3	3	2	2	2	2	3	2	3	3	3
no. of campaigns	1893	236	26	39	223	144	92	144	92	53	276	263	144	53	55	53
throughput time	0.68	0.8	0.8	0.8	0.6	0.7	0.7	0.6	0.6	0.6	0.6	0.7	0.6	0.7	0.7	0.7
FP-GC																
order frequency		16	6	6	16	12	12	12	6	6	16	16	12	6	6	6
no. of locations		10	10	10	10	10	10	10	10	10	10	10	10	10	10	10
PARAMETER VALUES FOR JIT																
BULK																
lot size (kg)	136	100	100	100	150	115	115	100	100	135	370	140	140	120	130	120
campaign size (no. of lots)	5.1	12	4	4	6	5	5	6	6	4	4	4	4	5	4	4
loss		0.08	0.08	0.08	0.08	0.08	0.08	0.08	0.08	0.08	0.08	0.08	0.08	0.06	0.06	0.06
demand (kg)	125.2	20.6	4.6	6.9	21.8	6.7	6.9	7.2	8.9	5.1	6.5	3.6	10.6	6.7	3.5	5.7
no. of lots	1031	206	46	69	145	59	60	72	89	37	17	26	75	56	27	47
no. of campaigns	190	17	12	17	24	12	12	12	15	9	4	7	19	11	7	12
throughput time	5.2	11	3	3	5	4	4	5	5	3	3	6	3	4	3	3
SP																
campaign size (M-units)	3.1	4.8	0.8	0.8	2.3	3.2	2	2.1	1.1	1	11.5	11.2	1.4	1.3	2.2	1.4
loss		0.05	0.05	0.05	0.05	0.05	0.05	0.05	0.05	0.1	0.1	0.1	0.1	0.1	0.1	0.1
demand (packs)	41.6	7.6	0.8	1.3	3.6	3.5	2.2	2.3	1.5	0.9	4.7	6.7	2.4	1.3	1.4	1.3
no. of campaigns	174	16	11	16	22	11	11	11	13	9	4	6	17	10	6	11
throughput time	5.5	11	3	3	5	4	4	5	5	3	3	6	3	4	3	3
FP-PC																
campaign size (K-packs)	6.7	11.3	3.3	5.0	5.3	6.9	4.4	4.6	5.8	3.3	6.6	9.4	4.6	5.0	5.3	20.0
loss		0.01	0.01	0.01	0.01	0.01	0.01	0.01	0.01	0.01	0.01	0.01	0.01	0.01	0.01	0.01
no. of campaigns	6040	646	243	242	647	484	484	485	243	243	647	646	485	242	242	61
throughput time	0.1	0.2	0.1	0.1	0.1	0.2	0.1	0.1	0.1	0.1	0.2	0.2	0.1	0.1	0.1	0.3

Table 7.2.3: Basic numerical input parameters for CLASSIC and JIT. For JIT, only the values that differ from CLASSIC are listed. The first numerical column contains either the average or the total of the specific values for each individual product. Note that not all values shown are input parameters. Production throughput times, number of campaigns and lots, and dependent demand are calculated by QED. As shown, the total independent demand volume of the base case model is 14.4 million fully-finished packages, which is a relatively small operation. It should be stressed that the campaign sizes for CLASSIC are taken from the industrial case investigated, which uses a sophisticated 'optimization' algorithm. No attempt was made to optimize the campaign sizes for JIT.

CLASSIC		TABLETS			FILMDRAGEES					DRAGEES				CAPSULES		
		1	2	3	4	5	6	7	8	9	10	11	12	13	14	15
AS																
TPC	**78.4**	**54.0**	**54.0**	**44.0**	**60.0**	**25.0**	**25.0**	**60.0**	**60.0**	**140.0**	**34.0**	**90.0**	**30.0**	**115.0**	**115.0**	**270.0**
BULK																
VPC	39.2	27.0	27.0	22.0	30.0	12.5	12.5	30.0	30.0	70.0	17.0	45.0	15.0	57.5	57.5	135.0
TPC	88.6	62.6	65.7	53.1	70.4	35.0	37.6	73.2	71.2	158.5	42.5	107.9	36.6	118.1	118.0	278.8
SP																
VPC	0.30	0.22	0.29	0.26	0.32	0.17	0.19	0.24	0.32	0.52	0.17	0.17	0.21	0.42	0.29	0.69
TPC	0.55	0.35	0.56	0.49	0.62	0.25	0.29	0.43	0.63	1.08	0.25	0.24	0.36	0.80	0.51	1.43
FP-PC																
VPC	0.83	0.87	1.14	1.04	0.64	0.52	0.56	0.47	0.63	1.04	0.34	0.52	0.42	1.27	0.86	2.07
TPC	1.86	1.74	2.63	2.34	1.55	1.04	1.19	1.15	1.55	2.49	0.78	1.01	1.01	2.79	1.87	4.80
FP-GC																
VPC	0.83	0.87	1.14	1.04	0.64	0.52	0.56	0.47	0.63	1.04	0.34	0.52	0.42	1.27	0.86	2.07
TPC	2.02	1.87	2.85	2.53	1.67	1.12	1.27	1.24	1.66	2.67	0.84	1.09	1.08	3.01	2.02	5.34
MARKET																
FULL	**8.92**															

JIT

FP-GC																
VPC	0.83	0.87	1.14	1.04	0.64	0.52	0.56	0.47	0.63	1.04	0.34	0.52	0.42	1.27	0.86	2.07
TPC	1.99	1.85	2.76	2.56	1.81	1.13	1.33	1.24	1.69	2.61	0.81	1.05	1.12	2.88	1.93	5.04

Table 7.2.4: Active substance costs and average sales price (**bold**) in SFr. per unit. The VPC per kg of bulk product is taken to be half of the TPC value for AS. The TPC value of bulk includes the other half. The non-weighted average TPC for AS is SFr. 78.4 per kg. As shown, the non-weighted average sales price used for the calculations is SFr. 8.92 per pack. The specific values, which intentionally are not shown, range from a minimum of SFr. 4.90 to a maximum of SFr. 16.56. QED calculates the VPC and TPC values of the other stages; they depend on numerous other factors and, therefore, vary from case to case. The VPC and TPC values shown are for the base scenario with the volume at 100% of the base mode case, see §7.3.1.

	INVESTMENT COSTS						
	EQUIPMENT	BUILDING	INFRA.	LAND	SPACE	AVAIL. HRS.	HRLY RATE
BLENDER	0.65	1.26	0.26	0.09	180	1430	189.03
GRANULATOR	2.55	0.91	1.02	0.07	130	1430	434.88
FETTE PT 2080	0.72	0.18	0.29	0.01	25	1540	111.40
FETTE 3002	0.60	0.25	0.24	0.02	35	1500	100.88
DRYCOTA MANESTY	0.49	0.18	0.20	0.01	25	1610	75.70
ENCAPSULATOR	0.86	0.32	0.34	0.02	45	1420	146.28
GLATTCOTER	0.97	0.21	0.39	0.02	30	1630	134.30
PELLEGRINI	0.85	0.21	0.34	0.02	30	1790	108.12
TROMMELN	0.08	0.11	0.03	0.01	15	1600	16.83
SEIDENADER	0.17	0.18	0.07	0.01	25	1500	38.42
HARTNETT	0.19	0.18	0.08	0.01	25	1540	40.51
LABORATORY	0.20	0.09	0.08	0.01	25	1400	40.00
SERVAC PH2	1.50	0.40	0.60	0.04	80	1600	235.95
CARTONER	0.80	0.40	0.32	0.04	80	1600	140.55

Table 7.2.5a: Total investment cost per equipment item. Included are the costs of the basic equipment item; auxiliary equipment (*Gemeinkosten der Fertigung*) taken as a fixed percentage of the basic equipment cost—see table 7.2.5d; and building space. The fifth column specifies the space requirements in square meters. The sixth column specifies the planned available hours per shift. The final column specifies the hourly equipment rate calculated by QED.

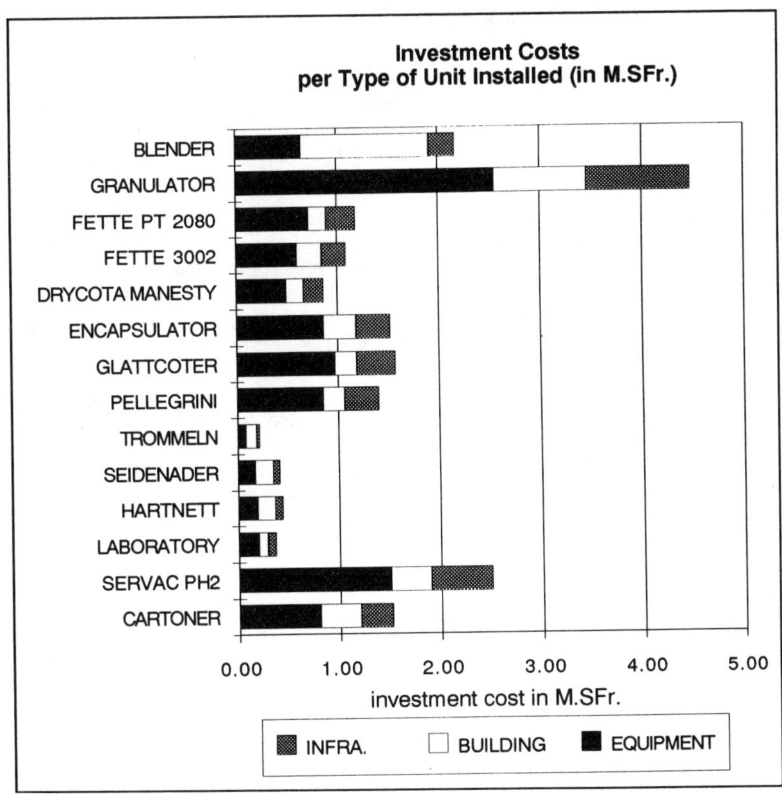

Table 7.2.5b: Total investment cost per equipment item as a bar chart.

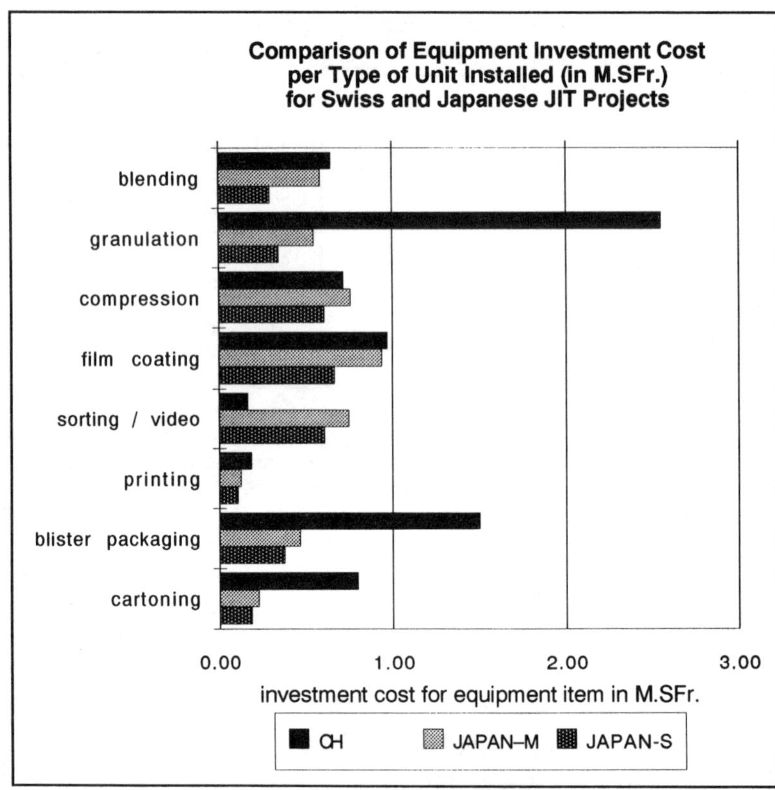

Table 7.2.5c: Comparison of equipment investment cost for Swiss and Japanese just-in-time projects. The bar chart puts the figures for the equipment items shown in table 7.2.5a—**CH**—next to the comparable items selected in Japan. **JAPAN-M** refers to the medium-sized equipment for batch sizes of 200 kg; and **JAPAN-S** to small-sized for batch sizes of 100 kg. For an overview of the Japanese project see §8.6. The Japanese figures are based on the exchange rate of June, 1989: SFr. 1 = ¥ 85. The Japanese figures show that smaller equipment items are somewhat cheaper. The subsequent analysis makes the conservative assumption that the cost of large and small equipment items are the same, i.e. irrespective the batch or lot size. See §7.3.2 for a further discussion on lot sizing.

		equipment	infrastructure	building space
fabrication	unit investment	see table 7.2.5a	40%	SFr. 7'000 / m2
	economic life	15	15	30
	R&M	3%	1%	1%
quality control	unit investment	SFr. 200'000	30%	SFr. 3'500 / m2
	economic life	10	15	30
	R&M	3%	1%	1%
packaging	unit investment	see table 7.2.5a	30%	SFr. 5'000 / m2
	economic life	15	15	30
	R&M	3%	1%	1%
warehouse	unit investment	SFr. 500		SFr. 2'000 / PP
	economic life	15	15	30
	R&M	3%	1%	1%

Table 7.2.5d: General parameter values for calculating the annual cost of capital investment in fixed assets. The investment cost for infrastructure items is taken as percentage of the investment in equipment. Also included in the table are the parameter values for calculating the annual costs for repairs and maintenance—R&M. These are specified as a fixed percentage of the total investment. The alternative is to base R&M on operating hours. QED's approach penalizes JIT.

Components of Group Company Order Delivery Times	CLASSIC	JIT
planning cycle (divided by 2 for the total)	30	7
time bucket	1	1
frozen period	14	2
processing of group company order	3	1
retrieval of packaging material from warehouse	7	0.5
production throughput time for fully-finished packaged	*< 1*	*< 1*
delay until export packaging	4	0.5
overall throughput time for export packaging	3	1
delay until shipment to group company	21	2
physical transportation	2	2
group company order delivery time	**71**	**14**

Table 7.2.6: Input parameters and their values for group company order delivery times. All values are expressed in days. Since the lead time for filling group company orders includes components that are not explicitly modeled by QED additional input parameters are required. QED uses the group company order delivery times for calculating the safety stock levels in the group companies. See chapter 6 on the specific values and chapter 5 on the logic.

7.2.5 QED Output Parameters

FIXED ASSETS	
TOTAL	**50,040,450**
FABRICATION	22,869,000
QC	760,000
SP	10,160,000
FP	6,487,500
WAREHOUSE	9,763,950

CURRENT ASSETS	
TOTAL	**22,933,166**
PM	3,703,525
BULK	4,830,945
SP	3,938,077
FP-PC	2,284,024
FP-GC	8,176,596

VOLUME **100%**

FLOW TIME
13.78

PF
5.63

DCPF
4.77

CAPITAL COSTS & DEPRECIATION			
	TOTAL		**6,074,282**
	FABRICATION	2,819,754	
	QC	107,198	
	SP	1,290,107	
	FP	800,847	
	WAREHOUSE	1,056,376	
COST OF CAPITAL TIED-UP IN STOCKS			
10%	STOCKS	2,293,317	**2,293,317**
DIRECT LABOUR			
	TOTAL		**2,297,991**
	FABRICATION	674,171	
	QC	163,394	
	SP	705,400	
	FP	563,850	
	WAREHOUSE		
	MATERIAL HANDLING	191,176	
REPAIRS & MAINTENANCE			
	TOTAL		**730,716**
	FABRICATION	236,001	
	QC	15,350	
	SP	220,000	
	FP	125,350	
	WAREHOUSE	134,015	
TRANSPORTATION			
	TOTAL	285,600	**285,600**
CUSTOMS DUTIES			
	TOTAL	1,011,555	**1,011,555**
PLANNING & CONTROL			
	TOTAL		**704,602**
MATERIALS & ENERGY			
	TOTAL		**18,049,707**
	FABRICATION	8,789,862	
	SP	6,294,645	
	FP	2,965,200	
COST OF SLOWMOVERS			**1,452,634**
LOST BUSINESS			**434,304**

DISCOUNTED NET CONTRIBUTION	GROSS REVENUE –TOTAL COSTS –FIXED OVERHEAD NET CONTRIBUTION	GROSS REVENUE	TOTAL COSTS
32,678,890	**38,575,591**	**102,729,000**	**33,334,709**

Table 7.3a: QED output panel for CLASSIC with volume at 100% of the base case model. QED calculates costs on an annual basis. *Fixed assets are reported at acquisition cost. The costs related to inventory amount to 8.5 M.SFr., which is 25% of the total cost. Interest charges amount to 27% of these 8.5 M.SFr. For every SFr. that is tied-up in stocks, CLASSIC pays 0.37 SFr. per annum.*

FIXED ASSETS			**CAPITAL COSTS & DEPRECIATION**		
TOTAL	**74,347,800**		TOTAL		**9,197,456**
FABRICATION	47,339,000		FABRICATION	5,848,063	
QC	1,900,000		QC	267,995	
SP	10,160,000		SP	1,290,107	
FP	11,057,500		FP	1,370,286	
WAREHOUSE	3,891,300		WAREHOUSE	421,006	
CURRENT ASSETS			**COST OF CAPITAL TIED-UP IN STOCKS**		
TOTAL	**8,273,053**	10%	STOCKS	827,305	**827,305**
PM	360,636				
BULK	0		**DIRECT LABOUR**		
SP	3,331,654		TOTAL		**3,047,951**
FP-PC	378,934		FABRICATION	1,002,048	
FP-GC	4,201,829		QC	403,487	
			SP	684,150	
			FP	771,200	
			WAREHOUSE		
			MATERIAL HANDLING	187,066	
			REPAIRS & MAINTENANCE		
			TOTAL		**875,135**
			FABRICATION	344,650	
VOLUME	**100%**		QC	38,375	
			SP	220,000	
			FP	218,700	
			WAREHOUSE	53,410	
			TRANSPORTATION		
			TOTAL	275,400	**275,400**
			CUSTOMS DUTIES		
			TOTAL	1,022,319	**1,022,319**
			PLANNING & CONTROL		
			TOTAL		**310,035**
			MATERIALS & ENERGY		
FLOW TIME			TOTAL		**17,157,307**
4.63			FABRICATION	8,250,218	
			SP	6,054,849	
PF			FP	2,852,240	
5.89					
			COST OF SLOWMOVERS		
DCPF					**202,094**
5.59		**GROSS REVENUE**			
		–TOTAL COSTS	**LOST BUSINESS**		
		–FIXED OVERHEAD			**146,051**
DISCOUNTED NET		**NET**			
CONTRIBUTION		**CONTRIBUTION**	**GROSS REVENUE**	**TOTAL COSTS**	
36,866,255		**38,849,246**	**102,729,000**		**33,061,054**

Table 7.3b: QED output panel for PURE JIT with volume at 100% of the base case model. QED calculates costs on an annual basis. Fixed assets are reported at acquisition cost. *The costs related to inventory amount to 2.1 M.SFr., which is 6% of the total cost. Interest charges amount to 38% of these 2.1 M.SFr. For every SFr. that is tied-up in stocks, PURE JIT pays 0.25 SFr. per annum.* These summary figures and percentages, for both CLASSIC and PURE JIT, exclude the discounted value of income, and material damage and loss due to materials handling.

7.3 Evaluation of the Basic Concepts and Alternatives under different Scenarios

This section and its sub-sections contain the experimental results. As shown in figure 7.3, the analysis has been grouped into four areas. The first set of experiments compares the CLASSIC concept with the most radical form of the just-in-time concept, PURE JIT. The second set investigates two pragmatic alternatives of PURE JIT. The two remaining sets of experiments assess the impact of the input parameters and the assumptions of QED: one focuses on cost-based factors, the other on quantitative parameters. Clearly, the experiments presented here investigate but a small selection of the aspects of the manufacturing system that could in principle have been investigated.

CLASSIC vs PURE JIT	**group I**
• volume • number of shifts • changeover times • campaign sizes	**§ 7.3.1**
Alternatives for PURE JIT	**group II**
• POOL JIT – PURE JIT with pooled resources • CLASSIC LOT JIT – PURE JIT with CLASSIC lot sizes	**§ 7.3.2**
Cost-based factors: CLASSIC vs PURE JIT	**group III**
• economic life of equipment • cost of active substance • cost of capital • cost of equipment vs labour content	**§ 7.3.3**
Assumptions: CLASSIC vs PURE JIT	**group IV**
• demand variability • package sizes	**§ 7.3.4**

Figure 7.3: Overview of the experimental analysis. Each sub-section deals with a separate group of experiments.

As noted, the experiments generally compare the results of two different concepts. Nearly all experiments cover the volume dependency of the difference in the results. Volume, which is always expressed as a percentage of the base case, turns out to have a very significant impact on the outcome. Moreover, volume is the cause of what seems to be an anomaly in the results. A small increase in volume may require a disproportionately large increase in the fixed assets base. Putting it differently, the fixed asset base is a step function of the volume. The return on assets as measured by the performance factor is therefore not a continuously increasing function of volume. In order to 'iron out' the effects, it is necessary to repeat the experiments for different sizes of the manufacturing system.

The presentation of each set of experiments is highly structured and consists of the following components:

- the purpose of the experiments
- graphical representations of the numerical results of the experiments in the form of standardized E-Charts[69]
- detailed explanations and comments in the captions of the E-Charts
- a summary of the results and the conclusions to be drawn from these

Different graphical views of the same numerical results have been chosen to provide additional insight into the relationships between the relevant factors and to allow the reader to draw conclusions that may not coincide with those presented in the discussion. As a result, the total volume of results may initially appear to be larger than it actually is. The sections are largely independent of each other; however, the reader who would like to obtain a detailed understanding will occasionally have to cross-refer to other sections.

The E-Charts combine some of the values for QED's financial output parameters, shown in figures 7.4a and 7.4b. Specifically, the values for

- capital cost & depreciation
- direct labour
- repairs & maintenance

are added for the basic stages in the manufacturing process

- FABRICATION – fabrication of bulk products
- QC – quality control of bulk products
- SP – semi-finished packaging
- FP – fully-finished packaging

---

[69]E-Chart stands for EXCEL or Experimental Chart. It is introduced for having the convenience of starting a new sequence of figure numbers. Note that the numbers of the E-Charts have been aligned with the numbers of the sections and groups, see figure 7.3.

7.3.1 Evaluation of the Basic Concepts: CLASSIC vs PURE JIT

Besides presenting the detailed results for the scenario that provides the starting point for all of the subsequent sets of experiments, this section investigates the impact of

- number of shifts
- changeover times
- campaign sizes

The latter two are particularly important because they concern decision variables where the just-in-time concept calls for very different input values. The results also shine light on the 'optimality' of current campaign sizes in the CLASSIC case, which are taken from the industrial case investigated.

Purpose ***Base Scenario***

The *base scenario*, as its name indicates, forms the starting point for all of the experiments carried out in this chapter. The *base scenario* takes the parameter values, as described in §7.2, and varies the volume from 50% to 300% of the base model case. With the volume set at 300% of the base model case, QED simulates a manufacturing operation three times as large as the one required for the top 18 class A products taken from the actual case. The purpose of the experiments is to show the dependency of the results on the size of the manufacturing system. In order for the results of the two different approaches to be comparable, CLASSIC and PURE JIT are subjected to identical experimental conditions. As will be shown in other experiments, the difference between the two approaches depends not only on the volume but also on many other factors and assumptions.

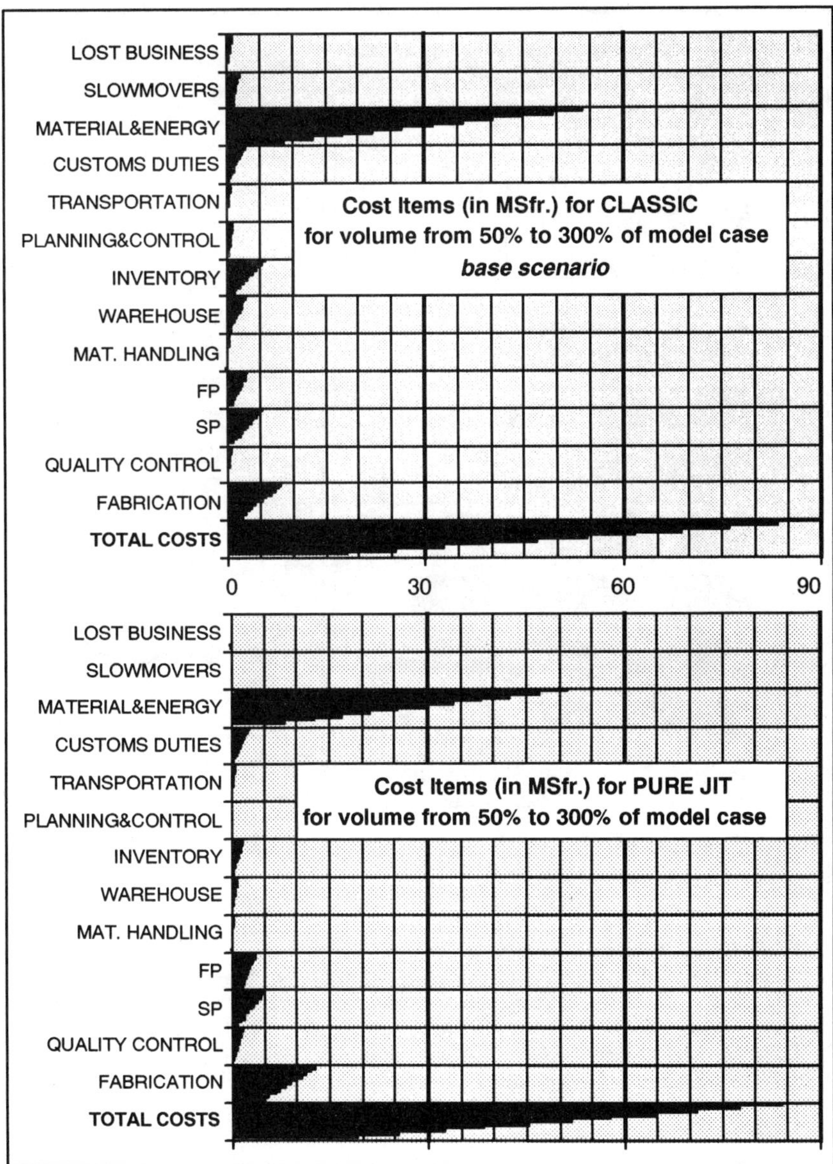

E-Chart I-1.1: Total annual costs and costs for individual cost items for CLASSIC and PURE JIT with the sales volume increasing from 50% to 300% of the model case. This chart is intended to display the magnitude and growth of each of the cost items in relation to the others. E-Chart I-1.3 displays the differences in the values for each cost item between CLASSIC and PURE JIT.

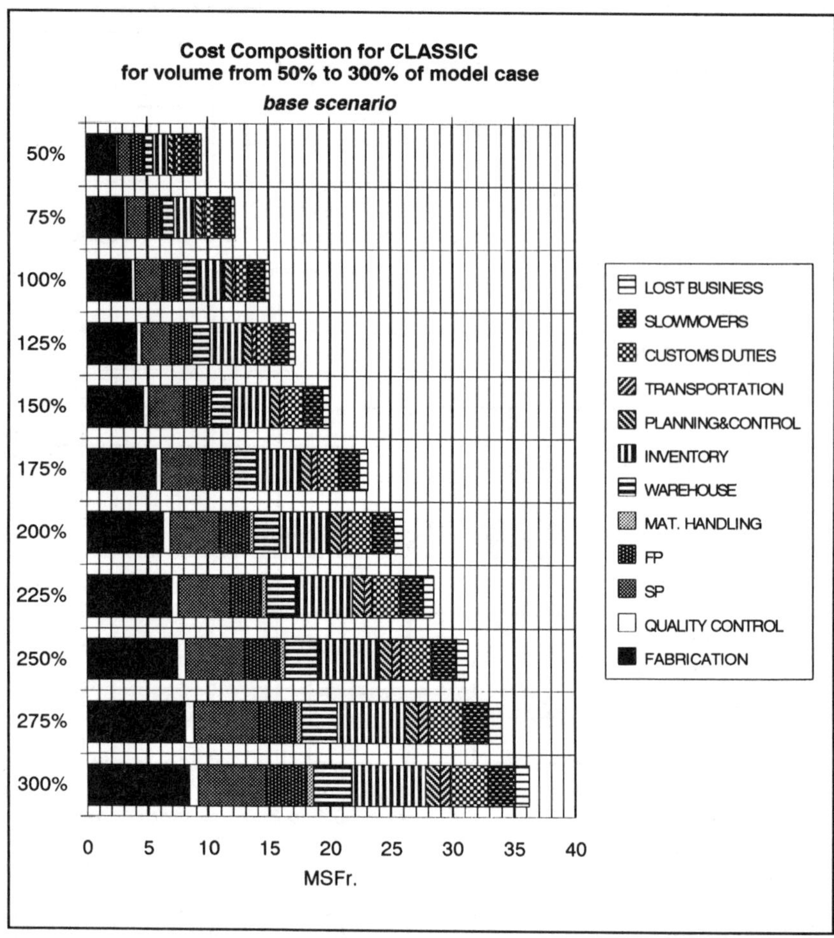

E-Chart I-1.2a: Composition of annual costs for CLASSIC with the sales volume increasing from 50% to 300% of the base model case. The share of production-based cost items—FABRICATION, QUALITY CONTROL, SP and FP—equals approximately 50% of the total costs. The total costs—excluding MATERIALS&ENERGY—increase fourfold, whereas the volume increases sixfold. Compare these with the same figures for PURE JIT shown in E-Chart I-1.2b.

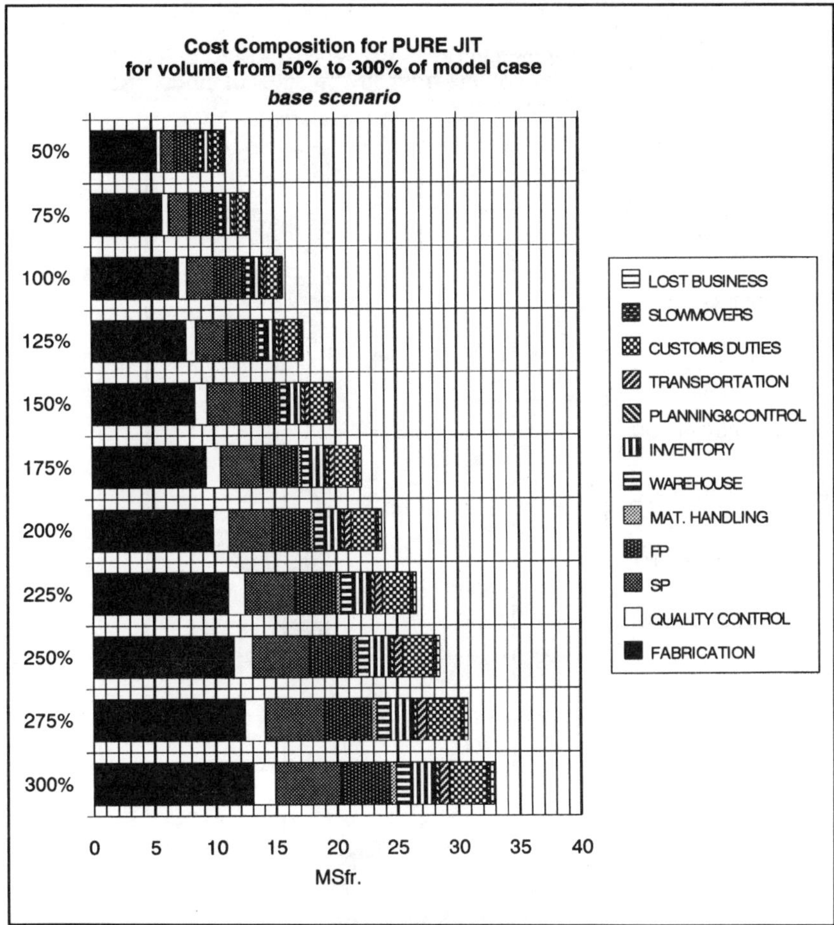

E-Chart I-1.2b: Composition of annual costs for PURE JIT with the sales volume increasing from 50% to 300% of the base model case. The share of production-based cost items—FABRICATION, QUALITY CONTROL, SP and FP—equals approximately 75% of the total costs. As expected, the production costs of PURE JIT are much higher than those of CLASSIC, both in absolute and relative terms. However, the total costs—excluding MATERIALS&ENERGY—increase only threefold, whereas the volume increases sixfold. The total costs for PURE JIT increase more slowly than those of CLASSIC. The cause of this relatively slow increase, which is investigated in E-Charts II-1.4 and II-2.5 in §7.3.2, is simply and intuitively the fact that the utilization of fixed production assets in a small PURE JIT manufacturing operation is very low.

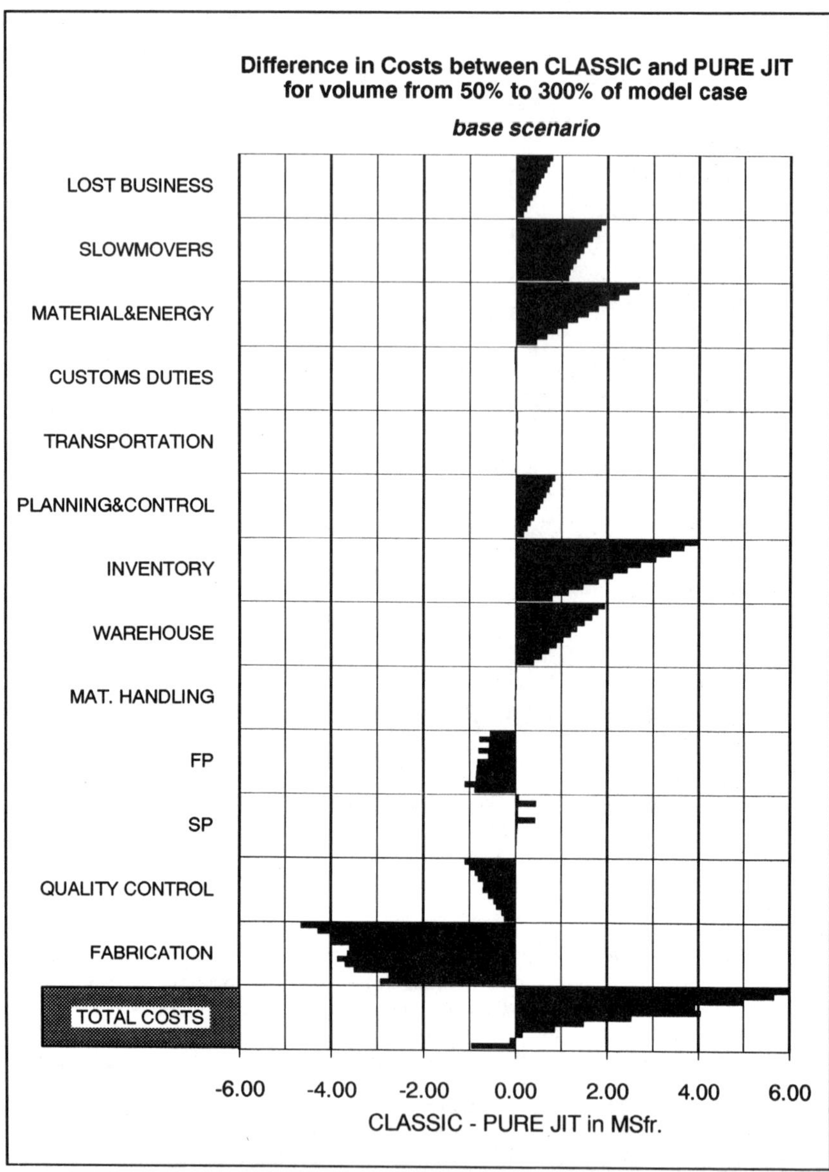

E-Chart I-1.3: Difference in annual costs between CLASSIC and PURE JIT with the sales volume increasing from 50% to 300% of the base model case. The values shown for the individual cost items are the costs for CLASSIC minus those for PURE JIT. As the volume ranges from 50% of the model case to 300% the difference in the total costs changes from -1.0 M.Sfr. to 6.0 M. Sfr. in favour of PURE JIT. This chart fails to show that the difference in total costs between the two concepts is a small in relative terms. The difference ranges between -5% to 7% of the total costs of CLASSIC.

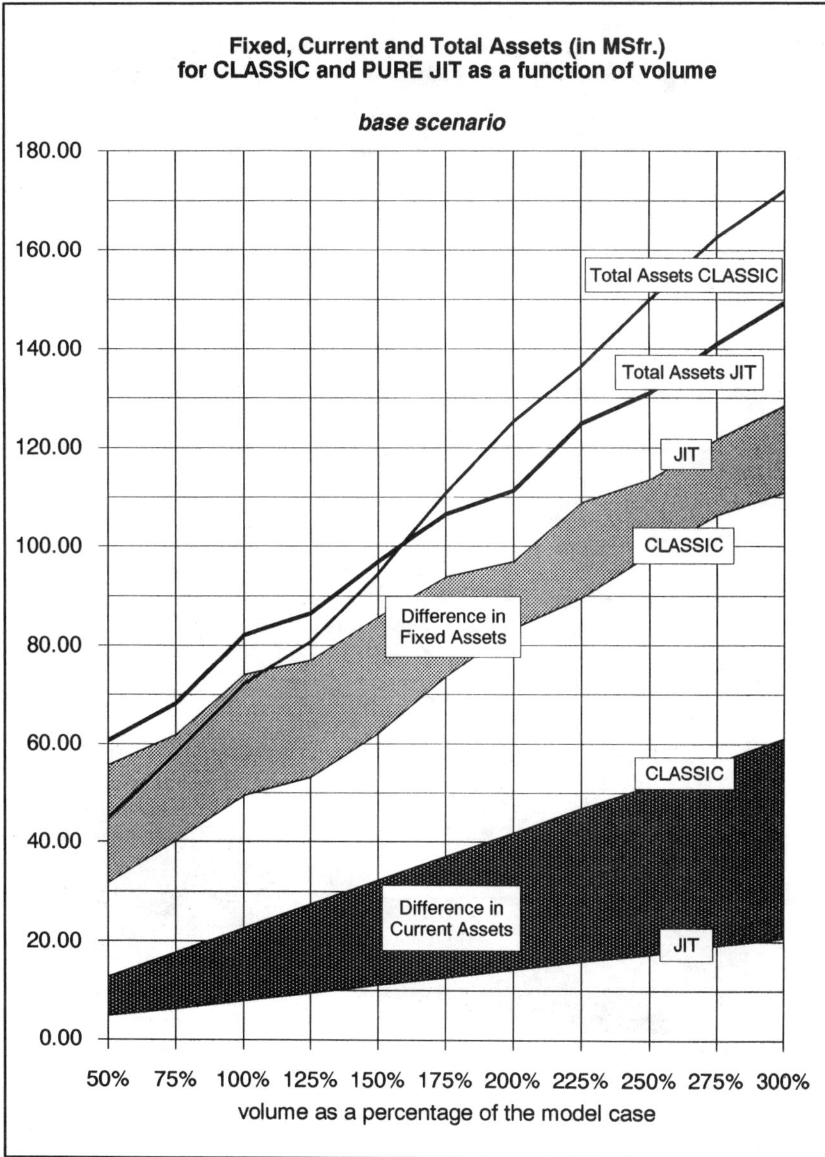

E-Chart I-1.4a: Asset base for CLASSIC and PURE JIT with the sales volume increasing from 50% to 300% of the model case. This chart displays the changing composition of the balance sheet for the two concepts. It is the key to understanding the increasing difference in total costs as the volume increases. It also explains the cause of the erratic shape of the difference in costs for the production areas and hence the total costs. Fixed assets are shown at their initial value—acquisition costs—and include the investment in warehouses in the parent company and the group companies. E-Charts II-1.4 and II-2.5 show production assets only.

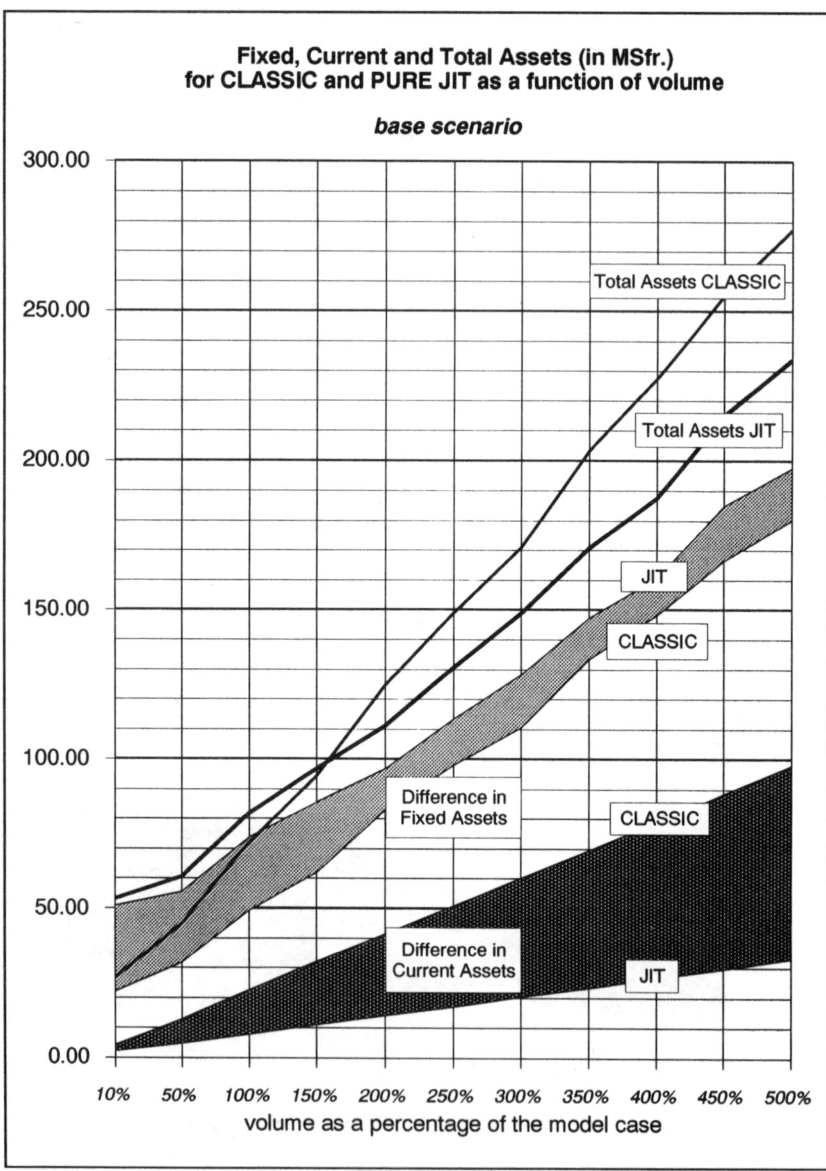

E-Chart I-1.4b: Asset base for CLASSIC and PURE JIT with the sales volume increasing from 10% to 500% of the base model case in steps of 50%. After 350% the difference in fixed assets appears to increase again. E-Chart II-2.5, which shows the production assets and increases the volume to 900%, confirms this and explains the underlying trend.

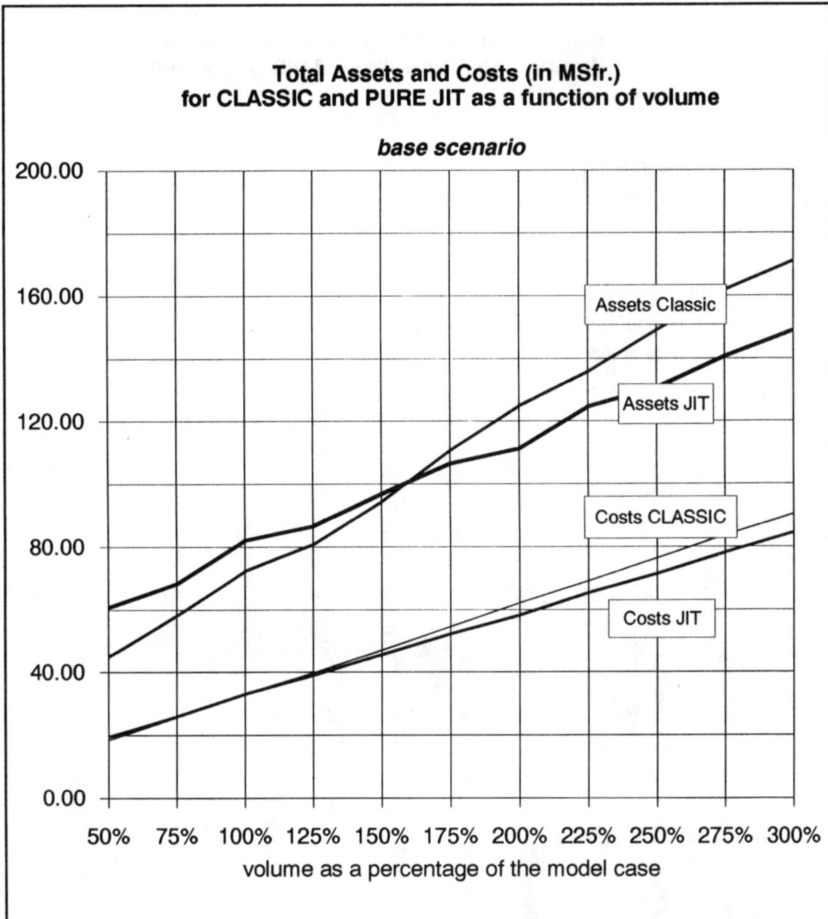

E-Chart I-1.5: Total assets and total costs of CLASSIC and PURE JIT with the volume increasing from 50% to 300% of the base model case. The difference in total assets is larger in relative and absolute terms than the difference in total costs. This holds in particular if fixed assets are taken at half their acquisition cost. Valuing fixed assets at half their acquisition cost would be consistent with the way the capital costs for fixed assets are calculated: in QED, these reflect the average annual costs over the economic life of the investment.

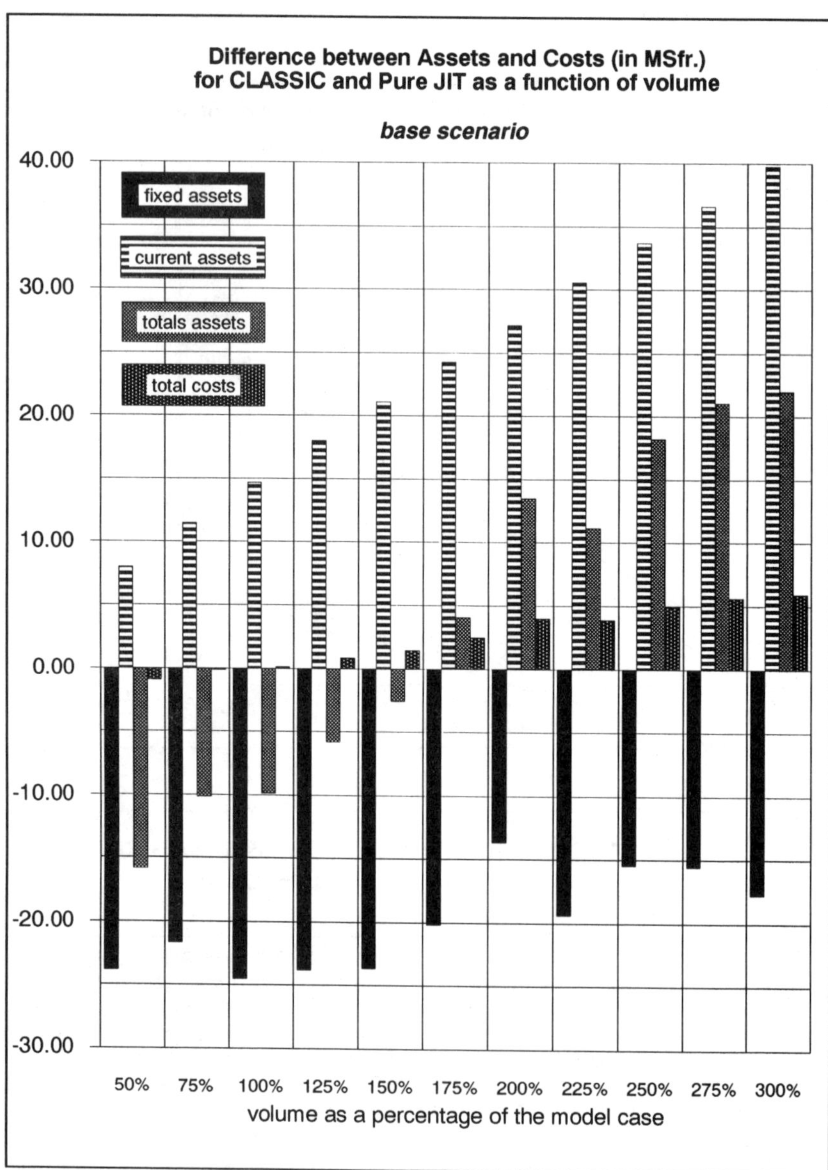

E-Chart I-1.6: Difference in assets and total costs between CLASSIC and PURE JIT with the volume increasing from 50% to 300% of the base model case. The difference in fixed assets stabilizes as the volume increases. If fixed assets are taken at half their acquisition value, then this difference will be even smaller. Since the performance factor does just that, the crossover in favour of PURE JIT occurs at a smaller volume than we might have guessed on the basis of the curves for total assets and total costs—see E-Charts I-1.7a and I-1.7b.

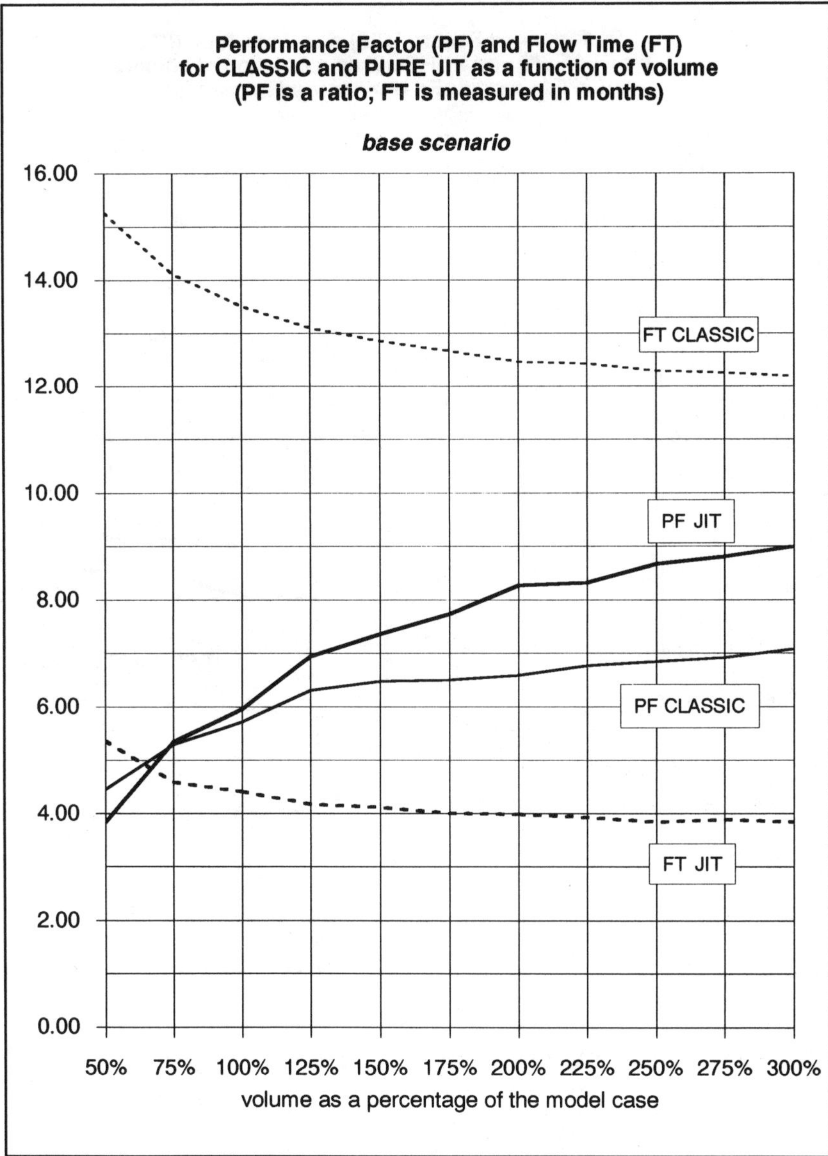

E-Chart I-1.7a: Performance factor and flow time for CLASSIC and PURE JIT with the volume increasing from 50% to 300% of the base model case. As noted, the crossover in the performance factor in favour of PURE JIT occurs at a surprisingly low volume. The performance factor appears to be approximately proportional to the inverse of the flow time, which is calculated as the accumulated inventory coverage for the four stages in the manufacturing system.

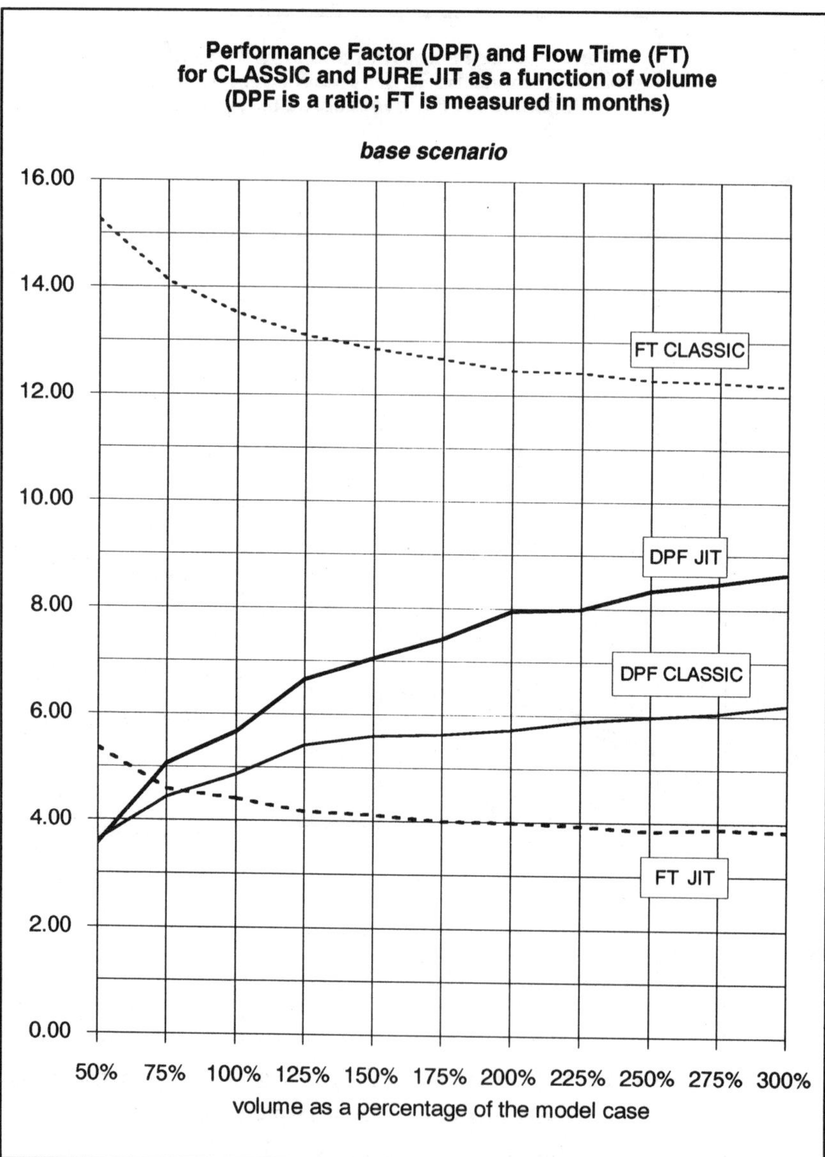

E-Chart I-1.7b: Discounted performance factor and flow time for CLASSIC and PURE JIT with the volume increasing from 50% to 300% of the base model case. By discounting a part of sales income as a function of the flow time the crossover in favour of PURE JIT is shifted in the direction of smaller operations. In addition, the gap between CLASSIC and PURE JIT for the volume at 300% has widened from 2 to 2.5 points, which in this case is a change from a 30% to 40% difference.

Discussion ***Base Scenario***

The most obvious result from this set of experiments is that the prime financial indicators are highly dependent on the volume. This applies in particular also to the difference between CLASSIC and PURE JIT. The scenario clearly turns in favour of PURE JIT as the volume increases. The volume at which the curves for CLASSIC and PURE JIT intersect varies with the indicator used. The conclusion, which squares with common intuition, is that a manufacturing system based on the same or similar principles as PURE JIT and implemented in the kind of environment investigated must have a certain minimum size in order to be financially attractive. This is not to say that the principles are applicable to high-volume products only. The volume dependency is a direct consequence of the (poor) utilization of fixed production assets.

The difference in performance factor, either PF or DPF, can largely be attributed to the smaller average annual asset base of the PURE JIT concept. The difference in total costs is relatively small. An important implication of this situation is that in the case of an existing factory, even if it is a large one, the overall cost advantages of the just-in-time concept are unlikely to justify the additional investment in fixed production assets. This certainly applies to the specific case investigated here.

The PURE JIT concept shifts the composition of the balance sheet heavily towards fixed production assets. Because of the emphasis placed on fixed cost absorption, and hence utilization, by cost accounting systems, these assets have traditionally come under most management scrutiny. Managerial skepticism towards investments in 'surplus' capacity is not only understandable but also consistent with the direction set by cost accounting systems.

The inclusion of the group companies and the investment in warehouses in the calculations makes a significant difference. The breakdown of tied-up capital in inventories and the consequential fixed assets in warehouses for the different stages with the volume at 100%, see E-Chart IV-2.1, shows that:

- if the group companies are excluded from the model, the difference in total assets would increase from 10.0 to 16.0 MSfr. in favour of CLASSIC; the total costs for PURE JIT would then be at least 0.6 MSfr. higher than those of CLASSIC (with the volume at 100% the total costs are nearly equal, as shown in E-Chart I-1.6)
- if it is assumed, either implicitly or explicitly, that there is already plenty of warehouse space available, i.e. the investment in warehouses is excluded from the fixed assets, then the difference in total assets would also increase to 16.0 MSfr. in favour of CLASSIC

This underscores a well-know point: the myopic functional view favours a classical operation. The additional production cost introduced by independent production lines and small batch sizes will generally outweigh the local benefits in inventory-related costs.

Purpose ***2 Shift Operation***

The purpose of the scenario *2 shift operation* is to assess what impact the number of shifts that the system operates has on the financial indicators of CLASSIC and PURE JIT; and, especially on the difference in performance.

The number of shifts is an input parameter of QED. However, it is not a straightforward decision variable, since the decision is constrained by governmental regulations and labour market conditions. The packaging lines in the Stein works are mainly operated by women. In Switzerland, women are not allowed to work night shifts in factories; only day and evening shifts. Moreover, a severe labour shortage continues to restrict the options open to management.

The *2 shift operation* is identical to the *base scenario* except that production equipment is used for two shifts per weekday. Otherwise the experimental conditions are identical. The volume is again increased from 50% to 300% of the base model case. The same set of E-Charts, with identical scaling for direct comparison in most cases, is shown.

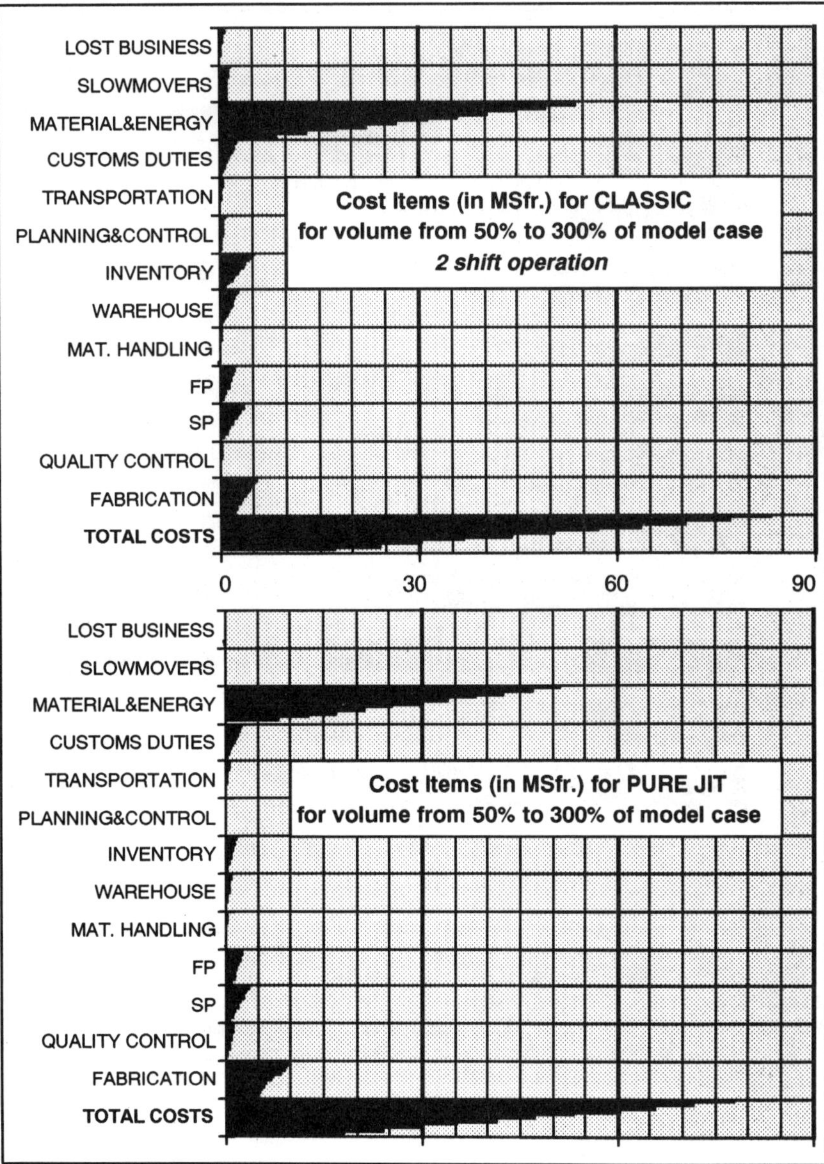

E-Chart I-2.1: Total annual costs and costs for individual cost items for CLASSIC and PURE JIT with the sales volume increasing from 50% to 300% of the model case. This chart is intended to display the magnitude and growth of each of the cost items in relation to the others. E-Chart I-2.3 displays the differences in the values for each cost item between CLASSIC and PURE JIT.

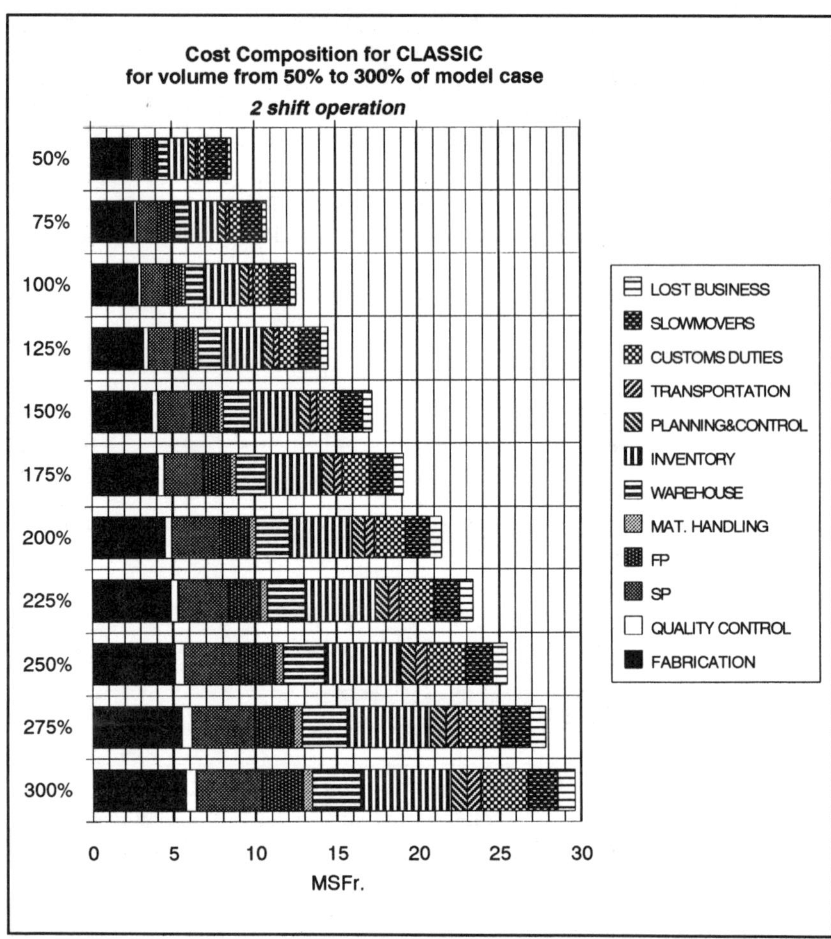

E-Chart I-2.2a: Composition of annual costs for CLASSIC with the sales volume increasing from 50% to 300% of the base model case. The share of production-based cost items—FABRICATION, QUALITY CONTROL, SP and FP—equals approximately 44% of the total costs, compared to 50% for the 1 shift operation in the *base scenario.* Note the difference in scale in comparison with I-1.2a.

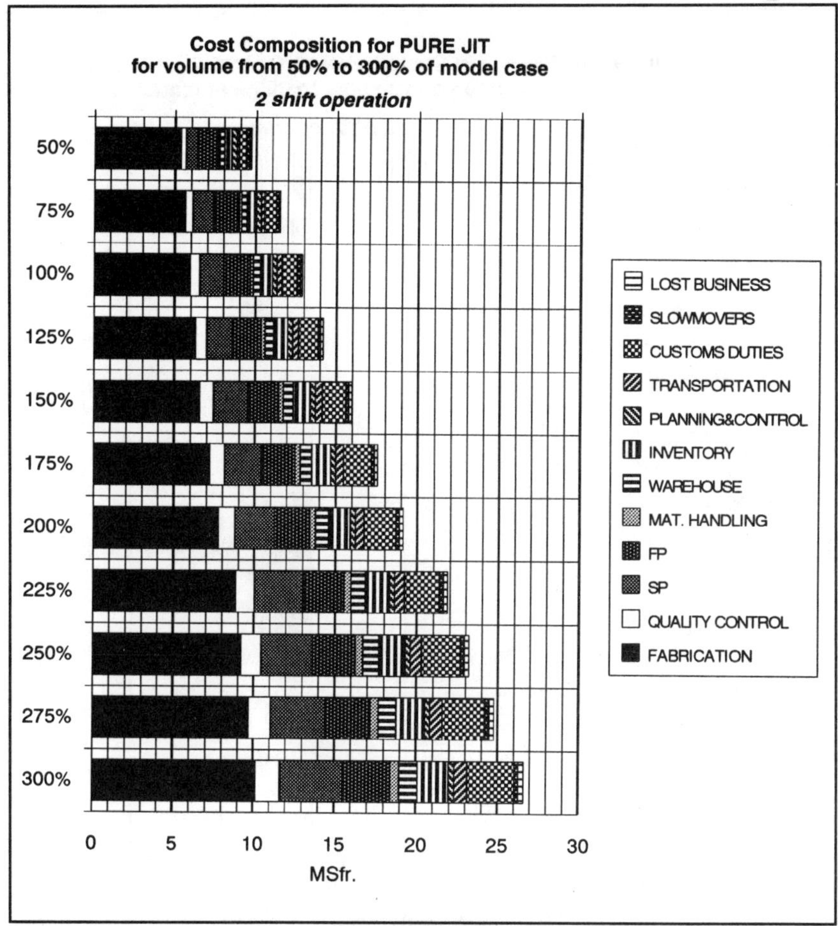

E-Chart I-2.2b: Composition of annual costs for PURE JIT with the sales volume increasing from 50% to 300% of the base model case. The share of production-based cost items—FABRICATION, QUALITY CONTROL, SP and FP—equals approximately 70% of the total costs, compared to 75% for the 1 shift operation in the *base scenario*. Note the difference in scale in comparison with I-1.2b.

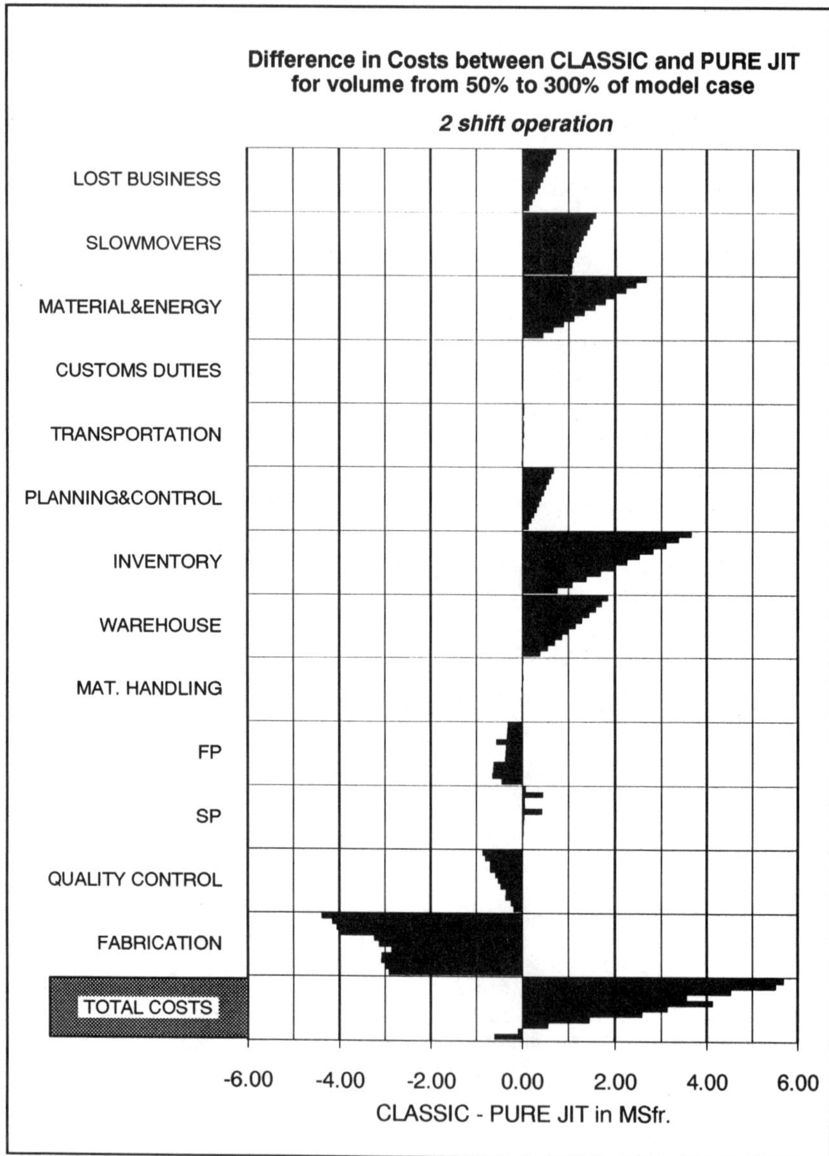

E-Chart I-2.3: Difference in annual costs between CLASSIC and PURE JIT with the sales volume increasing from 50% to 300% of the base model case. The values shown for the individual cost items are the costs for CLASSIC minus those of the PURE JIT. As the volume ranges from 50% of the model case to 300% the difference in the total costs changes from -0.6 M.Sfr. to 5.6 M. Sfr. in favour of PURE JIT, compared to the larger range of -1.0 MSfr. to 6.0 MSfr. for the 1 shift operation in the *base scenario*

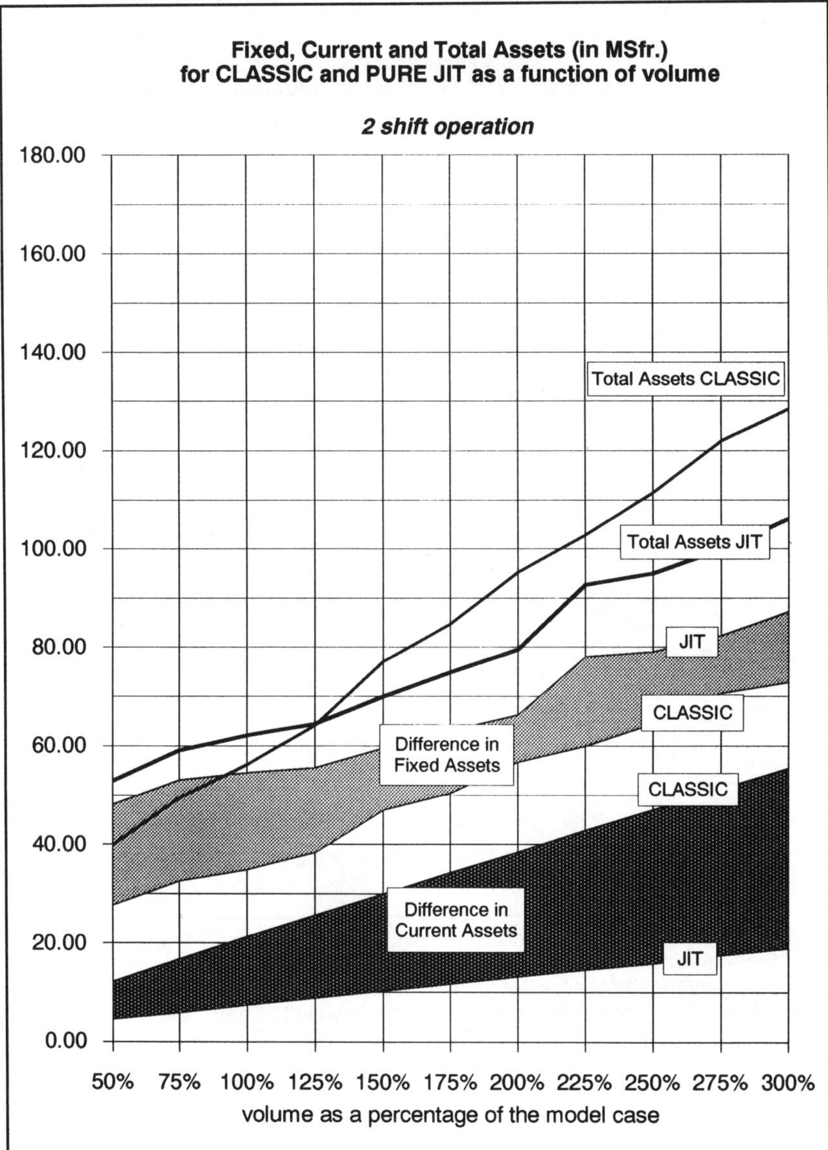

E-Chart I-2.4: Asset base for CLASSIC and PURE JIT with the sales volume increasing from 50% to 300% of the base model case. This chart displays the changing composition of the balance sheet for the two concepts. The total asset base for both concepts is, as expected, much lower in the *2 shift operation*. Note in particular the slope of the fixed assets curves.

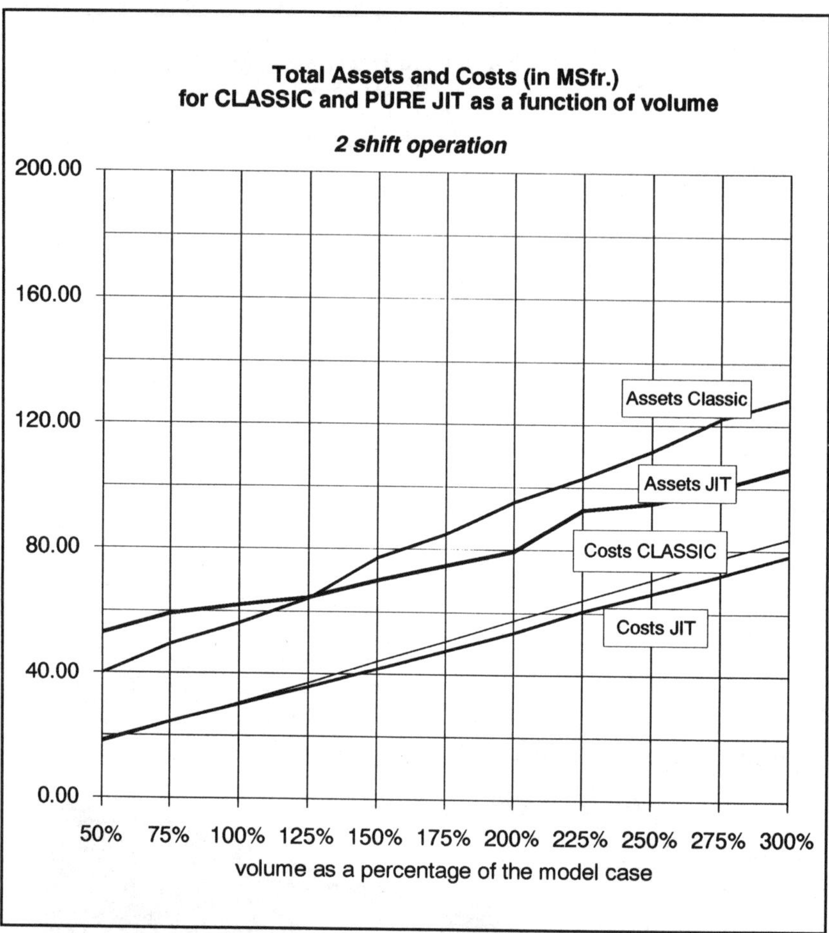

E-Chart I-2.5: Total assets and total costs of CLASSIC and PURE JIT with the volume increasing from 50% to 300% of the base model case. In comparison with the *base scenario* the total asset base for both concepts is considerably lower. The differences in total assets and total costs are shown in E-Chart I-2.6.

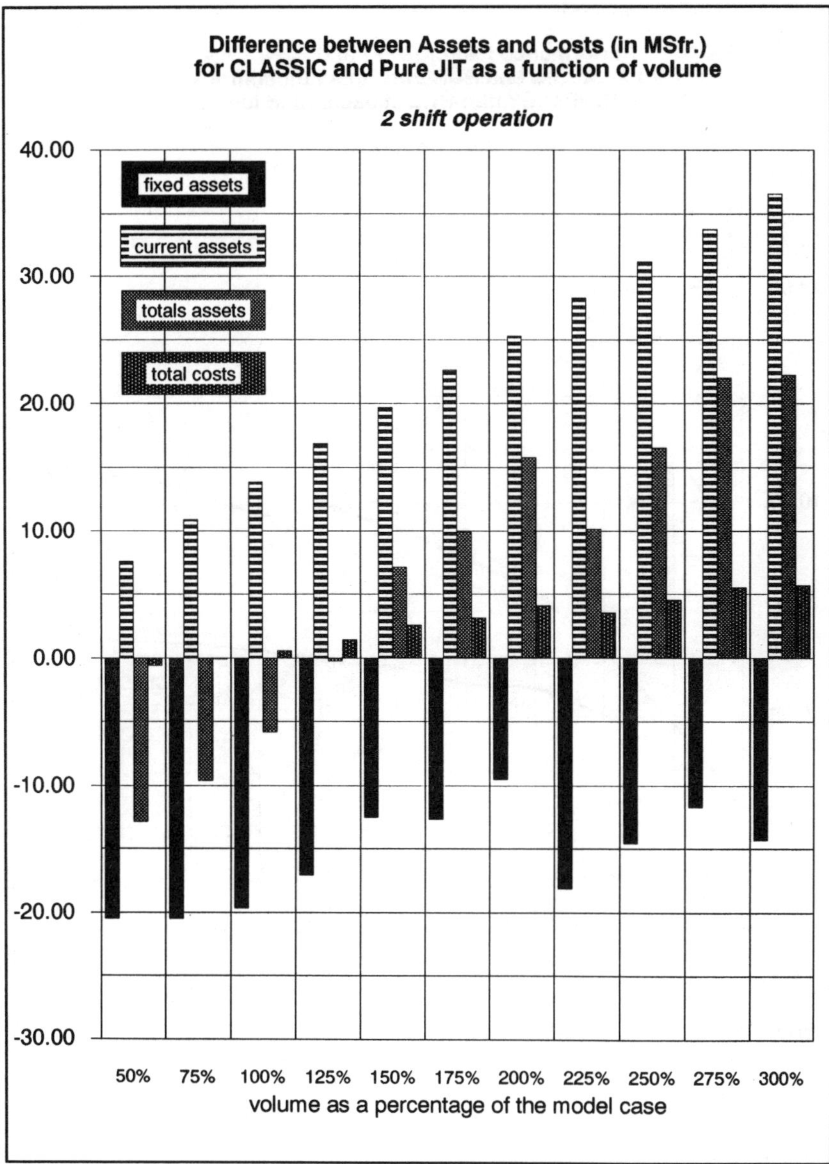

E-Chart I-2.6: Difference in assets and total costs between CLASSIC and PURE JIT with the volume increasing from 50% to 300% of the base model case. The difference in total assets has increased somewhat in favour of PURE JIT by the introduction of 2 shifts. On the other hand, the difference in total costs has become marginally smaller.

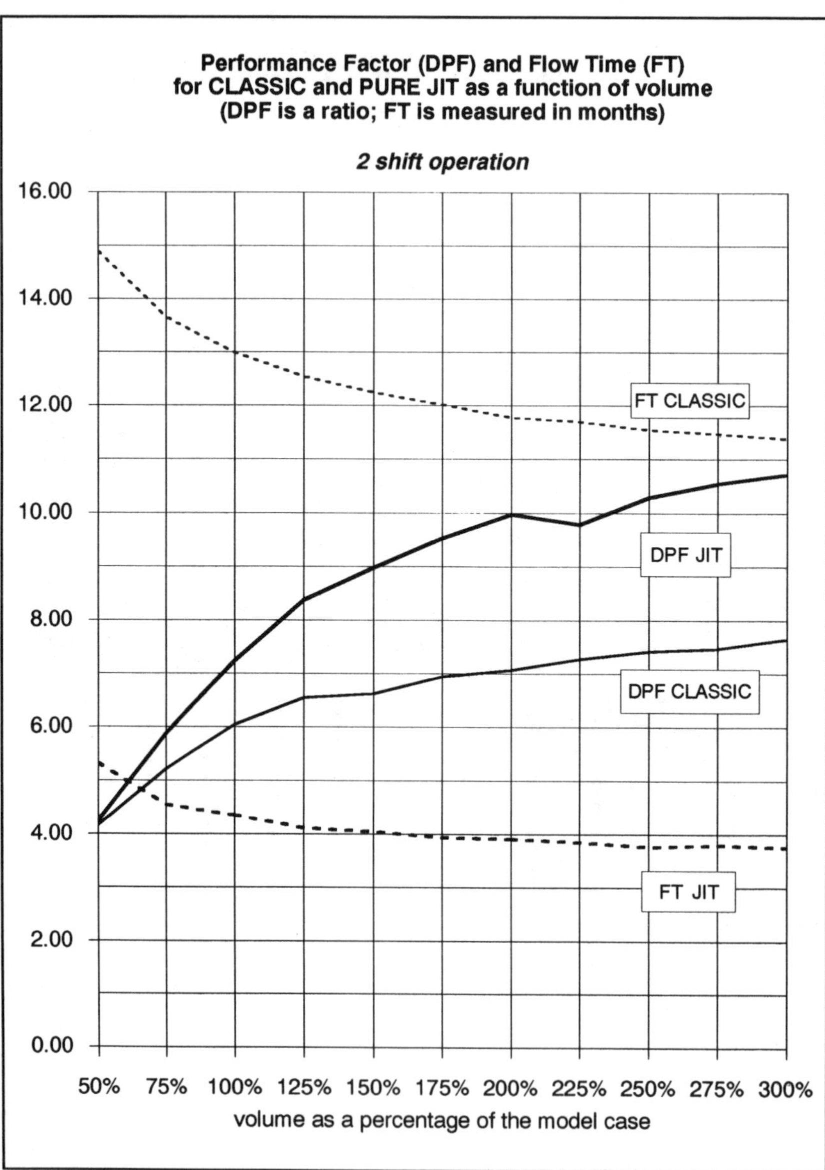

E-Chart I-2.7a: Performance factor and flow time for CLASSIC and PURE JIT with the volume increasing from 50% to 300% of the base model case. The point at which the PF curves intersect has not been changed by the introduction of 2 shift. The slope of both curves is substantially steeper. In comparison with the *base scenario,* the gap in performance factor increases more rapidly as the volume increases. With the volume at 300%, the difference in PF is approximately 25% greater.

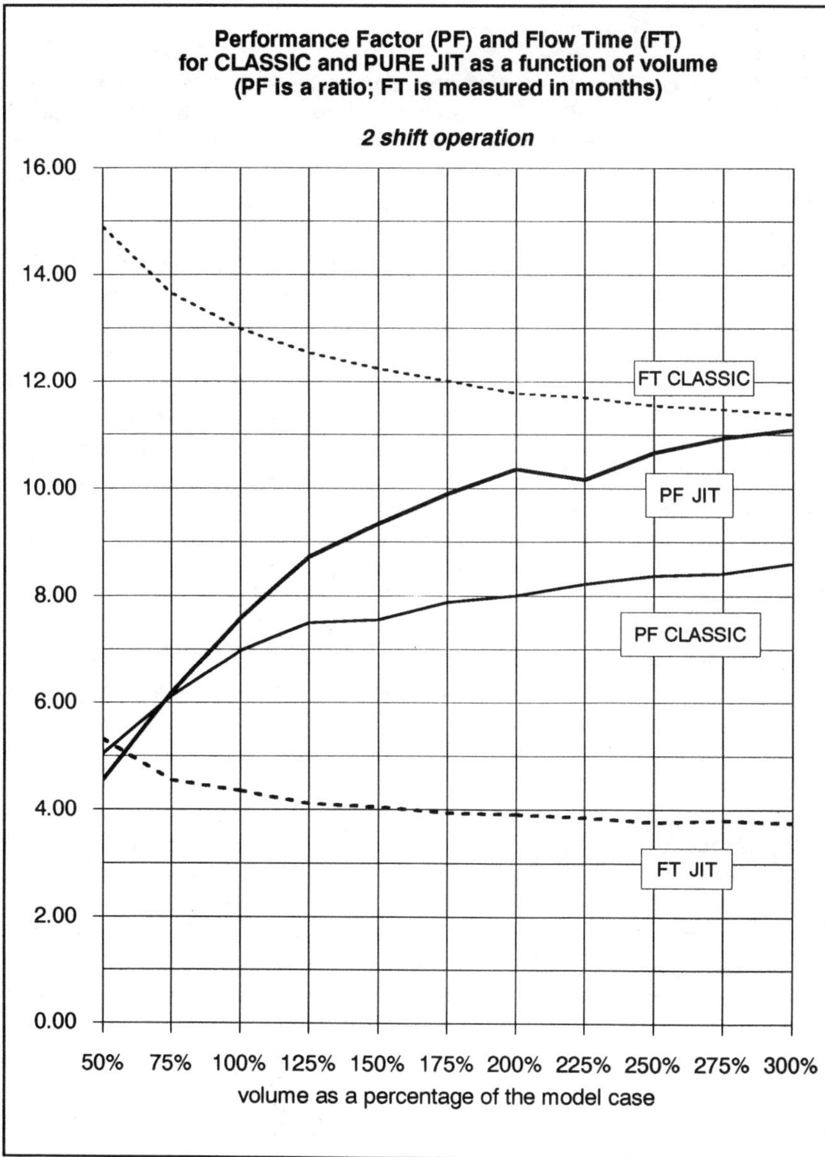

E-Chart I-2.7b: Discounted performance factor and flow time for CLASSIC and PURE JIT with the volume increasing from 50% to 300% of the base model case. The same comments apply to the curves for DPF: the introduction of 2 shifts significantly increases the difference in DPF between CLASSIC and PURE JIT.

Discussion ***2 Shift Operation***

The financial impact of the *2 shift operation* on the difference in performance between CLASSIC and PURE JIT is clearly shown by the performance factor, either PF or DPF. PURE JIT benefits most from an additional shift. The difference in PF is up to 25% greater. Although the total asset base and total costs are much lower for the *2 shift operation* in both cases, the two performance factors improve by a relatively smaller amount.

Some care needs to be exercised when drawing conclusion from these experimental results. Obviously, the performance factor improves with the number of shifts. However, the experimental scenario is not a realistic one. As mentioned, there is a labour shortage at present, which is predicted to last for at least for some time. In simple numerical terms, no additional labour hours are required by the *2 shift operation*. The implicit assumption is that the labour utilization remains unchanged. Furthermore, some form of compensation must be provided for shift work. It may also be more difficult to attract qualified personnel. It is, therefore, necessary to reduce the labour content of the production processes at the expense of higher equipment costs. In other words, the underlying strategy must be to de-couple the the size of the labour force from the production volume. This has other advantages as well, to mention the added flexibility in terms of medium-term demand fluctuations.

The performance factor (DPF) for CLASSIC with the volume at 100% increases from 5.6 to 7.2 by the introduction of a second shift. The experimental results on equipment costs in relation to labour content, see §7.3.3, indicate that a 50% increase in the equipment cost would decrease the DPF by circa 25%. Subtracting 25% from 7.2 gives a DPF of 5.4, which is already less than 5.6, the value for the *base scenario*. The same set of experimental results indicates that the impact of reduced labour content—the term labour productivity is misleading, but commonly used—on the performance factor is likely to be weak. The impact depends on the labour content reduction in relation to the increase in investment. According to the production staff who supplied the input for the *base scenario*, the equipment selected already represents "top of the line" technology; automating the production process any further would require a disproportionately large increase in investment.

Purpose ***Campaign Sizing***

In the *base scenario,* campaign sizes vary with the square root of the production volume. This section repeats the basic set of experiments while keeping campaign sizes at all levels constant as the volume increases. *Constant campaign sizes* is the name of the scenario. If the volume is greater than 100% of the model case, then this is equivalent to reducing the campaign sizes, and *vice versa*. This is illustrated and explained in E-Chart I-3.1.

The second and more important set of experiments under this heading varies the campaign sizes in fabrication in order to assess the sensitivity of this decision variable with respect to the overall financial performance measures. The values used for campaign sizes of CLASSIC are taken from the industrial case investigated. A sophisticated implementation of a dynamic lot sizing[70] algorithm for 'optimizing' campaign sizes calculated these specific values. Although the assumptions and the treatment of input parameters of the two models are too different to make any direct comparison of the results questionable, it is possible to comment on the application of this campaign sizing technique and to clarify the extent to which it stocks the flow of goods.

In the case of PURE JIT, the base model campaign sizes were set by classifying the products according to their production volume and selecting a higher frequency for the larger products. No attempt was made to optimize the campaign sizes by taking cost factors into account.

It should be stressed that the campaign sizes are changed uniformly for all products in the subsequent set of experiments. This is crude and obviously leaves some room for fine-tuning, but that is not the point of the experiments and this section.

---

[70]Strictly speaking campaign sizing

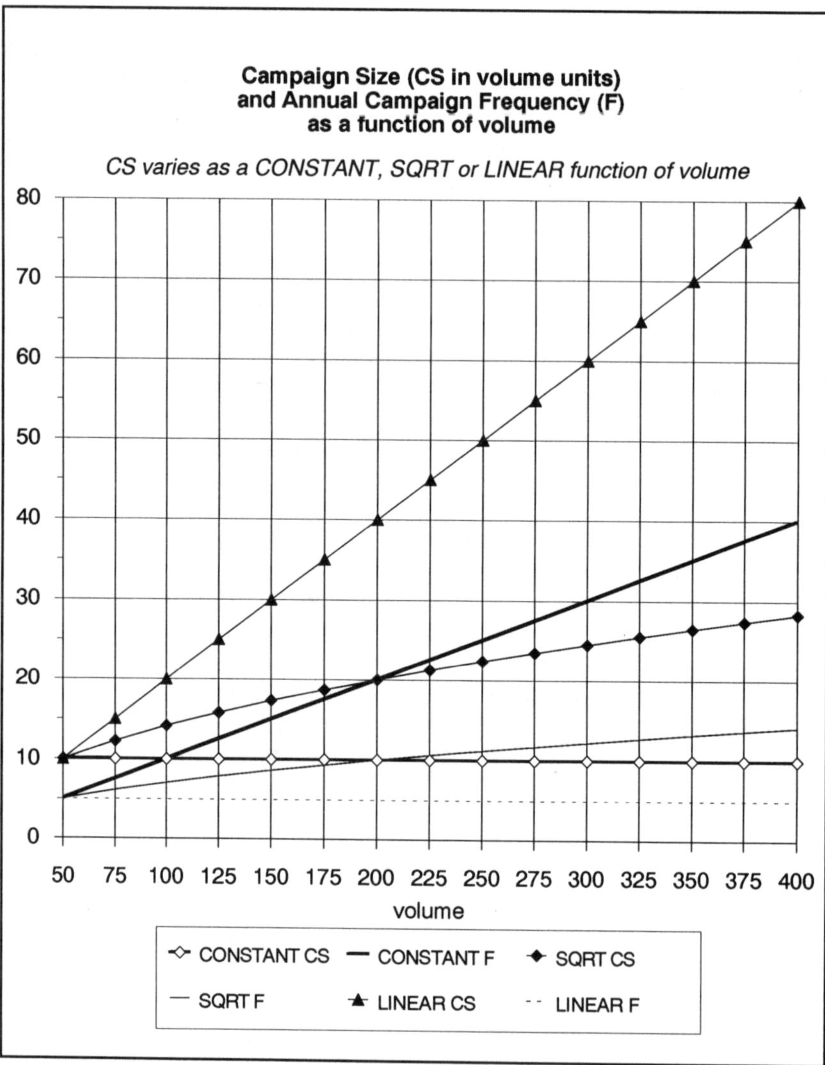

E-Chart I-3.1: Campaign sizes and campaign frequency as a function of volume. This chart is not the output of QED. It shows the effects of the assumed relationship between campaign sizes, frequency and volume. In the *base scenario,* campaign sizes at all production levels are increased with the square root of the production volume. If the campaign sizes are kept constant, the frequency increases linearly with the volume, as illustrated in this chart. E-Charts I-3.2 through I-3.4 show the results for this variant of the *base scenario.* This variant—*constant campaign sizes*—amounts to a decrease in the relative size of the campaigns as the volume increases above 100% of the base model case. Conversely, the variant in which the campaign sizes are increased linearly with the volume, which is not investigated, amounts to a decrease.

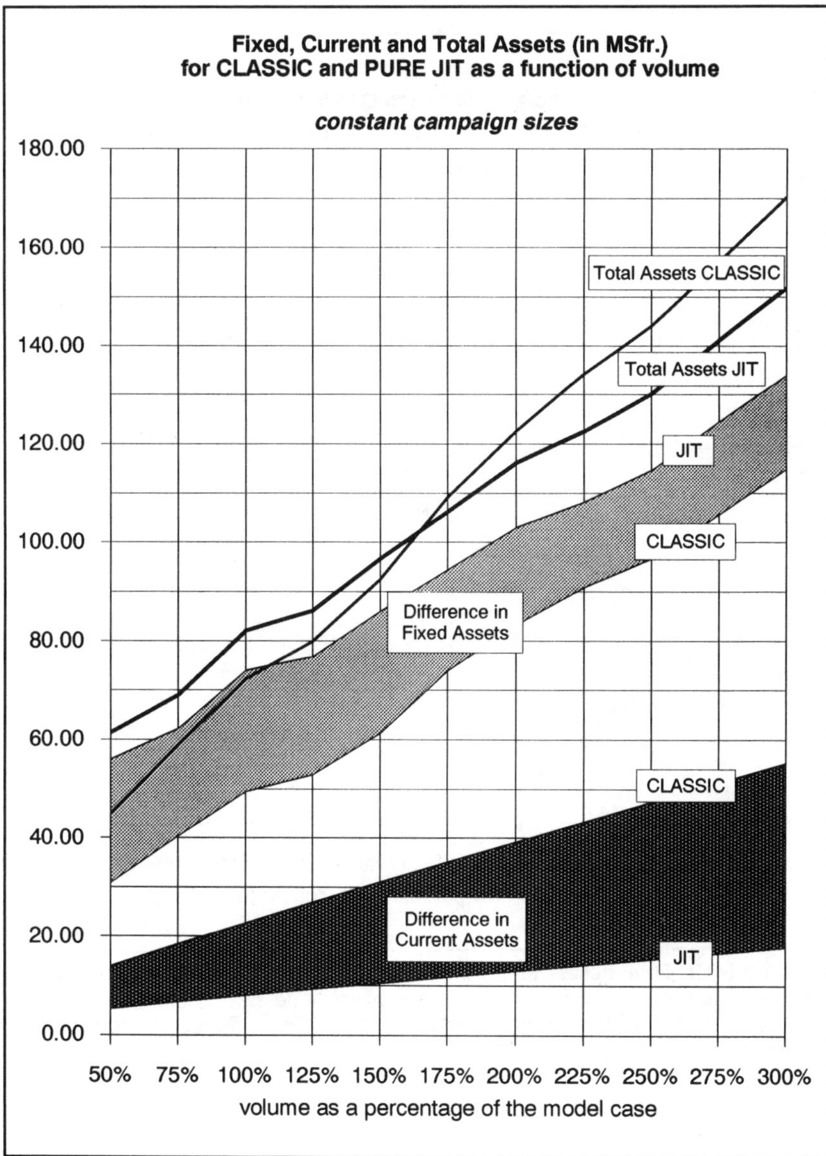

E-Chart I-3.2: Asset base for CLASSIC and PURE JIT with the volume increasing from 50% to 300% of the base model case. The results do not appear to be different from the *base scenario.* A direct comparison with E-Chart I-1.4a reveals, however, a small change in the composition of the balance sheet. The *base scenario* has less current assets and more fixed assets; the total assets are approximately the same. This holds if the volume is greater than 100%; below this value, the campaign sizes are in effect increased by not varying the campaign sizes when the volume decreases.

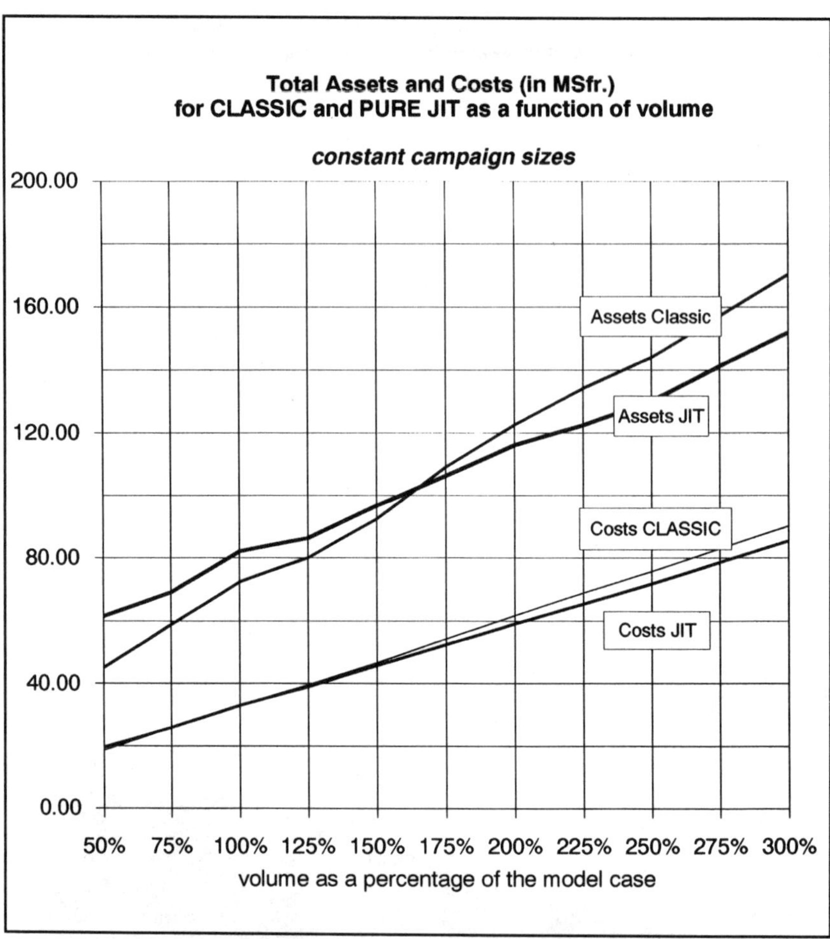

E-Chart I-3.3: Total assets and total costs for CLASSIC and PURE JIT with the volume increasing from 50% to 300% of the base model case. Again, the results do not appear to be different from the base scenario. The difference in total costs is somewhat smaller than for the *base scenario*, see E-Chart I-1.4a

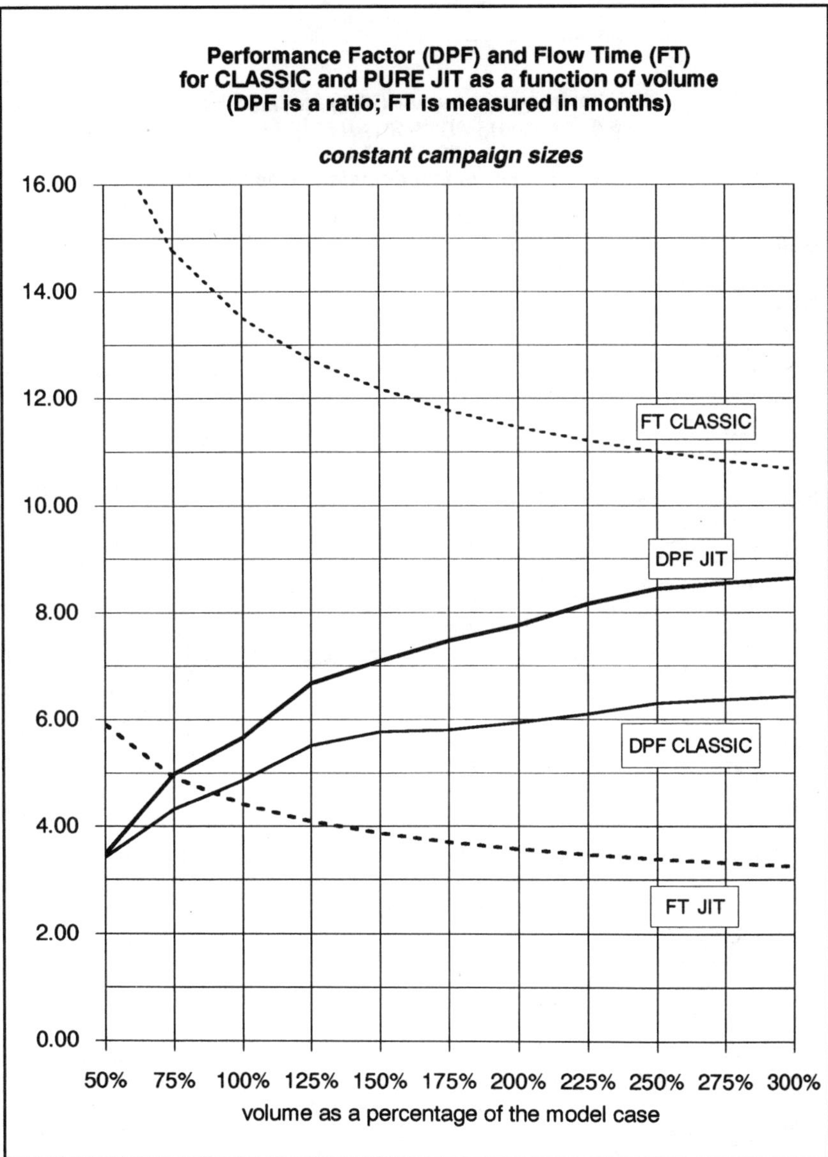

E-Chart I-3.4: Discounted performance factor and flow time for CLASSIC and PURE JIT with the volume increasing from 50% to 300% of the base model case. In comparison with the *base scenario* the discounted performance factor for CLASSIC and PURE JIT is somewhat higher since the stock levels, as shown by the different flow times of the two scenarios, are higher than under the *base scenario*—see E-Chart I-1.7b.

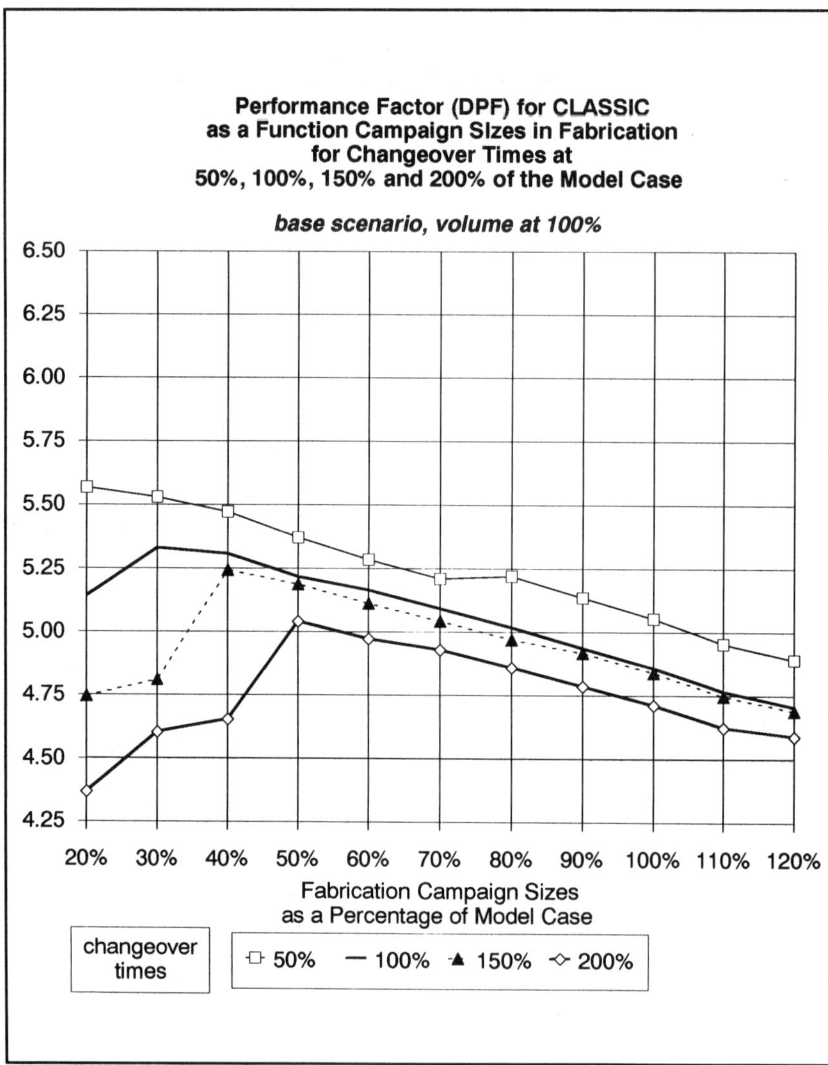

E-Chart I-3.5: Discounted performance factor (DPF) for CLASSIC as a function of the campaign sizes in fabrication, which increase from 20% to 120% of the base model case. Changeover times vary from 50% to 200% of the base model case. Taking DPF as the prime financial indicator, the 'optimal' campaign sizes of the base model case are about three times too large: DPF reaches its peak at 30% for the base model changeover times. As expected, the DPF maximum shifts to larger campaign sizes with increasing changeover times.

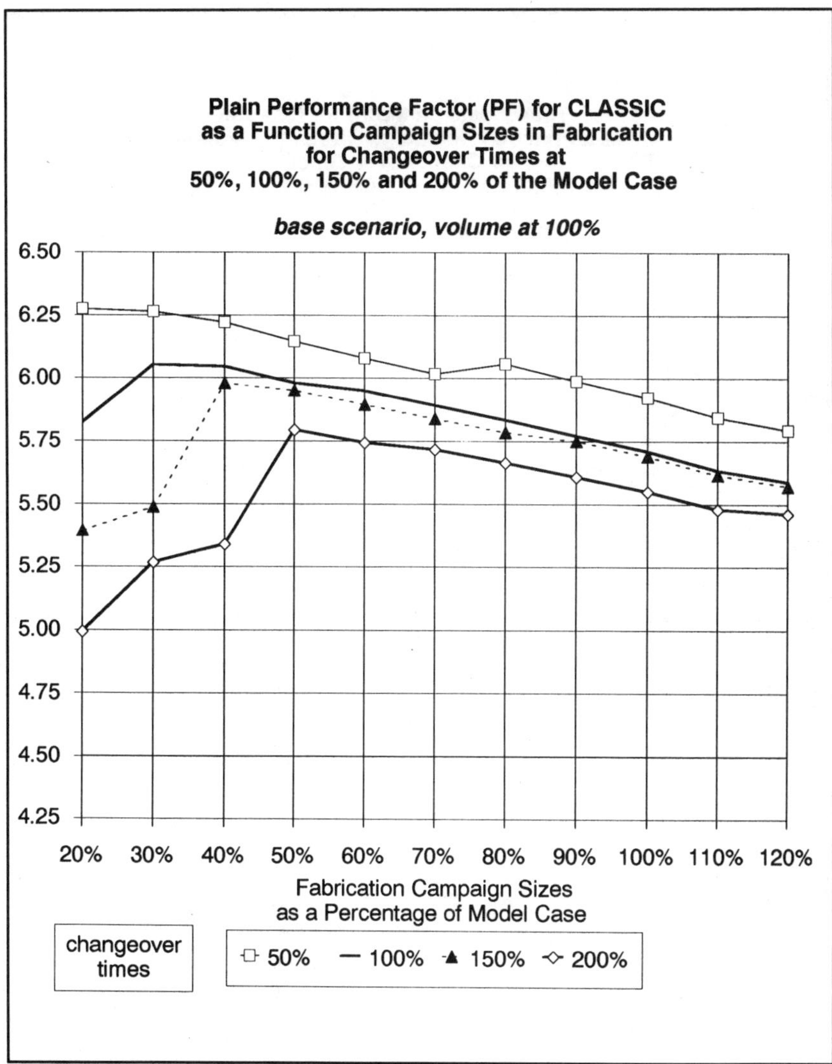

E-Chart I-3.6: Plain performance factor (PF) for CLASSIC as a function of the campaign sizes in fabrication, which increase from 20% to 120% of the base model case. Changeover times vary from 50% to 200% of the base model case. The use of PF instead of DPF only changes the slope and the level of the curves. The maximum values are obtained at the same campaign sizes.

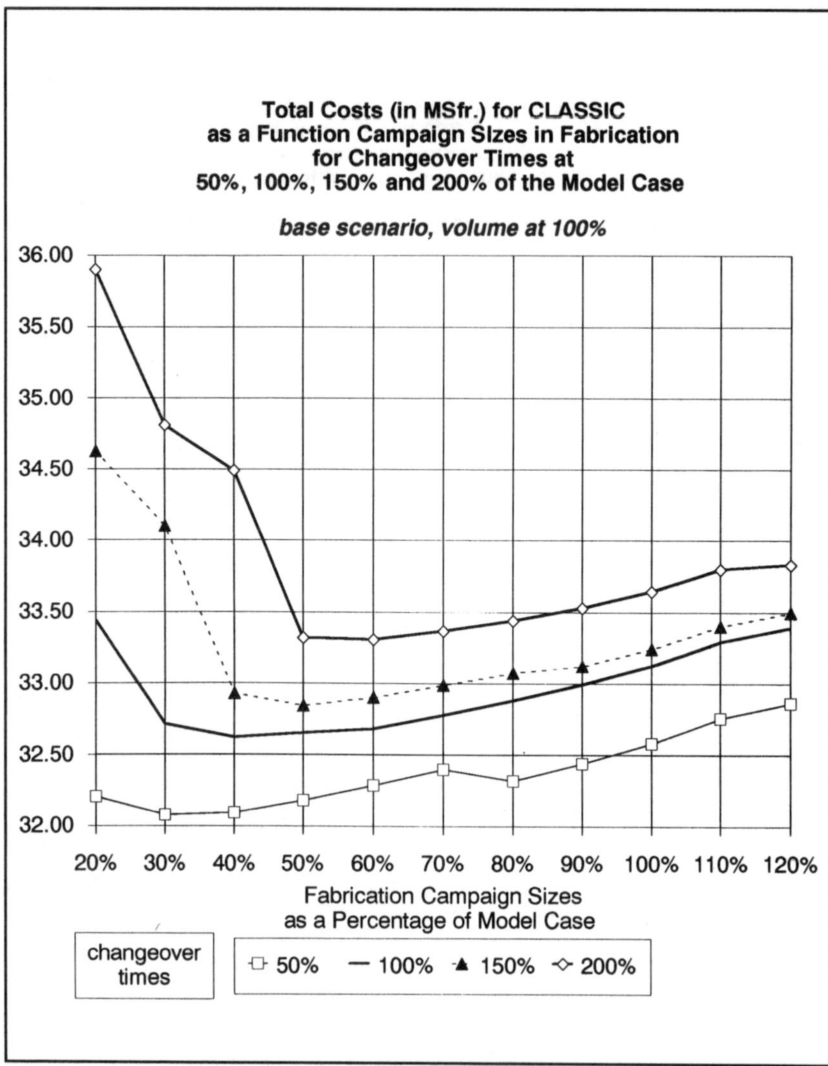

E-Chart I-3.7: Total costs for CLASSIC as a function of the campaign sizes in fabrication, which increase from 20% to 120% of the base model case. Changeover times vary from 50% to 200% of the base model case. The minimum total costs, as opposed to maximum PF or DPF, are obtained with larger campaign sizes. The shift to larger campaign sizes is about 10%—more in relative terms. This means that the choice of the performance factor instead of minimum total cost as the prime financial criteria results in smaller optimal campaign sizes.

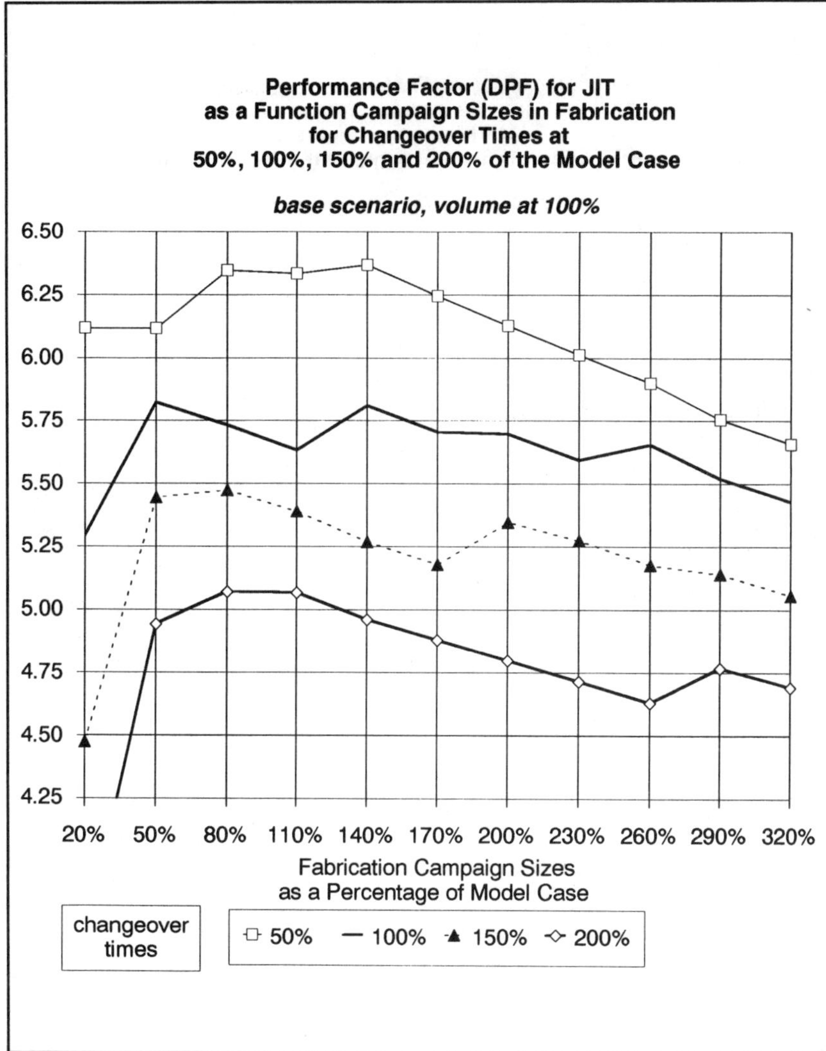

E-Chart I-3.8: Discounted performance factor (DPF) for PURE JIT as a function of campaign sizes in fabrication—ranging from 20% to 320% of the base model case in steps of 30%. Changeover times vary from 50% to 200% of the base model case. The eyeballed campaign sizes for PURE JIT do not appear to be too far of the mark. However, the results are less consistent than those for CLASSIC. This indicates that there is in fact some room to fine-tune the individual campaign sizes. What seems like an anomaly in the results is explained by the fact that a small decrease in the campaign sizes may require a step increase in the required capacity. The range within which the values for DFP beyond the turning point vary is small in comparison to CLASSIC. E-Chart I-3.9 zooms in on the area around the maximum values.

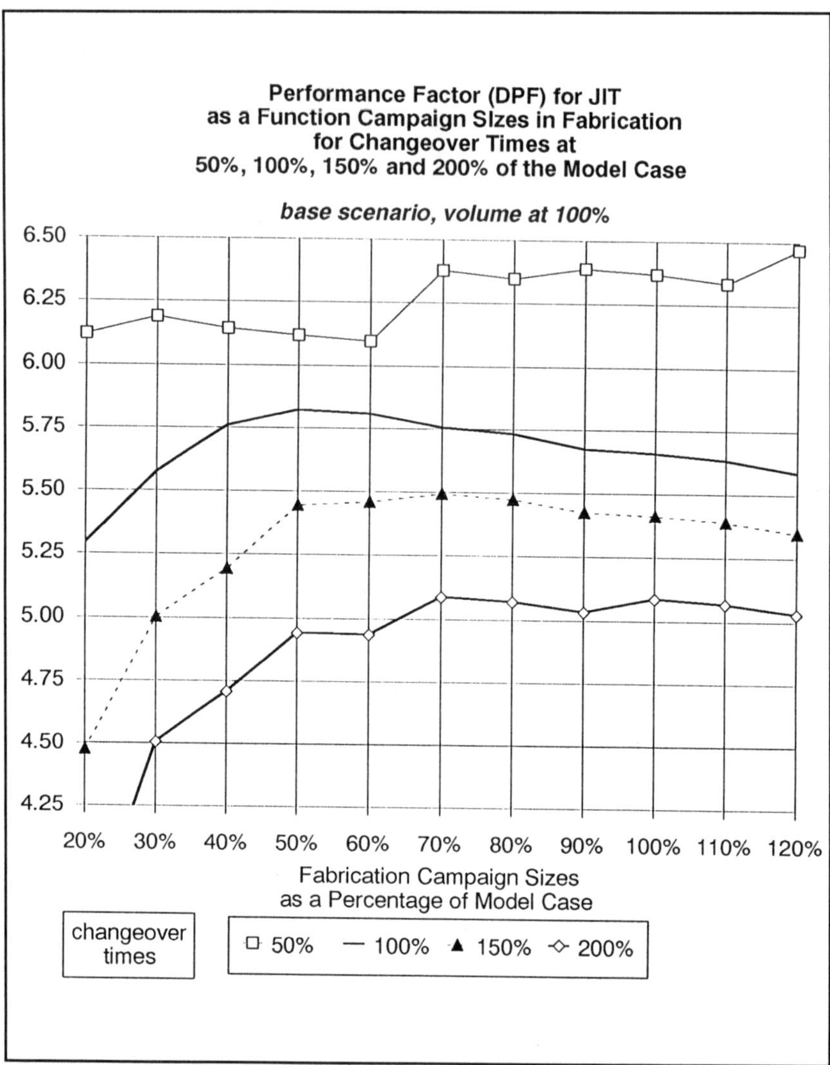

E-Chart I-3.9: Discounted performance factor (DPF) for PURE JIT as a function of campaign sizes in fabrication—ranging from 20% to 120% of the base model case in steps of 10%. Changeover times vary from 50% to 200% of the base model case. This E-Chart zooms on a section of E-Chart I-3.8.

Discussion ***Campaign Sizing***

The experimental results confirm that campaign sizes in fabrication have a significant effect on the financial indicators. The campaign sizes for CLASSIC need to be reduced to 30% of the values of the base model case to achieve the maximum DPF. This increases the performance factor DPF by 0.5 points, which amounts to a performance improvement of 10%. The total costs are minimal with campaign sizes at 40% of the values of the base model case. The cost reduction equals about 0.5 MSfr., which is less than 2% of the total cost of 33 MSfr. The conclusion that the use of DPF or PF as the prime optimizing criteria leads to smaller campaign sizes than the traditional "minimum total cost" approach concurs with the findings reported in [Pack 1989].

It is not hard to see how the implementation of the campaign sizing algorithm could arrive at the particular values for the 'optimal' campaign sizes. In the industrial case, the inventory related costs are estimated to be significantly lower. Depending on the parameter values, QED typically ends up with a pallet space cost for a fully automated warehouse (silo) of 300 Sfr. per annum. The industrial case from which the base model is derived reports and uses values that are less than 40% of this figure. Secondly, in QED, the cost of additional changeovers is fairly low for any equipment item that has sufficient surplus capacity. In the industrial case on the other hand, the implementation of the campaign sizing algorithm includes, depending on the utilization of the equipment, part are all of the equipment costs in the changeover penalty. This is generally considered to be a dubious practice[71] and a poor substitute for a solution to the capacitated lot sizing problem. Nevertheless, practitioners may feel that this is an acceptable pragmatic approach. The results presented here put the financial spotlight on its effects. The experiments are not detailed enough to allow any further conclusions to be drawn. It is clear that other aspects such as increased production throughput time play a role as well.

It is also of interest to realize that QED, as noted already, embeds a long-term view of the impact of the decision variables on financial performance. Applications of campaign sizing algorithms typically consider only the short-term effects of varying campaign sizes. In a sense, therefore, the analysis would evaluate the long-term impact of these short-term optimizations.

[71]The argument is that the equipment costs—depreciation and the cost of capital—are fixed, i.e. not influenced by the decision about campaign sizes. See also section 2.7 "Insight from Mathematical Models."

Purpose ***Changeover Times***

In the first set of experiments, the changeover times at all levels vary from 200% to 25% in terms of the base model case while campaign sizes are kept constant. As mentioned, keeping campaign sizes constant while the volume increases, is equivalent to a campaign size reduction with constant volume. In the second set, the campaign sizes vary with the square root of the product of the scalars for production volume and changeover time. For example, if the volume is doubled and changeover time reduced to 25% of the base case, then campaign sizes would be set at 70% of values of the base model case—$\sqrt{(2.0 \times 0.25)}$ is about 0.7.

These two sets of experiments assess the financial impact of a changeover time reduction programme. Clearly, changeover time could be coupled with the investment cost of equipment, see §7.3.3. Experience in other industries has shown that substantial reductions can achieved with some ingenuity—but relatively little effort—if enough emphasis is put on the importance of the improvements. This doesn't necessarily involve major capital investments.

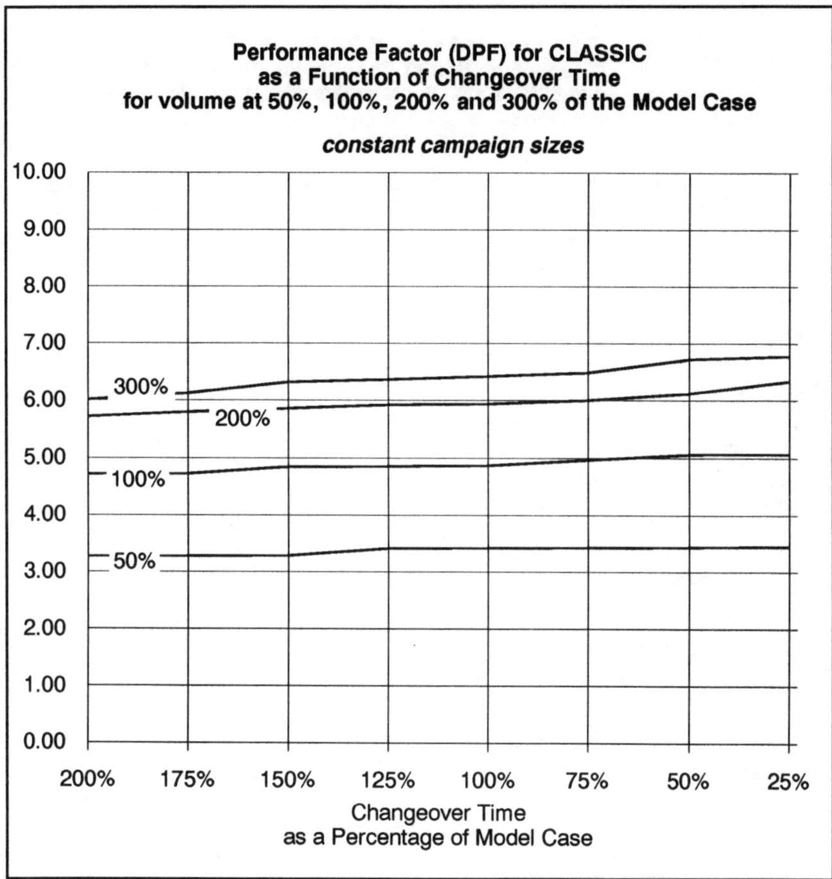

E-Chart I-4.1: Discounted performance factor (DPF) for CLASSIC as a function of changeover times with the volume at 50%, 100%, 200% and 300% of the base model case; campaign sizes are kept constant. The improvements in DPF are small, especially when the volume at 50% or 100%.

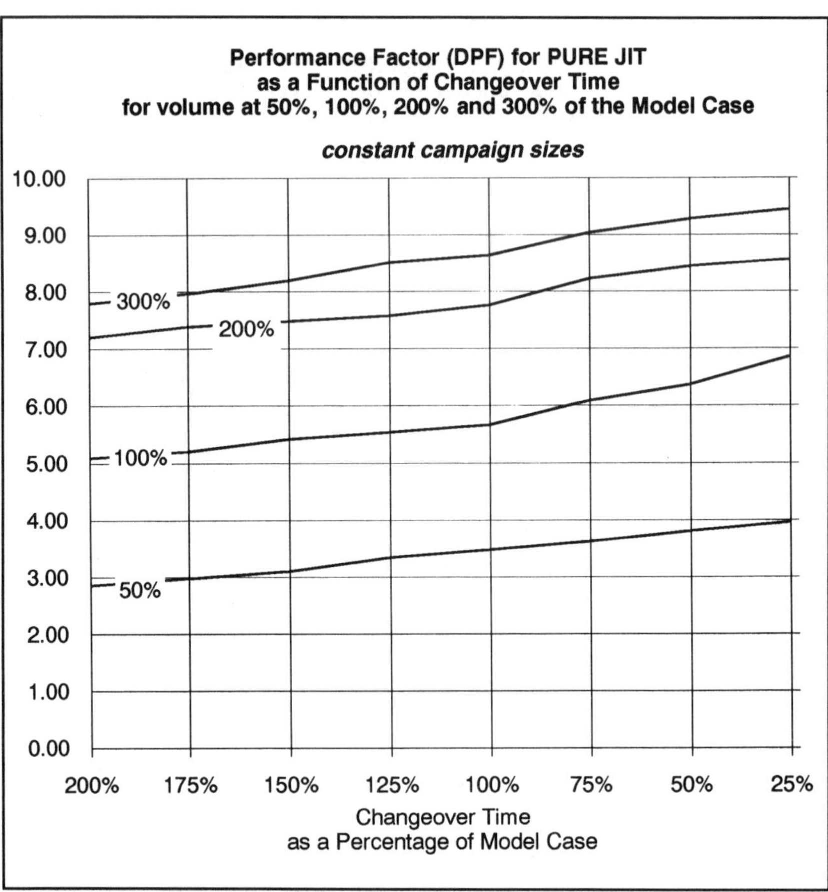

E-Chart I-4.2: Discounted performance factor (DPF) for PURE JIT as a function of changeover times with the volume at 50%, 100%, 200% and 300% of the base model case; campaign sizes are kept constant. In comparison with CLASSIC, the improvements in DPF are substantial. E-Chart I-4.3 shows this more clearly.

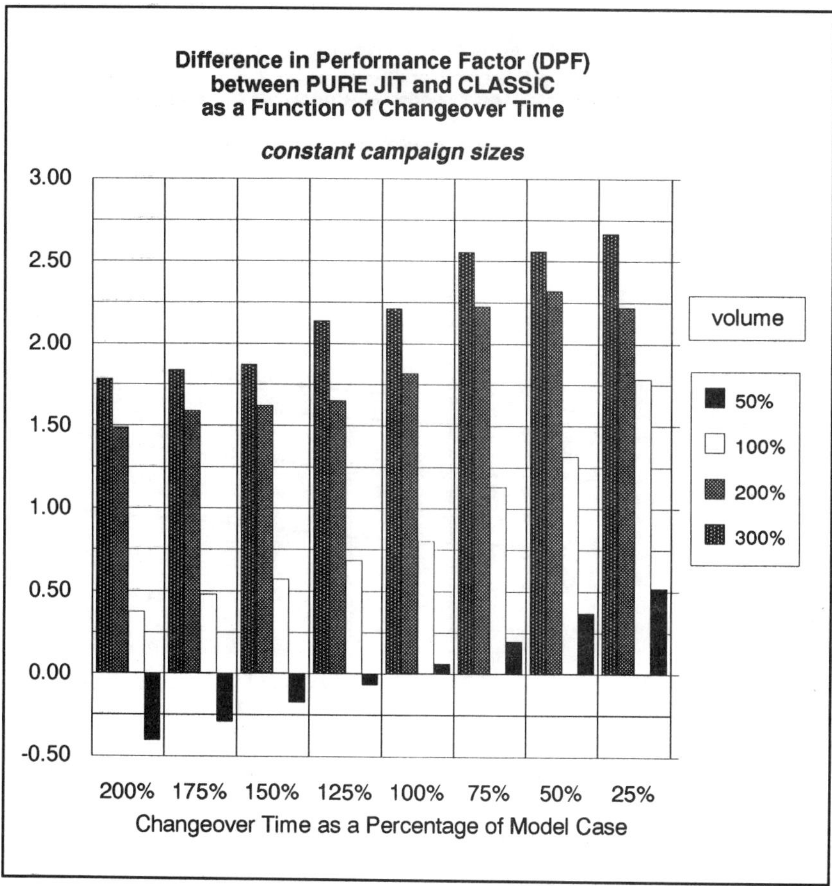

E-Chart I-4.3: Difference in discounted performance factor (DPF) between CLASSIC and PURE JIT as a function of changeover times with the volume at 50%, 100%, 200% and 300% of the base model case; campaign sizes are kept constant. In this scenario, the difference in DPF between CLASSIC and PURE JIT clearly increases as changeover times are reduced. For a comparison, see E-Chart I-4.6.

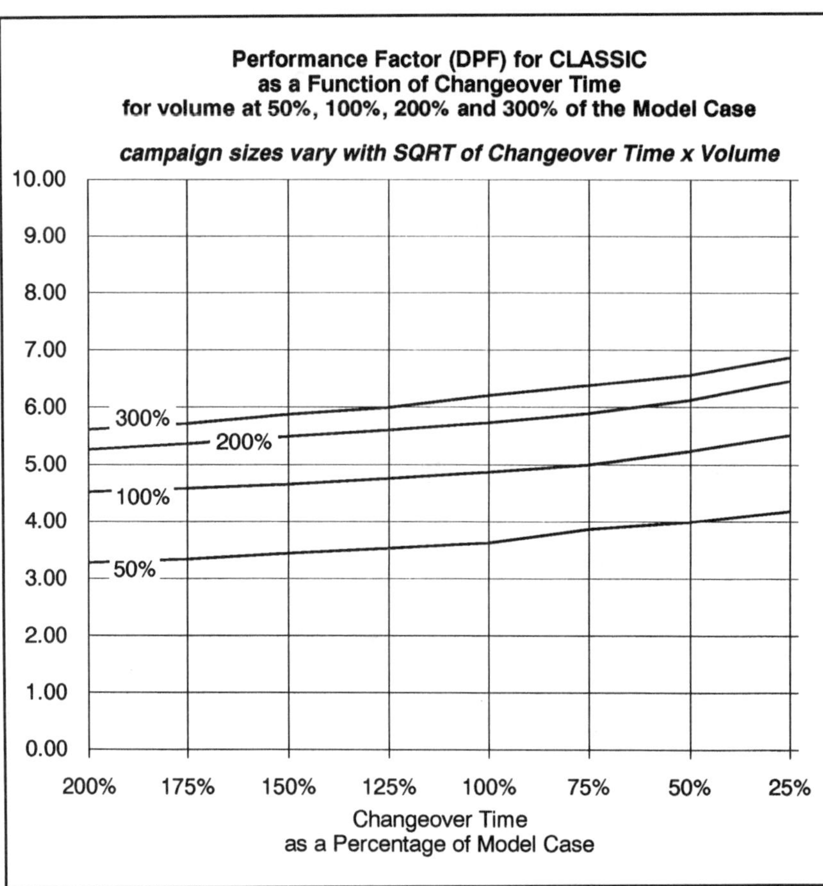

E-Chart I-4.4: Discounted performance factor (DPF) for CLASSIC as a function of changeover times with the volume at 50%, 100%, 200% and 300% of the base model case; campaign sizes vary with the square root of the product of the scalars for changeover time and volume. Under this scenario, there is a significant increase in DPF, regardless the volume.

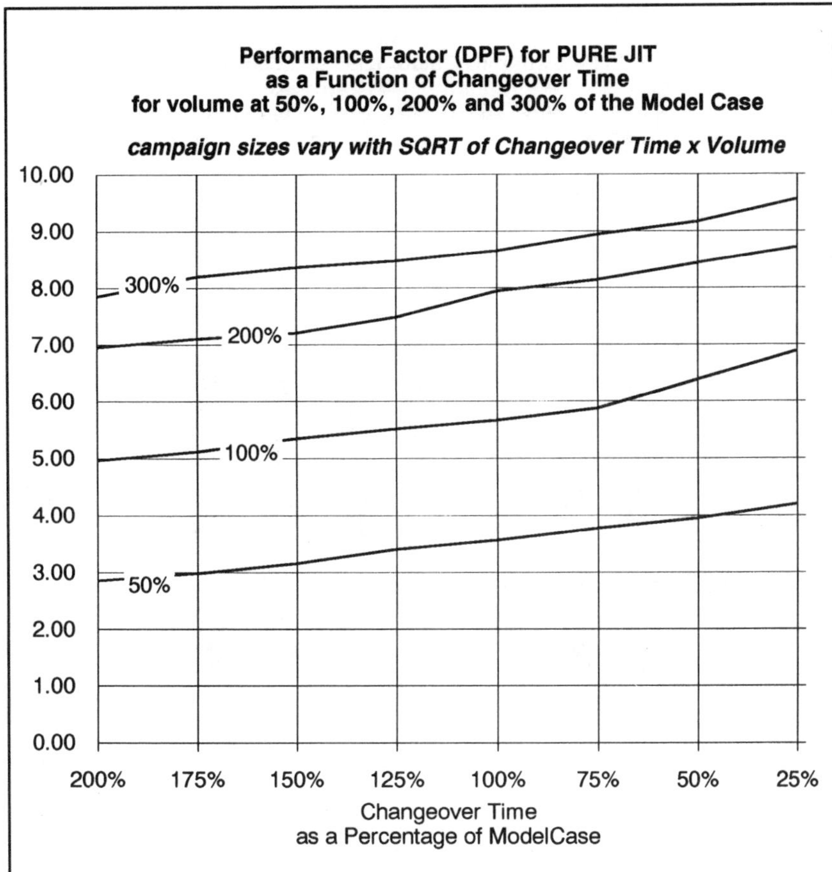

E-Chart I-4.5: Discounted performance factor (DPF) for PURE JIT as a function of changeover times with the volume at 50%, 100%, 200% and 300% of the base model case; campaign sizes vary with the square root of the product of the scalars for changeover time and volume. The increase in DPF does not level off as the changeover times are reduced; on the contrary, the DPF appears to increase somewhat more rapidly towards the tail end of the curves.

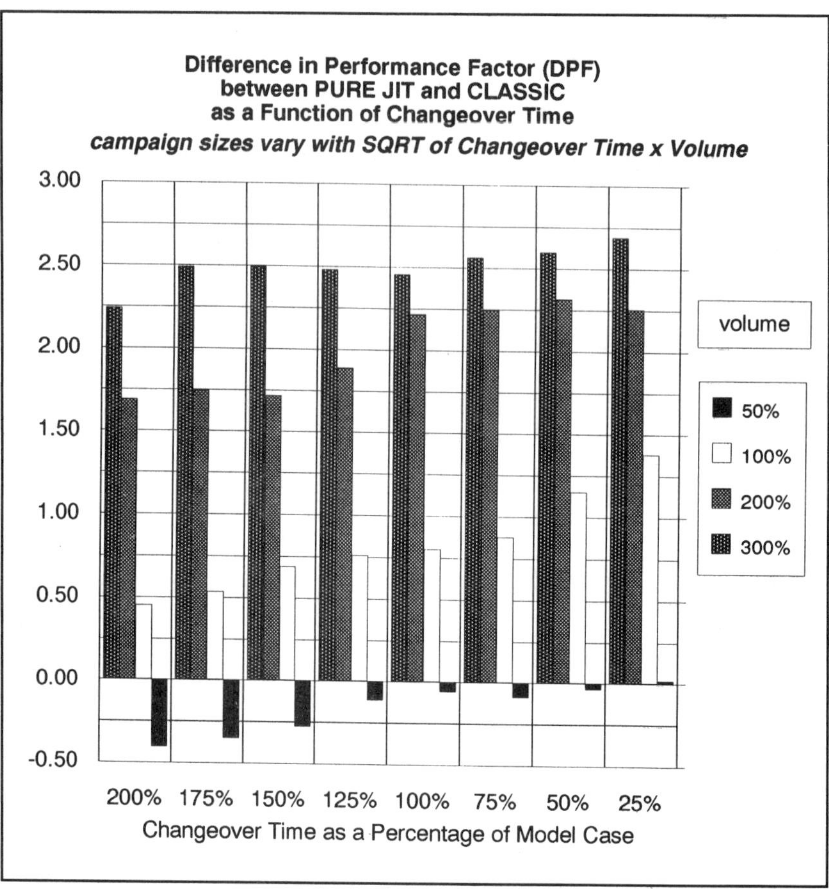

E-Chart I-4.6: Difference in discounted performance factor (DPF) between CLASSIC and PURE JIT as a function of changeover times with the volume at 50%, 100%, 200% and 300% of the base model case; campaign sizes vary with the square root of the product of the scalars for changeover time and volume. If the campaign sizes are coupled with the changeover time reduction, then the growth in the difference in DPF between CLASSIC and PURE JIT appears to be more modest. The cause, however, is the poorer DPF of CLASSIC with changeover times at values larger than the base model case.

Discussion ***Changeover Times***

The experimental results permit us to draw two major conclusions. First of all, there is no sign that the benefits of a changeover time reduction program taper off as the changeover times become smaller. On the contrary, for PURE JIT the slope of the DPF curve turns up somewhat as changeover times are reduced, i.e. increasing marginal returns. In the CLASSIC case, we achieve the full benefits only if we simultaneously reduce campaign sizes; further performance improvements, especially for CLASSIC, can be expected if we optimize the campaign sizes in conjunction with the reduction in changeover times. In summary, these results provide empirical support for the theoretical insight obtained by other researchers, see chapter 2.

The second conclusion that we can drawn is that PURE JIT appears to benefit more from reductions in changeover time than CLASSIC. A series of additional experiments would be required to show to what extent this is caused by the less than optimal campaign sizes of CLASSIC.

The difference in annual costs between CLASSIC and PURE JIT for quality control, see E-Chart I-1.3, indicates that the issue of changeover times is equaly relevant quality control. The penalty paid by PURE JIT for small campaign and lot sizes increases from 0.2 to 1.1 MSFr. per annum. With the volume at 300% of the base case model, the quality control costs of PURE JIT are more than double those of CLASSIC.

Interestingly enough, the QC department is currently testing newly-developed automated equipment for key analytic tests that would drastically reduce this penalty. First of all, the concept of changeover time is not applicable in its usual sense. The equipment takes any combination of samples. The number of campaigns has little influence on the processing time, since the changeover process is automatic. Secondly, the equipment runs unattended once it has started to process a series of samples. Thirdly, since roughly half of the investment costs are for the development of the process control software, an increase in the total number of lots to be processed should no longer result in a linear increase in quality control costs. In view of the potential benefits in a just-in-time environment, the quoted costs of the developments appeared to be modest. QED could verify this claim.

7.3.2 Pragmatic Alternatives for PURE JIT

The experiments in this section cover two pragmatic alternatives for PURE JIT. The analysis of the experimental results not only leads to a better understanding of these alternatives, but also provides insight into two rather different aspects of PURE JIT that both affect its conversion efficiency. In addition, the analysis permits conclusions as to the appropriateness of their application.

The alternatives are subjected to the set of conditions specified by the *base scenario*, described and used in earlier.

Purpose ***POOL JIT***

The purpose of the first set of experiments is to compare PURE JIT with a modified version of this basic concept. In sharp contrast with the usual just-in-time concept, this particular variant pools the production resources. It does not employ the independent production lines for each different product segment that just-in-time theory normally calls. The variant is referred to as POOL JIT.

The issue addressed by the POOL JIT variant is of considerable interest to practitioners and has divided them into its proponents and opponents. Its pros and cons have provoked lengthy discussions. The experimental results should help to rationalize the debate, which has been tarnished by a number of misconceptions about the mechanics and application of a kanban-like pull principle for directing the material flows. These misconceptions will be addressed shortly. The final decision, however, will remain a matter of managerial judgement since two important issues are hard if not impossible to quantify in financial terms.

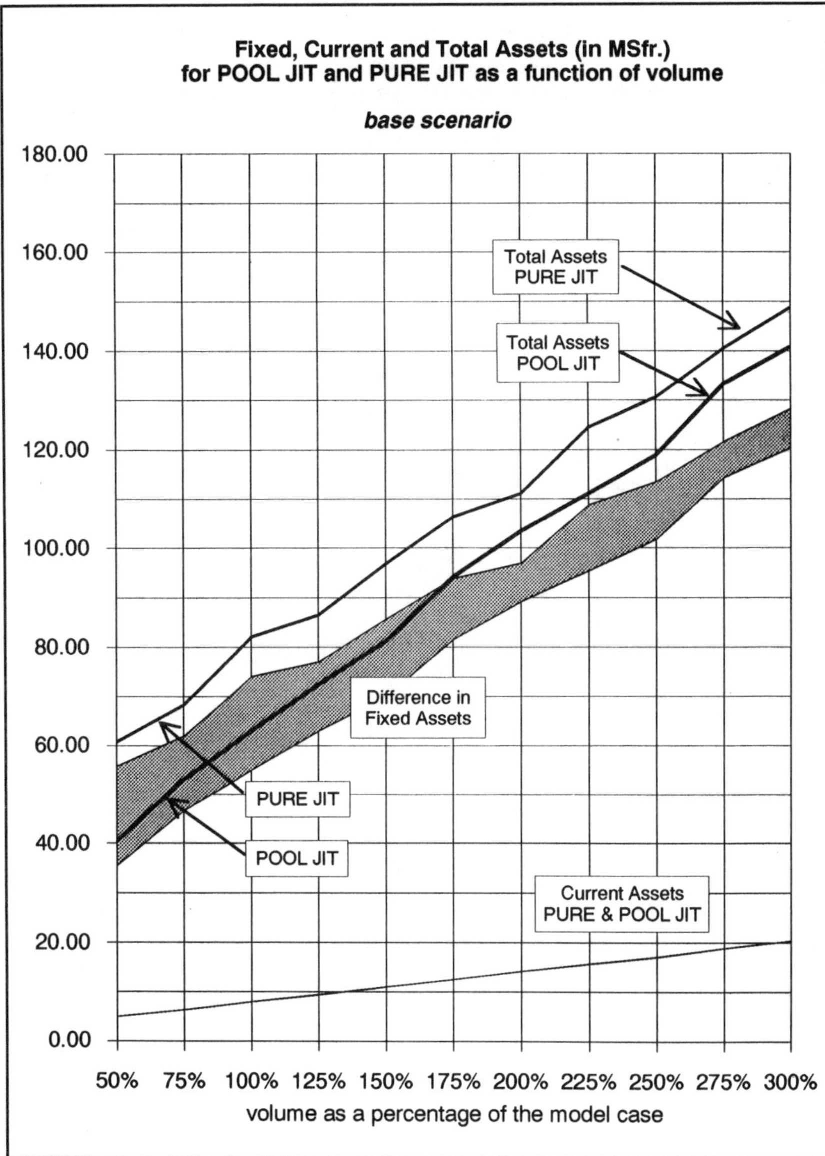

E-Chart II-1.1: Asset base for POOL JIT and PURE JIT with the sales volume increasing from 50% to 300% of the base model case. This chart displays that the initial gap in total assets between POOL JIT and PURE JIT decreases as the volume increases from 50% to 300% of the base model case. E-Chart II-1.4 shows the fixed production assets for a longer range. There is no difference in the inventory levels.

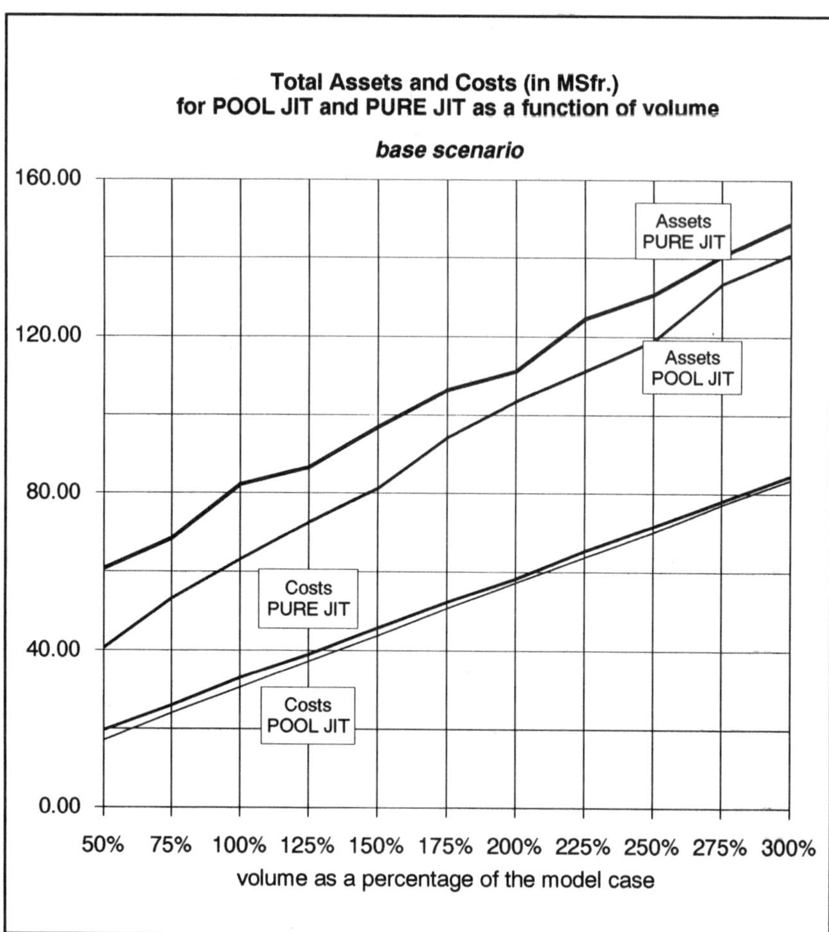

E-Chart II-1.2: Total assets and total costs of POOL JIT and PURE JIT with the volume increasing from 50% to 300% of the base model case. The additional capital costs for the fixed assets required by PURE JIT outweigh the lower costs for planning & control. The difference in total costs is small and decreases with the volume.

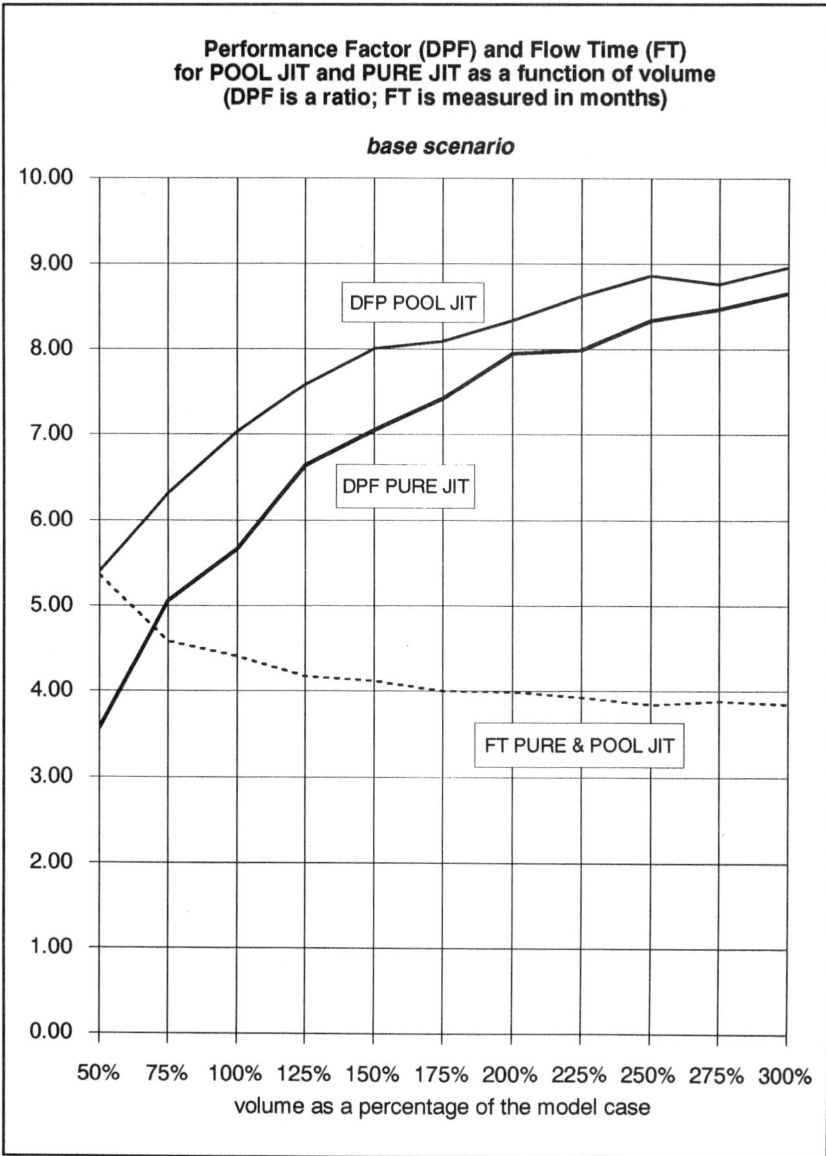

E-Chart II-1.3: Discounted performance factor and flow time for POOL JIT and PURE JIT with the volume increasing from 50% to 300% of the base model case. Given the closing gap between both the total assets and the total costs, the discounted performance factor of the two cases must also converge.

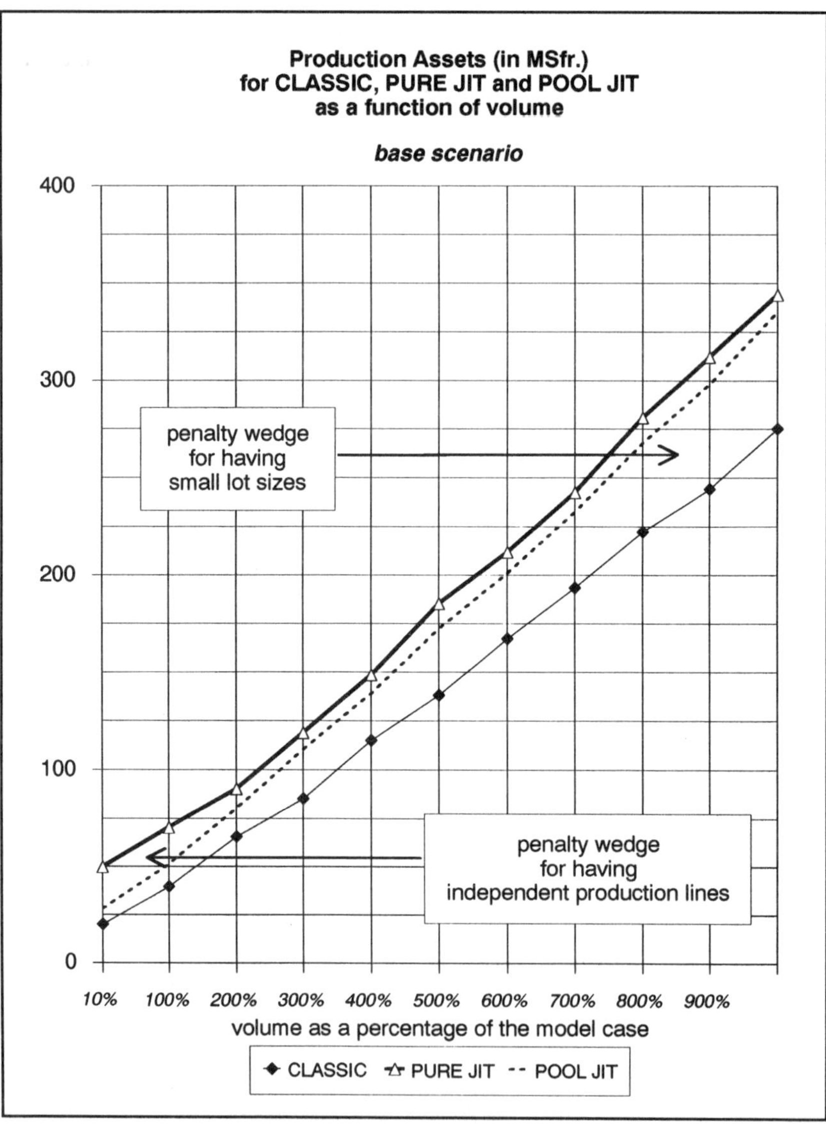

E-Chart II-1.4: Production assets for CLASSIC, PURE JIT and POOL JIT. This chart displays the fixed production assets, i.e. warehouses are excluded, for the volume increasing from 10% to 1000% of the base model case. Note that the values for the 10% observation are not drawn in exactly the right place. In theory, the curves for PURE JIT and POOL JIT converge, albeit very slowly. The gap between CLASSIC, on the one hand, and PURE JIT and POOL JIT, on the other hand, clearly widens as the volume increases. See E-Chart II-2.5 for a comment on the "penalty" wedges.

Discussion ***POOL JIT***

The experimental results show that the penalty for independent production lines is highest for small operations. This can hardly be a surprise. The difference in total assets between PURE JIT and POOL JIT decreases both in absolute and in relative terms as the volume increases from 50% to 300% of the base model case. The difference in production assets converges quite slowly. See figure 7.4 for an explanation. Thus, PURE JIT continues to pay a price for having independent production lines for any operation with a realistic size.

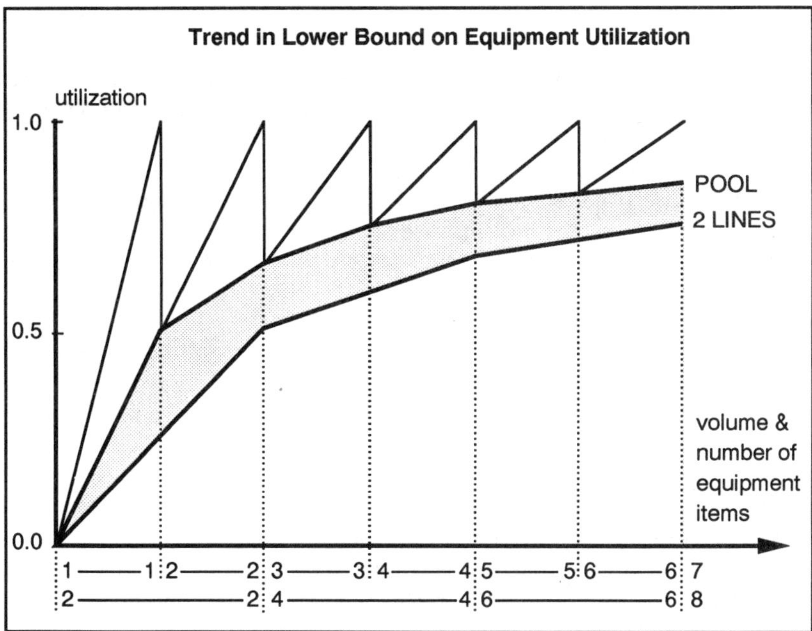

Figure 7.4: Trend in equipment utilization. The two thick curves for POOL and 2 LINES connect the points which express the minimum utilization, i.e. a lower bound on the utilization, of the equipment items required to handle a given volume. The bottom two rows show the number of equipment items. The ratios of pairs of numbers around the dotted lines determine the minimum utilization: if 'n' machines are fully utilized for a certain volume, then 'n + i' machines have a utilization of 'n / (n + i)'.

What are the additional pros and cons? It is generally taken for granted that operational scheduling for POOL JIT is more difficult. The implicit assumption, which seems plausible enough, is that the level of complexity is higher. The extent to which this is in fact reasonable depends on whether the pull principle is applied. If this is the case, then there is no need to schedule the individual steps in the overall process. The feedback cycles control the operation. Only the final stage and the arrival of packaging and raw materials should be scheduled. See for example

[Hall 1983, pp. 58-82]. As a just-in-time system approaches continuous flow manufacturing, scheduling becomes more and more like rate setting. The complexity does not increase. QED, therefore, assumes that planning & control costs are inversely proportional to the number of independent lines. For example, the costs for PURE JIT with four lines will be one fourth of the POOL JIT costs. These costs, however, are so small in relation to the other cost items that even a substantial increase will barely affect the total costs.

The above erroneous assumption also leads to the common point of view that a fully automated materials handling system is required to manage the complexity of a just-in-time system using the pool concept. The irony is, of course, that the implementation of such a system is then indeed complex. The reason for introducing independent production lines may be the need for just such a materials handling system. The argumentation runs in the other direction: an advantage of independent lines is that it may make automated materials handling simpler; and hence, technically feasible and economically justifiable.

A further true advantage of independent lines is that the flow is more clearly visible to production workers and supervisors. Quality problems can be traced more easily and quickly, and the consequences of breakdowns and other interrupts are immediately apparent. Moreover, production workers have a better chance to understand the impact of these problems on the overall process. QED does not quantify these benefits.

On the other side of the equation, we must recognize that any change in the product mix may unbalance the production lines. If the change is substantial, the impact may be difficult and time consuming to assess. Under the pressure of day-to-day business, crossovers may then be introduced as a stop-gap measure. The system quickly degenerates into a bastardized version of the original concept, while maintaining its disadvantages. In industrial practice, such compromises, i.e. crossovers, are known to slip in at the very outset.

In summary, PURE JIT will generally be most appropriate for large operations with relatively low volume products. Some aspects discussed above are not easily quantified, thus leaving room for managerial judgement.

Purpose — ***CLASSIC LOT JIT***

The purpose of the second set of experiments covered in this section is to assess the impact of lot (batch) sizes. To understand the impact of the small batches used by PURE JIT, it is necessary to be aware of two critical assumptions concerning batch processes:

- the investment cost of an equipment item for a batch process is entirely independent of its size
- the processing time is determined by the characteristics of the process and entirely independent of the batch size

This means that small batches are proportionally more expensive than large ones. Both assumptions, although considered to be realistic by the production managers in the Stein works that were interviewed, err on the conservative side and favour a classical operation with the large batch sizes that are typical for it. A recent article on "design cost factors for scaling-up engineering equipment" [Remer et al. 1990] confirms my claims. The empirical relationship between acquisition cost and equipment size is given by the following equation:

$$[cost_2 / cost_1] = [size_2 / size_1]^R$$

On the basis of their analysis of a large number of specific equipment items, Remer et al. determined average R values ranging between 0.63 and 0.82 for the 6 different types equipment types. The standard deviation ranged from 0.15 to 0.27. "Using the average R value of 0.68 [for general equipment], the rule of thumb is that doubling the size of a piece of equipment increase the cost by about 60% and tripling the size increases it by about 110%. [ibid, pp. 81-82]" See also table 7.5.2c in §7.2.4.

A further relevant characteristic is the restriction that batch sizes cannot be varied as easily and quickly as campaign sizes. For one, GMP regulations require all production processes to be registered. This applies also if the batch size of a process is changed.

The lot sizes for PURE JIT were determined by looking at the campaign sizes of a number of the smaller semi-packaged products in the class A segment of solid dosage forms. The question that needs answering is what is an appropriate batch size in relation to the size of the production runs. The campaign sizes for the selected products indicate that larger batches could have been used. However, if the product mix were to be enlarged to include smaller volume products, then large batches would possibly be inappropriate. The use of small batches for PURE JIT means that an increase in volume could also come from the inclusion of more, lower volume products, and not just from an increase in volume for the products selected

CLASSIC LOT JIT is identical to PURE JIT, except that it uses the same batch sizes as CLASSIC. In the basic set of experiments, the campaign sizes measured in terms of the number of batches are unchanged. QED automatically re-calculates the campaign frequencies, which end up being correspondingly smaller. In an additional set of experiments, labelled CLASSIC LOT JIT (*), the campaign sizes are on average reduced by the same factor that the batches sizes were increased. This means that the campaign sizes measured in terms of kg of bulk product are approximately equal to those of PURE JIT.

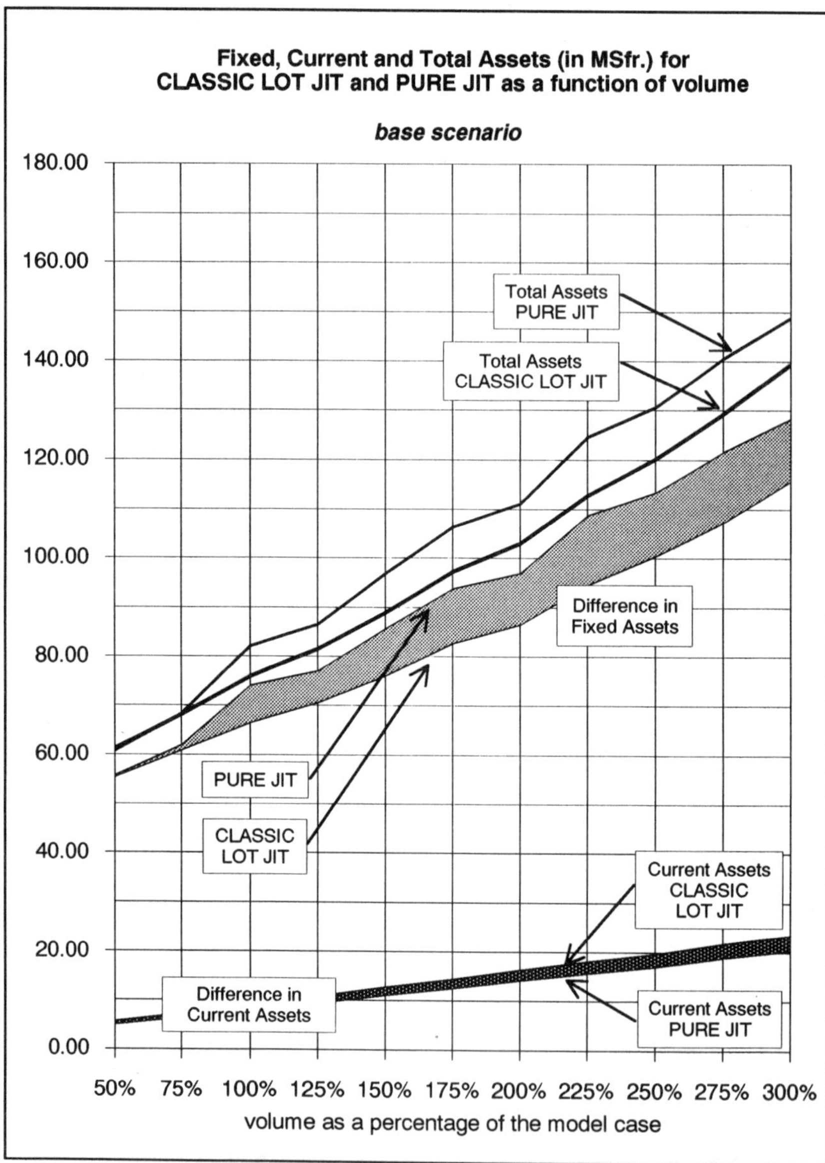

E-Chart II-2.1: Asset base for CLASSIC LOT JIT and PURE JIT with the sales volume varying from 50% to 300% of the base model case. The gap between the fixed assets for the two cases increases with the volume. The underlying trend in the production assets is clearly visible in E-Chart II-2.5. PURE JIT also requires more total assets because its advantages in terms of current assets do not outweigh the difference in fixed assets. The conclusions to be drawn from these results need to take into account that the selected product mix of the *base scenario* includes the largest class A products in the Stein works only.

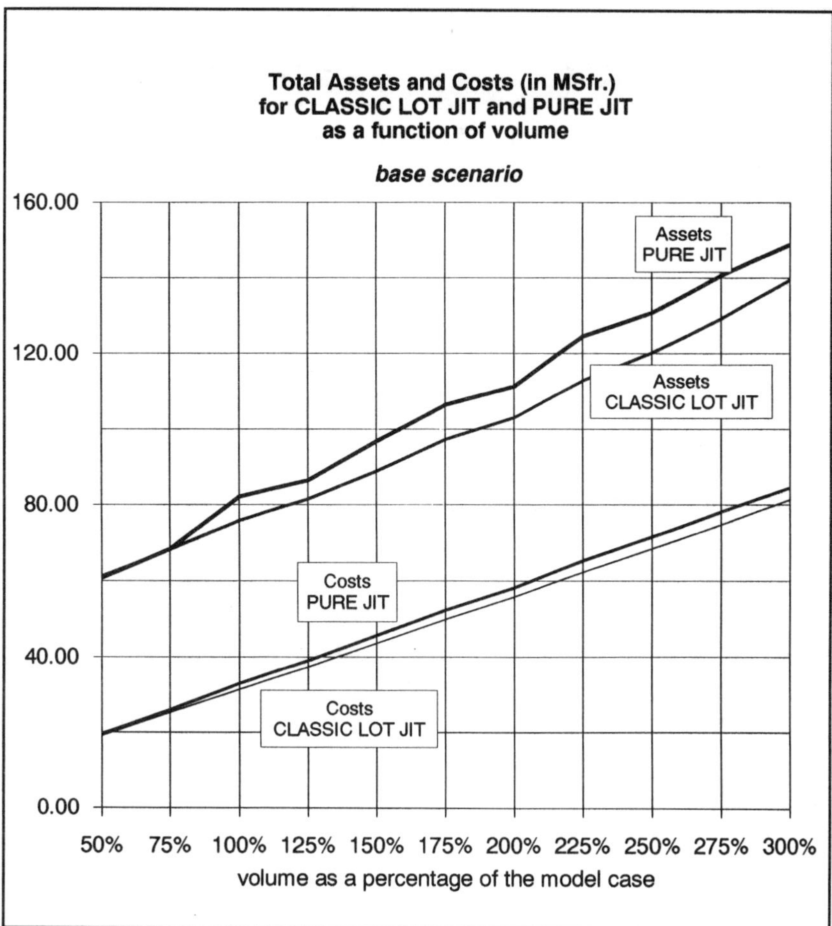

E-Chart II-2.2a: Total assets and total costs of CLASSIC LOT JIT and PURE JIT with the volume increasing from 50% to 300% of the base model case. The difference in total costs appears to stabilize as the volume increases. This is shown more clearly in E-Chart II-2.3.

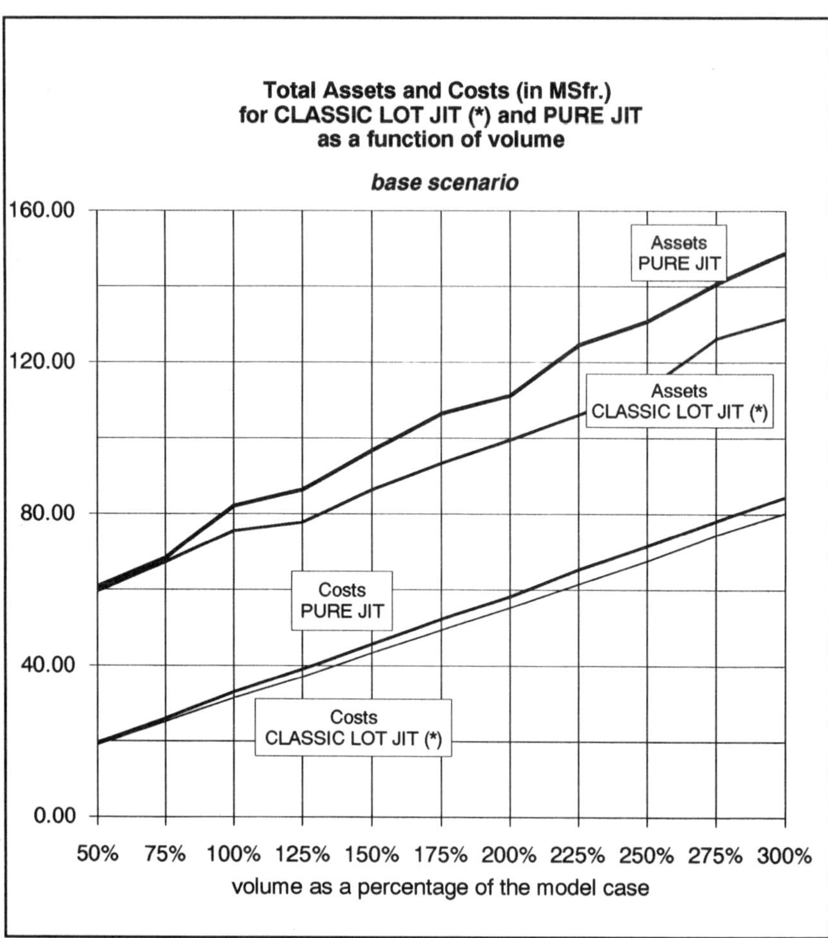

E-Chart II-2.2b: Total assets and total costs of CLASSIC LOT JIT (*) and PURE JIT with the volume increasing from 50% to 300% of the base model case. The difference in total assets is somewhat larger with this variant of CLASSIC LOT JIT, because the smaller campaign sizes result in less inventories. The inventory level has been reduced by about one month, as shown by the flow times for CLASSIC LOT JIT and its variant in E-Charts II-2.4a and II-2.5b, respectively. A comparison with E-Chart II-2.2a shows that the smaller campaign sizes do not noticeably affect the difference in total costs between CLASSIC LOT JIT and PURE JIT.

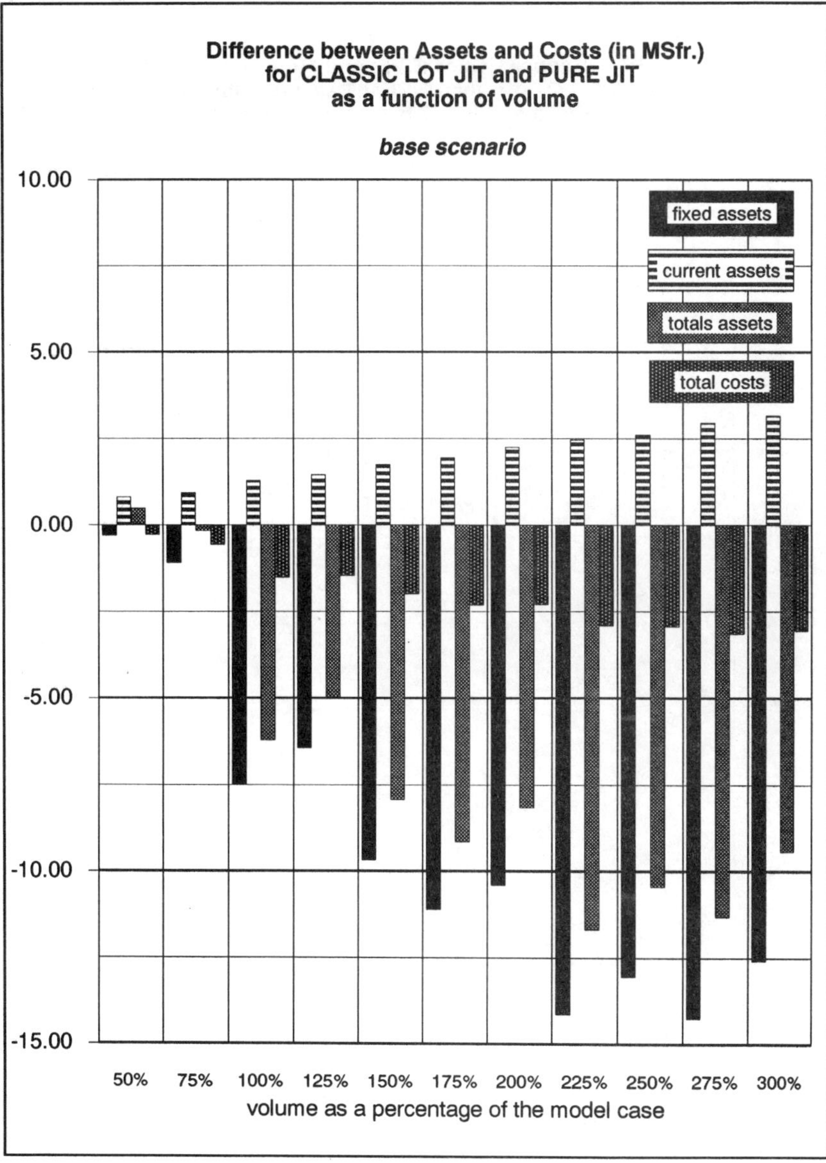

E-Chart II-2.3: Difference in assets and total costs between CLASSIC LOT JIT and PURE JIT with the volume increasing from 50% to 300% of the base model case. The differences in the total costs and total assets stabilize in the volume range shown.

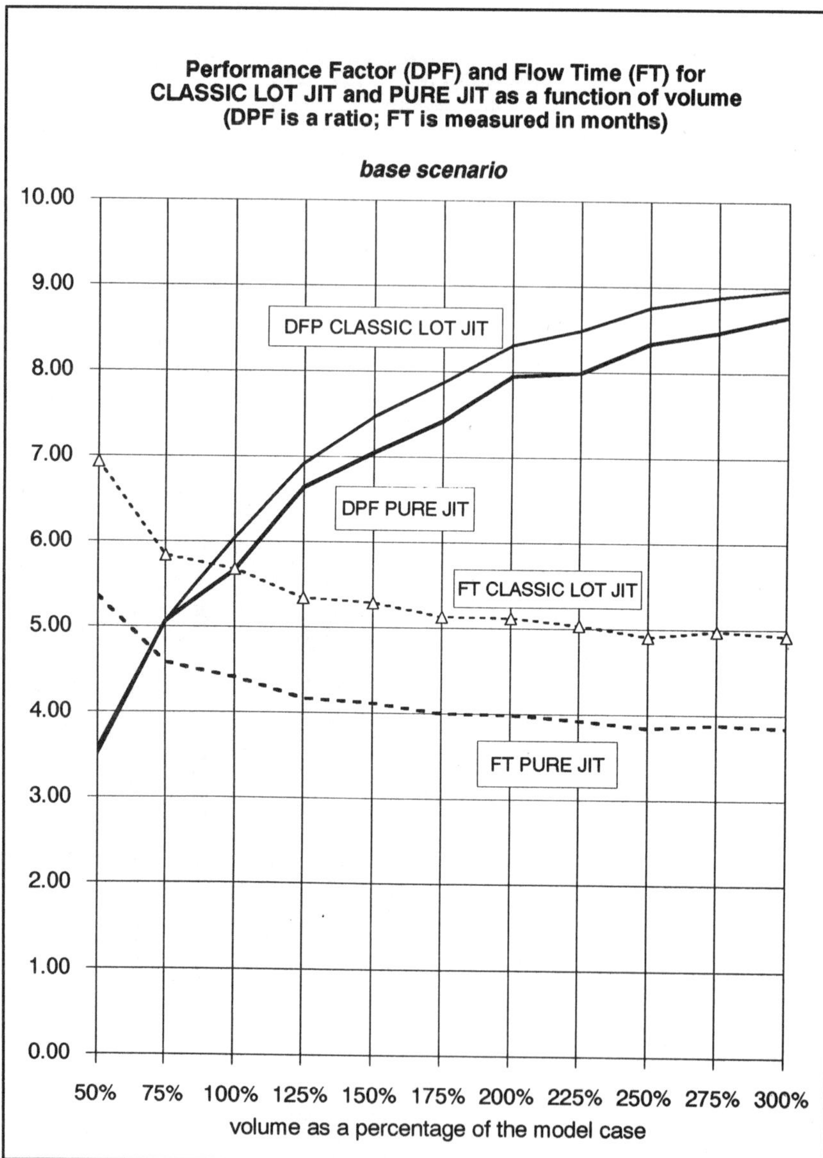

E-Chart II-2.4a: Discounted performance factor and flow time for CLASSIC LOT JIT and PURE JIT with the volume increasing from 50% to 300% of the base model case. As can be expected on the basis of the values for the total assets and costs shown in E-Chart II-2.3, the gap between the discounted performance factor for the two cases stabilizes in the volume range shown. Note that the scale of the axis for DPF and FT has been reduced from 16 to 10 units.

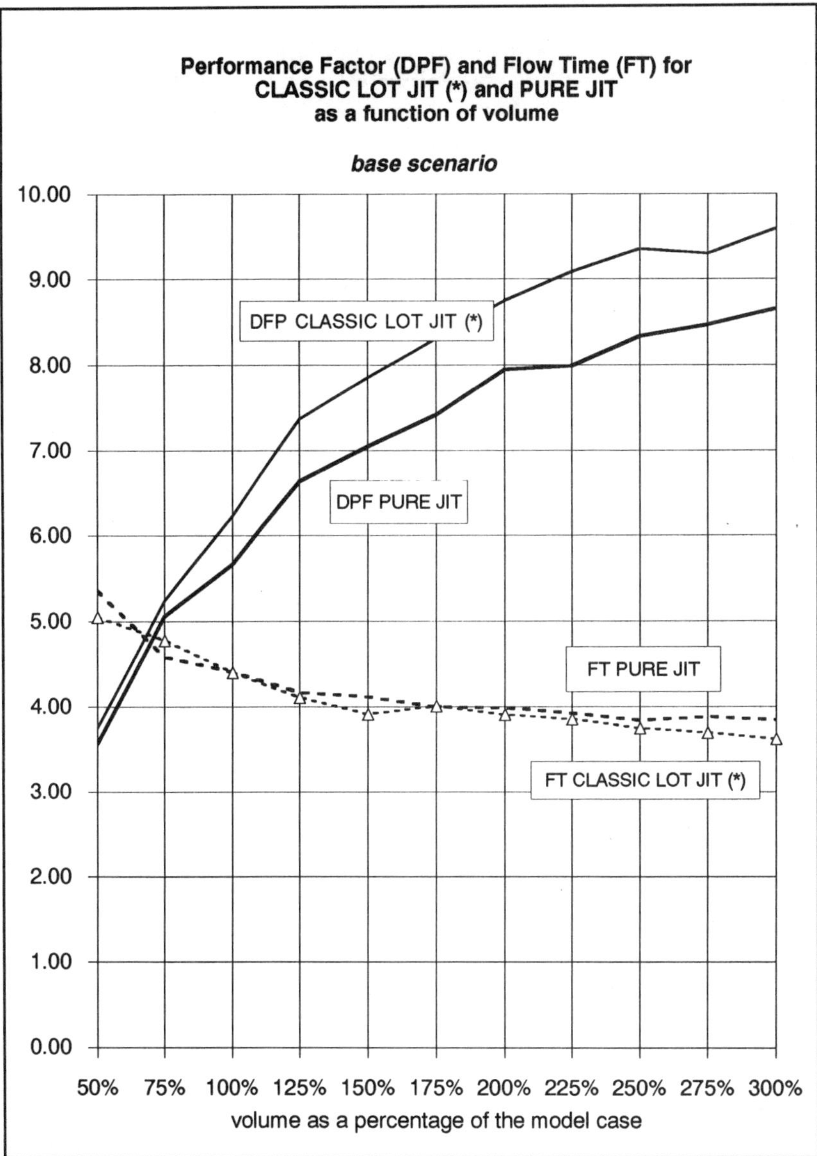

E-Chart II-2.4b: Discounted performance factor and flow time for CLASSIC LOT JIT (*) and PURE JIT with the volume increasing from 50% to 300% of the base model case. As shown by a comparison with E-Chart II-2-4a, the difference in DPF between CLASSIC LOT JIT (*) and PURE JIT is larger than the difference between CLASSIC LOT JIT and PURE JIT. By introducing campaign sizes that are comparable in size to those of PURE JIT the discounted performance factor is significantly improved. Note that the scale of the axis for DPF and FT has been reduced from 16 to 10 units.

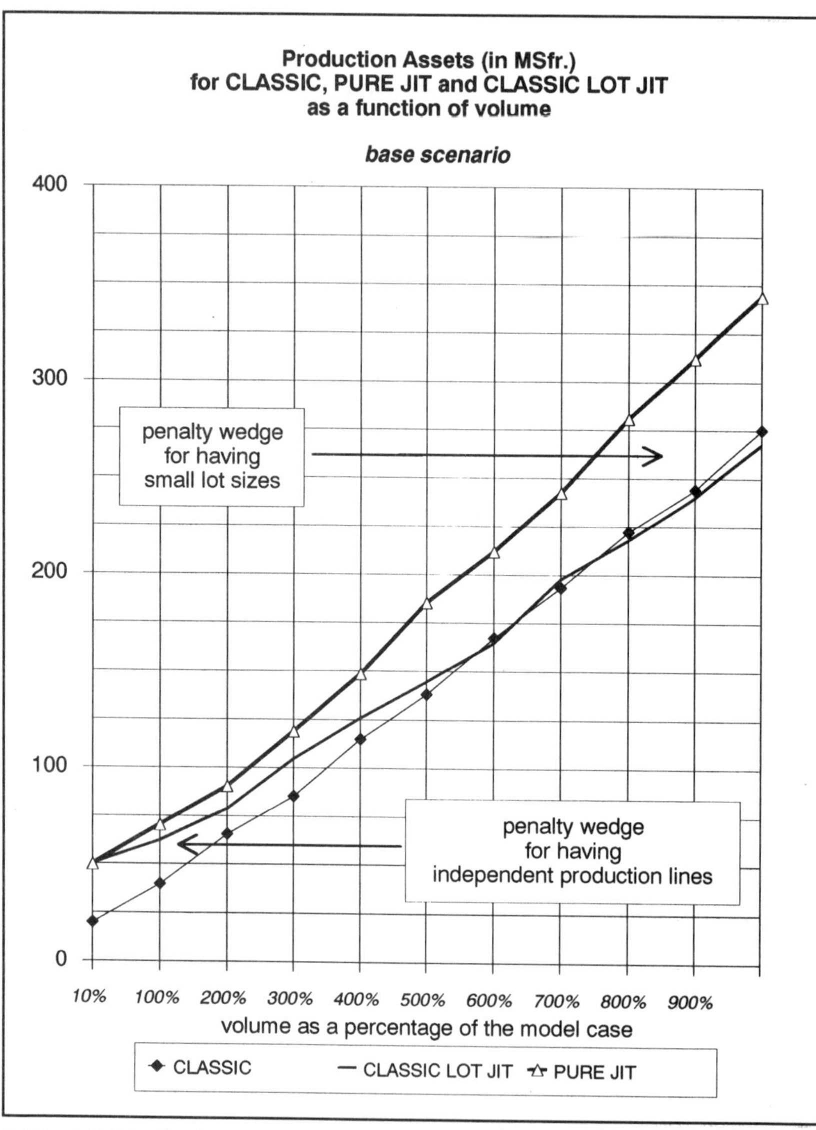

E-Chart II-2.5: Production assets for CLASSIC, PURE JIT and CLASSIC LOT JIT with the volume increasing from 10% to 1000% of the model case. The upper "penalty" wedge gives a rough indication of the price to be paid for the small lot sizes of PURE JIT in terms of production assets required. The lower "penalty" wedge, which compares CLASSIC LOT JIT with CLASSIC, does the same for the price to be paid for having independent production lines. The main reason the wedges only give a rough indication is that the costs of the characteristic element of the PURE JIT variants are not additive—the sum of the parts does not equal the whole.

Discussion ***CLASSIC LOT JIT***

Because the product mix used for these experiments represents the largest products in the class A of solid dosage forms, the experimental results need to be interpreted with some care. The conclusions can not be extended arbitrarily. If a volume increase is obtained through the addition of numerous lower volume products, the costs of overly high stock levels will outweigh the benefits of higher equipment utilization levels.

Ignoring the make-up of the product mix, it is safe to say that batch sizes in fabrication have a significant impact on the financial performance. For the investigated product mix, the campaign sizes of PURE JIT are unnecessarily small. However, the full benefits of using the same batches sizes as CLASSIC are only achieved if campaign sizes comparable to those of PURE JIT are used.

Given that the utilization of the manufacturing operation is low enough to absorb additional lower volume products, it appears advisable to use at least two different batches sizes in fabrication. This depends not only on the volume of the individual products, but also on the demand variability. The higher the demand variability is, the more the flexibility of small batches comes to the fore.

7.3.3 The Impact of Cost-Based Factors

It needs no saying that cost-based factors have a significant impact on the financial performance of both CLASSIC and PURE JIT. The analysis of the experiments with the impact of four different factors therefore focuses on the difference in performance between the two cases. The question analyzed is whether a change of scenario or assumptions pulls the two further apart. The four factors selected for analysis are:

- useful economic life of equipment
- cost of active substance
- cost of capital
- cost of equipment

The fourth set of experiments is particularly interesting because it is carried out in combination with a change in the direct labour content of production. The first three are carried out in combination with a change in volume.

Purpose ***Useful Economic Life of Equipment***

The purpose of this first set of experiments is to investigate the impact of the useful economic life of equipment in fabrication and packaging. The base case model uses 15 years in fabrication and packaging, and 10 years in quality control. As noted in §6.3.7, the useful economic life of packaging equipment in the existing facility appears to be substantially longer. The experiments vary the useful economic life from 25% to 200% of the base model case, i.e. from 4 to 30 years. The useful economic life of buildings is left unchanged at 30 years.

The experiments also shine light on the impact of the way in which QED calculates the annual cost of the capital investment in fixed assests. QED uses the annuity on the investment for this calculation. In the base model case, the interest charges already amount to 50% of the cost of the capital investment. This percentage increases further if the useful economic life is assumed to be longer. If the pay-back period of the total investment is much shorter than the useful economic life of the equipment, QED's method of calculating the cost of the capital investment may be questionable.

Because of the use of annuities, the outcome of this set of experiments depends also on the interest rate. The third set of experiments in this section investigates the impact of interest rates, but not in combination with the useful economic life of equipment. With QED it is possible, however, to assess the effects of varying both factors at the same time.

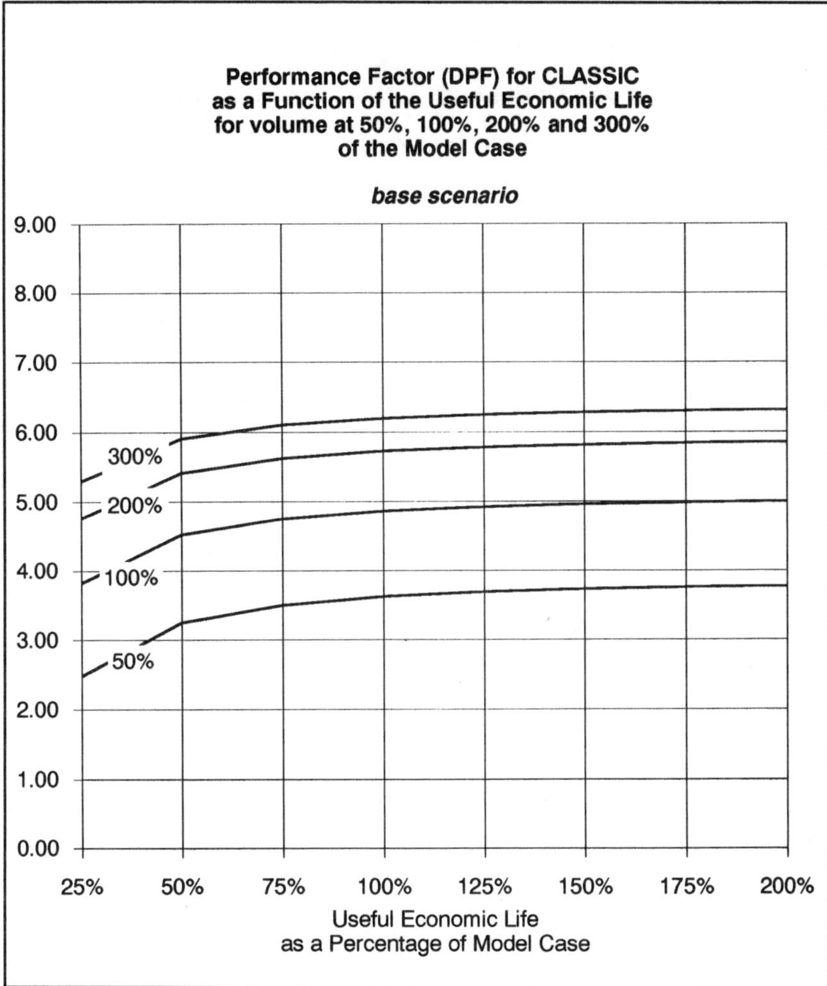

E-Chart III-1.1: Discounted performance factor for CLASSIC as a function of the useful economic life of production equipment for values ranging from 25% to 200% of the base model case. The improvement in DPF levels off because the interest charges increase with the length of the amortization period. The reduction in the annual depreciation charges decreases steadily.

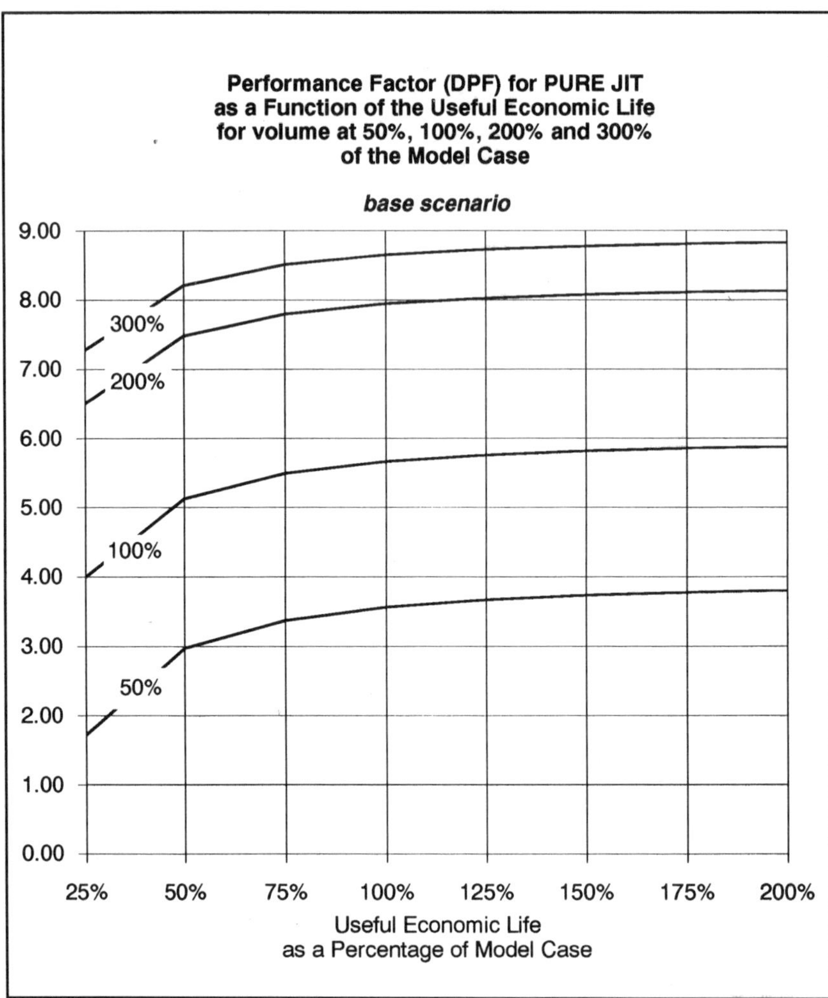

E-Chart III-1.2: Discounted performance factor for PURE JIT as a function of the useful economic life of production equipment for values ranging from 25% to 200% of the base model case. The same comments that were made for CLASSIC apply.

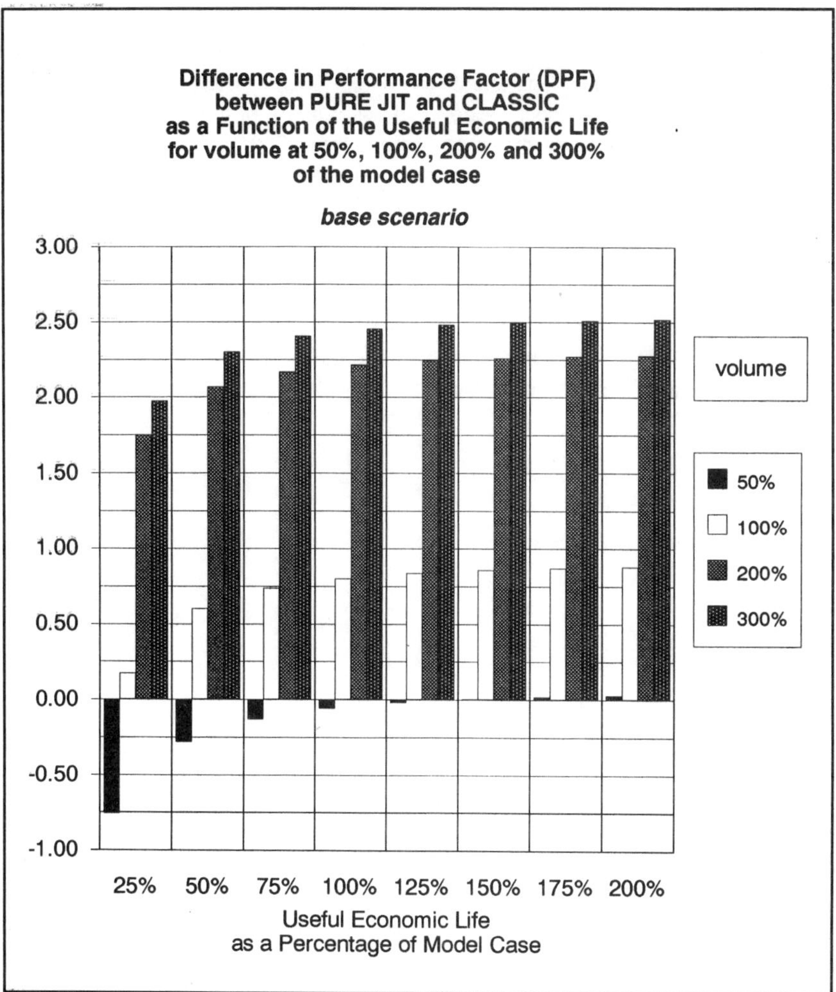

E-Chart III-1.3: Difference in discounted performance factor between CLASSIC and PURE JIT as a function of the useful economic life of production equipment for values ranging from 25% to 200% of the base model case. PURE JIT pays a higher penalty for a reduction in the useful economic life of equipment than CLASSIC. Morever, the effect becomes increasingly significant with further reductions and is stronger for smaller factories. The lower utilization of equipment in a small PURE JIT factory is the reason.

Discussion **Useful Economic Life of Equipment**

The results are intuitive. The longer the useful economic life of the equipment, the less weight carries the cost of the fixed asset share of the capital investment. Beause PURE JIT requires more equipment than CLASSIC, it pays a higher penalty. As the economic life of equipment decreases, the depreciation charges expressed as a percentage of the total cost of the capital investment in equipment increase. As noted in the captions of the E-Charts, this component of the cost of investment in capital equipment starts to increase rapidly.

The conclusion is that the difference between PURE JIT and CLASSIC is not neutral to the useful economic life of equipment. The choice of equipment, if it has a high share of new technological content with a presumably shorter useful economic life, needs to take this dimension into account.

Purpose **Cost of Active Substance**

The second set of experiments in this section varies the cost of active substances. It serves several different purposes. The cost of active substances used by QED reflect the present TPC values taken from the cost accounting system. As discussed, these are underestimates because they exclude, among other items, warehousing costs and the cost of capital in the chemical production of active substances. The difference probably lies between 20% and 30%. The first purpose of the experiments is therefore to assess the impact of this underestimate. The second purpose is based on the recognition that the product mix selected for the investigation is not a representative sample. The weighted average of active substance cost for the whole business or for a special segment may be considerably smaller or larger than the average value for the product mix selected. The third and most obvious purpose is to assess the impact of a true rise in the cost of active substance. Inflationary pressures or currency fluctuations may be the cause; or the cost of chemical production goes up because of additional investments in new facilities that reduce the ecological impact of chemical production on the environment. As noted in chapter 6, material and production costs are expected to increase further during the next decade. Although the experiment itself is a simple one, it is safe to conclude that the results are of interest. The focus is again on the difference between CLASSIC and PURE JIT.

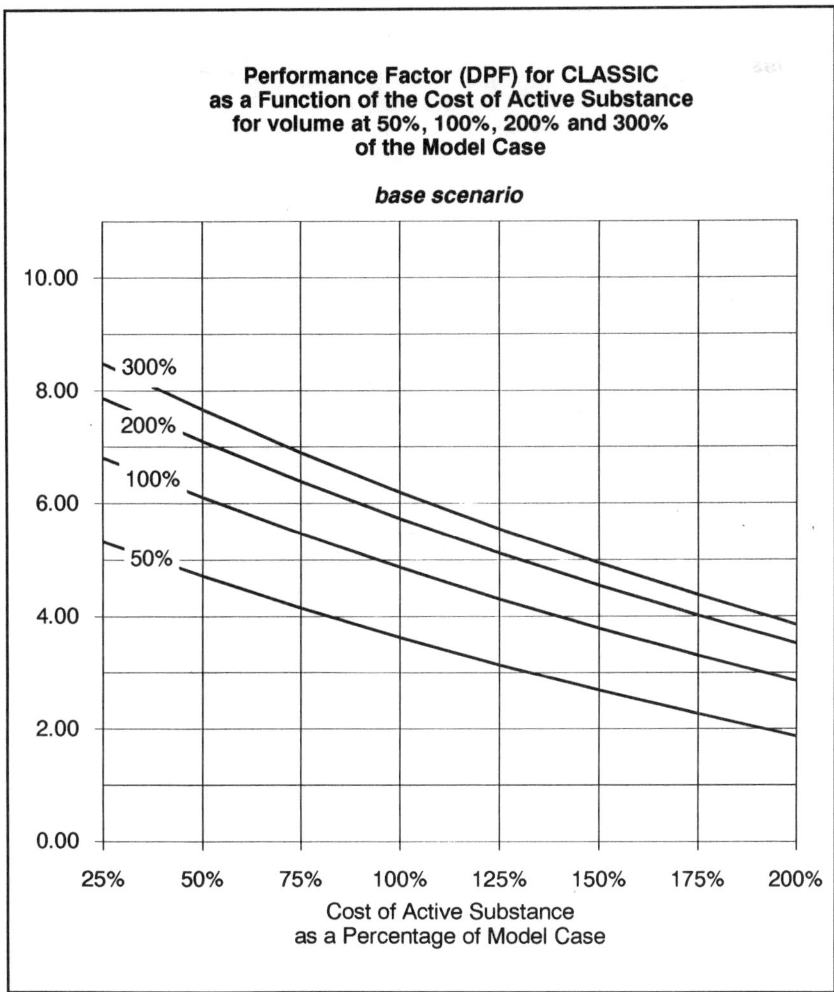

E-Chart III-2.1: Discounted performance factor for CLASSIC as a function of the cost of active substance for values ranging from 25% to 200% of the base model case.

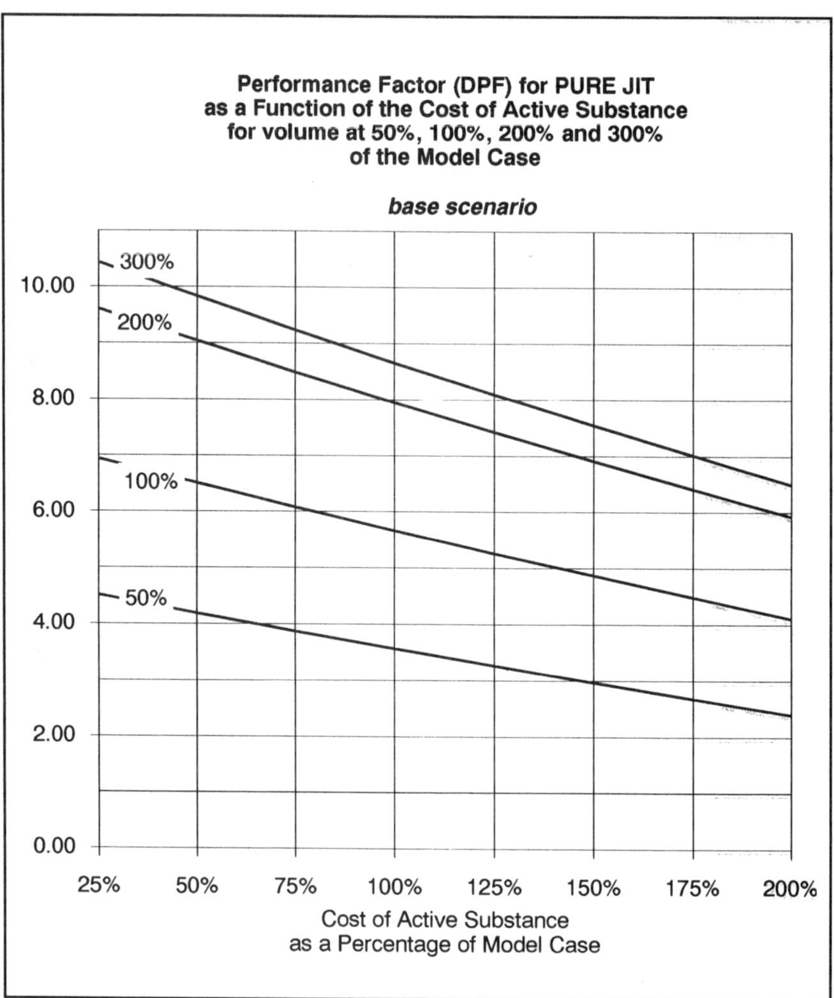

E-Chart III-2.2: Discounted performance factor for PURE JIT as a function of the cost of active substance for values ranging from 25% to 200% of the base model case.

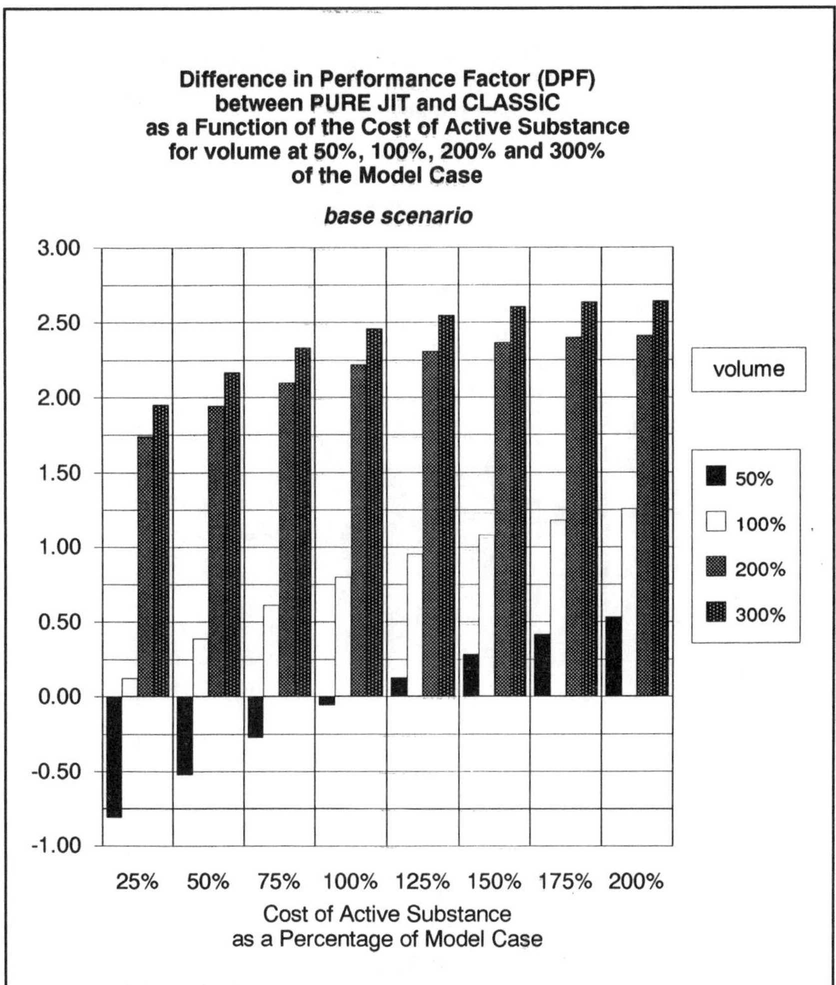

E-Chart III-2.3: Difference in discounted performance factor between CLASSIC and PURE JIT as a function of the cost of active substance for values ranging from 25% to 200% of the base model case. The higher the cost of active substance, the better PURE JIT performs. The increasing advantage does level off and is stronger for smaller volumes.

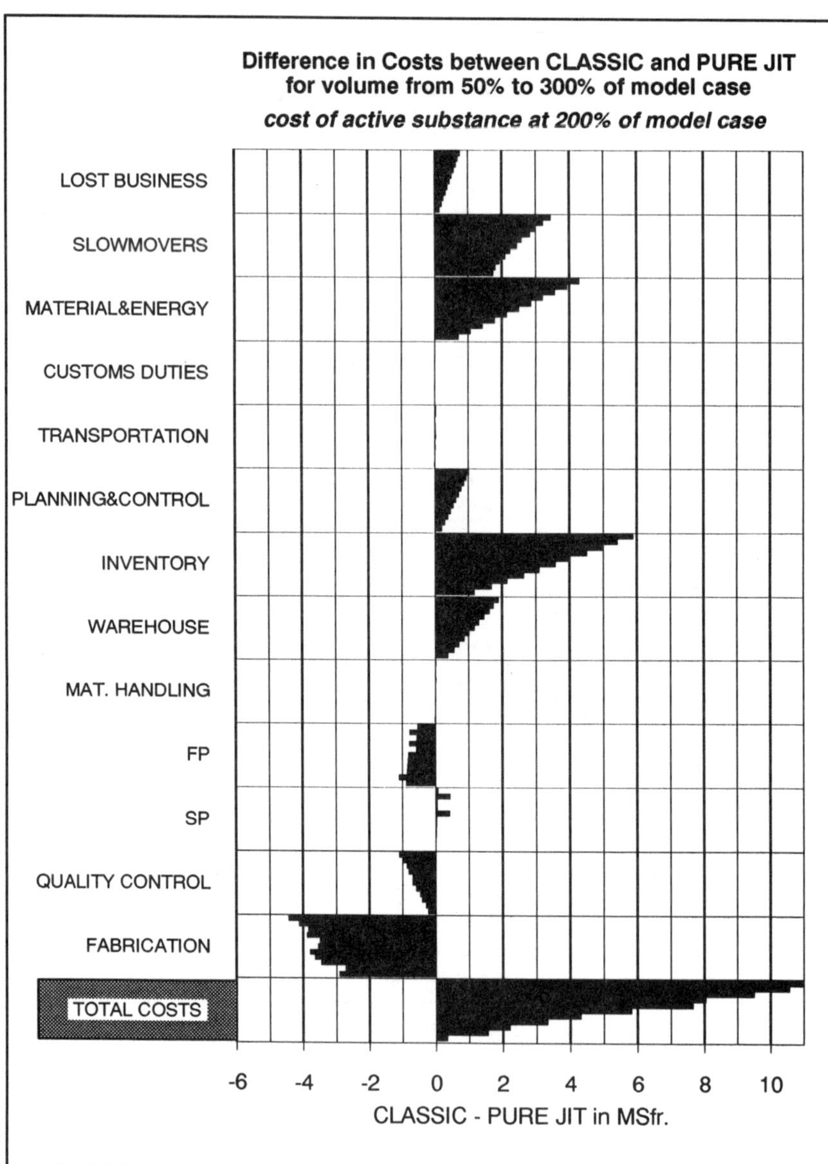

E-Chart III-2.4: Difference in annual costs between CLASSIC and PURE JIT with the cost of active substance at 200% of the base model case. The values shown for the individual cost items are the costs for CLASSIC minus those of the PURE JIT. As the volume ranges from 50% of the model case to 300% the difference in the total costs changes from 0.2 M.Sfr. to 11.2 M. Sfr. in favour of PURE JIT. This chart fails to show that the difference in total costs between the two concepts is a small in relative terms. The difference ranges between 0% to 9% of the total costs of CLASSIC. Compare with E-Chart I-1.3

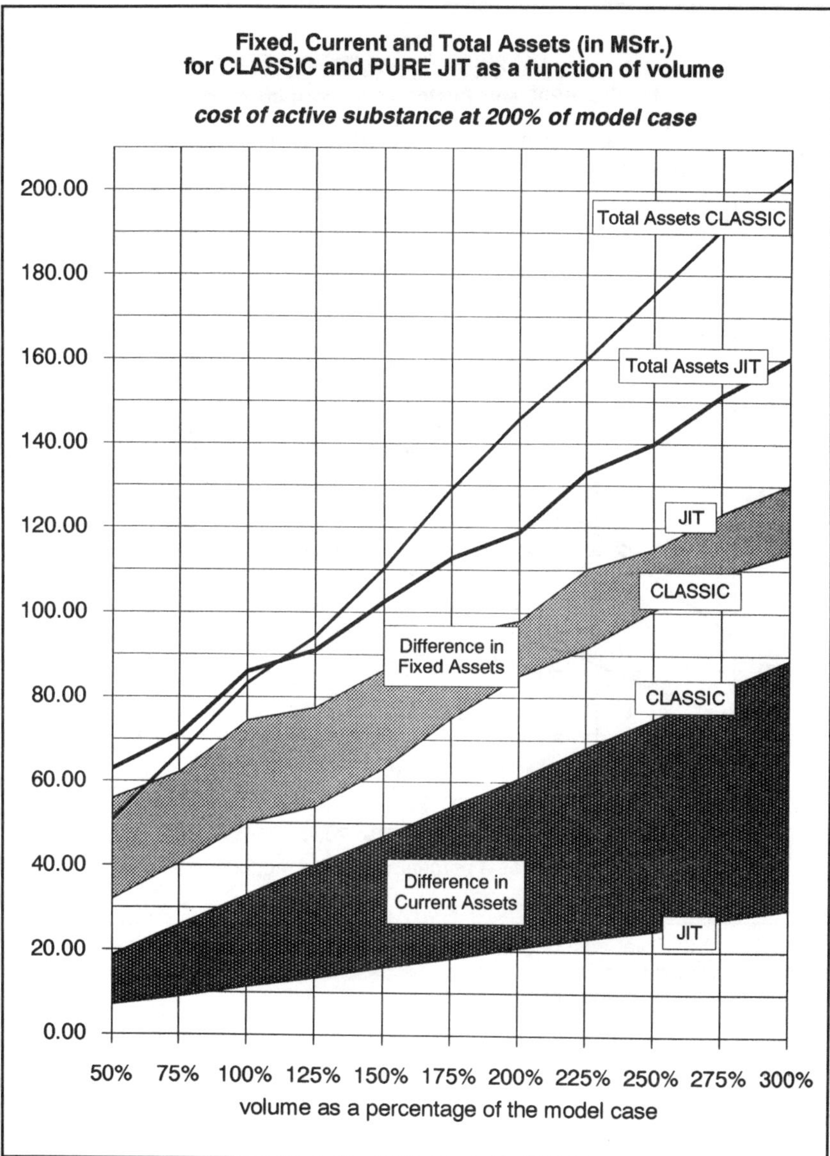

E-Chart III-2.5: Asset base for CLASSIC and PURE JIT with the sales volume varying from 50% to 300% of the base model case and the cost of active substance at 200% of the base model case. This chart displays the changing composition of the balance sheet for the two concepts.

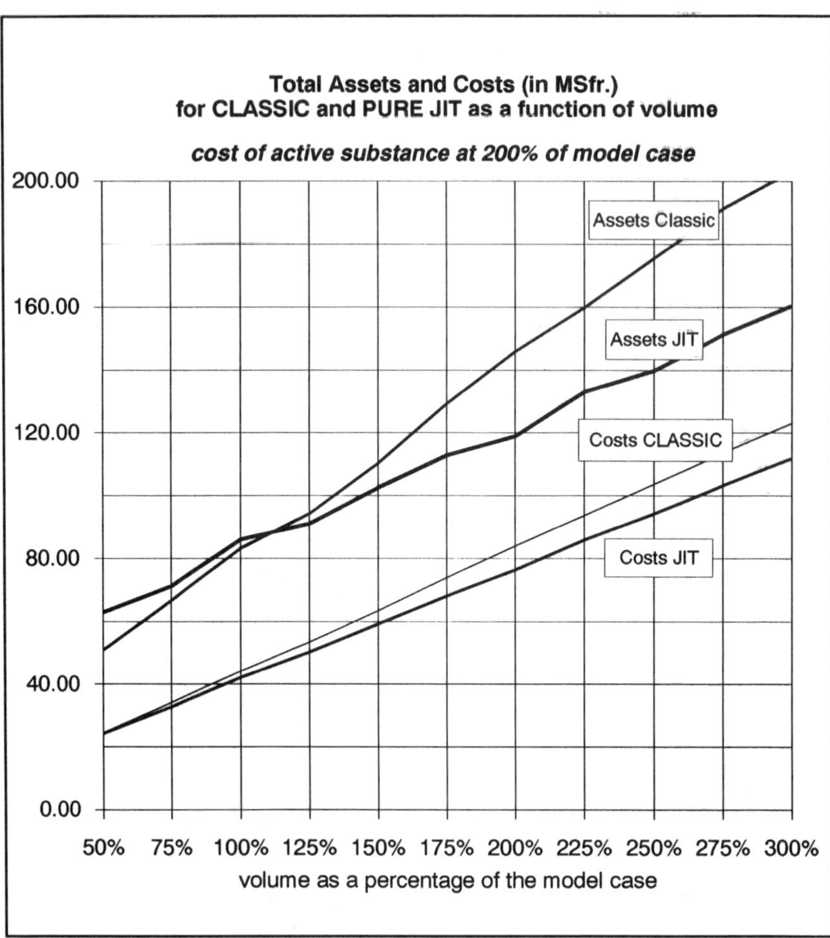

E-Chart III-2.6: Total assets and total costs of CLASSIC and PURE JIT with the volume increasing from 50% to 300% of the base model case and the cost of active substance at 200% of the base model case.

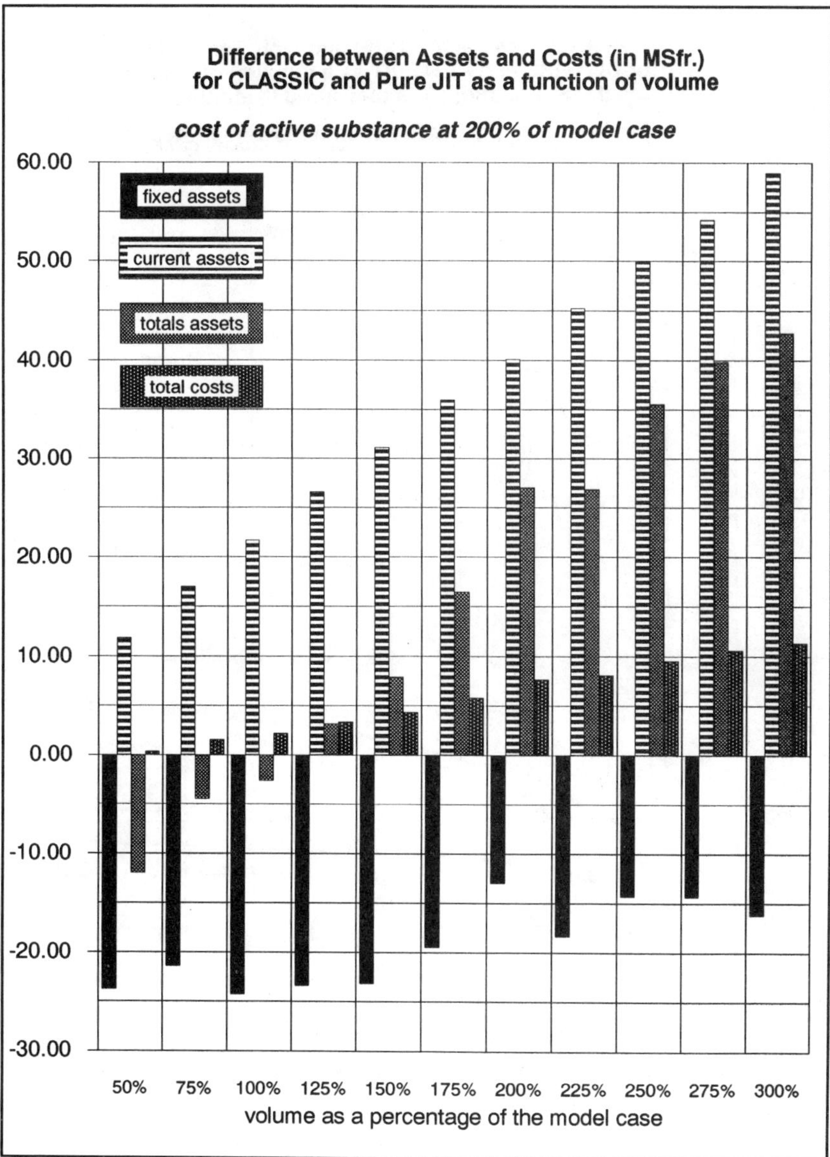

E-Chart III-2.7: Difference in assets and total costs between CLASSIC and PURE JIT with the volume increasing from 50% to 300% of the base model case and the cost of active substance at 200% of the base model case.

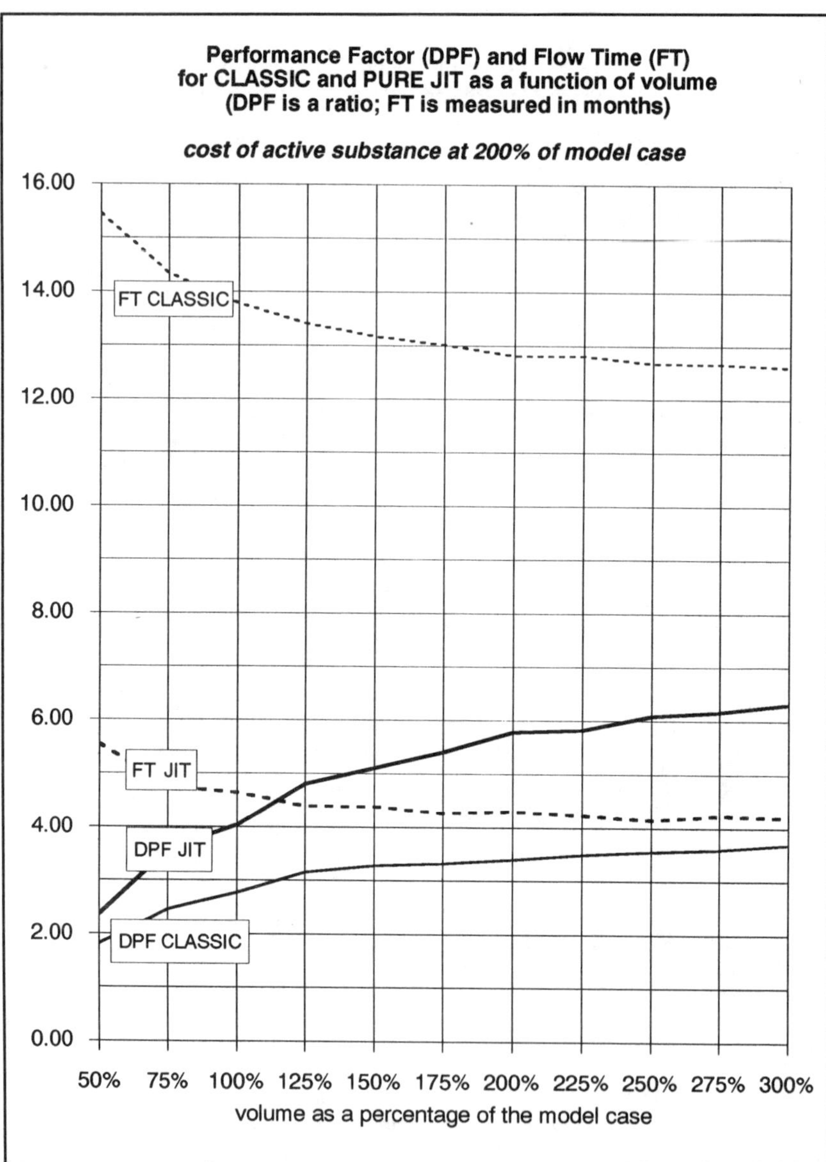

E-Chart III-2.8: Discounted performance factor and flow time for CLASSIC and PURE JIT with the volume increasing from 50% to 300% of the base model case and the cost of active substance at 200% of the base model case. A comparison of these results with those of the base model case, see E-Chart I-1.7b, shows that the difference in DPF between PURE JIT and CLASSIC is not only larger in absolute terms but especially also in relative terms.

Discussion ***Cost of Active Substance***

As expected, CLASSIC pays a higher penalty than PURE JIT in terms of overall financial performance for any increase in the cost of active substance. This applies in particular for smaller operations. For the base case model, a 25% increase in the cost of active substance results in a 12% increase in the difference in DPF between CLASSIC and PURE JIT. With the volume at 200% of the base model case, the 12% increase drops to less than 5%.

The use of TPC values taken from a cost accounting system that excludes significant cost items or the neglect of upward pressures on the cost of active substance will underestimate the benefits of PURE JIT or its variants. Assessing the current or projected cost of active substance is therefore a worthwhile activity.

Purpose ***Cost of Capital***

The next set of experiments varies the cost of capital from 7% to 14%. The base case model uses 10%. Investigated is the combined effect of a change in interest rate on current and fixed assets. Since these affect the difference in DPF between CLASSIC and PURE JIT in opposite directions, a preliminary set of experiments only takes the impact on the holding cost of inventories into account. Some additional insight is obtained in the combined effect by ignoring one of its components.

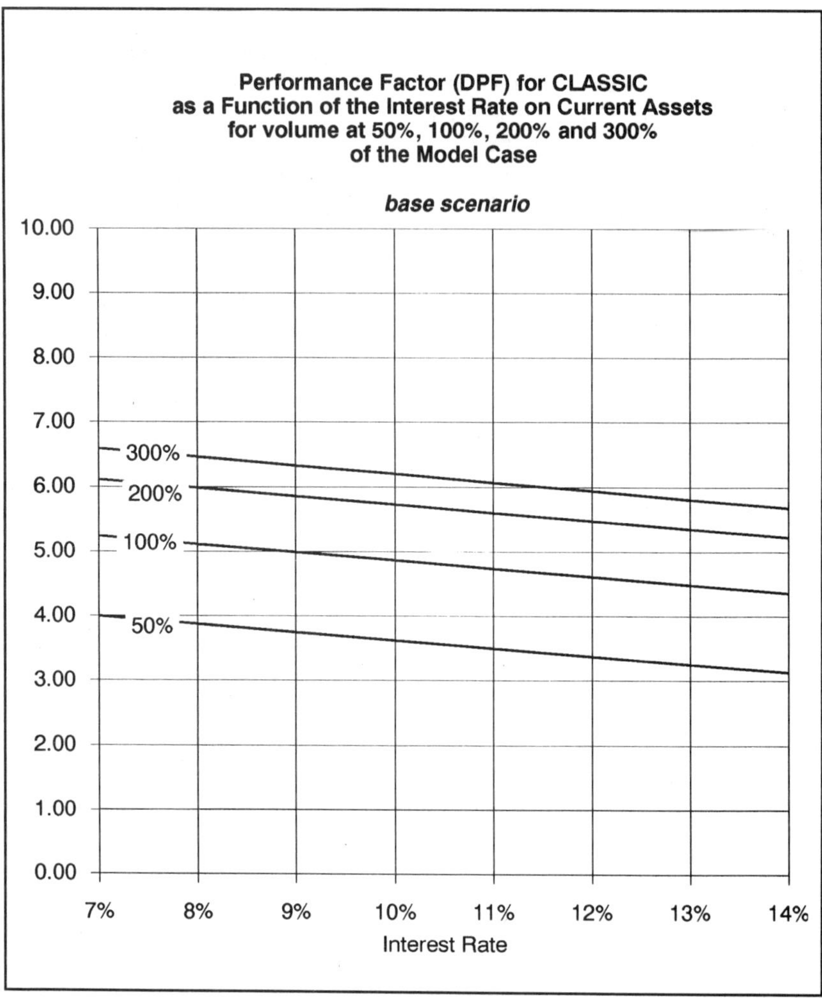

E-Chart III-3.1: Discounted performance factor for CLASSIC as a function of the interest rate on current assets for values ranging from 7% to 14%.

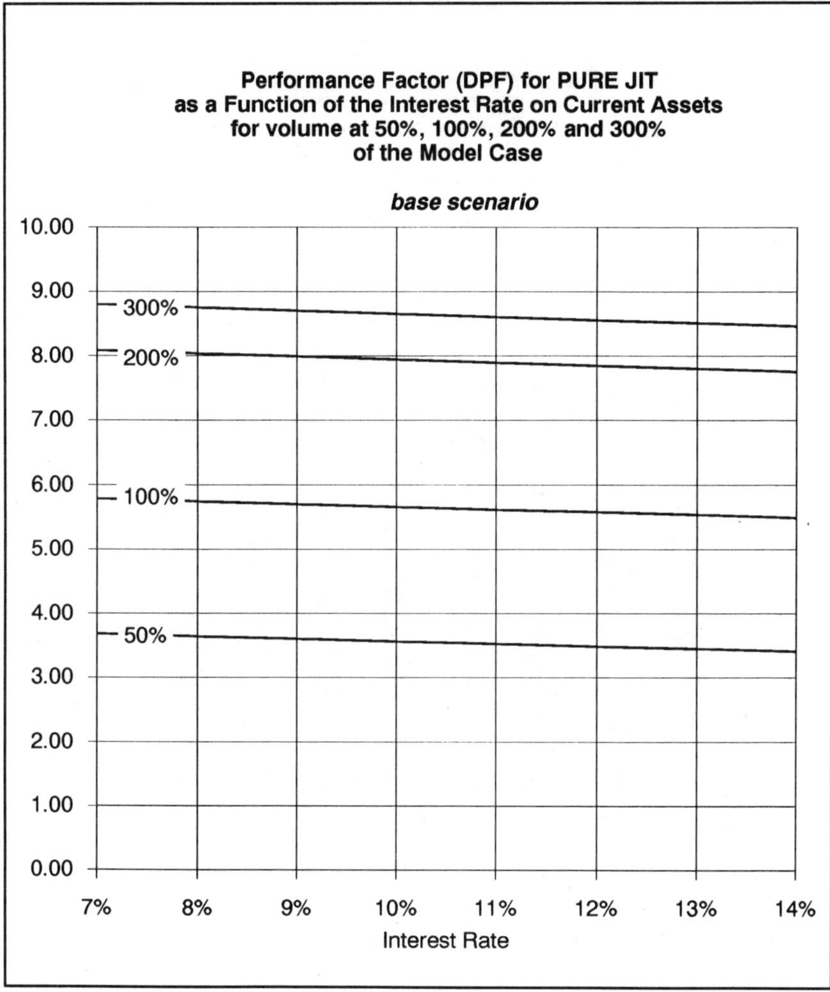

E-Chart III-3.2: Discounted performance factor for PURE JIT as a function of the interest rate on current assets for values ranging from 7% to 14%.

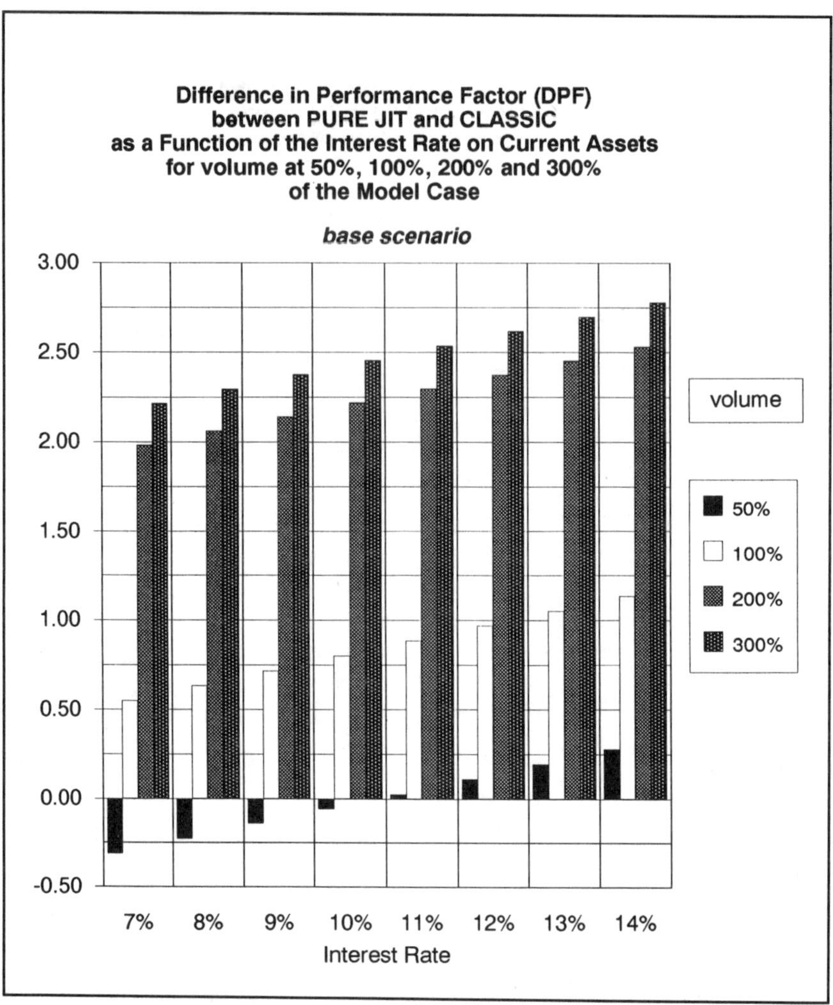

E-Chart III-3.3: Difference in discounted performance factor between CLASSIC and PURE JIT as a function of the interest rate on current assets for values ranging from 7% to 14%. The difference in DPF between CLASSIC and PURE JIT increases steadily with the interest rate. In contrast with most other investigated factors, the increases do not level off as the interest rate goes up, and are equally pronounced for all sizes of the operation.

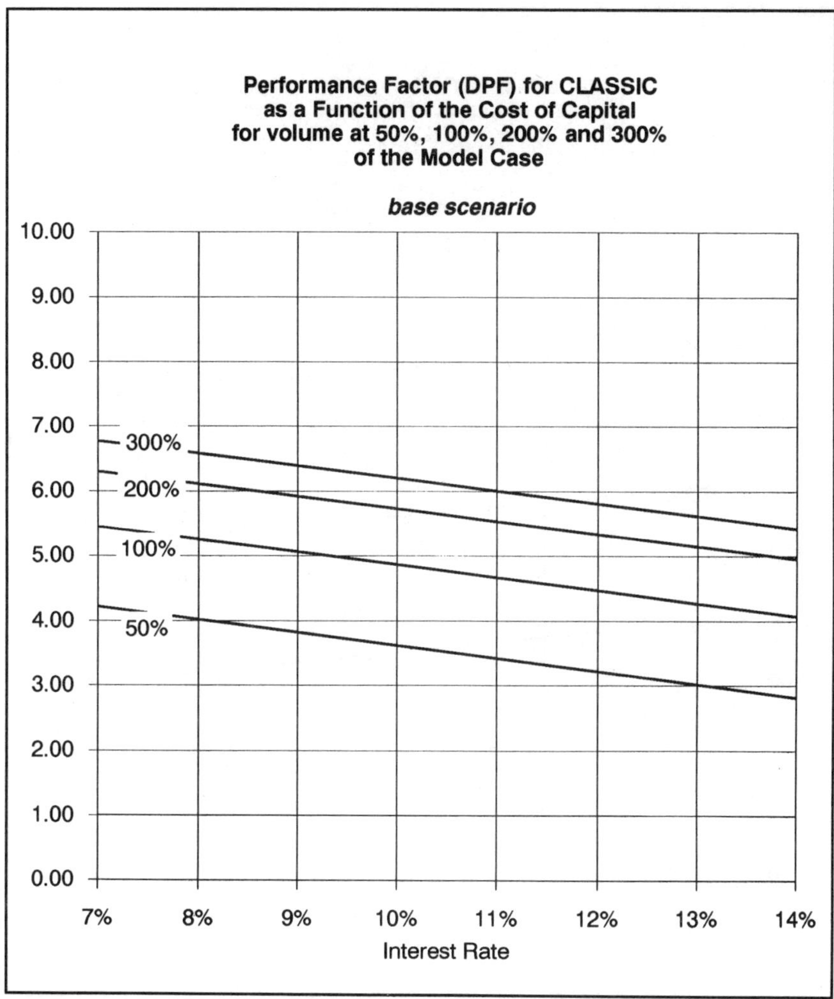

E-Chart III-3.4: Discounted performance factor for CLASSIC as a function of the cost of capital for current *and* fixed assets for values ranging from 7% to 14%. The DPF drops ca. 1.4 units over the range investigated.

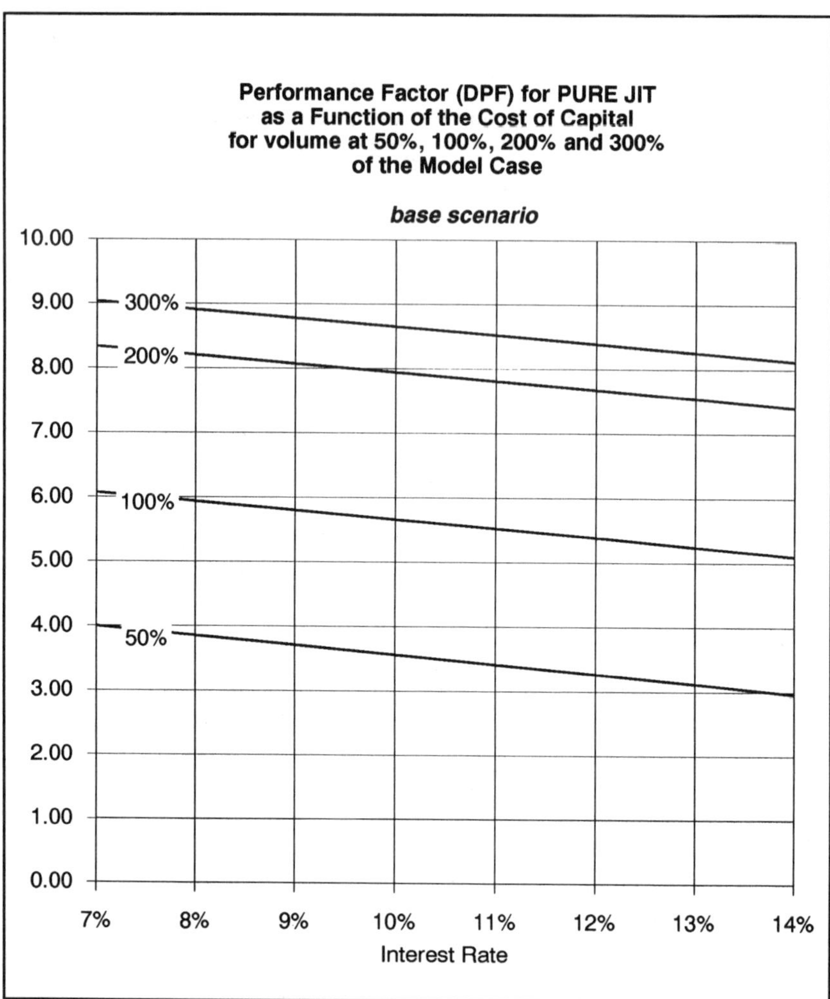

E-Chart III-3.5: Discounted performance factor for PURE JIT as a function of the cost of capital for current *and* fixed assets for values ranging from 7% to 14%. The DPF drops ca. 1.0 unit, in comparison with 1.4 units for CLASSIC, over the range investigated.

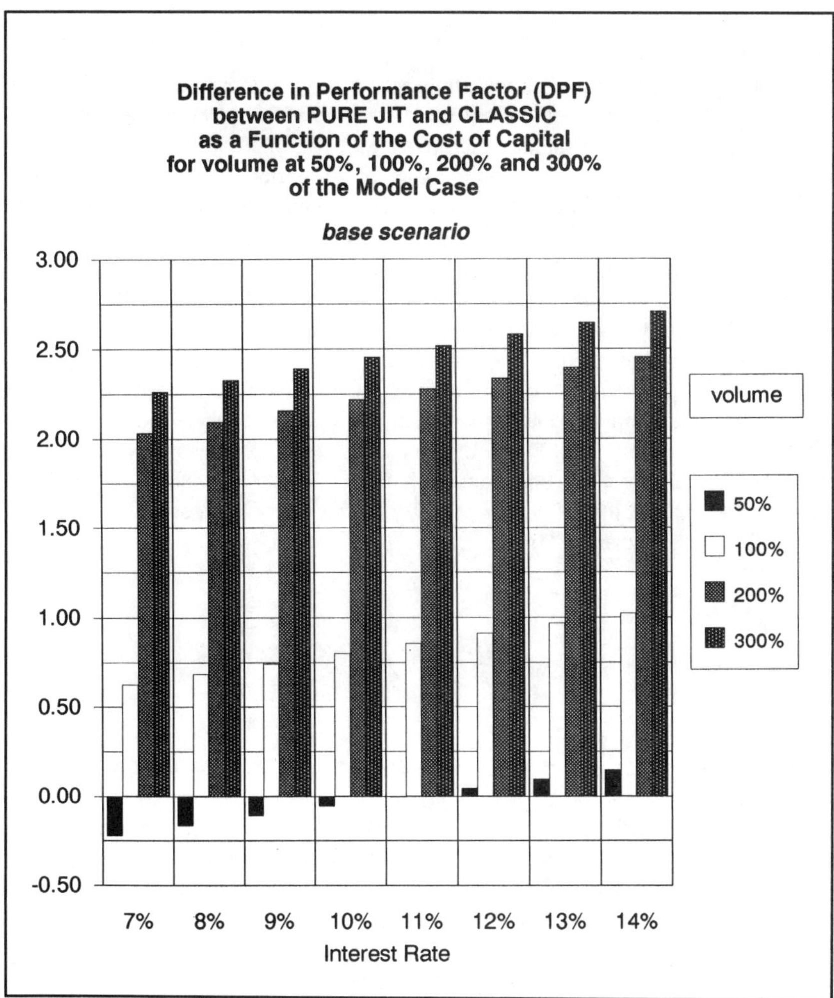

E-Chart III-3.6: Difference in discounted performance factor between CLASSIC and PURE JIT as a function of the cost of capital for current *and* fixed assets for values ranging from 7% to 14%. The difference in DPF between CLASSIC and PURE JIT increases steadily with the interest rate. A comparison with E-Chart III-3-3 shows that the aggregated effect is smaller. In contrast with most other factors investigated, the increases do not level off as the interest rate goes up. However, the increase is least pronounced for small operations. The poorer utilization of capacity in smaller operations is the cause.

Discussion ***Cost of Capital***

The experimental results clearly show that the additional total cost of holding stock outweigh the additional interest costs on fixed assets. One of the reasons is that the tied-up capital in stocks increases with the interest rate. This increase affects both the nominator and denominator of the performance factor ratio. This indirect increase in current assets is a specific example of a significant secondary effect. It justifies the complicated procedure of QED for accurately estimating the TPC values at every stage of the manufacturing process.

Setting the cost of capital is at least partially a policy decision. Since the difference in overall financial performance between CLASSIC and PURE JIT is not neutral to the cost of capital, the implications of this decision, especially in this context, need to be understood. This should not come as a surprise. What does or may surprise is the magnitude of the impact of the cost of capital. The difference in DPF between CLASSIC and PURE JIT increases by ca. 0.4 units over the interest rate range from 7% to 14%. For the base model case with the volume at 100% this is a 70% increase in the difference in DPF, i.e. for every interest rate increase of 1%, the difference grows by 10%.

Purpose ***Equipment Cost vs Labour Content***

The fourth and final set of experiments in this section varies the cost of equipment in combination with the labour content or, depending on the interpretation, the cost of labour. The experiments not only show that QED is capable of assessing the combined impact of varying two different inputs, but more importantly that this may be a worthwhile effort. The particular combination examined here focuses on investments in more highly automated equipment and its effects on labour productivity. The JIST project team in the Stein works selected the equipment items for the base model case in view of reducing the total labour content of production. Can we justify this selection in economic terms? Other factors such as the availability of skilled labour on the market play a role here. Unfortunately, QED neglects to calculate the total size of the labour force required. This wouldn't have been to difficult to compute since the total labours hours and the working hours per person are known. The experimental results ignores this dimension.

The experiments vary the labour content of production activities from 50% to 200% of the base model case. The investment cost of equipment is varied from 92% to 106% of the base model case. The reason for this small range will become apparent. A supplementary set of experiments examines a much larger range to show the underlying trend of the impact of the investment cost of equipment.

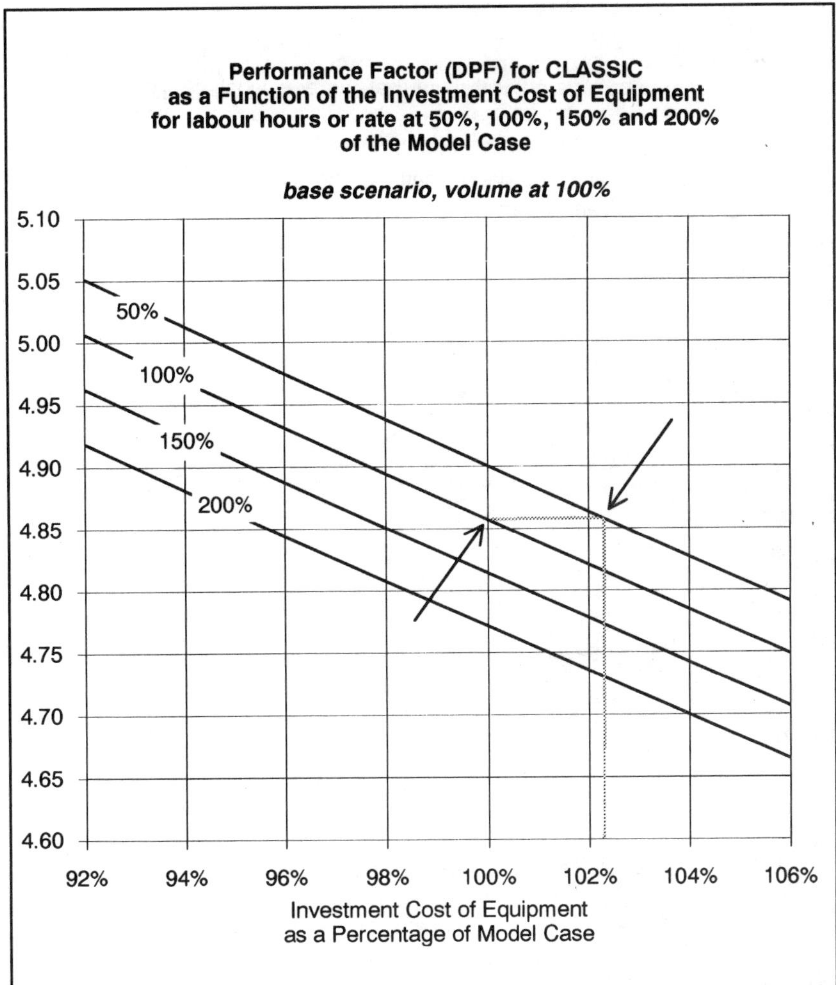

E-Chart III-4.1: Discounted performance factor for CLASSIC as a function of the investment cost of production equipment for values ranging from 92% to 106% of the base model case and standard labour hours or rate at values ranging from 50% to 200% of the base model case. A comparison of the two points marked by the arrows shows that a 2.4% increase in the cost of equipment must be matched by a 50% reduction in the labour contents or labour rate to maintain the same DPF. In economic terms, therefore, cheaper and less automated equipment appears to be much more appropriate than the equipment selected for the base model case. As shown in E.Charts III-4.4, the distances between these curves vary with cost of the equipment, i.e. the tradeoff ratio changes. There is some optimal balance between the cost of equipment and the labour content. This balance is achieved at much lower values for the investment cost of equipment.

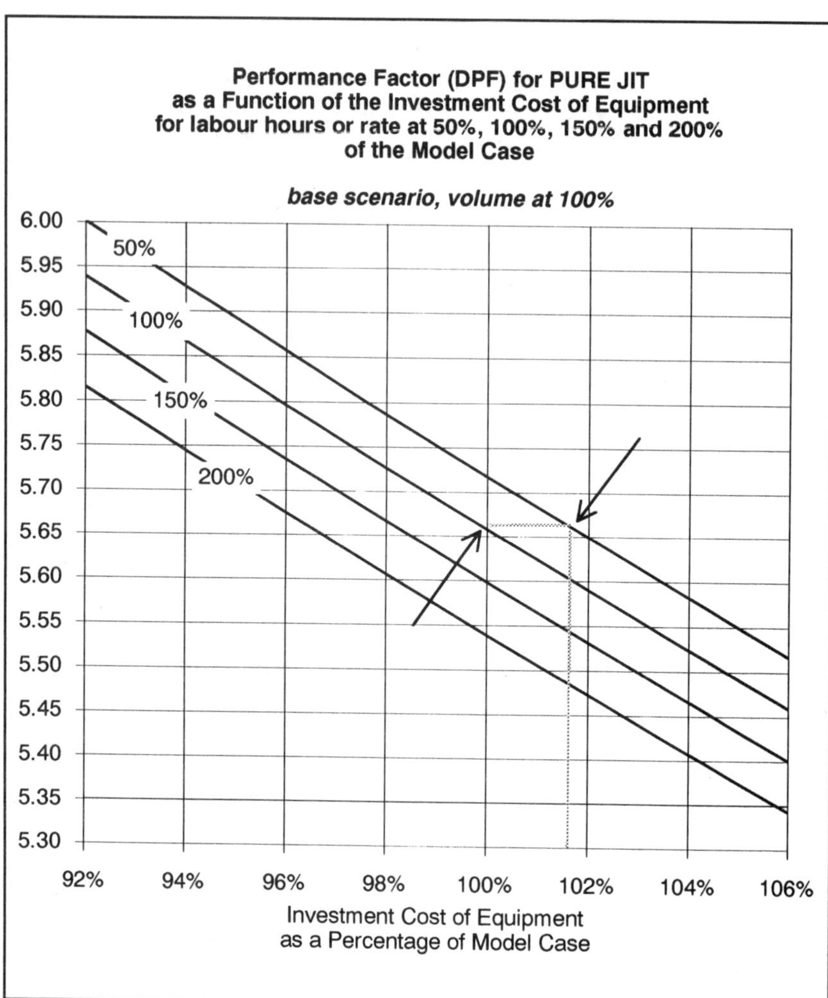

E-Chart III-4.2: Discounted performance factor for PURE JIT as a function of the investment cost of production equipment for values ranging from 92% to 106% of the base model case and standard labour hours or rate at values ranging from 50% to 200% of the base model case. A comparison of the two points marked by the arrows shows that a 1.5% increase in the cost of equipment must be matched by a 50% reduction in the labour contents or labour rate to maintain the same DPF. In economic terms, therefore, cheaper and less automated equipment appears to be much more appropriate than the equipment selected for the base model case. Moreover, this choice of equipment is even worse for PURE JIT than it is for CLASSIC.

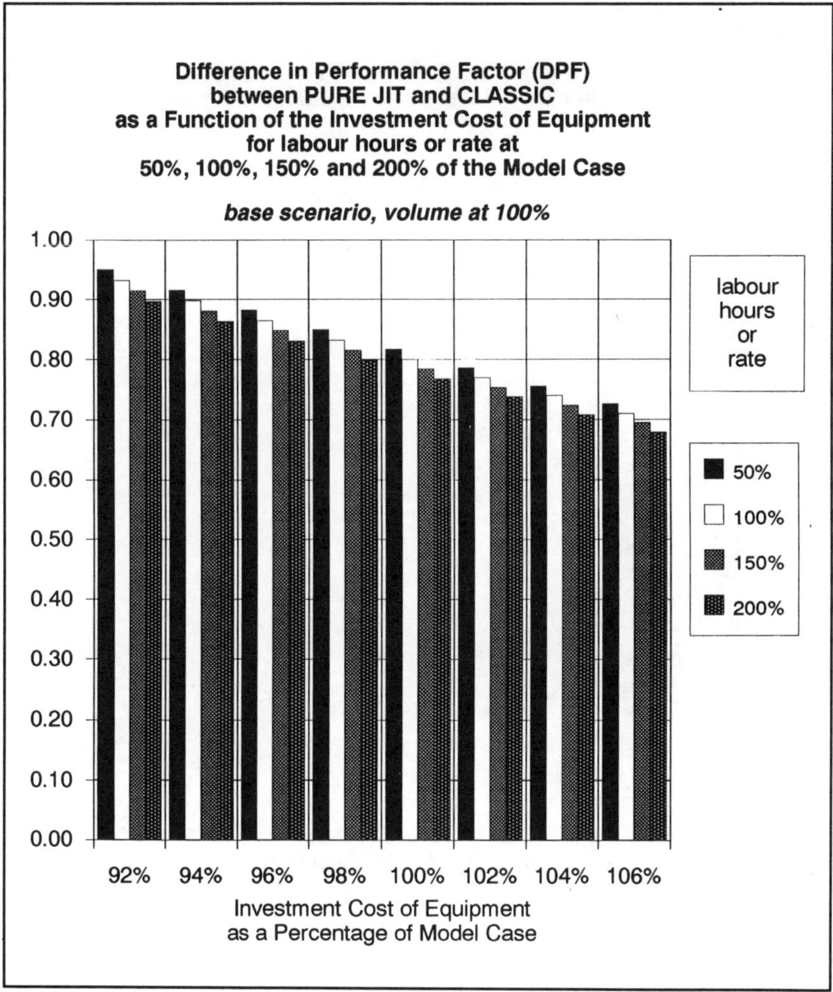

E-Chart III-4.3: Difference in discounted performance factor between CLASSIC and PURE JIT as a function of the investment cost of production equipment for values ranging from 92% to 106% of the base model case and standard labour hours or rate at values ranging from 50% to 200% of the base model case.

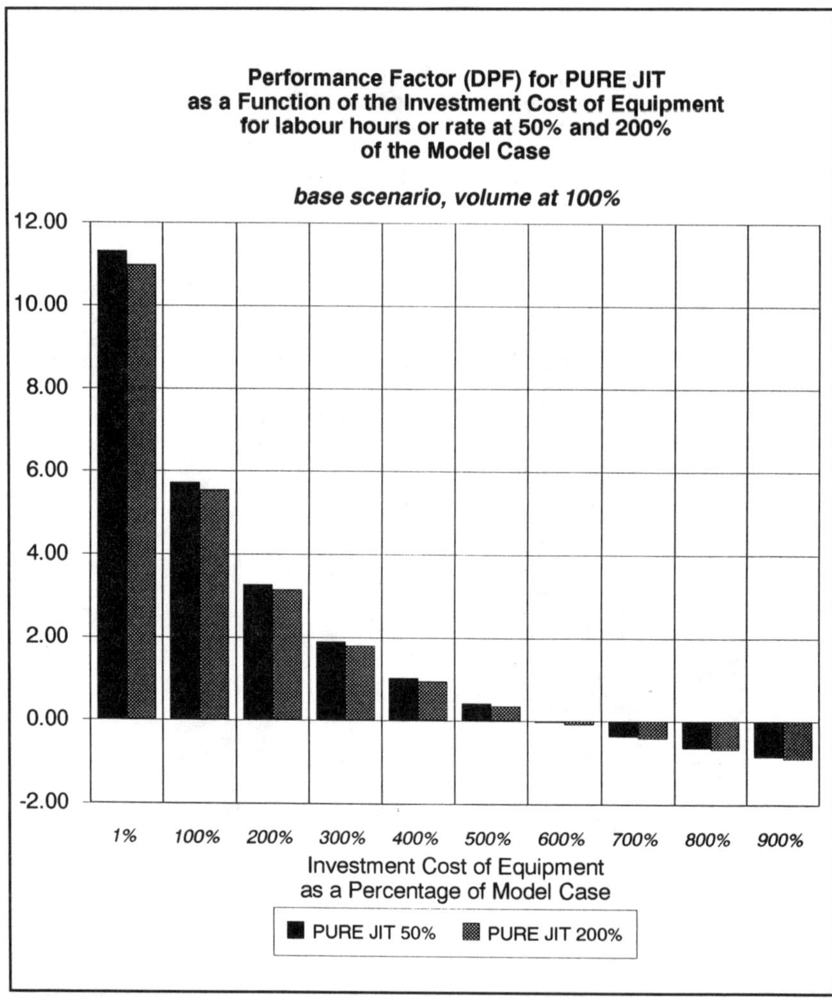

E-Chart III-3.4: Discounted performance factor for PURE JIT as a function of the investment cost of production equipment for values ranging from 1% to 900% of the base model case and standard labour hours or rate at 50% and 200% of the base model case. The values for DPF do not lie on a straight line and the distance between the two curves becomes increasingly smaller.

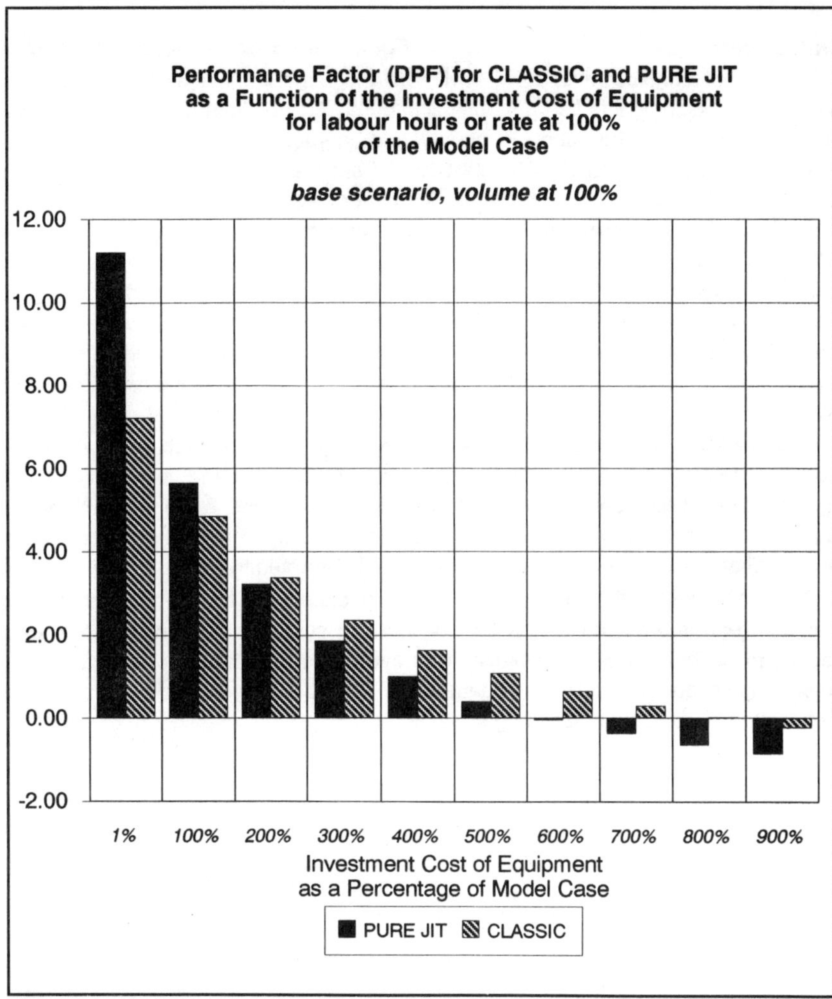

E-Chart III-3.5: Discounted performance factor for CLASSIC and PURE JIT as a function of the investment cost of production equipment for values ranging from 1% to 900% of the base model case and standard labour hours or rate at 100% of the base model case. Since PURE JIT requires more equipment capacity, it is much more sensitive to changes in the investment cost of equipment. If the equipment is twice as expensive as it is in the base model case, PURE JIT is no longer a lucrative proposition.

Discussion ***Equipment Cost vs Labour Content***

The major conclusion to be drawn from the experimental results is that the selection of equipment is far from optimal in purely economic terms. Less expensive equipment with a higher labour content would be substantially better. This applies to both CLASSIC and PURE JIT, but PURE JIT suffers most from this poor choice of equipment. Any justification for highly automated equipment must come from an altogether different corner. The short supply of labour in Switzerland, which has effectively had no unemployment during the past 10 years, is at issue here. Given that the situation in other European countries is much less rosy than in Switzerland and will likely remain so, any decision about the location of a new just-in-time factory will have to take the market supply of labour at different locations into account. In comparison, the differences in the hourly labour rate are hardly relevant for the decision.

The decision process needs to recognize that a low direct labour content decouples the size of the labour force from medium-term demand fluctuations. QED ignores the advantages of this kind of flexibility provided by highly automated equipment. It is worth pointing out that the choice of equipment is not a continuous spectrum as the curves in the E-Chart might be interpreted to imply.

The conclusions drawn here are at sharp odds with the information in the periodic reports provided by the cost accounting system, which invariably shows labour to be the largest cost block. This information reinforces efforts aimed at improving labour productivity. Together with the focus on capacity utilization, it defines the *de facto* manufacturing strategy.

7.3.4 Investigating Assumptions

The experiments in this final sub-section with experimental results investigate two selected areas where the quality of the model input would benefit from additional information and further data collection. A number of fairly crude assumptions needed to be made. Specifically, the experiments vary the relevant input parameters that determine demand variability and package sizes of finished products. In this way, the impact of the lack of detailed and accurate information about the input factors is assessed.

Purpose ***Demand Variability***

The first set of experiments varies both the variabililty of third party, independent demand in the group companies and the variability of dependent demand[72] at the production stages in the parent company. The variability of demand is one of the factors that determines safety stock levels. See §5.4 for a general discussion. For this set of experiments QED again assumes the forecast error to be equal to the demand variability. The forecast accuracy factor is set to 1.0, independent of the lead time. This is a further conservative assumption that favours a classical operation with long lead times.

The specific formula employed by QED for the safety stock levels in the group companies is shown in figure 7.5a. See [Williams 1984] for the derivation of the general formula. The base case model uses a k-factor of 2.3, which theoretically gives a service level—ability to deliver from stock—of approximately 99%, and a partially arbitrary value of 25 for the demand variability factor. Given the demand coverage in the group companies, the demand variability factor can be adjusted so that the output of QED matches these figures.

The specific formula for the safety stock levels for the production stages in the parent company has a further input parameter that specifies the order frequency. The base case model uses a k-factor of 1.2 for the bulk level and 2.3 for the semi-packaged level; and a value of 5 for the demand variability factor at both levels.

QED calculates the demand volume for a specific fully-packaged end-item in the group companies by dividing the total demand by the number of group companies and and the number of variants. Thus, QED assumes that the demand is divided equally between the end-item and the group companies. The total amount of safety stocks increases with the number of variants and group companies. The example calculations in figure 7.5b show this.

Since the safety stock formula for these experiments is somewhat more detailed than the one used for the other experiments, E-Charts IV-1.1 through IV-1.4 are

[72]There are numerous sources of internal demand variability. In the case investigated, a prime example is the notorious 'splitting' rule, which doesn't divide the quarterly forecast into three equal portions to arrive at monthly requirements. Although there is virtually no hard empirical evidence about the extent of internal demand variability, there are plenty of 'war stories' in circulation that indicate that relatively small changes in external demand are perceived to be much larger at the lower production stages. The degree of distortion is linked to the accumulated lead time and planning horizon.

included to show that the results for the base model case are nearly identical. E-Charts IV-1.5 through IV-1.7 contain the primary results.

A1	GCSafetyStock	Excel Macro for Safety Stock Level
A2	= ARGUMENT("k")	k factor, a function of the desired CSL
A3	= ARGUMENT("volume")	total annual demand
A4	= ARGUMENT("laverage")	average lead time (in days)
A5	= ARGUMENT("ldeviation")	standard deviation of the lead time
A6	= ARGUMENT("variability")	demand variability factor
A7	= 0.1 * SQRT(volume)	order size is proportional to the square root of the total demand
A8	= variability * A7 * A7	variance of order size
A9	= (volume/A7) / 365	order frequency (orders per day)
A10	= variability * A9 * A9	variance of order frequency
A11	= k*SQRT((A7*A7*laverage*A10) + (A9*laverage*A8) + (A9*A9*A7*A7* ldeviation*ldeviation))	textbook formula, which captures the demand variability during the fluctuating lead times
A12	=RETURN(A11)	

Figure 7.5a: EXCEL macro used by QED for calculating the safety stock level in the group companies. The macro has 5 arguments, which are referred to in the formulas. The processing order is strictly sequential. The variables **An** in the formulas refer to the results of the preceding sub-formula in cell **An**. The formula used by QED for the production stages in the parent company is identical, except that the order frequency is specified explicitly.

k volume (packs) lead time (days) lead time deviation demand variability	2.0 100'000 50 20 25	50'000	25'000	5'000
Safety Stock (packs)	23'210	11'797	6'031	1'313

Figure 7.5b: Safety stock levels in the group companies for some specific input values. Note that the safety stock level does not decrease proportionally with the demand volume. With a volume of 100'000 packs the average order size is calculated to be 32 packs.

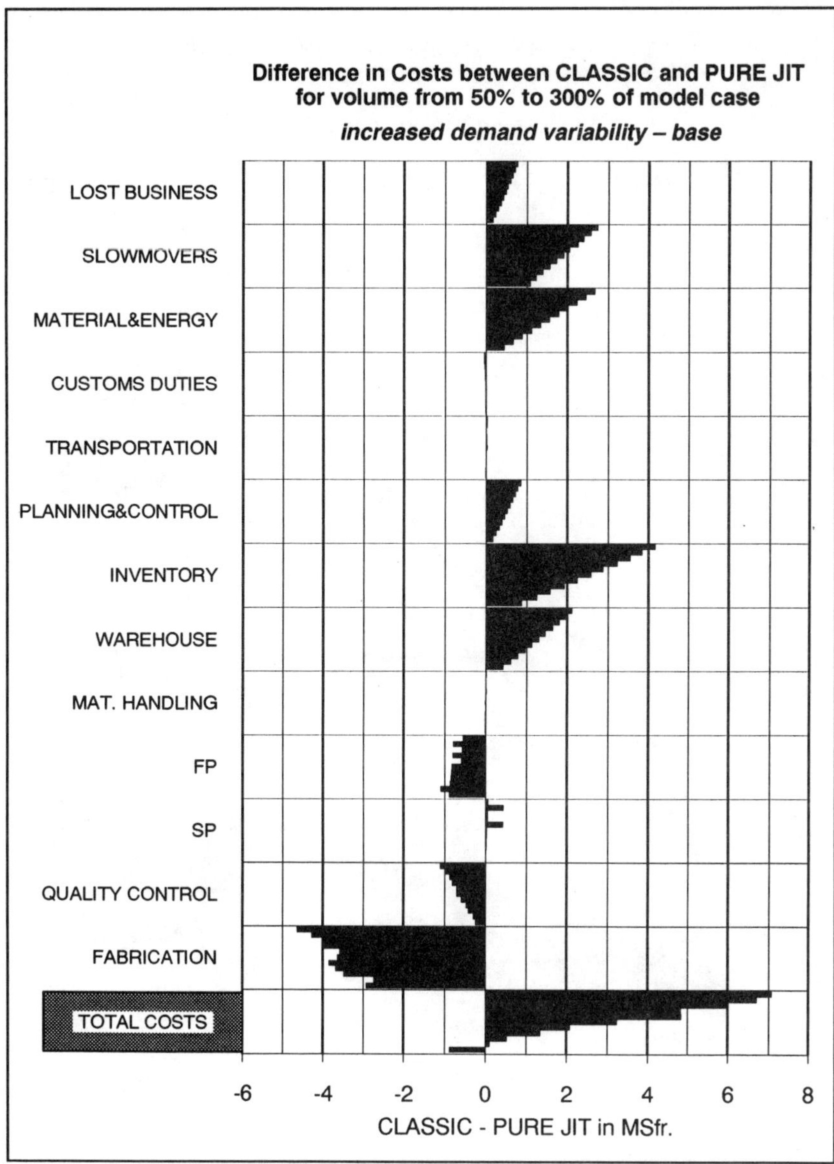

E-Chart IV-1.1: Difference in annual costs between CLASSIC and PURE JIT. The values shown for the individual cost items are the costs for CLASSIC minus those of the PURE JIT. As the volume ranges from 50% of the model case to 300% the difference in the total costs changes from ca -1 M.Sfr. to 7 M. Sfr. in favour of PURE JIT. *Since the safety stock formula for these experiments is somewhat more detailed than the one used for the other experiments, the next four E-Charts are included to show that the results for the base model case are nearly identical.* Compare with E-Chart I-1.3.

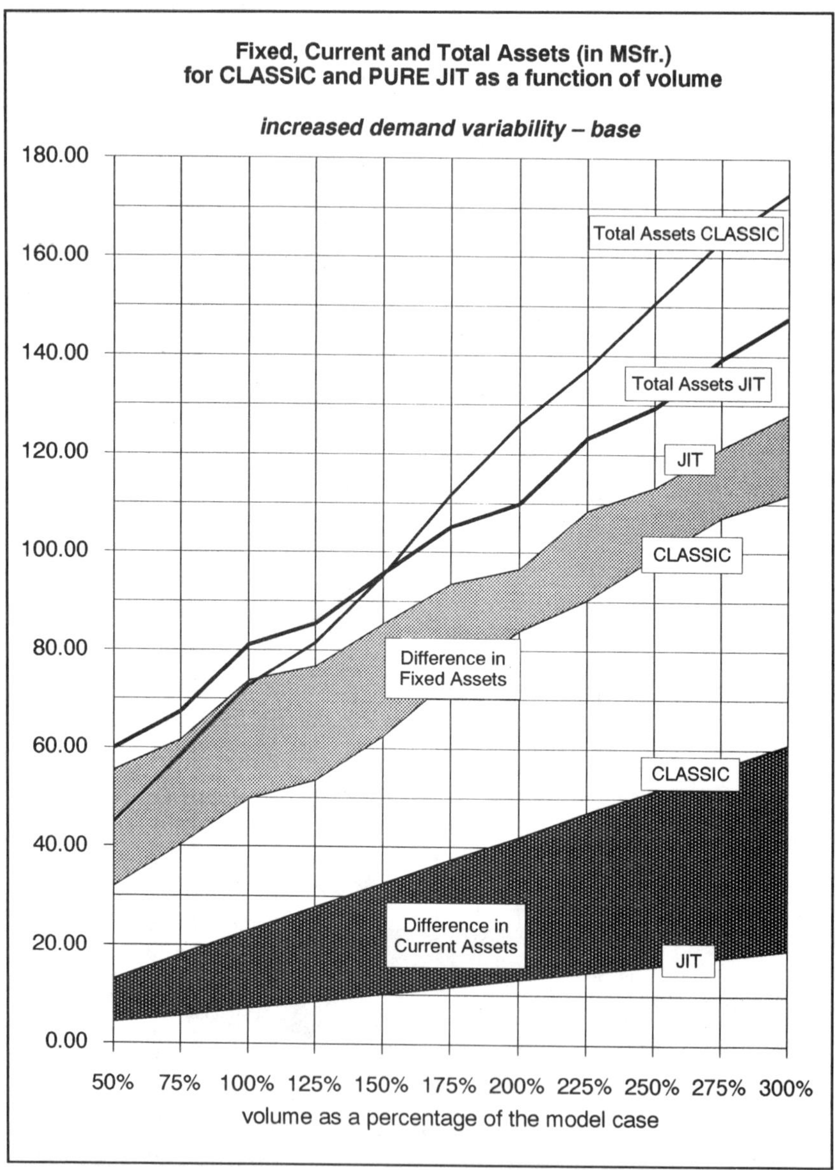

E-Chart IV-1.2: Asset base for CLASSIC and PURE JIT with the sales volume varying from 50% to 300% of the base model case. Compare with E-Chart I-4a.

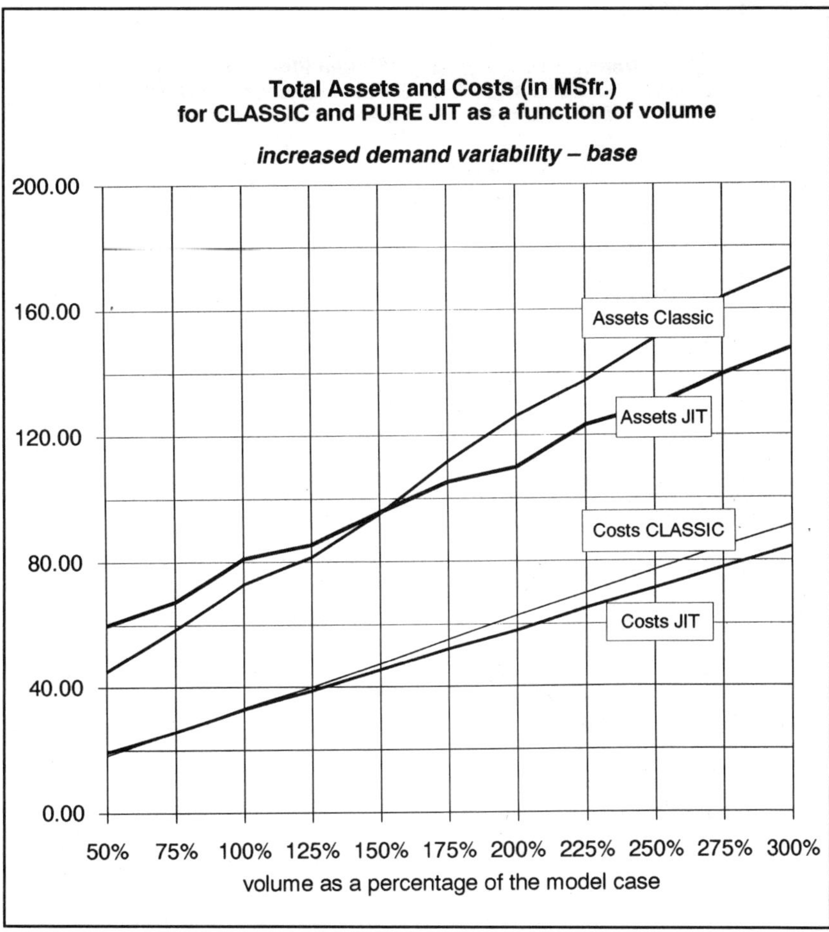

E-Chart IV-1.3: Total assets and total costs of CLASSIC and PURE JIT with the volume increasing from 50% to 300% of the base model case. Compare with E-chart I-1.5.

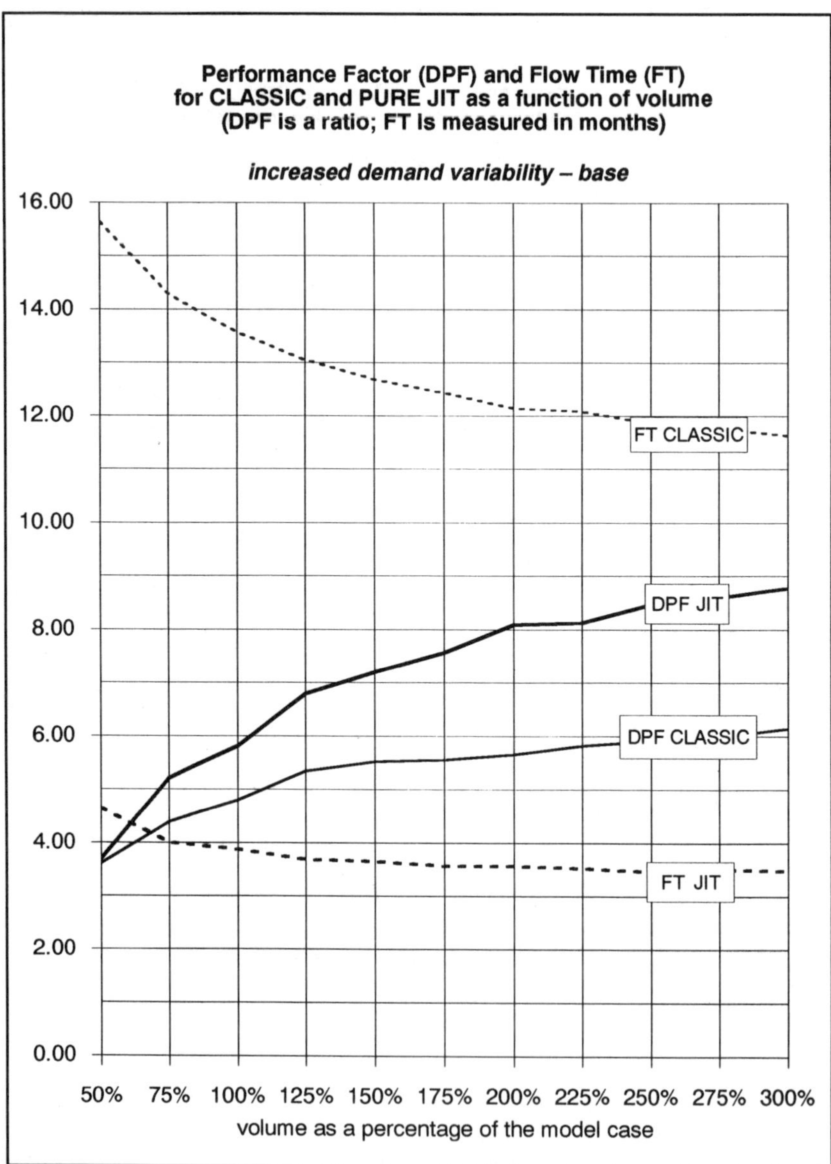

E-Chart IV-1.4: Discounted performance factor and flow time with the volume increasing from 50% to 300% of the base model case. Compare with E-chart I-1.7b.

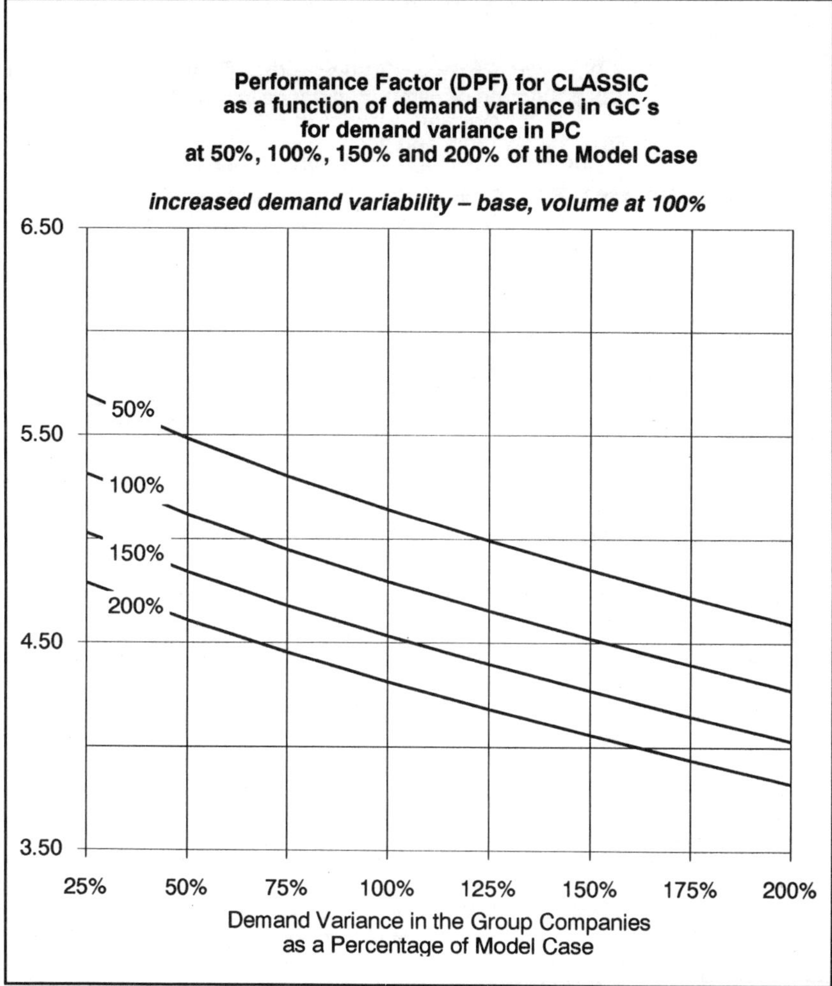

E-Chart IV-1.5: Discounted performance factor for CLASSIC as a function of independent demand variance in the group companies ranging from 25% to 200% of the base model case, and for dependent demand variance in the parent company at 50%, 100%, 150% and 200% of the base model case. The deterioration in performance, as measured by DPF, is surprisingly strong.

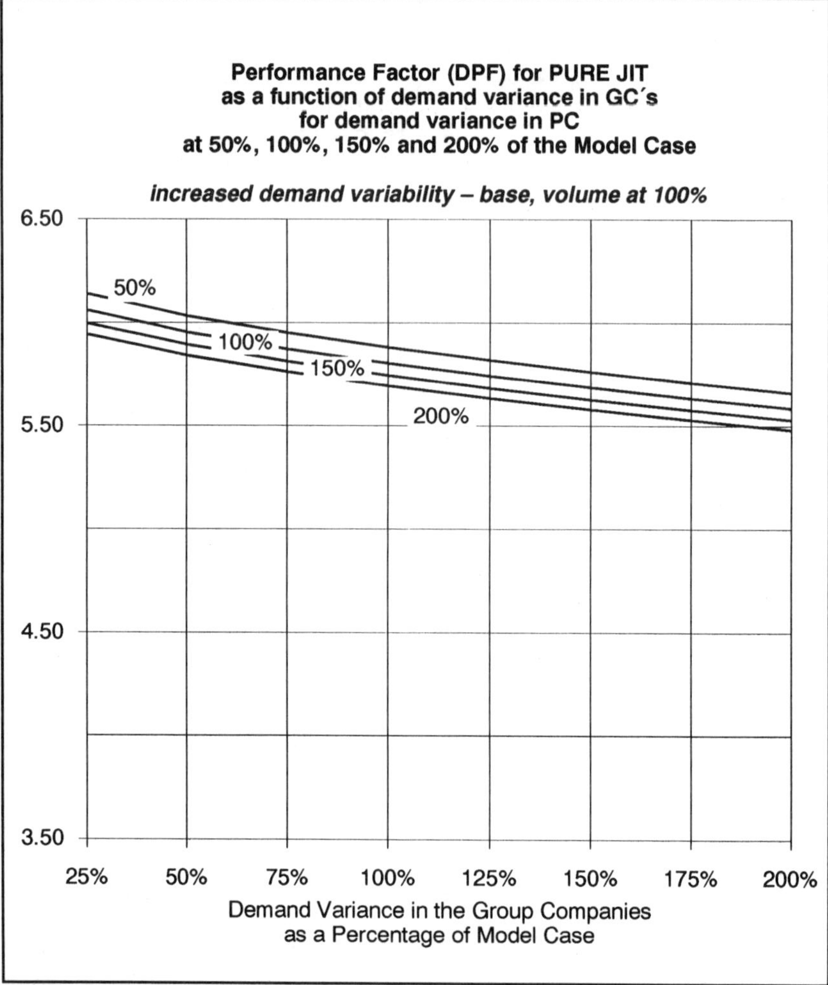

E-Chart IV-1.6: Discounted performance factor for PURE JIT as a function of independent demand variance in the group companies ranging from 25% to 200% of the base model case, and for dependent demand variance in the parent company at 50%, 100%, 150% and 200% of the base model case. The rate of deterioration in performance for PURE JIT is less than half that of CLASSIC.

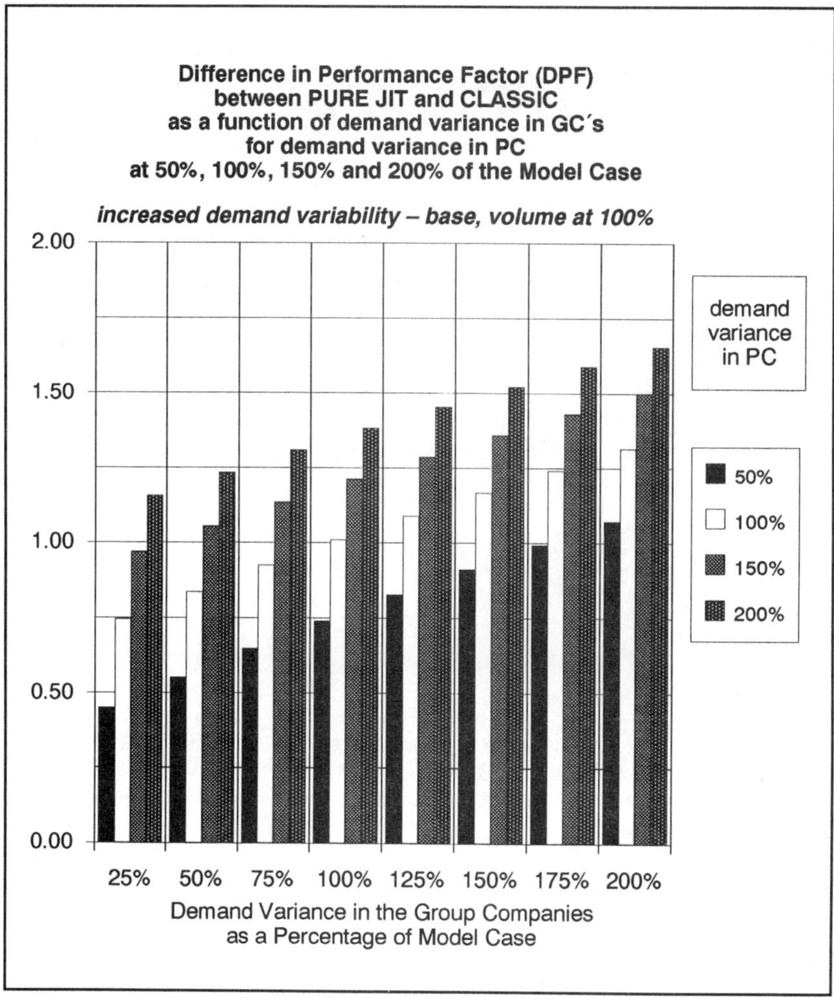

E-Chart IV-1.7: Difference in discounted performance factor between CLASSIC and PURE JIT as a function of independent demand variance in the group companies ranging from 25% to 200% of the base model case, and for dependent demand variance in the parent company at 50%, 100%, 150% and 200% of the base model case. The difference in DPF increases rapidly with the demand variance. The increases level off somewhat; but would be increasing if the standard deviation instead of the variance had been used.

Discussion ***Demand Variability***

The experimental results clearly show that both the variability of dependent demand in the parent company and independent demand in the group companies have a significant effect on the difference in DPF between CLASSIC and PURE JIT. CLASSIC is twice as sensitive to increases in the variance of the demand as PURE JIT. The results also show that if QED were to make the reasonable link between forecast accuracy and lead times, PURE JIT would look better still.

The strong dependency of the results on demand variability justifies further collection and analysis of demand data. The quarterly figures that are available today are obviously inadequate.[73] Nevertheless, the basic results and conclusions need not be called into question. The available data on service and stock levels justify the rough estimate of demand variability that QED uses.

Since a change in the target service level in the group companies has a similar effect on safety stocks as independent demand variability, we can also conclude that PURE JIT can establish an increase in customer service levels at lower costs than CLASSIC.

Purpose ***Finished Product Package Sizes***

A number of exogenous parameters will shift the balance of stocks towards the last part of the supply chain. Generally, this will have an unfavourable impact on the total cost of holding stock in the manufacturing system. The number of different variants of fully-packaged products and the number of group companies served from the parent company are two examples which have been mentioned already. A further, perhaps surprising example is the package size of fully-packaged products. The final set of experiments presented in this chapter doubles the average package size to investigate the difference in performance between CLASSIC and PURE JIT. The average selling price is assumed to stay the same.

---

[73]Demand variability and forecasting have been the subject of several OR projects in the past. One of the project reports shows that the quarterly forecast error for group company demand of 18 fully-packaged products, measured over a three year period, averaged at 230%. The figure was obtained by taking the average over the three year period of the absolute value of the quarterly forecast error put in relation to the effective demand. The use of statistical methods improved the forecasts, but only marginally, for little more than half of the 18 products investigated. The report attributes the lack of success to the long forecasting horizon resulting from the present lead times. I should add that in my view attempts to improve the forecast error at this level are at best doomed to failure and at worst ill-conceived. The bull is best taken by its horns. Reducing forecast horizons and eliminating the need for detailed forecasting of fully-packaged end-items is a more effective approach. The bulk product stage is the highest level at which statistical forecasting is likely to meet with success. An approach suggested to me by Mr. Tim Mantle requires the use of planning bills to aggregate finished product forecasts into bulk product forecasts. It has met with success at a distillery and bottler of whisky, where the diversity at the finished product level is also large. However, a past OR project which investigated precisely this idea, comes to less favourable conclusions.

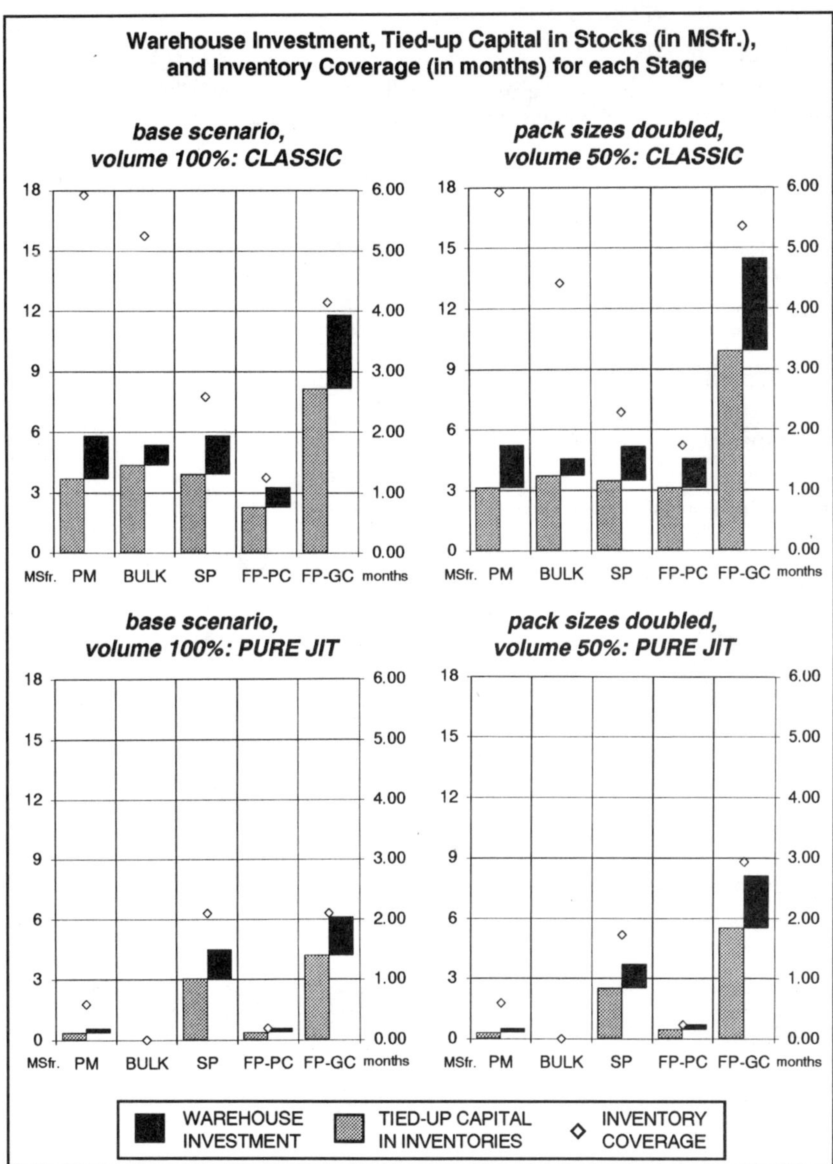

E-Chart IV-2.1: Warehouse investment, tied-up capital in inventories (both in MSfr.) and inventory demand coverage (in months) for the *base scenario* & *pack sizes doubled*. The *base scenario* is shown with the volume at 100% of the base model case and *pack sizes doubled* at 50% because the volume is measured in terms of fully-packaged products. There is a clear shift in inventory balance towards the group companies that occurs when the pack sizes are double the size of the *base scenario.*

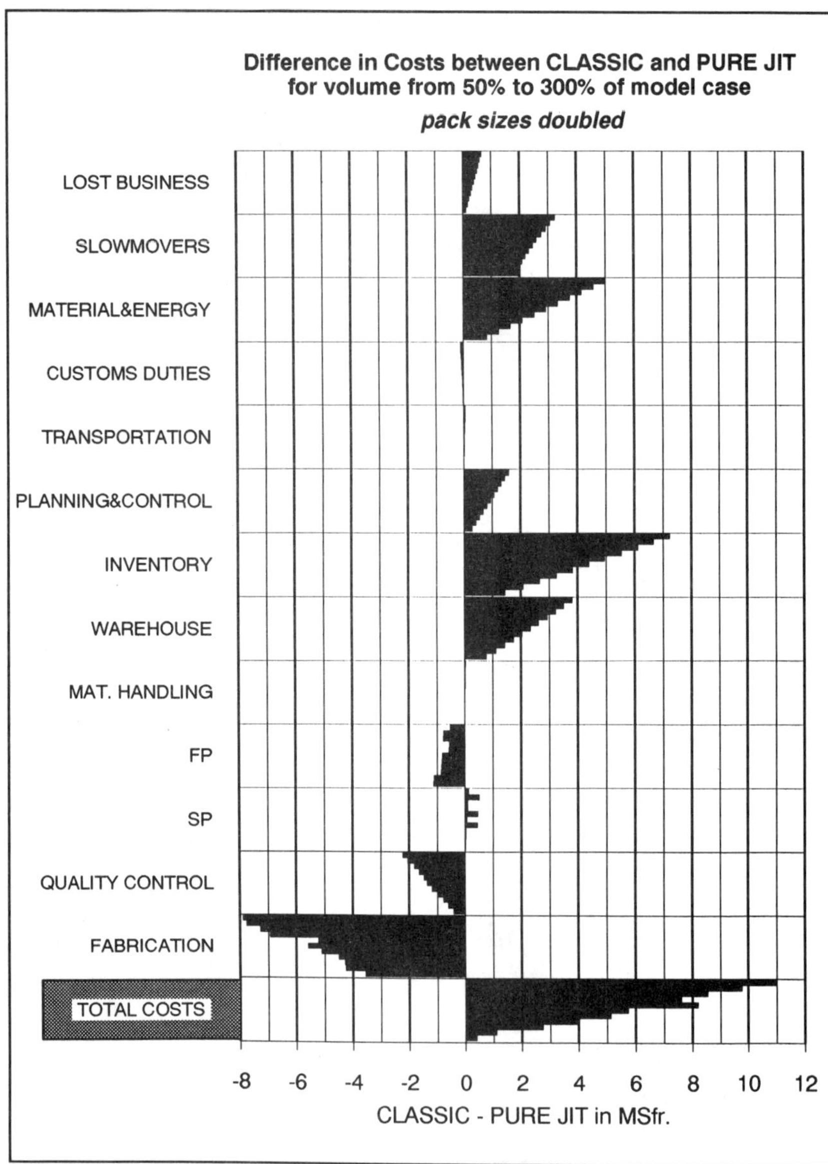

E-Chart IV-2.2: Difference in annual costs between CLASSIC and PURE JIT with the sales volume increasing from 50% to 300% of the base model case. The values shown for the individual cost items are the costs for CLASSIC minus those of the PURE JIT. As the volume ranges from 50% of the model case to 300% the difference in the total costs changes from ca -0.4 M.Sfr. to 11.0 M. Sfr. in favour of PURE JIT. At 150% the difference is 5.0 M.Sfr., which is approximately 16% less than the comparable volume of 300% in the *base scenario*.

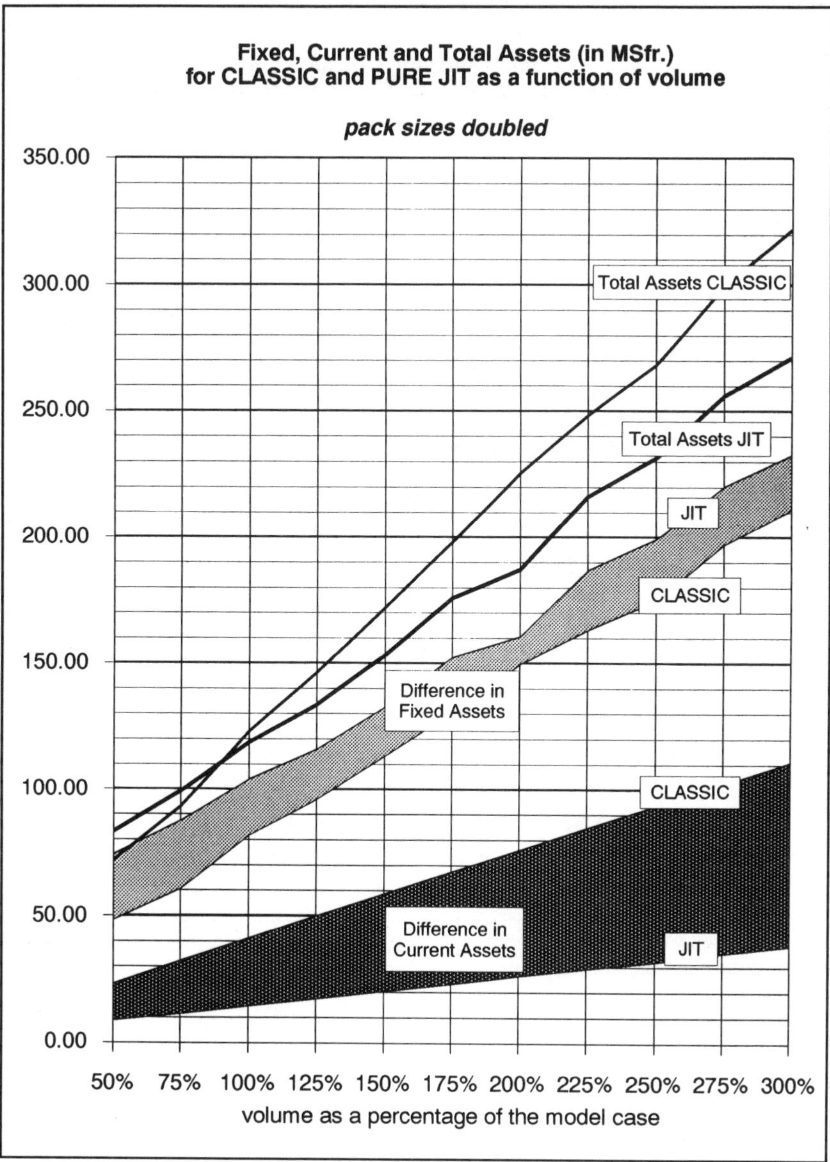

E-Chart IV-2.3: Asset base for CLASSIC and PURE JIT with the sales volume increasing from 50% to 300% of the base model case.

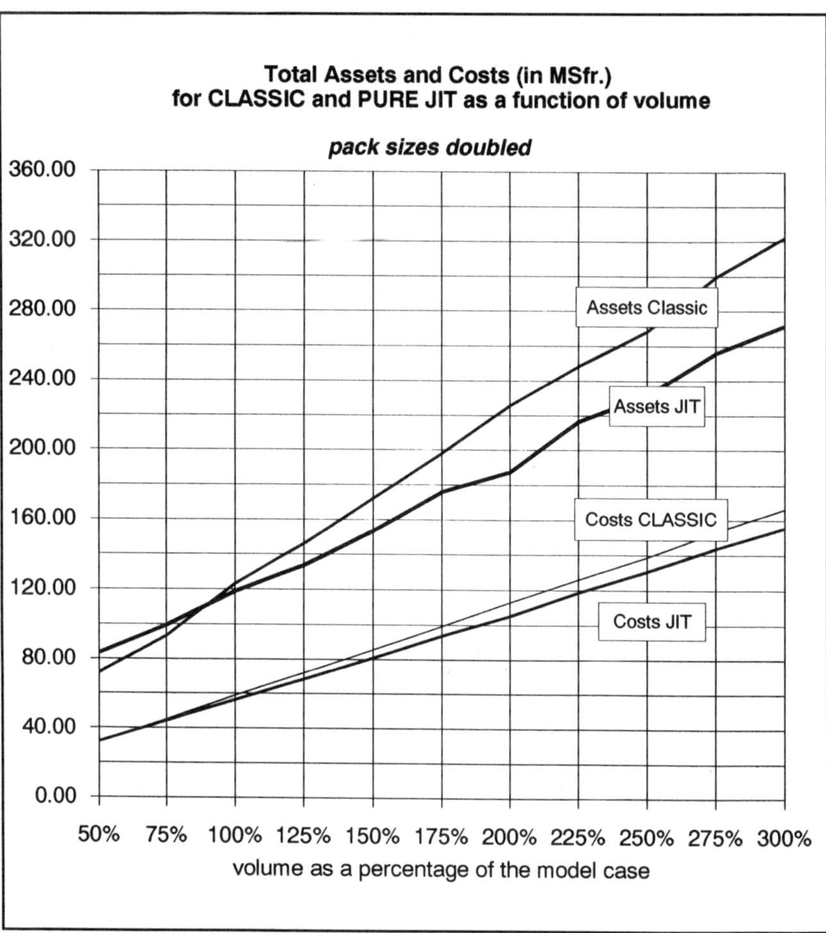

E-Chart IV-2.4: Total assets and total costs of CLASSIC and PURE JIT with the sales volume increasing from 50% to 300% of the base model case.

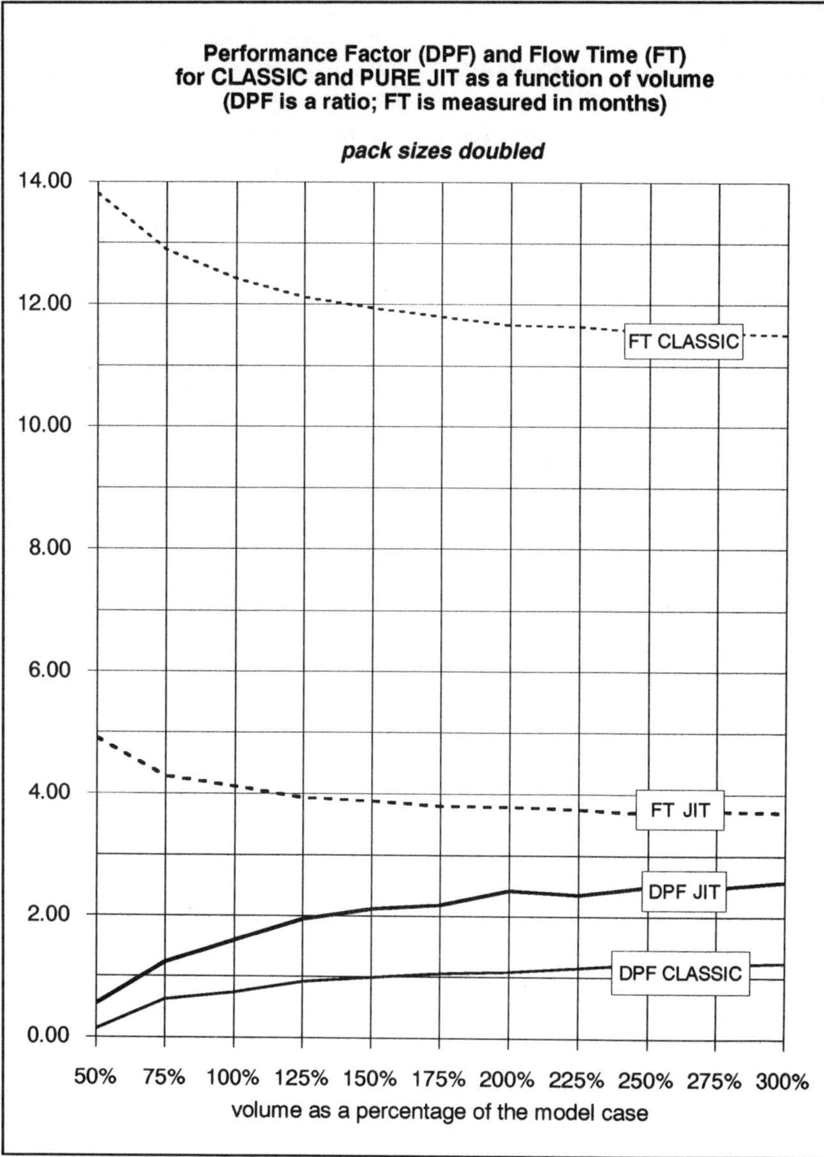

E-Chart IV-2.5: Discounted performance factor and flow time with the sales volume increasing from 50% to 300% of the base model case. Because the average sales price is left the same in this set of experiments DPF drops dramatically in comparison with the base scenario, see E-Chart I-1.7b. With the volume at 150%, the difference between PURE JIT and CLASSIC is only 1 unit, in comparison with 2.5 units in the base scenario with the volume at 300%. However, in this scenario, PURE JIT is 100% better than CLASSIC; in the *base scenario* with the comparable volume, it is only 40% better than CLASSIC.

Discussion ***Finished Product Package Sizes***

The interpretation of this final set of experimental results is hampered by the fact the production volume is not directly comparable with that of the *base scenario*. The average sales price was left the same, while the finished product package sizes was doubled. A comparison of the scenario *pack sizes doubled* with the *base scenario* at half the sales volume shows that the difference in financial performance between PURE JIT and CLASSIC narrows in absolute terms. However, in relative terms it increases.

7.4 Critical Assessment of QED and the Experimental Results

The range of experimental results contained in this chapter permit the conclusion that QED has achieved what it was designed to achieve. QED has established the link between low-level decision variables such as lot and campaign sizes, and segmentation decisions, on the one hand, and flow time and financial performance measures, on the other hand. As argued in the introductory chapters, this is a key issue in modern manufacturing. On the basis of this linkage, it was possible to differentiate the two basic manufacturing approaches investigated and draw significant conclusions about the economics of speed. QED was also able to show the degree to which different external factors influence the primary results.

If we accept the underlying modeling logic of QED, the results of the experimental sets appear to be both intuitive and consistent. It is the size of the benefits of the application of the just-in-time concept that surprise, given the composition of the balance sheet for the industrial case investigated—and especially as reported by the accounting system. The results also confirm that the reliance on cost or contribution alone is dangerous. The return on assets employed, as measured by the performance factor, differentiates the two cases more clearly.

The logic of QED also lends itself to application in other cases. Moreover, the total implementation effort is modest and a standard electronic spreadsheet fulfills the technical implementation requirements. From an academic point of view, it would be valuable to apply the technique underlying Forrester's industrial dynamics. Two important aspects that would benefit from its application are the estimates of costs of slow-movers and lost business, i.e. the impact of demand volatility. However, the returns in additional insight into the different dynamics of the two alternatives would probably not justify the much larger model implementation effort required for a case as complex as the one investigated. My assessment of the feasibility of using Stella, which is a tool that provides a most convenient user-interface for systems dynamics modeling, showed that it would be extremely cumbersome to develop a model for a multi-stage and multi-product case with which an equivalent range of experiments and sensitivity analysis could be carried out. The key difficulty concerns the ability to parametrize the size of the operation modeled, which also applies to discrete-event simulation models. For the purposes of a rough-cut financial analysis, as decribed in chapter 3, a less sophistcated but more pragmatic approach will have to do.

8 Conclusions, Current Trends and Outlook

8.1 Overview

This final chapter begins by rounding off the previous chapter: it assesses the business implications of the extensive experimental results and analysis presented in that chapter. It then proceeds with a discussion of just-in-time implementation issues in an existing operation, which, as promised, focuses on what I see as a prime managerial dilemma. The next three sections outline current trends in the pharmaceutical production. Covered are developments at CIBA–GEIGY in the EEC and Japan, as well as a just-in-time project at the Kaiseraugst works of Hoffmann-La Roche Pharmaceuticals in Switzerland. These developments substantiate the business implications that will be discussed shortly. The final section takes a bit broader perspective of the just-in-time concept by reviewing its status in the general context of supply chain management.

8.2 Strategic Impact of the Experimental Results: A Summary

The experimental results contained in §7.3 have been presented in a fashion that should permit the reader to draw conclusions independently of the discussion following each set of experiments. The reader who has taken advantage of the opportunity to question and, hopefully, confirm my conclusions will find that this section presents little in the way of new facts. The length of §7.3 should, however, justify the following summary of the primary results in more general terms. Although the analysis is restricted to a single industrial case, I also venture to sketch the general impact of these results on competitive manufacturing strategies in the industry.

The application of the just-in-time concept in the pharmaceutical will change the shape of the cost-delivery frontier.[74] The just-in-time concept ensures more rapid and reliable delivery service at lower total cost. Firms that once were at or near the efficient frontier and are not in a position or otherwise fail to adopt the concept will find it increasingly difficult to maintain the competitive position of their products once the patent protection period has run out.

Small firms marketing a full range of dosage forms for a few active ingredients may well be at a disadvantage because the volume in fabrication and packaging is too low in relation to the number of segments required to justify the disproportionally large investment in fixed assets. Small firms are therefore under the highest pressure to increase equipment flexibility and to reduce changeover times without at the same time investing additional assets in more sophisticated equipment, which would only put them at a further disadvantage. Of course, the pressure to innovate is known not to be a bad thing by itself, on the contrary. The pool concept investigated in §7.3.2, although it is a thorn—beam?—in the eye of just-in-time theorists, may be a viable alternative for small operations.

---

[74]See §2.4 for a discussion of the concept of the cost-delivery frontier.

The combination of the application of the basic elements of the just-in-time concept with judicious investments in highly flexible equipment[75] will put those large firms at an advantage that are capable of restructuring their operations quickly. Restructuring entails, among other things, specialization. Operations will need to focus on specific ranges of dosage forms: there clearly is a critical size above which the application of the concept becomes increasingly lucrative. The allocation of packaged products to manufacturing sites by criteria such as sales volume or, worse, active ingredient is ill-suited to take advantage of the economics of speed.

The numerous implications and the changes in manufacturing strategy these call for come at a time when the general business conditions in the EEC are still in a state of flux. The question is whether the management decisions that have been made already and those that still need to be made are putting a firm into a position to take advantage of the opportunities offered by both the liberalization in the EEC and the economics of speed to the fullest extent. The 1990's will tell.

The specific financial results presented are sufficiently clear-cut that they should put the justifiable concerns of management about the cost-effectiveness of the just-in-time concept at rest. Despite the unfavourable composition of the asset balance sheet, which I believe is one source of these concerns, the just-in-time concept will reduce the total asset base. To capture the overall benefits, a broader financial view, which must include stock levels and warehouses in the group companies or at decentral locations, is indispensable. A myopic view favours a classical operation..

The results show that the penalty for the delay in income that results from holding stocks, which goes beyond the usual interest charges on tied-up capital in stocks, is significant. The application of conventional investment appraisal methods, which by their very nature account for the time value of money, ought to recognize this

The analysis is on the whole very conservative. It underestimates the benefits of the just-in-time concept on several counts. In particular, the impact on market share doesn't enter the calculations—there is no data on which to base a sound quantitative analysis. It should also be stressed that the effects of a changeover time reduction programme, although such a programme is an integral component of the concept, are excluded from the experiments, except for those specifically dealing with the issue. They confirm the importance of changeover time reductions. Although the evidence it not wholly conclusive, the efforts invested in a changeover reduction programme show *increasing* marginal returns, which would confirm the insight obtained from mathematical models, see §2.7.

The pervasive attitude of factory managers, ingrained by the current cost accounting system, that puts the emphasis on high capacity utilization and the

---

[75]A particularly interesting kind of flexible equipment items are packaging machines that perform the printing of packaging material on-line. Such machines, if they were available or developed, would reduce the range of packaging materials dramatically, and decrease the reliance on supplier partnerships, and, in general, simplify the implementation of the just-in-time concept. The results presented in chapter 7 justify skepticism towards investment in highly automated equipment. This particular kind of investment forms an exception.

reduction of period cost in production clearly does not align with a manufacturing strategy designed to exploit the economics of speed. The just-in-time concept invariably requires more fixed assets, even if warehouses are included, than a traditional operation. Moreover, this attitude influences a number of operational decisions as much as medium- and long-term investments decisions. The evidence provided shines an altogether different light on the optimality of current campaign sizes. The lack of attention paid to changeover time reduction stands out in a similar fashion.

There is an apparent conflict that centers around the degree to which equipment should be automated to reduce the direct labour content. In economic terms, the necessary investments in expensive equipment are questionable. The shortage of labour on the market may nevertheless justify such investments if the decision about the location of the manufacturing operation is fixed. Other advantages of automated equipment play a role as well. Care must be taken that the information provided by the cost accounting system, which shows labour to be the largest cost block, doesn't distort the investment decisions.

Higher investments in fixed production assets make the introduction of a second or third shift more attractive. As shown, this holds especially for the just-in-time concept. But, any additional shift requires additional labour. The experimental design is too simple for any definitive conclusions.

The overall benefits of the just-in-time concept are by no means spectacular. Depending on several internal and external factors, the reduction in total annual costs may be quite modest. However, in most realistic industrial cases, these reductions can be expected to remain significant.

The return on assets employed distinguishes the two opposing alternatives much more clearly than total cost does. The choice of financial performance measure is a particularly important one in the context of jus-in-time.

To summarize, there is a strong inverse correlation between flow time and return on assets. By establishing the link between speed and financial performance, this thesis has answered the original question: the tortoise not only wins the race, but also makes more effective and efficient use of resources in doing so. Future investments and manufacturing strategies in the industry should reflect this.

8.3 Implementation Issues: A Managerial Dilemma

The comparative financial analysis performed with QED shows that the construction of a new manufacturing operation should be based on the application of the principles of the just-in-time concept. The traditional concept is a poorer alternative. The construction of a just-in-time fabrication and packaging operation should not be any more difficult than a traditional operation. Because of the segmentation into independent production lines, design problems will be simpler.

The application of the just-in-time concept in an existing traditional operation is proving to be much more difficult. The first question is whether in such a case the improvements in performance justify the additional investments. To answer this question we need to know how much of the existing fixed assets, including building space and infrastructure, can be or need to be taken over for the product range selected. The selection of a suitable product range with which to start is a difficult question, that we cannot circumvent in the implementation of the just-in-time concept in an existing operation. Opinions will diverge on whether a re-design of the material and information flows, and the required additional investments, aimed at improving and replacing a part of an existing facility provide the necessary returns. In general, the magnitude of the benefits will be too small to support any such efforts and investments. The experimental results contained in §7.3 appear to be in agreement with this conclusion.

Unfortunately, the decision not to apply the just-in-time concept to an existing manufacturing operation entails a serious medium-term risk that threatens to erode the future competitive basis of traditional capacity-oriented operations. The implications of the financial analysis that were put forward in the previous section make it abundantly clear that new just-in-time facilities will eventually operate from an advantageous competitive position. The current developments outlined in the next two sections indicate that this isn't merely an academic prediction but that the basis of competition will in fact change quite dramatically over the next decade. The failure to apply the concept may therefore jeopardize the continuation of operations at existing facilities and locations. Thus, the question is not so much whether but when to change. The longer an active decision is delayed, the greater the temptation to invest in non-value-added solutions that merely cover up the symptoms of an operation that lacks a flow-oriented perspective aimed at speed. The inherent weakness of purely financial investment appraisals is at issue here. The literature on investments in new technologies has widely recognized this. Thus, the dilemma that the just-in-time concept poses a manager of a traditional existing operation is not a truly new one. It is an instance of a kind of dilemma that a successful business has resolved before.

The previous discussion has largely ignored the practicality of implementing the just-in-time concept in an existing facility. What are the chances of success *across the board?* Forgetting the partial and limited successes that have been achieved to-date, the realistic and frank answer must be that in the empirical case investigated, which is unlikely to be wholly untypical of other industrial cases, they are slim indeed. Although this judgement is coloured by the perceptions and attitude of experienced management and staff in the Stein works, the totality of solutions that must be found and implemented represents an seemingly unsurmountable set of interrelated problems that sap the available resources and motivation. Since just-in-time is a multi-faceted concept, there are no instant solutions that conveniently pop up from the theoretician's drawers. The application of the basic principles of the concept in each individual case generates a broad range of entirely different issues. Chapter 6 has discussed these. It is clear that solutions should not be designed around existing concepts, facilities and structures controlling the flow of material and information, which themselves need to be revamped. Here lies the difficulty. Can an organization learn to restructure its existing operations and mobilize the inertia, which has built up over the years, to do so?

The next two sections indicate that things are indeed much easier if there is a clean drawing board from which the design and implementation can proceed.

8.4 Just-in-Time at CIBA–GEIGY Pharmaceuticals in the EEC

On the basis of an assessment of the current developments in the EEC, CIBA–GEIGY has put in place a new European production policy. This policy covers the construction of modern production facilities; matching changes in the organization, which will unfold over the next couple of years; the creation of a central logistics function for demand and supply management on the basis of the MRP II concept, and a major re-registration effort. Clearly, the implications and benefits are long-term and of strategic importance for the pharmaceutical division. In addition, the policy and its realization are not without risks.

One integral component of this policy addresses pharmaceutical production in Spain, France and Italy. The existing equipment and facilities in these countries no longer meet the projected business requirements and are not suited to take advantage of the opportunities offered by the liberalization of regulations in the EEC. The EFI project, which was publicly announced by CIBA–GEIGY in 1989, foresees the construction of three new and specialized production facilities in these countries. Spain will be producing low-volume solid dosage froms, France liquid and semi-liquid dosage forms, and Italy high-volume solid dosage forms. Specialization—but here based on product volume, *nota bene*—is a key element of the overall concept, which is designed to improve the response to market requirements and reduce or at least maintain current production costs. To capitalize fully on the potential synergy effects and economies of scale, it will be necessary to pursue the harmonization of the product range. The detrimental effects of country specific requirements are considerable. All in all, the EFI project requires investments more than 200 M.SFr. for the fabrication and packaging of roughly 150 million fully-finished packages annually.

Since the facilities in Spain and Italy both produce fully-packaged solid dosage forms directly from active substance, a comparison of the major characteristics is meaningful and instructive. The facility in Spain adheres most closely to the elements of the just-in-time concept. In view of the experimental results reported in chapter 7, the facility in Italy, which will be located in the vicinity of Naples, has a number of characteristics—see table 8.1—which raise design questions that cannot be answered here. The product mix and the specific equipment requirements for fabrication are at issue. Although both facilities aim at short production throughput time, the difference in philosophy that is made plain by the values given in table 8.1 will in all likelihood result in longer average production throughput times and planning lead times for the Italian facility. Its reliance on sophisticated computer controlled operations for both production planning and the shop floor control will be much higher. The choice of a high degree of automation appears surprising given the geographic location. Since both facilities eliminate the intermediate storage of bulk and semi-packaged products in the warehouse, the accumulative planning lead times will be several times shorter than those for traditional facilities.

	Spain	Italy
product class	low-volume (B & C)	high-volume (A)
max. annual output (M. Packs)	40	60
projected capacity utilization '96	75%	85%
no. of shifts	2	2
batch size (kg)	150	450
no. of batches per year	1600	800
no. of campaigns per year	740	~150
horizontal segmentation	on-line	on-line
vertical segmentation	independent lines	pool
flexibility of packaging equipment	high	medium to high
degree of automation	low	high
throughput time (no. of shifts)	4-10	5-10[76]
warehouse space (pallets)	5200	–

Table 8.1: A comparison of the facilities in Spain and Italy for solid dosage forms.

In close cooperation with the OR department, the technical operations department in the pharmaceutical division carried out a detailed simulation analysis with ProfiSEE of the facility to be built in Spain. The purpose of the simulation project was to provide the necessary input for the detailed investment proposal and to demonstrate the feasibility of achieving short throughput times in an on-line, flow-oriented production unit.

The factory layout modeled foresees 4 independent production lines each with 2 sublines, as shown in figure 8.1. Work stations are separated by buffers areas providing space for only 4 containers holding WIP. The model also covered container movement and washing as well as manpower requirments. Some more specific characteristics of the model and the project are given in the first column of table 4.6b in §4.10. Further relevant parameters are listed in table 8.1 above.

The factory was modeled to operate under a so-called shiftwise concept. This concept basically stipulates that a single batch is to be processed per shift. It is designed to ensure a smooth and easily understood flow of material through the factory and achieves an artificially balanced process by including pre-programmed idle times at each work center. The kanban approach is notably different. With the exception of dispensing, and granulation & blending, where 2 or 4 hours of processing time were specified, the processing times for the different stages were rounded to a multiple of 4 hours. The shiftwise comes at the expense of a further deterioration in equipment utilization. The degree will depend on the true level of imbalance of the process, see table 7.2.2 for 'unrounded' processing times.

[76]The average throughput time for an entire campaign is likely to be close to or larger than 10 shifts. Unfortunately, the report available to me doesn't state how this range was obtained. My rough estimate indicates that it may not take into account imbalances in the fabrication process.

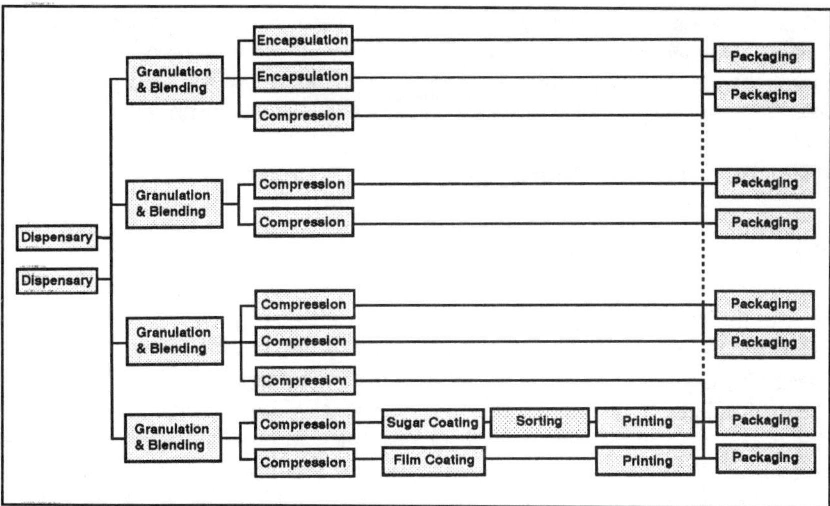

Figure 8.1: Segmentation concept and material flow for just-in-time facility in Spain. [Source: K. Braun, D. Kinrade, G. Oxé; "Final Report for OR 428," (CIBA–GEIGY internal report); February 1990]. Maximum capacity: ca. 40 million fully-finished packages annually. Packaging includes semi- and fully-finished packaging, excluded is export packaging. The dashed lines indicate that some crossovers are permitted inspite of the line concept. The problem is that the segmentation criteria used for fabrication are counter-productive in packaging, where package format plays a key role in reducing the number of major setups. The approach taken by Hoffmann-La Roche, see §8.5, avoids this problem by including all three stages in packaging and excluding fabrication. This segmentation concept has considerable merits: there is a single major segmentation criteria to stick to.

The simulation experiments provided detailed results for the following key items:

- throughput times – days of no. of shifts
- line utilization – percentage of working days in use
- utilization of equipment items – process and changeover time vs available time
- WIP levels and no. of containers required

The combination of the line and shiftwise concept resulted in an average throughput time of 3.3 days, equivalent to 7 shifts, with an average line utilization of 70% on the basis of 2 shifts per day and 5 working days per week. The utilization of the individual line ranged from 59% to 100%. The report doesn't fail to note that the load on the over-loaded lines will have to be shifted towards to the remaining lines. As expected, the average utilization levels of the individual equipment items was much lower than the line utilization. The levels ranged from a low of 35% to 70%. The bottleneck stage in the process varied from line to line.

These detailed figures are provided here to amplify once more that speed comes at the expense of poor equipment utilization. Although improvements in line and process imbalance are certainly achievable, and indeed essential, classical utilization levels of 80% are out of reach. The results of this detailed simulation study of a further industrial case are consistent with those presented in §7.3.2. The overall financial analysis of the economics of such low utilization levels, as developed and carried out in this thesis, appears to be a worthwhile effort.

8.5 Just-in-Time at Hoffmann-La Roche Pharmaceuticals

Hoffmann-La Roche finds itself in a rather similar position as CIBA–GEIGY as far as pharmaceutical production in the parent company is concerned. During the past twenty years, the group companies have swallowed the most 'lucrative' and easy parts of the business. The resulting changes in the composition of the production orders for packaged products have amplified the need for flexibility and delivery speed. The existing equipment and production management of material and information flows in packaging are no longer ideally suited to meet the demands placed upon the parent company. It is interesting to draw the parallels with the situation in the Stein works and to contrast and compare the proposals put forward.

Due to office space requirements at the central production site in Basel, Hoffmann-La Roche has decided to build a new factory in Kaiseraugst, which is twenty miles up the Rhine valley from the company headquarters in Basel. Besides releasing expensive space in Basel, the new facility will make it easier to conform to GMP regulations, will open up perspectives for future expansions and will allow the company to meet demand requirements in terms of speed and flexibility.

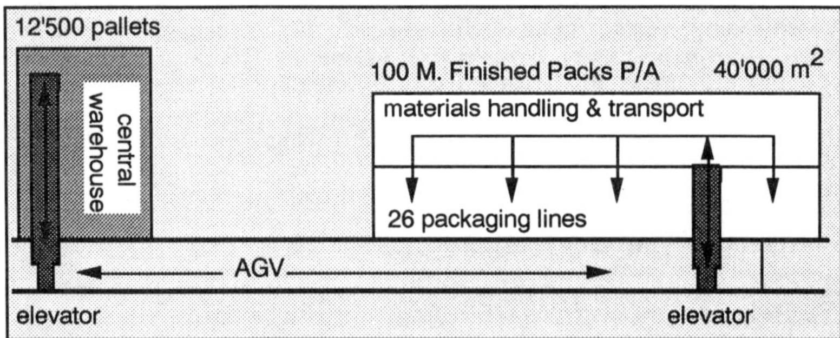

Figure 8.2a: New packaging plant for Hoffmann-La Roche pharmaceuticals. Materials will enter and leave the production building through the basement; packaging will take place on the main floor; materials handling and transport inside the plant is restricted to the first floor as much as possible. Automated guided vehicles (AGV) look after transportation from and to the warehouse.

The new facility, which is projected to be fully operational in the course of 1994, is to produce ca. 100 million presentation (fully-packaged) packs per annum for roughly 10'000 production orders with an average order size of 10'000 packs. A full range of dosage forms is covered. The total investment sum will exceed 100 M.SFr. Much of the existing equipment from the old facility will be taken over. Only gradually, will more flexible equipment replace the old equipment. The investment includes a central warehouse with fully-automated access to 12'500 pallet spaces, a smaller facility for manual warehousing, as well as a shipping and receiving area. The warehouse will store packaging materials, bulk and finished products. The warehouse capacity allows for the storage of bulk and finished products that are packaged at another site.

The objective of the project is to increase the speed and flexibility of packaging on the basis of an entirely new design of the information and material flows. The target is to reduce the present lead times for group company orders from ca. 8 weeks down to 3 weeks. The design of the operation of the plant relies on a pragmatic application of the just-in-time concept and involves the following principles:

- no intermediate storage of semi- and fully-packaged products
- formation of 26 independent packaging lines, segmented by dosage form and package format
- tight coupling of the three packaging steps, with a minimum amount of WIP and simple materials handling
- setup time reduction by improved methods and procedures, re-training of production personnel to perform minor setups, and the judicious use of spare equipment to perform setups while the alternate is running
- only full export-packaged boxes on the packaging lines produce and in the automated warehouse stocks
- unpacking of full export-packaged boxes and handling of non-standard orders both in the warehouse.
- responsibility for detailed production scheduling with the plant
- support for shop floor control provided networked PC's
- demand management and rough-cut requirements planning covered by the MRP II system AMAPS, including links to plant and warehouse systems
- responsibility for order shipment consolidation with the shipping agency
- component retrieval from the warehouse within 2 hours
- building of supplier partnerships to reduce packaging material stocks for selected items

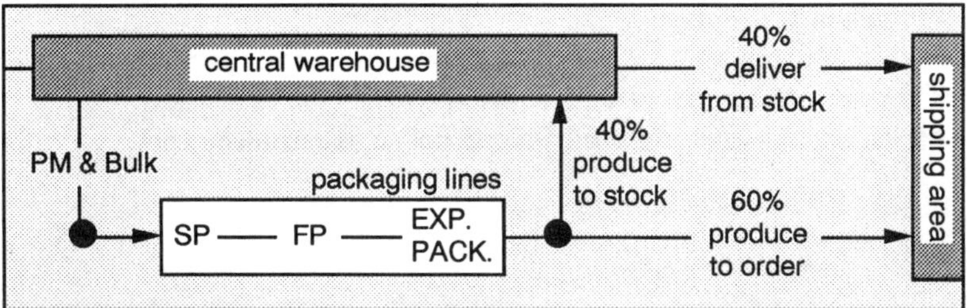

Figure 8.2b: Material flow for the new packaging plant. The plan calls for altogether 26 independent lines to cover a full range of dosage forms.

Hoffmann-La Roche is also using simulation modeling to support the design of the facility.and optimize the material and information flows. Besides the usual tasks faced by the implementation teams, the smooth transfer of production from the existing plant to the new one presents a major logistics problem. This is an ambitious and forward-looking project. It makes it clear that the just-in-time concept is establishing itself in the pharmaceutical industry and, as argued in §8.2, the basis of competition is shifting towards speed and flexibility.

8.6 Just-in-Time at CIBA–GEIGY Pharmaceuticals in Japan

Although the requirements placed on pharmaceutical production in a group company that predominantly serves its own markets are not comparable to the situation in the parent company, a few comments on the present situation in Japan[77] serve to round off the discussion on current trends in the industry.

CIBA–GEIGY's Sasayama plant has in the past introduced on-line production for the dosage forms suppositories and dry syrups of two main active substances, which together account for 30% of the sales volume. The construction of these production lines reduced the inventory for the two products to 18% of the total amount of capital tied up in stocks. The Sasayama plant, with an annual volume of ca. 1'000 million tablets, still fabricates and packages solid dosage forms in the convential, capacity-oriented way. Total inventory coverage—the figures quoted in the paper of Iwata for four main products are 3.7, 6.3, 5.5 and 10.8 months of demand—reflect the consequences.

Using simulation, the production department investigated the feasibility of the introduction of the on-line concept to reduce throughput times. The issues of interest in this simulation study match those covered in chapter 7. Covered are two cases: a medium-sized plant with 500 million tablets and 5 million packages annually, and a small-sized plant with 100 million tablets and 1 million packages. The product mix includes only 10 different fully-packaged products. For both cases two variants are analyzed: a single production line with a batch size of 200 kg, and 100 kg, respectively; and, alternatively, two independent lines with half the batch size. Campaign sizes were set to cover on average one month of demand. The results focus on:

- throughput time – days
- inventory for raw material and finished products – coverage and tied-up capital
- equipment utilization – process and changeover time vs available time
- equipment and plant efficiency – output per no. of changeovers[78]

---

[77]My comments are based on a paper and presentation of Mr. H. Iwata entitled "Lead time in pharmaceutical production: The effects on on-line production of solid dosage forms." It was presented in 1989 at the sixth international meeting of CIBA–GEIGY pharmaceutical production mangers.

[78]This is an usual and interesting measure: it draws attention to the importance of reducing the changeover time per campaign, but is open to abuse.

In addition, the capital investment required in each case was calculated.[79] The conclusions of the report state that the throughput times of the existing facility are approximately 4 times longer than those for the cases investigated. As measured by the output per total number of changeovers, the plant efficiency for the on-line concepts simulated, is worse than 50% of the existing facility. Not surprisingly, the importance of changeover times for the on-line concept is pointed out. The report recommends that the on-line concept, being a prime alternative, should be subjected to an in-depth analysis in the case a new facility is constructed. This analysis must cover various design decisions, the impact of desired customer service levels and flexibility, and the financial side of the coin.

The parallels with the issues in the parent company are clear. For the construction of new facilities the same direction will be adopted: speed of response at the expense of capacity utilization and efficient utilization of equipment. Finally, the present situation in pharmaceutical production in the country that brought the Western world the just-in-time concept isn't necessarily a whole lot better. How well do CIBA–GEIGY's Japanese competitors, which dominate the Japanese market, perform with regard to speed?

8.7 Just-in-Time in the Context of Supply Chain Management

Thy measure,
Thy treasure,
Thy pleasure?

Just-in-time is not a panacea for all problems in supply chain management. Taken as whole and in its pure form the concept has limited applicability in batch chemical processes, which come to mind first when we think about *die Chemischen.*[80] However, manufacturing in the chemical-pharmaceutical industry also covers the various delivery forms of the basic active substance and other specialty chemicals. Here lie the opportunities offered by the application of the concept.

Just-in-time is by no means a substitute for the MRP II concept or comparable materials management systems. On the contrary, these two concepts complement each other. As discussed, just-in-time improves the chances for successful realization of the MRP II concept, which are, by all empirical accounts, notoriously poor. It is not just fashionable to talk about synergies: just-in-time can contribute to supply chain management as a whole and obtain added leverage from other investment made in this area. The drive towards simplicity, which Taiichi Ohno emphasized from the start, is the key factor. Detailed production scheduling is a

[79]The investment cost of the selected equipment items, in comparison with the costs in the case investigated in chapter 7, throws up some interesting questions—see table 7.2.5c in §7.2.4. The total investment sum for the small-sized plant was estimated at 33 M.SFr. for the variant with1 production line and 39 M.SFr. for the variant with 2 production lines; the figures for the medium-sized plant are 64 M.SFr. and 67 M.SFr., respectively. Again, the cost of segmentation decreases with the size.

[80]The German term used by the population in Basel to refer to the three multi-national chemical companies that are based there.

whole lot easier for a just-in-time operation. Moreover, every intermediate product level that is taken out of the supply chain not only shortens it but also makes it is easier to plan and manage. At the same time, a just-in-time operation comes to a grinding halt much more quickly than a traditional operation when the supply of raw material breaks down. Continuity of supply and accurate aggregated demand forecasts, which the instruments of the MRP II concept are intended to deliver, are key factors on which the successful operation of the just-in-time concept depends.

The thesis has intentionally kept the two concepts apart. In industrial practice, the distinction between them appears to be blurring. MRP II plays the role of the big brother, gradually absorbing the key elements of the just-in-time concept that will allow it to move away from the unsatisfactory status quo in supply chain management.

A number of companies, including CIBA–GEIGY, have clearly recognized that improvements in supply chain management will not come about, or at least too slowly, unless they measure key performance indicators in a systematic and consistent manner. Key measures to be selected include not only those that have been used in this thesis to differentiate a classical operation from its just-in-time counterpart but also those outward-looking measures that assess the degree to which market needs and customer requirements are being fulfilled. Supply chain performance measurement of nonfinancial factors is necessary to counterbalance the impact of the focus on production costs and the utilization of fixed assets imposed by the cost accounting systems presently in place.

Up and till recently, developments in modern manufacturing have been divorced from those in accounting. There is some indication that cost accounting is catching up to the developments in manufacturing [Berliner et al., 1988], or, putting it differently, manufacturing is starting to acknowledge the impact of cost accounting.

There are many open issues. These begin with basic implementation questions:

- should supply chain performance measurement be developed into a full-fledged system *on par* with a cost accounting system or carried out in an *ad hoc* fashion? Is there a compromise solution?
- alternatively, should performance measurement be an integrated component of cost accounting systems to ensure that the information provided receives the same status and is used effectively?
- how are the specific and changing needs of the business segments taken into account?
- how does the cost of capital enter the process? Is it best to value inventory at variable products only for all or most purposes?

and do not end with more specific issues concerning suitable levels of aggregation, ownership and target setting. There are enough questions to fill a final section on future academic—and practical—work which is customarily included in a thesis. Hoping to do the patient reader who has come this far a favour, I am taking the liberty to skip such section.

References

Aggarwal, S., 1985, "MRP, JIT, OPT, FMS? Making sense of production operations systems," *Harvard Business Review,* Vol. 63, No. 5, pp. 8-13.

Anonymous, 1984, APICS Dictionary, American Production and Inventory Control Society Inc., Falls Church, Virginia.

Ansari, A., 1986, "Survey identifies critical factors in successful implementation of just-in-time purchasing techniques," *Industrial Engineering,* Vol. 18, No. 10, pp. 44-50.

Apple, J.M, 1977, *Plant Layout and Material Handling,* John Wiley & Sons, New York, 3rd edition.

Ashford, R.W.; Dyson, R.G. and Hodges, S.D., 1988, "The capital-investment appraisal of new technology: problems, misconceptions and research directions," *Journal of the Operational Research Society,* Vol. 39, No. 7, pp. 737-642.

Augusto, A.L.; Forrester, J. and Lyneis, J.M., (ed.) 1980, *Systems Dynamics,* Studies in the Management Sciences, Vol. 10, North-Holland Publishing Company, Amsterdam.

Baker, K.R.; Magazine, M.J. and Nuttle, H.L.W., 1986, "The effect of commonality on safety stock in a simple inventory model," *Management Science,* Vol. 32, No. 8, pp. 982-988.

Bahl, H.C.; Ritzman, L.P. and Gupta, J.N.D., 1987, "Determining lot sizes and resource requirements: A review," *Operations Research,* Vol. 35, No. 3, pp. 329-345.

Banks, J. and Malavé, C.O., 1984a, "The simulation of inventory systems: An overview," *Simulation,* Vol. ?, No. ?, pp. 283-290.

Banks, J. and Carson, J.S., 1984b, *Discrete-Event System Simulation,* Prentice Hall, Englewood Cliffs, NJ.

Bell, P.C., 1985, "Visual interactive modeling as operations researrch technique," *Interfaces,* Vol. 15, No. 4, pp. 26-33.

Bell, P.C., 1986, "Visual interactive modelling in operational research: Success and opportunities," *Journal of the Operational Research Society,* Vol. 36, No. 11, pp. 975-982.

Bell, P.C. and O'Keefe, R.M., 1987, "Visual interactive simulation – History, recent developments, and major issues," *Simulation,* Vol. 49, No. 3, pp. 109-116.

Bell, P.C.; Taseen, A.A. and Kirkpatrick, P.F., 1990, "Visual interactive simulation modeling in a decision support role," *Computers and Operations Research,* Vol. 17, No. 5, pp. 447-456.

Benton, W.C., 1985, "Product structure complexity and multilevel lot sizing using alternative costing policies," *Decision Sciences,* Vol. 16, No. 4, pp. 357-369.

Berliner, C. and Brimson, J.A.(ed.), 1988, *Cost Management for Today's Advanced Manufacturing: The CAM-I Conceptual Design,* Harvard Business School Press, Boston, MA.

References

Bertrand, J.W.M. and Wijngaard, J., 1986, "The structuring of production control systems," *International Journal of Operations and Production Management,* Vol. 6, No. 2, pp. 5-20.

Biggs, J.R., 1979, "Heuristic lot-sizing and sequencing rules in a multi-stage production-inventory system," *Decision Sciences,* Vol. 10, No. 1, pp. 96-115.

Bookbinder, J.H. and Locke, T.D., 1986, "Simulation analysis of just-in-time distribution," *International Journal of Physical Distribution and Materials Management,* Vol. 16, No. 7, pp. 31-45

Chakravarty, A.K. and Shtub, A., 1985a, "An experimental study of integer multiple lot sizes in multi-echelon production inventory systems," *International Journal of Production Research,* Vol. 23, No. 3, pp. 469-478.

Chakravarty, A.K., 1985b, "New technology investments in multistage production systems," *Decision Sciences,* Vol. 16, No. 3, pp. 248-264.

Cole, R.E., 1985, "Target information for competitive performance," *Harvard Business Review,* Vol. 63, No. 3, pp. 100-109.

Conway, R; Maxwell, W.L.; McClain, J.O. and Woron, S.L., 1987, *User's Guide to XCELL + Factory Modeling System,* The Scientific Press, Redwood City, CA.

Cooper, R. and Kaplan, R.S., 1988, "Measure costs right: Make the right decisions," *Harvard Business Review,* Vol. 66, No. 5, pp. 96-103.

Crosby, L.B., 1984, "The just-in-time manufacturing process: Control of quality and quantity," *Production and Inventory Management,* Vol. 25, No. 4, pp. 21-34.

Cusumano, M.A., *The Japanese Automobile Industry: Technology and Management at Nissan and Toyota,"* Harvard University Press, Cambridge, MA, 1986.

Dornan, S.B., 1987, "Just-in-time: The home-grown techniques comes home," *Production,* Vol. 99, No. 8, pp. 60-62.

Drucker, P.E., 1990, "The emerging theory of manufacturing," *Harvard Business Review,* Vol. 68, No. 3, pp. 94-102.

Eilon, S., 1984, *The Art of Reckoning: Analysis of Performance Criteria,* Academic Press, London, Great Britain.

Eilon, S., 1985, "A framework for profitability and productivity measures," *Interfaces,* Vol. 15, No. 3, pp. 31-40.

Egli, U.M. and Rippin, D.W.T., 1986, "Short-term scheduling for multiproduct batch chemical plants," *Computers & Chemicial Engineering,* Vol. 10, No. 4, pp. 303-325

Fincke, U. and Vaessen, W., 1988, "Reducing distribution costs in a two-level inventory system at Ciba–Geigy," *Interfaces,* Vol. 18, No. 6, pp.92-104.

Fine, C.H. and Hax, A.C., 1985, "Manufacturing strategy: A Methodology and an illustration," *Interfaces,* Vol. 15, No. 6, pp. 28-46.

Fleischmann, B., 1988, "Operations-Research-Modelle und -Verfahren in der Produktionsplanung," *Zeitschrift für Betriebswirtschaft,* Vol. 58, No. 3, pp. 347-372.

Forrester, J.W., 1961, *Industrial Dynamics,* John Wiley & Sons, Inc., New York.

Foster, G. and Horngren, C.T., 1987, "JIT: Cost accounting and cost management issues," *Management Accounting,* Vol. 68, No. 6, pp. 19-25.

Fox, M. and Smith, S., 1984, "ISIS–a knowledge-based system for factory scheduling," *Expert Systems,* Vol. No. 1.

Gold, B., 1985, "Foundations of strategic planning for productivity improvement," *Interfaces,* Vol. 15, No. 3, pp. 15-30.

Goldberg, A. and Robson, D., 1983, *Smalltalk-80: The language and its implementation,* Addison Wesley Publishing Company, Reading.

Goldratt, E.M.,1987, *The Theory of Constraints Journal,* Avraham Y. Goldratt Institute, New Haven, CT.

Geoffrion, A.M., 1987, "An introduction to structured modeling," *Management Science,* Vol. 33., No. 5, pp. 547-588.

Gröflin, H. and Schiltknecht, H., 1989, "PEPI: Ein innovatives Produktions-planungsinstrument in der chemischen Industrie," *OUTPUT,* Vol. 12, (special issue), pp. 33-38.

Hahn, C.K; Pinto, A.P. and Bragg, D.J., 1983, "'Just-in-time' production and purchasing," *Journal of Purchasing and Materials Management,* Vol. 19, No. 3, pp. 2-10.

Hall, R.W., 1983, *Zero Inventories,* Dow Jones-Irwin, Homewood, Illinois.

Harris, W, 1915, *Operations and Cost* (Factory Management Series), A.W. Shaw Company, Chicago, Chapter 4.

Hax, C.A. and Candea, D., 1984, *Production and Inventory Management,* Prentice-Hall Inc., Englewood Cliffs, New Jersey.

Hayes, R.H., 1981, "Why Japanese factories work," *Harvard Business Review,* Vol. 69, No. 4, pp. 57–66.

Hayes, R.H. and Wheelwright, S.C., 1979, "Link manufacturing process and product life cycles," *Harvard Business Review,* Vol. 57, No. 1, pp. 133-140.

Hayes, R.H. and Clark, K.B., 1985, "Explaining observed productivity differentials between plants: Implications for operations research," *Interfaces,* Vol. 15, No. 6, pp. 3-14.

Huang, P.Y.; Rees, L.P. and Taylor, R.W., 1983, "A simulation analysis of the Japanese just-in-time technique (with Kanbans) for a multiline, multistage production system," *Decision Sciences,* Vol. 14, No. 3, pp. 326-344.

Jäger, H., 1988, "Industrielle Logistik im Zeichen von 'Just-in-time'," *io Management Zeitschrift,* Vol. 57, No. 4, pp. 209-212.

Kanet, J.J., 1986, "Toward a better understanding of lead times in MRP systems," *Journal of Operations Management,* Vol. 6, No. 3, pp. 305-315.

Kaplan, R.S., 1984, "Yesterday's accounting undermines production," *Harvard Business Review,* Vol. 62, No. 4, pp. 95-101.

Kaplan, R.S., 1986, "Must CIM be justified by faith alone?," *Harvard Business Review,* Vol. 64, No. 2, pp. 87-95.

Kaplan, R.S., 1988, "One cost system isn't enough," *Harvard Business Review,* Vol. 66, No. 1, pp. 61-66.

Karmarkar, U.S., 1987, "Lot sizes, lead times and in-process inventories," *Management Science,* Vol. 33, No. 3, pp. 409-423.

Kirkpatrick, P.F. and Bell, P.C., 1989, "Simulation modelling: A comparison of visual interactive and traditional approaches," *European Journal of Operational Research,* Vol. 39, No. ?, pp. 138-149.

Krajewski, L.J.; King, B.E.; Ritzman, L.P. and Wong, D.S., 1987, "KANBAN, MRP, and shaping the manufacturing environment," *Management Science,* Vol. 33, No. 10, pp. 39-57.

Kreutzer, W., 1986, *System Simulation: Programming Styles and Languages,* Addison-Wesley, Reading, Mass.

Krüger, M., 1986, "Termin- und bestandsorientierte Logistik unter besonderer Berücksichtigung Japanisher KANBAN-Prinzipien," in [Wildemann 1986a], B1.

Loebel, A.E., 1986, "Just-in-time manufacturing: Implications for manufacturing resource planning," *Information Management Review,* Vol. 1, No. 4, pp. 45-53.

Lee, S.M. and Ansari, A., 1985, "Comparative analysis of Japanese just-in-time purchasing and traditional US purchasing systems," *International Journal of Operations and Production Management,* Vol. 5, No. 4, pp. 5-14.

Meyersiek, D.; Perraudin, M. and Roever, M., 1984, "Rationalisierungsreserven im Umlaufvermögen," *Zeitschrift für Betriebswirtschaft,* (Ergänzungsheft 2/84), pp. 17-29.

Monden, Y., 1981, "Adaptable Kanban system helps Toyota maintain just-in-time production," *Industrial Engineering,* Vol. 13, No.5, pp 28-46.

Mowshowitz, A., 1976, *The Conquest of Will: Information Processing in Human Affairs,* Addison-Wesley Publishing Company, Reading, MA, (Chapter 12).

Muller, E.J. and Schreffler, R., 1986, "How Toyota/GM makes cars by crossing the Pacific just in time," *Distribution,* Vol. 85, No. 10, pp. 53-60.

Musier, R.F.H. and Evans, L.B., 1990, "Batch process management," *Chemical Engineering Progress,* Vol. 86, No. 6, pp. 66-77.

Myers, M.S., 1987, "Don't let JIT become a North American quick-fix," *Business Quarterly,* Vol. 51, pp. 28-38.

Nakana, J. and Hall, R.W., 1983, "Management specs for stockless production," *Harvard Business Review,* Vol. 61, No. 3, pp. 29-46.

Ohno, T., 1988, *Toyota Production System: Beyond Large-Scale Production,* Productivity Press, Cambridge, MA.

O'Neal, C.R., 1987, "The buyer-seller linkage in a just-in-time environment," *Journal of Purchasing and Materials Management,* Vol. 23, No. 1, pp. 7-13.

Pack, L., 1988, "Gewinnmaximale oder rentabilitätsmaximale Losgrösse bzw. Bestellmenge," *Zeitschrift für Betriebswirtschaft,* Vol. 59, No. 1, pp. 5-26.

Piper, C.J. and Radford, R.W., 1985, "Process automation and just-in-time: Critical complements," *Business Quarterly,* Vol. 50, No. 4, pp. 109-114.

Philipoom, P.R.; Rees, L.P.; Taylor, B.W. and Huang, P.Y., 1987, "An investigation of the factors influencing the number of Kanbans required in the implementaion of the JIT technique with Kanbans," *International Journal of Production Research,* Vol. 25, No. 3, pp. 457-472.

Porteus, E.L., 1985, "Investing in reduced setups in the EOQ model," *Management Science,* Vol. 31, No. 8, pp. 998-1010.

Porteus, E.L., 1986, "Optimal lot sizing, process quality improvement, and setup cost reduction," *Operations Research,* Vol. 34, No. 1, pp. 137-144.

Remer, D.S. and Chai, L.H., 1990, "Design cost factors for scaling-up engineering equipment," *Chemical Engineering Process,* Vol. 86, No. 8, pp. 77-82.

Ritzmann, L.P.; King, B.E. and Krajewski, L.J., 1984, "Manufacturing performance - Pulling the right levers," *Harvard Business Review,* Vol. 62, No. 2, pp. 143-152.

Rippin, D.W.T., 1983, "Simulation of single- and multiproduct batch chemical plants for optimal design and operation," *Computers and Chemical Engineering,* Vol. 7, No. 3, pp. 137-156.

Rosenfield, D.B.; Shapiro, R.D. and Bohn, R.E., 1985, "Implications of cost-service trade-offs on industry logistics structures," *Interfaces,* Vol. 15, No. 6, pp. 47-59.

Rosenkranz, F., 1979, *An Introduction to Corporate Modeling,* Duke University Press, Durham, North-Carolina.

Saipe, A.J. and Schonberger, R.J., 1984a, "Don't ignore just-in-time production," *Business Quarterly,* Vol. 49, No. 1, pp. 60-66.

Saipe, A.J. and Schonberger, R.J., 1984b, "Just-in-time production: What are you waiting for?" *Industrial Management,* Vol. 8, No. 7, pp. 20-24.

Sauers, D.G., 1986, "Analyzing inventory systems," *Management Accounting,* Vol. 67, No. 11, pp. 30-36.

Schneeweiss, C., 1979, "Zur Problematik der Kosten in Lagerhaltungsmodellen," *Zeitschrift für Betriebswirtschaft,* Vol. 49, No. 1, pp. 1-17.

Schonberger, R.J., 1982a, "Some observations on the advantages and implementation issues of just-in-time production systems," *Journal of Operations Management,* Vol. 3, No. 1, pp. 1-11.

Schonberger, R.J., 1982b, "Why the Japanese produce Just in Time," *Industry Week,* Vol. 215, No. 5, pp. 56-60.

Schonberger, R.J. and Gilbert, J.P., 1983a, "Just-in-time purchasing: A challenge for U.S. industry," *California Management Review,* Vol. 26, No. 1, pp. 54-68.

Schonberger, R.J., 1983b, "Plant layout becomes product-oriented with cellular, just-in-time production concepts," *Industrial Engineering,* Vol. 15, No. 11, pp. 66-71.

Schonberger, R.J. and Ansari, A., 1984a, "'Just-in-time' purchasing can improve quality," *Journal of Purchasing and Materials Management,* Vol. 20, No. 1, pp. 2-7.

Schonberger, R.J., 1984b, "Just-in-time production – The quality dividend," *Quality Progress,* Vol. 17, No. 10, pp. 22-24.

Schonberger, R.J., 1984c, "Just-in-time productions systems: Replacing complexity with simplicity in manufacturing management," *Industrial Engineering,* Vol. 16, No. 10, pp. 52-63.

Schonberger, R.J, and Schniederjans, M.J., 1984d, "Reinventing inventory control," *Interfaces,* Vol. 14, No. 3, pp. 76-83.

Schonberger, R.J., 1987, "Frugal manufacturing," *Harvard Business Review,* Vol. 65, No. 5, pp. 95–100.

Sharman, G., 1984, "The rediscovery of logistics," *Harvard Business Review,* Vol. 62, No. 5, pp. 71–79.

Shycon, H.M. and Maffet, R.B., 1960, "Simulation - Tool for better distribution," *Harvard Business Review,* Vol. 38, No. 6, pp. 66-75.

Singhvi, S.S., 1979, *Planning for Capital Investments,* Planning Executives Institute, Oxford, Ohio.

Skinner, W., 1974, "The focused factory," *Harvard Business Review,* Vol. 52, No. 3, pp. 113-121.

Skinner, W., 1986, "The productivity paradox," *Harvard Business Review,* Vol. 64., No. 4, pp 55-59.

Stalk, G., 1988, "Time – The next source of competitive advantage," *Harvard Business Review,* Vol. 66, No. 4, pp. 41-51.

Steffen, R., 1987, "Flexibilitätssteigerung durch Rüstzeitsenkung," *io Management Zeitschrift,* Vol. 56, No. 11, pp. 507-511.

Stenger, A.J., 1986, "Just-in-time: Make sure you know what you're getting into," *Purchasing World,* Vol. 30, No. 3, pp. 64-67.

Sohal, A.S.; Keller, A.Z. and Fouad, R.H., 1989, "A review of the literature relating to JIT," *International Journal of Operations and Production Management,* Vol. 9, No. 3, pp. 15-25.

Sugimori, Y.; Kusonoki, K.; Cho, F. and Uchikawa, S., 1977, "Toyota production system and Kanban system: Materialization of just-in-time and respect-for-human system," *International Journal of Production Research,* Vol. 15, No. 6, pp. 553-564.

Suri, R. and De Treville, S., 1986, "Getting from 'just-in-case' to 'just-in-time': Insights from a simple model," *Journal of Operations Management,* Vol. 6, No. 3, pp. 295-304.

Swann, W.H., 1986, "The use of visual interactive simulation techniques for production scheduling," *Orion,* Vol. 2, No. 2, pp. 34-51.

Vaessen, W., 1989, "ProfiSEE: A workbench for visual interactive simulation modelling in the chemical-pharmaceutical industry," *OR Spektrum,* Vol. 11, No. 4, (Special Issue), first presented at *2. symposium on Simulationsmodelle als betriebswirtschaftliche Entscheidungshilfe,* March 1989, (A German translation is to appear in the proceedings)

Voss, C.A. and Robinson, S.J., 1987, "Application of just-in-time manufacturing techniques in the United Kingdom," *International Journal of Operations and Production Management,* Vol. 7, No. 4, pp. 46-52.

Wacker, J.G., 1986, "Can holding costs be overstated for just-in-time manufacturing systems," *Production and Inventory Management,* Vol. 27, No. 3, pp. 11-14.

Walleigh, R. C., 1986, "What's your excuse for not using JIT," *Harvard Business Review,* Vol. 64, No. 2, (March-April), pp. 38-54.

Warner, T.N., 1987, "Information technology as a competitive burden," *Sloan Management Review,* Fall 1987, pp. 51-61.

Wheelwright, S.C., 1981, "Japan, where operations really are strategic," *Harvard Business Review,* Vol. 59, No. 4, pp. 67-74.

Wijngaard, J. and Wortmann, J.C., 1985, "MRP and inventories," *European Journal of Operations Research,* Vol. 20, No. ?, pp. 281-293.

Wildemann, H., (ed.) 1986a, *Just-In-Time Produktion,* GFMT Verlag, München.

Wildemann, H, 1986, "Just-in-time Lösungskonzepte in Europa," in [Wildemann 1986a], A1.

Wildemann, H. and Carlson, J.G., 1987, "Implementing just-in-time concepts into European companies," *Engineering Costs and Production Economics,* Vol. 13, No. 1, pp 27-37.

Wildemann, H., 1988a, *Das Just-in-Time Konzept: Produktion und Zulieferung auf Abruf,* Frankfurter Allgemeinen Zeitung, Frankfurt am Main.

Wildemann, H., 1988b, *Die modulare Fabrik: Kundennahe Producktion durch Fertigungssegmentierung,* GFMT Verlag, München.

Wildemann, H., 1988c, "PC-Programm zur Inestitionsplanung und Wirtschaftlichkeitsrechnung", *Werkstatt und Betrieb*, Vol. 121, No. 1, pp. 35-39.

Williams, T.M., 1984, "Stock control with sporadic and slow-moving demand," *Journal of the Operational Research Society*, Vol. 35, No. 10, pp. 939-948.

Williams, K.; Williams, J. and Haslam, C., 1989, "Why take the stocks out? Britain vs Japan," *International Journal of Operations and Production Management,* Vol. 8, No. 8, pp. 91-105.

Wilson, H., 1934, "A scientific routine for stock control," *Harvard Business Review,* Vol. 13, No. 1, pp. 1-11.

Winton, J.M. et al., 1985, "Just-in-time: How suppliers adjust to new inventory strategies," *Chemical Week,* Vol. 137, No. 18, pp. 26-29.

Wortmann, J.C. and Monhemius, W., 1984, "Kanban – its use as a final assembly scheduling tool within MRP II," in *Operational Research '84,* Brans, J.P. (ed.), Elsevier Science Publishers, North-Holland, pp. 641-655

Zangwill, W.I., 1987, "From EOQ to ZI," *Management Science,* Vol. 33, No. 10, pp. 1209-1233.